Plugging
the
Microstate

Plugging the Microstate

A History of Technology Adoption, ICT Policy, and
Software Development in the Small Island State of Malta

Mario Aloisio

To *meine drei Schätze*:
Renate, Pascal, and Marcel.

CONTENTS

Rationales for an Office of Statistics ~ Formation of the Central Office of Statistics ~ National Income and Balance of Payments ~ Training, Expertise, and Knowledge Transfer ~ The First Machines ~ Expansion and Restructuring ~ Political and Economic Constraints ~ End of Mechanization

Efficiency Development in the Civil Service and a Failed Attempt at Creating a Government Computer Organization ~ Computerization at the Inland Revenue Department

List of Figures

List of Tables

List of Boxes

Preface

This book evolved from a doctoral dissertation completed in the summer of 2010. In revising the original dissertation text to make it accessible to a wider audience, I have carried out three principal tasks. The first exercise was to identify those dissertation chapters which could be broken down into sections that themselves would form the new book chapters. Having smaller chapters means being able to read (and digest) an entire chapter in a relatively short time. The only two original dissertation chapters which, it was felt, were better left untouched were those about the Central Office of Statistics (Chapter 1) and the Software Industry (Chapter 7), both essentially detailed case studies.

The second exercise was to include "information boxes" that provide supplementary material about some topic related to a chapter's content. I am conscious that many readers, even those knowledgeable in computing and information technology, often lack the computer history background. These boxes, it is hoped, will enable the reader to gain a fuller appreciation of chapter material.

The third exercise, somewhat complementing the second, was to include a glossary of terms used in the book. This book's audience can be varied, from computer practitioners to policy makers and politicians, to computer historians, IT teachers, and university students (perhaps reading government policy or computing with a history component). The glossary is meant to help the different types of reader comprehend some of the more technical terms.

Acknowledgements

This book (and the dissertation from which it derives) is the fruit of several years' research. It has been a long project, in the course of which I met, was introduced to, discussed with, and interviewed a number of persons, most new to me, and some I have known for years. In various ways, these people have contributed to this study, and to them I owe a debt of gratitude.

Beginning with Chapter 1, the following persons have been very helpful. The late Albert Galea, a former long-time Central Office of Statistics (COS) employee, was the first person to be interviewed. He recounted his early experience at the COS and answered a number of questions I put to him. He was glad that, after so many years, at least somebody acknowledged the pioneering data processing work carried out at the statistics office. Joe D'Amico was another former long-serving COS employee, introduced to me by Catherine Vella (who also works at the National Statistics Office, as the COS was renamed in 2000). Joe was kind enough to give up his time for me on a number of occasions. Enthusiastically, he explained how the early tabulating equipment worked; how strenuous it often was to spend long hours bent on the machines, resulting in frequent backaches; and the machine noise that one had to put up with. Maurice Abela, who was Principal Government Statistician in the 1960s, read the final version of the first Chapter for accuracy's sake. Other COS personnel who have been supportive include Sean Borg and Robert Tanti. To all of these I say thank you.

A lack of literature for Chapters 2 and 3 meant that I had to solicit assistance (again in the form of interviews) from a number of persons. Much of the account about the early work at Computime was compiled after a two-hour meeting with the only surviving founding director Mario Mizzi. Likewise, parts of the section on the Barclay's computerisation project would not have been written had it not been for David Grech who, having been closely involved in the project, recounted much of his experience. For the section on the Inland Revenue, help was forthcoming from Godfrey Calleja who worked there almost from the time the first computer was introduced in that department. The section about Megabyte was written after a brief meeting with Karm Galea (one of the company's founding directors) and James Forte (software manager). For the final section of Chapter 3, it was felt I should briefly interview Patrick Pullicino because of his experience with Philip Toledo Ltd in the late 1960s and 1970s, at a time when accounting machines in Malta were very popular. Philip Toledo Ltd has been a leading office accounting and computer firm, at one time with sole distributorship of NCR and Hewlett Packard machines. I was interested in finding out through this meeting why this company was slow to secure its first computer sale.

Chapter 5, which gives a brief account of computing at the University of Malta, the only Maltese university, was written after systematically going through the University's *Annual Reports* and *Bullettins*, and an interview (followed by a subsequent meeting) with Prof. Paul Micallef of the Faculty of Engineering. Again, for accuracy's sake and in order to ensure that nothing important has been missed, Micallef was shown the draft version of this section, which required minor changes.

No persons were interviewed for the software industry chapter (Chapter 7), but I must thank all those who responded to my company profile e-survey. In alphabetical order, these are: Dr. John Abela (Ascent Software), Noel Beck (HOB Software Ltd), James Bonello (Crimsonwing), James Deguara (Anvil Software Ltd), John de Giorgio (Shireburn Ltd), Dr. Gege Gatt (Icon Studio Ltd), Angelica Micallef Trigona (GFI Software Ltd), Dr. Mark Sammut (Cursor Ltd), David Schranz (Dakar Software), and Yuzhou Zhu (Tenovar Ltd). James Bonello also kindly let me see his MBA thesis on software outsourcing before it was made available for public inspection. He also gave me permission to reproduce one of the figures from his thesis. Thanks also go to Sonya Pecorella and Ralph Attard of Malta Enterprise for accepting to meet me to discuss software industry-related issues. Other persons I wish to thank are Daniela Armeni of the University of Malta and MCAST's Stefania Aquiliana for promptly furnishing me with statistics data used in Table 7.7; and Fr. David Cilia, Anthony Aquilina and Michele La Ferla of The Archbishop's Seminary for replying to my e-mail to confirm the year when their college first introduced computers for educational purposes.

For Chapters 9 and 10, I must thank Robert Sultana, director of the University's former Computer Services Centre (now IT Services), who agreed to briefly meet me to clarify a couple of points about the Malta Internet Exchange; and Stephanie Scicluna of the Malta Communications Authority who promptly provided me with MCA literature. Michelle Bonello and Moira Mifsud, both of the Intellectual Property Registration Directorate, have also given their time to discuss with me issues related to software copyright and patents in Malta, the subject of Chapter 12.

There are four more persons that deserve a special mention. Apart from seeing draft and final (or near-final) versions of the original dissertation chapters and making invaluable suggestions and constructive criticism, my former supervisor, Prof. Martin Campbell-Kelly, has never failed to be inspirational. Through a number of relevant conferences, seminars, and meetings, Martin also introduced me to some of the world's leading computer historians. Dr. Steve Russ, my mentor, also always found the time to discuss my progress and simultaneously provide encouragement; and — at the *Viva* stage — Prof. Gerard Alberts, my external examiner, suggested further minor improvements which could be — and have been — made to the originally submitted thesis. Finally, my wife Renate was tolerant and supportive, having persevered for the project's lifetime.

— Mario Aloisio
Santa Venera, Malta.

Abbreviations

ADP	Automatic Data Processing
ASYCUDA	Automated Systems for Customs Data
ATM	Automatic Teller Machine; Asynchronous Transfer Mode
BDS	Business Development Systems Ltd (Maltese firm)
BCS	British Computer Society
BEd	Bachelor of Education
BSA	Business Software Alliance
BSc	Bachelor of Science
BTM	British Tabulating Machine Company
CAPDD	Commonwealth Action Programme on the Digital Divide
CBS	Central Bureau of Statistics (the Netherlands)
CCTA	Central Computing and Telecommunications Agency (UK)
CDC	Control Data Corporation
CEO	Chief Executive Officer
CFTC	Commonwealth Fund for Technical Co-operation
CHOGM	Commonwealth Heads of Government Meeting
CIB	Computers in Business (Malta) Ltd
CII	Computer Implemented Inventions
CIMU	Central Information Management Unit (Malta)
COMNET-IT	Commonwealth Network of Information Technology for Development
CP/M	Control Program for Micros
CSC	Computer Services Centre (University of Malta)
CSG	Chief Secretary to Government
COS	Central Office of Statistics (Malta)
DAEs	Dynamic Asian Economies
DBMS	Database Management System
DEC	Digital Equipment Corporation
DOI	Department of Information (Malta)
EC	European Commission
ECDL	European Computer Driving Licence

ECU	European Currency Unit
EDB	Efficiency Development Branch (Establishments, Malta)
EDP	Electronic Data Processing
EEC	European Economic Community
EESC	European Economic and Social Committee
EPC	European Patent Convention
EPO	European Patent Organization/Office
ERDF	European Regional Development Fund
ERP	Enterprise Resource Planning
ESF	European Science Foundation
ESIB	The National Unions of Students in Europe
ESIS	European Survey of Information Society Projects and Actions
ESPRIT	European Strategic Programme for Research in Information Technologies
ETACS	Extended Total Access Communication System
ETC	Employment and Training Corporation (Malta)
EU	European Union
FDI	Foreign Direct Investment
FOI	Malta Federation of Industries
FP	Framework Programme
FSK	Frequency Shift Keying
GBP	Great Britain Pound
GDP	Gross Domestic Product
GMR	General Miscellaneous Reports (at the NAM)
GSM	Global System for Mobile communication
GNP	Gross National Product
GUI	Graphical User Interface
HMG	Her Majesty's Government
HMSO	Her Majesty Stationery Office
HND	Higher National Diploma
HP	Hewlett Packard Ltd
IANA	Internet Assigned Names Authority
IBM	International Business Machines
ICL	International Computers Limited
ICT	International Computers and Tabulators Company; Information and Communications Technology
IDA	Industry Development Act (Malta)
IDC	International Data Corporation

IDPM	Institute of Data Processing and Management
IRC	Innovation Relay Centre
ISDN	Integrated Services Digital Network
ISP	Internet Service Provider
ISSP	Information Systems Strategic Plan (Malta)
IP	Intellectual Property
IPR	Intellectual Property Right
IPSE	Institute for the Promotion of Small Enterprises (Malta)
IT	Information Technology
ITU	International Telecommunications Union
LLD	Doctor of Laws
MAGNET	Malta Government Network
MAP	Micro Enterprise Acceleration Programme
MCA	Malta Communications Authority
MCAST	Malta College of Arts, Science and Technology
MCS	Management Computer Services Ltd (Maltese firm)
MCST	Malta Council for Science and Technology
MDC	Malta Development Corporation
METCO	Malta External Trade Corporation
MITTS	Malta Information Technology and Training Services
MIT&I	Ministry for Information Technology and Investment (Malta)
MLP	Malta Labour Party
MNC	Multinational Corporation
MSU	Management Systems Unit (Malta)
NAM	National Archives of Malta
NATO	North Atlantic Treaty Organization
NCC	National Computing Centre (UK)
NCR	National Cash Register
NIC	Network Information Centre
NII	National Information Infrastructure
NSIT	National Strategy for Information Technology (Malta)
NSO	National Statistics Office (Malta)
OCR	Optical Character Recognition
OECD	Organization for Economic Co-operation and Development
OEM	Original Equipment Manufacturer
OR	Operations Review (Malta)
OTR	Office of the Telecommunications Regulator (Malta)

O&M	Organization and Methods
PGCE	Postgraduate Certificate in Education
PN	Partit Nazzjonalista (Nationalist Party, Malta)
PC	Personal Computer
PCT	Patent Cooperation Treaty
POS	Point of Sale
PSK	Phase Shift Keying
PSRC	Public Service Reform Commission
RAD	Rapid Application Development
R&D	Research and Development
RISC	Reduced Instruction Set Computer
RPI	Retail Price Index
RTDI	Research, Technological Development and Innovation
SME	Small to Medium Enterprise
SSB	Single Sideband
STC	Swatar Training Centre
ST&C	Standard Telephones and Cable
TLD	Top Level Domain
TRIPS	Trade-Related Aspects of Intellectual Property Rights
EUROTEL-DEV	European Telecommunications Development (Project)
UNCITRAL	United Nations Commission for International Trade Law
UNCTAD	United Nations Conference on Trade and Development
UNDP	United Nations Development Programme
UNESCO	United Nations Educational, Scientific, and Cultural Organization
UNIDO	United Nationas Industrial Development Organization
UOM	University of Malta
WIPO	World Intellectual Property Organization
WTO	World Trade Organization

Introduction

This study traces the history of computing, data processing and information technology in Malta. Like other microstates, Malta neither had the capability nor the resources to produce computers. Therefore, this study is predominently about computer technology adoption and IT-related policy. Since the policy-making process involves decisions taken at the ministerial level, some political issues are included in the account. As will be seen, politics has played its fair share in the uptake of new technology.

As a tiny Island and a former fortress colony serving as a naval base, Malta does not share, and has not shared, the same common features that characterise much bigger countries: economies of scale, natural resources, and a wide range of industries are lacking in Malta. The Island also tends to depend on international trade more than large economies do, again primarily on account of its smallness (Briguglio, 1985). In a way, these deficiencies make a study of Malta's economic, social and other factors the more interesting, and their problems the more challenging. The subject of small island states has, in the last two decades or so, received considerable attention, and a number of scholarly studies have been conducted involving Malta.[1] These have shown that in order for small economies to be sustained

---

[1] See, for example: Bowe, Briguglio & Dean (1998); Borda (1999); and Baldacchino & Milne (2000). Between March 17 and 19 of 1999, a workshop entitled "ICT Strategies for Island and Small States" was also held in Malta. It was sponsored by UNESCO, the Commonwealth Secretariat, and the Government of Malta, and organized by the (Malta) National Commission for IT, the Institute for Island and Small States (University of Malta) and the Commonwealth Network of IT for Development (COMNET-IT). See *http://www.comnet-it.org/pubs/reports/isiwkshp/iswreport/iswkrpnd.html.html* for the full report of this workshop.

and be competitive in the global economy, a shift from the traditional manufacturing industry to a services industry is the way forward. That is why, beginning from the late 1980s, Maltese politicians and policy makers began a drive to develop a services industry, for which it was recognised that a solid, all-encompassing, infrastructure was a prerequisite. Information and communications technologies formed part of that infrastructure. The telecommunications sector, in particular, was given special attention because that is where the new business potential lay: e-commerce, voice and video telephony, and knowledge-based industries would ensure that Malta no longer remains an island economy.[2]

In its favour, Malta's strategic location in the middle of the Mediterranean has, apart from attracting invaders, made it a hub of international trade: its proximity to North Africa has served as a bridging commercial link between neighbouring north-African countries and the rest of Europe. More recently, the heavy investment in ICT and education, coupled with a stable political environment and a mild climate, have also encouraged foreign firms, including multinationals, to locate to Malta. A number of these companies are high-technology firms and software developers.

Another advantage of a small state is that it is generally easier to bring key decision-makers together because of the physical concentration of people. Thus, when the National Strategy for Information Technology (NSIT) came to be drafted in 1992, it proved to be fairly straightforward to gather groups from academia, industry and the field of policy making to work together on its design. Over one hundred experts are known to have worked on the NSIT, which (in contrast with that of Singapore, for example) was developed in a bottom-up way, from the grassroots up.

In spite of the vast literature about historical topics involving Malta, and dealing with its political, economical, administrative, and

---

[2] All industries are to some extent dependent on knowledge inputs. However, some industries rely more on knowledge than others. The term "knowledge-based industries" usually refers to those industries which are relatively intensive in their inputs of technology and human capital (OECD, 1999). Examples of these include communications, finance, insurance, and manufacturing industries like aerospace, chemicals and biotechnology, and consumer electronics.

social aspects,[3] nothing substantial about Maltese computing history had been written when this project was begun in the autumn of 2004.[4] This is perhaps not surprising given that computing is a relatively young discipline and computer technology was adopted relatively late in Malta. However, the author felt then that the time was ripe for a detailed investigation of this subject matter, and a proposal was written to undertake the project as a doctoral dissertation, the latter having been completed and subsequently turned into the present book.

In a nutshell, this study reveals that Malta's take up of computers was initially very slow and then fairly rapid, rather than gradual. Although Malta made great strides in the Informatics area, it was late in devising and adopting a plan for an informatics-based infrastructure. Up to quite recently (the 1980s), Malta was considered a developing country with most of its revenues deriving principally from tourism and low-cost, export oriented, manufacturing. IT policy was unheard of before 1990, when the first Information System Strategic Plan was drafted.

This research also appears to give credance to studies that show that effective ICT adoption has an impact on economic growth. Malta's transition from a developing to a developed state came about following an aggressive IT strategy that was simultaneously complemented by a process of liberalisation and privatisation. The latter were part of an exercise in preparation of Malta's EU membership in 2004, and the adoption of new technologies formed part of that process. Had Malta not made attempts in the 1990s to join the EU, it is doubtful if the ICT sector would have developed to the extent it did.

Interestingly, this study also shows that even in a small island state diffusion and deployment of computing technology can follow different diffusion models over time.

---

[3] Apart from the general histories of Malta, some specialised Malta-related works include, in alphabetical order, a history of: astronomy; banking; broadcasting; the civil service; the constitution; education; medicine; the Police Force; politics; printing; and public transport.

[4] The article by Alex Mifsud, entitled "Computing in Malta" (Mifsud, 2000) which was specially written for the millennium launch of a collection of papers on the Maltese political, social, ecological and economic developments, was the only concise piece of related literature available at the time.

Book Overview

Shortly after the Second World War, which is the point at which this book narrative begins, at least three organizations in Malta felt they could do with an Automatic Data Processing (ADP) System, as the punched-card tabulating and early computer systems were then known. These three organizations were Simonds Farsons Cisk, a large brewery with roots going back to the 1880s; the Malta Dockyard (later to become The Malta Drydocks) which, before being sold in 1959 to the British engineering firm of C. H. Bailey (and subsequently acquired by the Maltese Government), belonged to the British Colonial Government; and the then newly formed Statistics Office. Although the Central Office of Statistics (as the Statistics Office officially came to be called) had just been set up, it expanded fairly rapidly, so that by the 1960s—in spite of its small workforce in comparison to that at the Dockyard (thousands of employees) and Farsons (hundreds of employees)—it was by far the "heaviest" tabulating equipment user of the three.

The War, which left heavy casualties and widespread destruction, necessitated the gathering of new census data for which it was acknowledged that an ADP system would prove useful both in terms of data processing efficiency and data analysis. As Malta—like other countries affected by World War II—tried to realign its international economy in the post-war period, statistics became increasingly a tool for economic planning, thus magnifying its status as a scientific discipline capable of reliable projections. As data sets became ever larger, it also became increasingly necessary to employ the "newer methods" of data processing. It was a strong argument for those at the Central Office of Statistics (COS) to promote the ADP system and simultaneously justify its high running costs.

Chapter 1 therefore opens with a case study of the COS's early work, the first government institution to have used tabulating and sorting equipment. Chapter 1 looks at how, and why, tabulating equipment was introduced, the success stories, technology transfer, and the problems encountered in the process. Since Malta was then a British colony, the British connection is also examined.

In the 1970s Malta saw little computing developments. Apart from a handful of computer installations, described in the second and third chapters, the computer scene throughout practically the entire decade was "dull" with little progress. Two events worthy of note, however, took place that merit investigation. These are the attempt in the late 1960s to create a government computer centre, or "organization" as it was then referred to, described in Chapter 2; and the relatively late and surprisingly long-lived and historically significant time-sharing era, which came about directly as a result of two Maltese firms set up in 1979-1980 specifically to provide a computer time-sharing service. In this period (1979-1981) three other local firms also started offering "turnkey" solutions. The story of time-sharing together with an account of two private firms is told in Chapter 3.[5]

An identification of the first computer users gives one an insight into the type of businesses that mostly felt the need for either full computerisation or at least the use of a computer bureau. Not surprisingly, most were large companies who could afford the high cost then associated with computers, however a few smaller firms also made use of remote and online time-sharing. Interestingly, as late as the 1990s, this type of computing mode was still being used, an example of organizational inertia.

An examination of the first fifteen or so computer installations, carried out as part of Chapter 3's exercise, reveals that the main computer supplier was the British company ICL (which set up an office in Malta in 1947) and that—particularly in a small market like that of Malta—it was initially difficult for other computer firms, or their agents, to make inroads.

Worldwide in computing history, the period spanning roughly the mid-1980s to the mid-1990s saw an unprecedented rise in personal computing as well as a paradigm shift in the use of the technology. The main events include: the proliferation of the PC and its continued massive use; the emergence of networking with a corresponding

---

[5] The mid-1970s was also a period when scientific calculators, some programmable, were introduced in local secondary and sixth-form (post secondary) schools, the former MCAST Polytechnic and the University. For a number of years these hand-held calculators formed part of the equipment found in science laboratories. Some of these calculators used reverse polish notation, a postfix notation which students were unaccustomed to and which therefore had to be explained to them. Today, postfix notation is mentioned at the sixth-form and first year undergraduate level computing courses as part of the compiler theory module.

move away from computer centralization, including downsizing; the emergence of client/server computing; the rise of Management Information Systems, which saw their beginnings in the 1960s, but matured into an academic discipline and gained widespread industry acceptance much later; a continued and increased deployment of computers in the financial sectors (e.g. the rise of Bank ATMs) and by manufacturing firms, both as automation tools and in the management of productivity; and—in the later part of this period— the beginning of the widespread use of the Internet.

The fourth, fifth and sixth chapters trace much of these developments as they happened in Malta. The adoption of computers, the computing models and the use of the new visual programming languages and DBMSs, for example, followed roughly that of developed countries, although perhaps lagging by two or three years. As Chapter 4 shows, the introduction of computers in Maltese schools (especially in state schools) was a slow process. Even the University (of Malta), the only university on the Island, was late in launching its first undergraduate degree programme in computing. Chapter 5 is dedicated to the development of computer science at Malta's only university. This chapter is then followed by another chapter that recounts the setting up of the Government Computer Centre in 1981, and the eventual shift to decentralisation as local area (and, subsequently, wide area) networks gained popularity roughly a decade later. The narratives on the MSU and MITTS, the national bodies that were instrumental in diffusing information technology in the public sector, form part of Chapter 6.

Chapter 7 is dedicated to Malta's nascent software industry. In the mid- to late 1990s a number of foreign software firms showed interest in setting up a base in Malta, the British company Magus (later renamed Crimsonwing) being perhaps one of the best examples. Reasons given by these foreign companies to locate in Malta varied from Malta's political stability to a good telecommunications infrastructure, but the educational level of the young Maltese, their ambitions, and their foreign-language skills were among the prime reasons for choosing Malta as the place to do business.

By this time, the local software houses that started up some decade and a half earlier had also expanded, so that together with other local firms that were created in the 1990s to offer Internet and web services, a software industry was in the making. By the turn of the Millennium, the industry was fairly mature. Based on a company profile e-survey and an investigation of other sources, in 2005 some one hundred software firms altogether employing about one thousand professionals were in existence. In 2005, the revenues generated amounted to about 1.5% of GDP, again quite significant, although still behind a number of advanced countries. Chapter 7 examines how this industry came about, the players involved, its modest success, and government's role in its promotion. Since a number of software industry studies of particular countries have appeared in the last two decades or so, it has been possible to compare Malta's indigenous software industry with those of other countries. Indeed, this has been one of the objectives of Chapter 7.

Chapters 8, 9 and 10 give an account of the development of the Maltese telecommunications sector. A nation's basic utility, telecommunications is today also one of a nation's economic pillars. Initially seen as primarily essential for large business concerns, it now touches every aspect of society. Information economies are completely dependent on a sound telecommunications infrastructure, failing which economic growth could be severely hampered. Indeed, it has been shown that economic growth is linked to a nation's advanced telecommunication system (see, for example, Baer, 2001: pp. 362-363; and Torero & von Braun, 2006: pp. 12-13 and p. 27).

Telecommunications in Malta has a long history, going back to the first telegraphic experiments in the 1860s involving submarine cables, but since this early period is hardly relevant to this book's subject matter, only a relatively short chapter (Chapter 8) is dedicated to this period, the emphasis therefore being placed on the more recent events beginning from about 1980 (described in Chapters 9 and 10).

Two aspects are primarily examined. The first concerns telecommunications as a utility, its infrastructure and service provision, including the technologies used and the players involved. The second is the related topics of regulation, liberalisation and privatisation. Like most European countries, the telecommunications sector—since its nationalisation in 1974—was a public monopoly and, again following much of Europe, Malta began in the late 1980s the process of liberalisation. Although then not a European Union member, Malta had long aspired to join (it became a member in 2004), so that much of the relevant policies and telecommunication liberalisation laws were directly modelled on the EU directives.

Chapters 11 through 13 evaluate information technology policy and government's involvement in the IT sector. Prior to 1990, no concrete IT policy was in place, and it was only with the first Information System Strategic Plan (ISSP) of 1991 that IT was placed on a solid foundation. The 1991 ISSP, followed three years later by a national information technology strategy, was to initiate a series of ambitious computerisation and policy programmes that would set the course for the subsequent heavy investment in computing technology, and that would make Malta part of the information superhighway. To implement its vision, the Maltese authorities had to face complex policy and institutional reforms, such as competition issues, universal access procedures, funding mechanisms and regulatory reforms that also involved the convergence of telecommunications and the media. Legislation related to intellectual property also had to be drawn up. This involved the complicated and controversial issues of software patents and copyright, a section to which is dedicated as part of Chapter 12. In the spring of 2003 a Ministry for Investment, Industry and Information Technology, under the lead Ministry for Competitiveness and Communications, was created to oversee many of the changes envisaged. Headed by a minister that must at least be remembered for being technology "savvy", IT almost took a new dimension, as the battle to win the digital divide saw various schemes being introduced that promoted IT's diffusion and widespread adoption.

Finally, Chapter 14 concludes with a review and analysis of the research findings. It highlights, and comments on, what are believed to be the crucial milestones that shaped Malta's computing and information processing history. The implications of those events are examined in the light of the policy-making process. Generally, it is found that the extent, timing and sequence of the policy decisions are determinants for success.

Part I

Computing with Tabulating Machines

Part I
Computing with Tabulating Machines

Punched card tabulating and sorting machines are often considered to be the precursors of computers. Ever since Herman Hollerith demonstrated their potential when he used them, in the summer of 1890, to process the United States Population Census, these machines rapidly found applications in other economic sectors and private institutions. From government statistics departments to insurance agencies, to the Nautical Almanac and the Military, for over half a century punched card tabulating machines were used to process data in a way no other equipment previously could.

In Malta, at least four organizations are known to have installed tabulating equipment, namely, the former Malta Dockyard, the former Central Office of Statistics (COS, now the NSO), Farsons, and the Archdiocese of Malta (known locally as the Archbishop's Curia, or simply as "il-Curia"). We know very little about the installations at three of these institutions but, fortunately, the working reports kept by the Statistics Office contain small sections about this Office's use of the machines, so that—following a systematic analysis of these documents and interviews with two former COS employees who programmed and operated the machines—a clear picture could be built of the COS's involvement with tabulators. The opening chapter recounts the story of the statistics office and this organization's "Machine Accounting" section that was responsible, amongst other things, for data processing with tabulators.

1

Computing at the Central Office of Statistics, 1947-1970

In 1800, after a brief spell of French occupation, Malta passed to Britain and formally became a British colony some years later. With a British presence that would last for almost one hundred and eighty years,[6] it was only natural for the Maltese to inherit much that was British, particularly the administrative machinery; and whenever Malta needed expert advice—as when government intended taking measures to improve the economic infrastructure—the expertise invariably came from the ruling country. During the early years (1947-1950) of the Malta Statistics Office's existence expert statisticians were also brought over from London to transfer their knowledge and help build the solid foundations. It is one of the many links with Britain involving the Statistics Office.

Regarding population density, Malta ranks amongst the highest in the world, and this held true even a century ago when—at about only 200,000—the population was half what it is today; but the fact remains that the numbers are small, which led some to question the need for a central statistics bureau, more so for the enactment of a statistics law. In fact, the proposal of the first Statistics Act in 1950 met with some resistance, and it was not before 1955, some eight years after the Statistics Office had been established, that the bill became law when it was finally passed through parliament.[7]

---

[6]   Malta obtained its independence in 1964 but British military presence lasted until 1979.

[7]   In 1955 the Statistics Office became officially the Central Office of Statistics (COS, for short). More recently, following the enactment of the Statistics Act of

Although the reasons for opposing a Statistics Bill are now of historical importance only, the story is significant because it is not an isolated case and certainly not one that is unrelated to the events that led to the enactment of the British Trade Act of 1947 (on which the Maltese Act was modelled) and the establishment of Britain's Central Statistics Office some years before in 1941. The British Act was long in coming because it had met considerable opposition, with some of the arguments put forward against its introduction being not too far removed from those submitted by the Maltese politicians of the day. Here was another link. In fact, the Maltese Statistics Office's formation has some connections and parallels with that of Britain (and a few other European countries that were involved in the war) and these are brought out in the story that follows.

The aim of this chapter, beyond highlighting these connections is to recount the story of one of the earliest application of data processing equipment in Malta, of a government entity that was the first to have used such equipment locally and in so doing shape the future of information processing in Malta.[8]

Rationales for an Office of Statistics

Prior to 1947 when the Statistics Office was created, no government department was responsible for all of the nation's statistics. However, a number of departments had had a long tradition of keeping some statistics relevant to their particular function. Thus, both the Health and Customs departments kept internal annual records from documents that were collected throughout the year, for example the number of yearly deaths in the case of the Health section, and records of foreign trade in the case of the Customs department.

For a number of years, the department of Agriculture also held annual surveys of agricultural activities (under the provisions of the Agricultural Returns Ordnance 1935), and the department of Labour likewise held various surveys into workers' earnings for the

---

2000, the COS was renamed the National Statistics Office (NSO). See the NSO's home page at *http://www.nso.gov.mt* for the latest statistics on Malta.

[8] The only other small data processing installation at the time was that of Simonds Farsons Cisk Ltd., a local brewery. See, for example, Galea (1981).

compilation of a retail price index (Camilleri, 2000).[9] Other departments which have actively compiled statistical data include the Emigration Department (set up in 1921), the Treasury, and the Public Registry. As far as population (and other) censuses are concerned, the normal practice was for government to set up a temporary census office until the data had been collected and manually processed. The office would be closed once the exercise had been completed.

Before the last century, basic but important official statistical data was compiled and published in the "Blue Books", the first of which entitled *The Blue Book of the Colony of Malta* came out in 1851. The Blue Books were akin to the current *Abstract of Statistics* and typically included information like demographic data relating to births, deaths and marriages; education data on the number of private and state schools and the number of "scholars"; financial information including amount of bank deposits; land sales; trade statistics and a host of other information that could have been useful for the Island's administration.

It is appropriate to reflect on what computing equipment was available in Malta in the late 1940s when the Office (henceforth referred to as COS, for Central Office of Statistics) was still in its infancy. At the time, three firms worthy of note had presence in Malta: Olivetti and the National Cash Register company (NCR) which were represented by local agents; and the British Tabulating Machine Company (BTM) which had just established a base in Malta, working from a small office in Valletta, Malta's capital.

The Italian firm of Olivetti had long made a name for itself in the office business sector by being the first Italian firm to mass produce high-quality typewriters, marketed globally.[10] Although founded in 1908 and represented in Malta at least since the 1940s, the company did not produce any electromechanical data processing and tabulating machines.

---

[9] The first scientific enquiry into the patterns of household expenditure which is on record is the one carried out by the Commissioner of Labour and Emigration in 1936. Some 100 workers' households were selected and a "cost of living" Index with January 1937 as the base month was constructed. The first full scale household budgetary survey was not carried out until 1971, when a new index with 1971 as base year was introduced. See Camilleri (1996).

[10] For a brief history of Olivetti see *http://www.olivetti.nu/history.htm*.

NCR, in Malta since 1946, needs little introduction. In business since the 1890s, NCR grew rapidly in the early 1900s with its huge sales of cash registers.[11] In the 1920s it started diversifying into mechanized accounting and by the 1940s a number of punched-card products suitable for automatic data processing were produced by the company. Its first computer, the CRC 102A was launched in the early 1950s as a result of its acquisition of another American firm called Computer Research Corporation.

The third computer company in Malta at the time was BTM, later to become ICL.[12] BTM's links with IBM are well known: in 1908, shortly after the London-based BTM company was formed, an agreement was reached between it and the American firm for BTM to have exclusive rights to work the Hollerith patents in Britain and the Empire in exchange for a (substantial) payment of 25% of its revenues to the American company (Campbell-Kelly, 1989a: pp. 10-13).[13] BTM also had links with Sperry Rand to sell the latter's products.

The data processing equipment that BTM was selling in the late 1940s when the Statistics Office had just started operating were therefore predominantly IBM machines, for example models like the Type 405 alphabetic accounting machine and the Type 77 collator, and machines of BTM's own design such as the Senior Rolling Total Tabulator (Campbell-Kelly, 1989b: pp. 90-92). As BTM had already a small office in Malta (practically next to that of the COS, as it happened)[14] and as IBM machines of the type just mentioned were very popular worldwide, not to mention the close ties that existed between the Maltese and British governments it was perhaps natural for the British company to have been chosen as the sole supplier of tabulating equipment by the Office.

---

[11] See, for example, Cortada (1993: p. 65); and Campbell-Kelly & Aspray (2004: p. 23).

[12] The BTM company started operating in Malta in 1947 (*Informatics*, 1985, 12: p. 13). In 1959 BTM merged with Powers-Samas to become ICT, which in turn merged with English Electric in 1968 to become ICL. Interestingly, the BTM company was also the one that, during World War II, built the Bombe machines (based on designs by Turing and Welshman) used at Bletchley Park to help in deciphering encrypted German naval Enigma messages.

[13] A chapter about the development of ICL is also given in Rose (1971). The authoritative work on ICL is Campbell-Kelly (1989b).

[14] BTM's office was located at 45 Ordnance Street [Triq l-Ordinanza], Valletta, about two hundred metres away from the COS's premises.

Formation of the Central Office of Statistics

The first official intimation that Government intended opening a new statistical service was conveyed by Circular No. 12/46 calling for applications to fill the post of Government Statistician (*Report on the working of the Central Office of Statistics (Incorporating the Electoral Registry) for the Year 1961*: p. 1 (henceforth *COS Report 1961*); and Lieutenant-Governor's Office Circular No. 12/46) (see Figure 1.1). The post was filled by Captain George Stivala who had formerly worked as a civil servant 'First Class Clerk' (*The Malta Government Gazette*, 1947: p. 301). Stivala's principal task was setting up the COS, so that with his appointment and the recruitment of one clerical officer and two temporary clerks, the COS effectively started operating in April 1947.

Initially, the new department was given temporary accommodation with the Public Relations Office at 5 Merchants Street (now Triq il-Merkanti), Valletta, but in April 1948 new premises were provided at 201 Old Bakery Street (Triq l-Ifran). Even before the small staff was relocated to the new building, the Department lost no time in publishing that same year its first *Statistical Abstract of the Maltese Islands*. This abstract is a compendium of statistics on the development of the country in the demographic, social and economic fields covering the period 1936-1946.

The first major exercise was the 1948 Census of the Maltese Islands, the 11th of a series started on 21 March 1842.[15] It was taken partly, if not chiefly, as a result of the aftermath of war. To quote from the introductory letter of this census report by the Census Officer (and chief government statistician) to the Minister of Finance:

> Both by reason of normal evolution, as well as through the upheaval of war, the post-war period is characterised by unusual problems, new needs and peculiar circumstances. For that reason, it will be found that, in the 1948 Census, much fresh ground has been

---

[15] In England the first decennial census of population was taken in 1801. See Agar (2003: p. 81).

explored which former Censuses left untouched (*Census of the Maltese Islands, 1948*: p. I).[16]

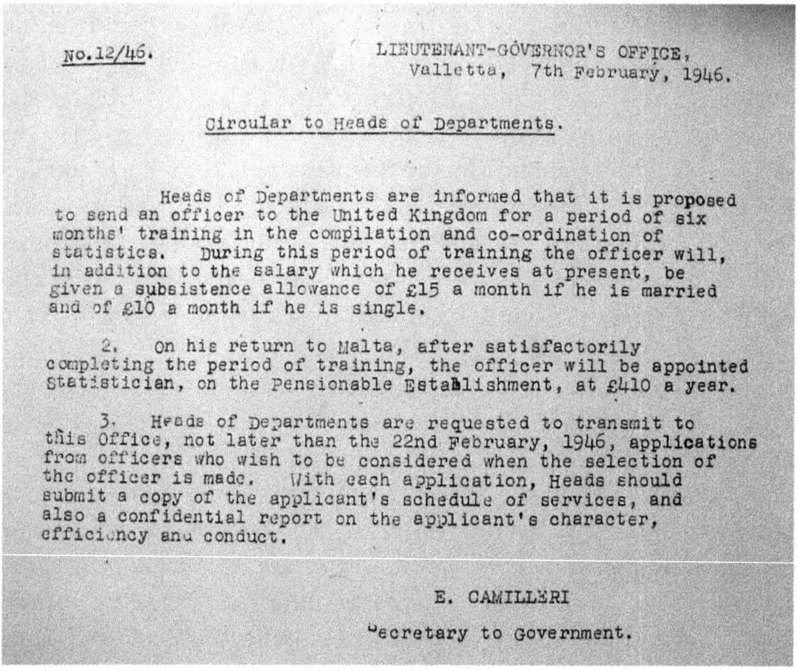

No.12/46.
LIEUTENANT-GOVERNOR'S OFFICE,
Valletta, 7th February, 1946.

Circular to Heads of Departments.

Heads of Departments are informed that it is proposed to send an officer to the United Kingdom for a period of six months' training in the compilation and co-ordination of statistics. During this period of training the officer will, in addition to the salary which he receives at present, be given a subsistence allowance of £15 a month if he is married and of £10 a month if he is single.

2. On his return to Malta, after satisfactorily completing the period of training, the officer will be appointed Statistician, on the Pensionable Establishment, at £410 a year.

3. Heads of Departments are requested to transmit to this Office, not later than the 22nd February, 1946, applications from officers who wish to be considered when the selection of the officer is made. With each application, Heads should submit a copy of the applicant's schedule of services, and also a confidential report on the applicant's character, efficiency and conduct.

E. CAMILLERI
Secretary to Government.

Figure 1.1
Circular No. 12/46 calling for the appointment of the first Malta Government statistician.
Source: *Lieutenant-Governor's Office Circular No. 12/46*, Chief Secretary to Government documents, National Archives of Malta [NAM:CSG 22/13].

The importance of this particular census is elaborated further in the "administrative" section of the report:

> ... A serious problem arose out of the continuous bombing from the air to which the Islands were subjected during the years 1941 to 1943. Many dwellings were destroyed and large numbers of people moved away from urban areas either in search of safety

---
[16] Letter dated 22 December 1948.

or to start a new home in lieu of a destroyed one. This abnormal movement of population and destruction of habitable dwellings has created problems to the public authorities never experienced before (*Census of the Maltese Islands, 1948*: p. V).

The abnormal movement of population is revealed in the census figures which show that whereas, in 1931, 22.9% of the total population lived in the Urban Harbour Area, only 11.5% inhabited this region in 1948. As just quoted, during the war many of those who lived in the Harbour Area had to leave their urban dwellings to seek refuge in the less dangerous rural areas. Interestingly, this demographic shift also had socio-economic implications. By the end of World War II the rural community had come into contact with the people outside their village, thus absorbing their ideas, and since a fair number of urban dwellers did not return to their original cities or towns, an urban mentality left its mark upon the younger members of the community (Pollacco, 2003: pp. 30-31).

The report's administrative section also alludes to the economic role of statistics and their importance for planning:

... the comprehensive and detailed information which has been collected cannot but serve to assist the Government in dealing with the urgent problems confronting it, such as reconstruction, housing, emigration, education and social services. All these problems involve a long term policy and it would obviously be futile to attempt to plan ahead without a basis of solid facts (*Census of the Maltese Islands, 1948*: p. V).

Prior to the war, censuses were taken at regular ten-year intervals up to 1931. Owing to the outbreak of the war, the 1941 census was missed, and hence for the first time in the space of a century a break of seventeen years occurred between two censuses.

In 1950—the year the first tabulating machines were introduced (more on this later)—legislation for an Act to provide for the establishment of a 'Central Office of Statistics' and 'for the supply of information thereto' (*Legislative Assembly Debates*, 1950), was moved by Arthur Colombo, finance minister of the then ruling Malta Labour

Party. The proposed Bill was withdrawn because no agreement could be reached by the main political parties involved.[17] Why was the Bill opposed? The Legislative Assembly Debates of that same year provide some answers. One opposition minister (Enrico Mizzi of the Nationalist Party) saw the Bill as an imposition by the British Government, an "enabling" law which gave the Governor in Council the power to amend it as and when required. Enabling laws, it was argued, were dangerous: the "Supplies" law enacted two years earlier to combat the black market was being used by Government to impose and prohibit importation to the detriment of the population and against import liberalisation. Owing to the fact that the Bill was moved by the finance minister, another opposition minister (Joseph Hyzler of the Democratic Action Party) was sceptical about it and was sure it had fiscal connotations; he also had reservations because the Act included items such as Immigration which was a "reserved matter".[18] For him, the Bill also meant an increase in the number of government employees at a time when stringent economy was called for.

In defence, Finance Minister Colombo stated that he was piloting the Bill only because the Office of Statistics fell under his Ministry. He explained how the Bill was modelled on Britain's Statistics of Trade Act 1947 and that the scope of the Bill was purely statistical so that better (economic) planning could be made. Indeed, this Act and an earlier 1939 Production Act both served as models for similar Acts that came out in Malaysia in 1949, in Jamaica in 1946, in New Zealand in 1945, and in Northern Rhodesia in 1948. He was in favour of centralisation because he believed that some departments (for

---

[17] The main political parties were the Democratic Action Party, the Labour Party and the Nationalist Party.

[18] When Malta was a colony, it was also a diarchy. The colonial self-government constitution of the British Empire gave limited legislative power to a legislative body elected by eligible voters in a given colony. Such an assembly could legislate in areas deemed of secondary importance to British Imperial interests (for example, taxation, housing, education and public health), but more sensitive areas such as defence, currency, telegraphy and external trade qualified as "reserved matters" and needed approval of special councils and committees and ultimately the Governor who represented the British monarch. The consequence of "reserved matters" rendered Malta completely dependent on Whitehall as regards currency control, international trade relations and civil aviation and, because of this, development in industry and trade was hard to achieve. See, for example, Pollacco (2003: p. xiii); and Pirotta (1987: Vol. 1, pp. 77-78).

example, Income Tax) were not equipped to perform statistics — the statistics required would be better done by people trained for the purpose.

Opposition to statistical surveys, statistically-related Acts, or an establishment of a central government statistical bureau is, of course, nothing new. For example, when Arthur Bowley, an academic statistician prominent at the newly established London School of Economics (first half of the 19th century) suggested employing "compulsory powers" to collect statistics, British miners rejected efforts by the Board of Trade to enforce these powers (Agar, 2003: p. 76). Likewise, ambitious education and religious censuses taken in the UK in 1851 both faced fierce opposition (*ibid.*: p. 83). The argument relating to the increase in the number of government employees which was expensive at a time when the economy was in a parlous state was also one reason put forward against the creation of Britain's Statistics Office although in the British case constitutional problems were more subtle (Agar, 2003: p. 246).

At this point it will be instructive to digress slightly and introduce the reader to the main political parties then active (since two of these will be encountered in later chapters). Although this will not necessarily explain why certain decisions were made regarding the acceptance, or rejection, of computing technology and modern ways of administration, it might throw light on an apparent paradox of political choices: why, for example, the Labour Party — by nature typically internationally oriented — has apparently played a shortsighted, protectionist and anti-modernist role (see Chapters 3, 4, 7 and 8); whereas, by contrast, the Nationalist Party — one might think internally oriented — appears to have been more open to modernization.

Shortly after the war, the Maltese political scene was still wrapped in uncertainty (Pirotta, 1987: Vol. 1, p. xv). The Nationalist Party (PN) — which would later become a major force — was unpopular because of its association with Italy. Its long-time leader Enrico Mizzi (who, during the war, was interned and deported to a Ugandan detention camp) was pro-Italian and of the opinion that Malta has much to benefit from Italy given Malta's geographical nearness and former friendship. It had long insisted that Italian should remain Malta's main language. It is little wonder that he viewed the proposed statistics bill as another imposition by the British Government.

The Democratic Action Party (DAP) was a newly formed party which essentially had a pro-British inclination. Its party members consisted of prominent Maltese business and professional persons who resisted any form of taxation that could conceivably have reduced the party members' wealth. This might explain the DAP's concern about the statistics bill to which they attached fiscal connotations.

The Constitutional Party (CP), for many years led by Lord Gerald Strickland and later by his daughter Mabel, was very Imperialist and loyal to the Crown. Following Strickland's death in 1940, however, it lacked leadership and became incapable of finding a place within the framework of the political re-alignment that was then (mid-1940s) taking place (*ibid.*: p. 31).

The Labour Party (LP) represented the working class and had close ties with the Workers Union. Whilst not pro-British, it preferred English as the language of instruction;[19] and it had at one time also proposed Malta's integration with Britain (which had begun a controversy with local church authorities). This party was more utilitarian and socialist, and it was depicted by the other parties as having Marxist ideologies because of its links with the Fabian Society of London (*ibid.*: p. 144). At that time the LP was progressive in the sense that it put forward several policies to improve the educational system and introduce social benefits, including old age pension, and health and unemployment insurance. It also frequently clashed with the Church.

In politics, disagreement among the same party members is not uncommon, leading to rivalry and sometimes also to a shift in political ideologies. This was the case with politics in Malta in that period. For reasons beyond the scope of this study, the DAP and the CP had dissolved by the 1950s.[20] Political rivalry and disagreements between Paul Boffa (LP's one time leader and Prime Minister) and

---

[19] Paul Boffa, then leader of the Labour Party, had stated that from a utilitarian and practical point of view, English was more useful than Italian: it would be of major benefit to workers seeking employment, especially given: a) the opportunities provided by HM services to Maltese workers; and b) the frequent emigration to English-speaking countries like Canada and Australia. See Pirotta (1996: p. 390).

[20] They fared badly in the 1947 general elections, which the MLP won.

Dominic Mintoff (also an LP member) eventually led to Boffa being ousted as party leader and the LP to split.[21] This resulted in the newly formed Malta Labour Party (MLP) headed by Mintoff. The split also profited the PN which won the 1950 elections.

In time, and following Enrico Mizzi's sudden death on 20 December 1950, the Nationalists' association with Italy became less of an issue. It gained popularity as its relations (under the leadership and premiership of Giorgio Borg-Olivier in the 1950s and 1960s) with Britain improved. By the mid-1950s the MLP had reorganised itself and managed to win the 1955 elections. From then onwards the MLP and the PN had established themselves as the two major political parties on the Islands.[22, 23]

National Income and Balance of Payments

Two items, National Income and Balance of Payments figure prominently in the annual publication of a country's National Accounts. The *national income* is the total money value of all incomes received by persons and enterprises in the country during a year, the sum of incomes earned by factors of production (labour, capital, land and entrepreneurship) as rewards for their participation in the production of goods and services—the GNP at factor cost less depreciation. The *balance of payments* is a statement of the economic transactions of a country with the rest of the world during a given period and may be regarded as a report of the outflows and inflows of

---

[21] Two important matters over which Boffa and Mintoff clashed concerned the Royal Navy Dockyard discharges, and Malta's claim for Marshall Aid (the European Economic Recovery Programme) which Britain denied Malta. See Chapter 8 of Pirotta (1987) and Chapter 3 of this book.

[22] Although the two parties were rivals, both were unanimous in emphasizing Malta's rights regarding aid (financial or otherwise) from Britain to build Malta's basic infrastructure following the Island's destruction from heavy aerial bombardment. They also both aspired to have a constitution that would give the Maltese government autonomy on managing the Maltese economy without colonian fetters. This was partly achieved through the 1961 Blood Constitution which empowered the Malta government to conduct external trade negotiations with foreign countries without the limitations of reserved matters.

[23] In a small island colony, the ideologies of the political parties which develop as a result of colonialism (as in the case of Malta) are more complex than have been painted in the necessarily brief account given here. See, for example, Frendo (1979).

foreign exchange from and into a country. National income and balance of payments are extremely useful indicators of a nation's well-being, and their estimates are therefore critical. A country's balance-of-payments performance is determined by the economic policies adopted by other countries as well as by its own policies. Local policies, in turn, can only be made in the light of accurate statistical information, so that the gathering of data and the role of any Statistics Office in performing these estimates cannot be overemphasised.

In 1955 the COS for the first time prepared these estimates for the previous year (*COS Report 1956-57*: p. 4). The estimates formed the basis of a number of tables which appeared in a famous report by the late Oxford economists Thomas Balogh (later Lord Balogh) and Dudley Seers, known simply as the Balogh Report (Balogh & Seers, 1955).[24] The Balogh Report dealt with the fundamental problems the Island was facing in that period and was drawn in consultation with the COS at the invitation of the report's authors by the Maltese government. Its terms of reference were:

(i)   to carry out a general survey of Malta's economic situation;

(ii)   to suggest how Malta's economy could be strengthened by capital development plans;

(iii)   to indicate to what extent Malta could legitimately expect economic aid from Great Britain; and

(iv)   to state what economic measures should be adopted to implement a closer union with Britain in conformity with the views of the Malta Government.

Balogh and Seers were chosen because of their expertise in Economic Statistics but possibly also because Dom Mintoff, then Malta's Premier, who invited them was an Oxford scholar himself and may have known them personally. Moreover, the left-wing Balogh's views coincided with those of the prime minister Mintoff (Pirotta, 1987: Vol. 1, p. 77).

Balogh's and Seer's calculations of the Maltese national product referred to the single year 1954 but in 1957, on the advice of the

---

[24] A very brief summary of this report may also be found in *The Malta Year Book 1956* (pp. 195-198).

United Nations expert Rupert Burge, a second study of the national accounts was undertaken covering the years 1954-56. This led to the very first publication of *The National Accounts of the Maltese Islands* (COS, 1957).[25] A year later Burge, who was sponsored by the UN Department of Economic and Social Affairs, also presented his report for the years 1954-57 (*COS Report 1957-58*: p. 9).[26] The 1954-56 study showed that the average per capita income for that period, at c. GBP105 (GBP: Great Britain Pound), compared well with capita incomes of most Mediterranean countries and was well above those of many places in Africa, Asia and Latin America.

The reasons for the importance of accurate statistics regarding National Income have already been noted;[27] in Malta's case were further reasons for its calculation, for example, the reductions in Dockyard employment levels and other HM Services as a result of Britain's post-war decolonization and demobilization process were bound to markedly reduce the national income of the Maltese.[28] Another reason for gathering statistics in general was that between c. 1945-1965 emigration was an accepted form of demographic control; in this period the rate of emigration was at times so fast that it led to lack of skilled manpower resources in Malta.

The COS's involvement in the estimates of the National Accounts says something about its role as a supplier of not only "informative" but also "administrative" statistics. The COS was instrumental for economic planning. Over the years, the number of bodies requesting statistical information multiplied, the demand coming from both government and private bodies as well as from international agencies such as the World Health Organization and the International Labour Organization.

---

[25] It is interesting to note that the measurement of the national income of the UK by official sources was first carried out in 1941. In the Netherlands the National Accounts—important then for determining Marshall aid—were first published in 1948. See, for example, van Maarseveen (1999: p. 27).

[26] See also Spiteri (1997: pp. 23-30).

[27] For the importance and uses of the National Income Statistics see Harvey (1998: pp. 337-340).

[28] HM Services refer to labour carried out by Maltese workers (mainly in Malta) for the UK's defence departments. See, for example, Pollacco (2003: pp. 5-6).

Training, Expertise and Knowledge Transfer

The employment of statistical techniques and the operation of new machinery both call for specially trained personnel and entail a level of qualification that can only be gained by undergoing a course of training. Between 1954 and 1957, following calls for applications, a number of higher executive and clerical officers were sent to England to gain academic qualifications in Economics and Statistics and thereby fill the posts of junior and senior statisticians (*COS Report 1956-57*: p. 2).

The training of these officials abroad was necessary and urgent because although the estimates for the year 1956 provided for four posts of statisticians, for a number of years no suitably qualified candidates could be found to fill these posts (*ibid.*: p. 2). As an interim solution two of the posts were temporarily filled by clerical officers. Additionally, for the upcoming 1957 population census, expert assistance was sought by recruiting the services of E. H. Slade, an expert on census-of-population problems and who had served as statistician in the General Registrar's Office in London (*ibid.*: p. 2). He was seconded to the COS in May 1956 to take charge of the Demographic Statistics Section, a new COS section dealing with a branch of statistics about which little was known in Malta at the time. In the course of Slade's four years with the department, the foundations for a proper and accurate appraisal of Malta's demographic characteristics were laid (*COS Report 1960*: p. 3).

Burge's expert advice on economic matters and Slade's service at the Malta Statistics Office may be taken as an early example — indeed an early form — of skills and service transfer and the development of tacit knowledge. The training of Maltese officials in Britain and the introduction of tabulating equipment new to Malta at the time also exemplifies technology transfer. Until at least the middle of the last century technology was mainly exported and imported in the form of equipment and machinery, drawings and formulae and human migration. It was only later — beginning perhaps from the early 1970s — that productive knowledge tended to be supplied across frontiers in a package form when big firms (transnational corporations), encouraged amongst other factors by the import substitution policies of recipient countries, began exploiting foreign markets through direct investment rather than through exports.[29] As with numerous developing countries, Malta experienced both modes of transfer: the "human" type form in the post-war years and before; the more "direct" form later when large foreign manufacturing firms began operating locally.

In the case of Malta, which was a developing country under colonial rule, much of the early technology and knowledge acquisition came from the ruling country, in this case Britain,[30] although in later years the local industry included a number of non-British foreign firms. Technical assistance in various sectors could also be sought from around the world through many technical aid programmes offered by international bodies (such as the United Nations), which Malta had joined. Clearly, Malta's particular form of analysis, be it economical or statistical, was modelled on that of Britain, initially at least.

The First Machines

Although in many other countries, tabulating equipment for statistical purposes had already become popular by the first few decades of the twentieth century (see Box 1-1), in Malta the first few, post-war, statistical publications were produced manually, using traditional, mechanical calculators and typewriters. For example, the Population Census of 1948 referred to above, was done completely manually (that is, without using tabulating equipment) (*Census of the Maltese Islands, 1948*: p. VIII).[31] However, in December 1949, a contract was signed

---

[29] See, for example, Dunning (1971) and White (1983). For more recent studies on technology transfer and innovation see Howells (1998) and Hartley & Rashman (2007).

[30] Although the UK's Department of Technical Co-operation was established in 1961, technical assistance by the UK to its colonies for economic development had been formally recognised since 1950 when the Secretary of State, Mr. James Griffiths, addressed a confidential Circular Despatch to Colonial Governments intended 'to give a broad picture of the source and nature' of technical assistance and of 'the way in which the various forms which it takes can contribute to the development of the Colonies'. By 1957 it was accepted policy that HMG should continue to provide technical assistance to former Colonial territories as they became independent. See Morgan (1980: pp. 236-239).

[31] That the 1948 Census was done manually is further confirmed in the *Preliminary Report of the 1957 Census* (p. 3), which states that 'Analysis in that kind of detail [referring to, for instance, the number of dwellings having various number of

between the COS and BTM for the supply of punched-card machines.[32]

The equipment was delivered and made operational in October 1950 (*COS Report 1956-57*: p. 9), which year proved a development milestone for the Office: the new sorting and tabulating machines enabled the department to more effectively produce statistics on various sectors of Malta's economy. As far as the COS was concerned, the ADP installation, albeit small, probably ranked in importance with the Statistics Act of 1955, which effectively authorised the department to obtain information directly from members of the community.

It has not been possible to ascertain the exact number and type of machines the Office acquired when the first contract with the BTM company was signed, but the first official *Report on the Workings of the Central Office of Statistics* — that for the financial year ending 31 March 1957 — mentions that the Office was equipped with 10 mechanical punches (operated by female employees), verifiers, at least one sorter, and at least one tabulator. The tabulator was an adding, listing and printing machine which produced a printout of the required statistical figures. These were then passed to the printing section for further checks by clerical staff before the corrected figures would be reproduced by other equipment (for instance, a "varitype writer") for final printing (*COS Report 1962*: p. 2).

Other office equipment included two Varityper machines, two typewriters fitted with microtypes, an electrically operated duplicating machine, and a multilith printing machine. The Varitypers and typewriters were used to reproduce the tabulated figures on duplimats or stencils which were then, in turn, reproduced in printed form by the duplicator and a small printing unit. Originally, the itemised output from the tabulators was printed as purely numeric codes — that is, without showing the item description. This tabulated output was then passed to the (usually female) clerks who would manually write down the description against the numeric Standard International Trade Classification codes, which description

---

rooms, and accommodating various number of households and persons] is now possible by the use of punched-card machinery. Nearly all of our statistical work in Malta is done today on such machines but at the time of the 1948 Census they had not been introduced.'

[32] Appendix C explains the function of the different tabulating machines that were used at the COS.

was then typed and used for the final printing purposes. Because this procedure was time consuming and error-prone, it was modified so that the description would be tabulated directly instead. A photoscopic machine was then used to photograph the large tabulated sheets so that they could be reproduced on the multilith printing machine.[33]

Until 1956, the number of reports produced was still relatively small: five main publication titles (containing a total of under 500 tabulations) of which fewer than 1,000 copies were published. However, in subsequent years the number of publications increased considerably, and some machines had to be replaced by better ones whilst others had to be purchased or hired in order to keep up with the demand. By the end of 1964, for example, the number of published copies amounted to more than 12,000 (13 different publication titles), together comprising approximately 802 statistical tables and 77 graphs (*COS Report 1964*: p. 5). These figures are remarkable considering the small size of Malta, which then had a population of just over 320,000 inhabitants.

Box 1-1
The Emergence of Punched-Card Tabulation

The invention of punched-card tabulating and sorting machines is attributed to the American mechanical engineer, statistician, and entrepreneur Herman Hollerith. Hollerith first encountered the problem of manually processing huge amounts of data in 1879 when he began working for the US Bureau of the Census in Washington shortly after graduating from Columbia University. Observing the immense volume of clerical work necessary to produce tabulated results from the 1880 raw census data which took over six years to process, he realised that without some mechanical means it would take even longer to process the next (1890) census data, by which time the results thus produced would be of little use. It was this experience that drove him to design and build his counting and sorting equipment.

Hollerith's machines worked by using data represented on cards punched with holes, whereby a particular hole pattern would represent a particular piece of data. According to Hollerith, the idea of using punched holes came

---

[33] In Malta, this process was first conceived at the COS by Albert Galea and Maurice Abela. Telephone conversation with Albert Galea on 20 March 2006.

to him when he was on board a train with a punched ticket that contained passenger data encoded in the punched holes. However, others before him—for example Joseph Marie Jacquard and John Shaw Billings—had already made use of, or suggested using, perforated cards: to control the pattern of hooks and needles for use in weaving in the case of Jacquard, and to count and sort the 1880 census in the case of Billings who put forward the suggestion. No tabulating machines were built for the 1880 census but by 1886 Hollerith machines were already employed to handle the mortality records of the city of Baltimore.

Was Hollerith alone in trying to create an electromechanical system for the 1890 census? For about two decades following the 1890 census Hollerith (and the company he founded, the Tabulating Machine Company, later to become IBM) had no direct competition. For the 1890 census a commission had been set up to select by competition the best alternative solution to the manual system of tally sheets then in use, and the only two other inventors who entered the competition proposed very different methods that were still manual. Hollerith's system won the competition so that the 1890 census was carried out by machines that the engineering firm of Western Electric produced to Hollerith's design. Hollerith's new system had the advantage that once the cards had been punched (manually, using a key punch), the counting and sorting could be handled mechanically. Using the new system the final results of the 1890 census—which comprised about 11 million schedules, one for each family—were announced just one year later.

From about 1911 onwards another company began producing tabulating machines. This was the Powers Accounting Machine Company formed in 1911 by James Power, Hollerith's successor at the Census Bureau. In 1927 the Powers company was purchased by a successful organisation called the Remington Rand Corporation, and although the latter had strong organizational capabilities and was a major competitor to IBM, it still always came second to the giant.

Who were the major users of tabulators, apart from the US Bureau of Census and statistical organisations? By about the 1920s, many corporate firms and government departments that handled large amounts of data had installed tabulating equipment and continued to use them well into the second part of the twentieth century. They included life insurances, the military, the railways, major astronomical observatories, telecommunications companies, and various manufacturing industries. Of course, the popularity of tabulating machines was their power: they were in a class of their own because they could be externally "programmed" (using plugboards and plug wires) and therefore directed to automatically carry out a finite sequence of operations. Tabulating machines can thus be seen as the forerunners of the modern digital computer.

Expansion and Restructuring

Water and Electricity Billing, and the Machine Accounting Division

Up to 1956 the COS had three main functions: the collection and compilation of statistical records; the compilation and publication every six months of a revised register of electors; and the conduct of elections, both general and casual (*COS Report 1956-57*: p. 1). The staff complement for that year amounted to 52 persons, which included 3 statisticians, 2 higher executive officers and 2 junior statisticians. In February 1956, on the retirement of the principal electoral officer and electoral register, the Electoral Office was incorporated with the COS. This event, coupled with the enactment of the Statistics Act in May 1955, saw a rapid expansion in personnel over the previous years.

The COS now consisted broadly of two divisions, a Statistics Division, and the Electoral Registry Division. The Statistics Division was further subdivided: the technical and clerical staff section responsible for the collection, compilation and analysis of statistical studies; the punching and tabulating section (also referred to simply as the "Machine" section) responsible for the processing of data; and the printing section.

With the increase in the number of commissions and committees sitting on various economic and social questions, demands for statistical work increased (*COS Report 1957-58*: p. 5). Government, private business firms and foreign organizations were all requesting up-to-date statistics from the Office. In fact, the COS was beginning to operate in a general consultancy role. When, for example, it foresaw the rapid expansion of the Water and Electricity Department as a result of the new power plant and the standardisation of the distribution system which was about to ensue, the COS was quick to point out that 'mechanization of the billing system would be conducive to the higher efficiency apart from being the most economical way to meet the situation' (*ibid.*: p. 14). The recommendation for the mechanization of the Water and Electricity Billing was formally made by a Committee and accepted by Government.

In 1957, therefore, following this recommendation, and because new machinery would be needed for this purpose, it was thought more appropriate to separate the machine section from the Statistics Division and create a new "Machine Accounting Division". The rationale was that as mechanization would likely be introduced for other government jobs—which it eventually was—it would make sense to have all the machinery centralized at the Office. Such an arrangement had the added advantage, it was argued,

> that should one of the [new] machines [for the Water Works] develop temporary defects, the present statistical equipment installed in the Office could to some extent be used on the Water Works job. The same benefits would accrue to the Statistics Office with the preparation of statistical tabulations (*COS Report 1957-58*: pp. 14-15).

Thus came into being the Machine Accounting Division.[34]

In 1958 the Machine Accounting Division consisted of 16 employees: 1 Higher Executive Officer, 1 Machine Room Supervisor, 2 Senior Machine Operators, 11 Clerk Typists and a Labourer. Also, by this time, the Office had moved to 1 Windmill Street (Triq l-Imtiehen) in a building which formed part of 3 Old Mint Street (Triq Zekka), and an adjacent house was taken over to provide office space for the new machine division (see Figure 1.2). Moving the office was essential since the Office now also incorporated the personnel from the Electoral Registry. By 31 March 1958, the authorized staff complement was 76 although only 58 posts were actually filled. For many years the Windmill Street address remained the COS's main functional premises in spite of subsequent attempts to move to a modern and more spacious building.

In the Report for the financial year 1957/58, the total expenditure incurred by COS is given as GBP37,509 which excludes GBP1,822 needed in connection with the setting up of the New Machine Division. To put these figures into context, the average yearly salary

---

[34] A parallel may be drawn here with what happened at the Central Bureau of Statistics (CBS) of the Netherlands when, in 1941, following the transfer of agricultural statistics from the Ministry of Agriculture to the CBS, office equipment was substantially expanded and a separate "Machine Processing Department" was therefore created. See, for example, Kellenbach (1999: p. 65).

in Malta at that time was about GBP200, the post of supervisor/operator with the COS for that year carrying an annual salary of GBP210, and that of executive officer GBP254.[35] The following year, the figure for the Machine Accounting Division shot up to GBP8,663, of which GBP3,512 went toward salaries.

Figure 1.2
The Central Office of Statistics building at Windmill Street.
Source: Author's collection

Type of Equipment Used

It is appropriate here to briefly summarize the equipment being used (see Figure 1.3). For the purpose of the Water Works project, the COS decided to undertake the mechanization process in two stages: a pilot scheme which lasted for about 18 months, and then a full scheme which lasted for about 18 months, and then a full scheme when more machines were hired and purchased. For the pilot

---

[35] "Examination for Executive Officers", *The Review*, 27 August 1957, No. 44, p. 6.

scheme, the following equipment was recommended (and used): two Alpha mechanical punches, two verifiers, one reproducing summary card punch, a sorter, collator, electronic calculator, pre-sensing gang summary punch, alphabetical numerical tabulator and a posting machine.

The additional equipment for the complete scheme included a mechanical punch, an alpha mechanical verifier, a sorter and a collator. It was further recommended that the equipment for the pilot scheme would be hired but that the punches, verifiers, reproducing summary card punch and the posting machines would be purchased outright when the full scheme was to be introduced. For the supply of machines for the Water and Electricity project, tenders were called for and the contract again given to ICT.

According to the late Albert Galea,[36] an ex-COS employee who had worked on the Water and Electricity billing, the pilot scheme had gone according to plan and was completed in time with no major problems, as far as he could recall (although customer complaints about bills were later made). By the end of 1961, 60 districts, out of a total of 98, had already been mechanised.

To operate machines such as these naturally required a certain amount of training, so in 1958 four locally recruited officers, who were to be directly connected with the planning, implementation and operation of this scheme, underwent courses of training at ICT's school at Cookham in England (*COS Report 1957-58*: p. 15).[37] This college, named the Moor Hall School, was established in 1950 for all BTM commercial and operator training (Connolly, 1967: p. E-18).

During the initial stages of the Water and Electricity billing project, the COS personnel were also assisted by experienced ICT staff, particularly by ICT's then local manager, Max Wenner, who according to Galea worked closely with the two government departments involved to get the project off the ground. The initial phase entailed a review of the entire manual structure to establish the methods employed by meter readers and account keepers in presenting the bills to the public. The systems analysis also revealed that "load programming", then considered a new working concept, had to be introduced in order 'to make the most economical and

---

[36] Interviewed on 13 October 2004.
[37] One of the officers who attended the course was Galea himself.

effective use of the calculating and tabulating machinery' (*COS Report 1958-59*, p. xiii).

Figure 1.3
Employees working on some of the equipment mentioned in the text.
Source: *Report on the Working of the Central Office of Statistics, 1956/57.*

Need for More Processing Power

Following the successful mechanisation of the Water and Electricity billing, several other jobs, external to the statistical work, were earmarked for mechanisation and eventually executed. The undertaking of these services to other departments enabled full use of the equipment and simultaneously justified the services' high cost.

In 1959, in parallel with the Water and Electricity billing project, a start was made to mechanise the treasury accounts. However, this work was soon abandoned because accounting machines were introduced and used at the Treasury Department itself.

In 1964, work on the first telephone billing was started. This work commenced following an investigation carried out by a Working

Committee (presided over by the officer in charge of the Statistics section) who drew up a report for the Postmaster General. Originally planned to be performed on the senior rolling tabulators, the telephone billing was initially done on the Type 903 tabulator but was later transferred to the 1004 data processor (which was also used for the water and electricity billing—see Figure 1.4). Processing went as far as the preparation of subscriber's history sheets, a ledger, and payments records. The bills were issued for the first time in 1966. Within two years, the Sliema district involving 6,750 accounts was fully automated (*COS Report 1968*: p. 5). Plans to extend the billing to other districts were disrupted in 1971 when a new government was elected whose attitude towards computers was markedly negative, as I will explain shortly.

Other jobs of significance which commenced in the early 1960s included the Public Works cost accounting system, the retail price index and the Pitkali system.

Pitkali refers collectively to the fruit and vegetable market centres where farmers gather to sell their products, and the Pitkali system, done on behalf of the Department of Agriculture, aimed to mechanically produce a statement of the amount due to each farmer and the corresponding payment by cheque (obtained from sales vouchers transcribed on punched cards). By the end of 1961, approximately half the Pitkali markets had been mechanised. Within a few years an average of 1,400 cheques per month for the farmers were being issued.[38]

At the market centres where the deals between farmers and the middlemen were negotiated, government officials would record the transactions. These transactions in the form of sales vouchers would then be transcribed on the punched cards. It is conceivable that, at times, an insufficient number of government officials would be available for audit purposes, leading to either abuse or more genuine errors.

The late 1960s witnessed considerable interest in the calculation of the retail price index (RPI) as a result of the general rise in domestic prices. Consequently, the COS exerted much effort on mechanising its calculation. The RPI calculation is often done as a measure to control inflation and its harmful effects it produces. The RPI's construction

---

[38] See, for example, the 1966 and 1968 COS Reports.

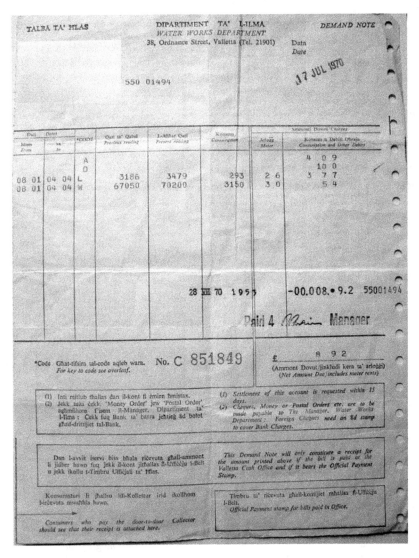

Figure 1.4
A water and electricity bill issued by the 1004 data processor in 1970. The client address has been hidden for privacy reasons.
Source: Provided to the author by Joe D'Amico.

typically entails the controlled gathering of statistical data from a representative sample of the population which is asked to maintain a careful budget of expenses over, for example, 1 month's time. On the basis of the survey, retail goods and services are then broken down into a number of categories to each of which is attached a weight according to its importance in total consumer expenditure. The weight assigned to each category is effectively the category's percentage of the total expenditure. The price index is then the total of the weighted indexes. This exercise is first done for a base year when each category's index is set to 100 so that the price index for the base year is also 100.[39] As prices change, so the index for each category is adjusted accordingly.[40] Owing to the assigned weights, the RPI gives a reasonably good indication of how prices (and therefore the cost of living) have changed in comparison to the base year. Indeed, the RPI has now come to be regarded as one of the most important economic indicators.

The RPI estimate carried out at the COS in the 1960s, although not the first attempt,[41] was the first in Malta to be worked out using the latest electronic punched-card calculators then available. The steps involved in its determination are also suitable for automatic calculation: the fact that the RPI needed to be calculated and published frequently made it ideal for the punched-card calculators, which were programmable. These jobs, in addition to the normal statistical work that by the mid-1960s had also
increased in volume, necessitated newer and faster equipment. Some of the machines had also been in continuous service for well over a decade and, apart from their considerable depreciation, had become unreliable 'due to frequent breakdowns' (COS Report 1968).

In 1966, therefore, the COS made another important decision, that of acquiring a Univac 1004 computer, primarily to replace the tabulators.[42] The event was important and historical, a great step

---

[39] Each category's weighted index is simply the weight of the category multiplied by its index.

[40] Thus, if in the base year the price of a certain commodity (or category) is x cents, and it rises to $1.2x$ the following year, the index for that commodity is changed from 100 to 120.

[41] In 1935 the Department of Labour already held the first partial survey into workers' earnings for the compilation of a retail price index. See Camilleri (1996) for an explanation of how the retail price index for Malta is compiled and the applications to which it can be put.

[42] The 1004 was one of many computer models produced by the Sperry Rand Corporation of America, a major rival of IBM and one of the few companies to have produced computers before Big Blue did so. It was a small core memory computer (ferrite core memory was by now already appearing in a number of

forward in the use of more modern technology and one that may perhaps also be counted as another COS milestone.

Delivered by ICT (the former BTM company which by now had merged with Powers-Samas and was renamed International Computers and Tabulators) in December 1966 and made operational some time later, this data processor had already sold well both in the United States where it was first conceived and in Europe. Together with a second 1004 ordered by the COS itself some years later, these two computers appear to have been the only machines of their type to have ever been installed in Malta.

COS Expenditure

Table 1.1 summarises the COS expenditure for the years 1959-1970. This table has two main sections, the expenditure for the machine division and that incurred by the rest of the Office, both given against total expenditure. The heading "Other Expenses" under the machine division refers mainly to equipment rentals. The policy that the COS adopted was to purchase and rent, although—particularly for the big machines such as the sorters, tabulators and data processors—leasing was by far the most common option.[43, 44]

---

computers) which used solid state (i.e. transistorised) components in its CPU and therefore was categorised as a UNIVAC Solid State machine. In this respect, it was also a 'second generation' type of computer. In Europe, the 1004 was sold as the ICT 1004, this being the model installed at the COS. This model took the standard 80 column cards.

[43] Although no records of actual financial transactions giving rental and other charges could be traced, the overall yearly expenditure on the machines alone have also been inferred from two other sources. A 1972 government report, for example, states that the hiring of machinery and equipment at the COS was costing government 11,625 Maltese Liri (abbreviated LM where 1 LM was roughly equivalent to GBP 1.05) per annum. *Reports on the Working of Government Departments* (1972: pp. 29-30).

[44] The second source comes from an ex-COS employeed. Asked if he could recall how much the COS were paying for the equipment at about 1970, Joe D'Amico, who worked in the machine division, was very specific: in the early 1970s the two 1004 machines were leased for LM875 (c. GBP920) monthly for 177 hours of use, and if this number of hours were exceeded, a further fee was charged (interview with D'Amico on 4 May 2005). With a rate of exchange of LM1 = US$2.6709 (March 1972), the monthly rental charge of LM875 was equivalent to about US$2337.

Important to note from this table is the following:

(i)   rental expenses were initially almost always more than personal emoluments of the machine section staff;

(ii)   the average yearly figure for rentals of approximately GBP10,000 represented about the equivalent of the yearly total income of about twenty employees; and

(iii)   the machine section expenditure seems to have levelled by the end of the 1960s to about 22% of the overall total expenditure, even though the number of employees as well as the number of publications (not shown) continued to rise. This might be interpreted as an improvement in office efficiency, the result of which could have been years of gained work experience (hence improved working methodologies) and better (faster) machinery.

Political and Economic Constraints

By the end of the 1960s the volume of work had increased to such an extent that a second data processor and faster sorting equipment had to be leased. One data processor could now be dedicated to the statistics production and another to the accounting jobs. With the new sorters (such as the type 314/0) and collators, the combined sorting capacity was of the order of 2,750 cards per minute (*COS Report 1969*: p. 31). The 1970 COS annual report also reveals that over 1.9 million punched cards were used for statistically-related jobs and approximately 2.2 million cards for billing work (excluding summary cards created during the various stages of the processing of jobs) (*COS Report 1970*: p. 24). Overtime frequently had to be resorted to in order to cope with the work load.

Apart from the strain of trying to cope with the sheer work capacity, several problems seriously affected the working conditions and efficiency. The first, and perhaps most acute, was the lack of office space. The problem of housing the computing machinery which was massive and occupied considerable floor space was very real and one that apparently was never properly solved. This problem of space

TABLE 1.1
Malta's Central Office of Statistics Expenditures, 1959-1970

Year	Total Employees	--- MACHINE SECTION ---			--- REST OF OFFICE ---		COS Total Expenditure	MS Expenditure as % of TE (TE)
		Salaries	Other Expenses	Expenditure Machine Section (MS)	Salaries	Expenditure Rest of Office		
1959	?	4,309	7,914	12,223	22,006	28,265	40,488	30.2
1960	83	5,562	9,882	15,444	24,660	32,378	47,822	32.3
1961	?	7,113	9,449	16,562	23,786	40,439	57,001	29.1
1962	87*	7,670	9,682	17,352	26,849	80,848	98,200	17.7
1963	82	8,253	10,078	18,331	27,393	36,664	54,995	33.3
1964	91*	7,325	7,151	14,476	30,480	67,886	82,362	17.6
1965	94	7,898	10,863	18,761	32,564	46,009	64,770	29.0
1966	96	8,310	11,121	19,431	35,442	106,987	126,418	15.4
1967	99	8,591	11,388	19,979	38,788	66,292	86,271	23.2
1968	101	8,719	7,892	16,611	39,721	61,199	77,810	21.3
1969	109	10,154	8,552	18,706	43,782	61,430	80,136	23.3
1970	138	12,359	8,936	21,295	53,374	82,701	103,996	20.5

Notes   1. In 1966 GBP58,272 were spent on the General Election.
        2. An asterisk in the second column indicates that this was the staff complement authorized in the Estimates for that year and therefore not necessarily the actual number of employees.
        3. In 1969 the Machine Section was renamed Data Processing.

Source   Compiled from the annual COS Reports.

was commented upon on a number of occasions. As early as 1961, for example, a report noted that the lack of office space effectively meant a check of expansion, especially in the machine accounting section. The report for that year recommended that the machines should ideally 'be housed in a very large hall which permits the grouping together of the machines according to their functions' (*COS Report 1961*: p. 4). The machines—then located at Windmill Street—were spread in various small rooms, on different floors.

We find similar complaints reiterated in at least two other reports, for example in the 1963 report and again in that for 1968. This last report makes it clear that the lack of working space was not only causing overcrowding but also a fall in operating conditions as a result. The staff complement in 1968 had already exceeded 100. Continuing, the report noted that alternative accommodation in Valletta was not secured while the project to erect suitable premises in Floriana had still not materialised (*COS Report 1968*: p. 19).[45]

The substandard accommodation led to two other problems, namely noise and dampness. According to Albert Galea and Joe D'Amico (another former COS employee) the level of noise was deafening, which caused much concern. The 1965 report noted that 'notwithstanding the steps taken to reduce machine noise and vibrations, their total elimination was difficult to achieve' (*COS Report 1965*: p. 15). The report did not elaborate on what steps were taken to dampen the noise. The fact that the machines were housed in old buildings whose floors were not ideally suited to take heavy loads and vibrations probably exacerbated the situation.

A related problem was the dampness. The premises where the equipment and the punched cards were stored were very damp. This, combined with the high relative humidity of the Maltese climate, frequently warped the cards and made them thicker. Because the machines had a "feeler" to gauge the thickness of the cards as they passed their sometimes tortuous path from hopper to stacker, the

---

[45] In fact it was only at the end of 1999 shortly before the COS became the NSO that suitable premises were found for the department. Although machine space was now not an issue, the volume of publications kept by the NSO—essentially an entire library—itself was one good reason for acquiring ample office space. The NSO is now housed in a historical building (refurbished to high standards), next to the War Rooms at Lascaris, Valletta.

cards would sometimes be rejected by the card feeder mechanism;[46] or, they would be let through and then get stuck halfway between the hopper and stacker of the sorter, collator or calculator.[47]

End of Mechanisation

If, after so many years of failed persuasion, there had been some hope of acquiring a larger and more appropriate building that would one day perhaps have housed more modern equipment (such as a minicomputer system), these hopes must have been shattered in June 1971. That year saw a change of government and a concomitant change in attitude toward computers and politics in general. For reasons that will remain unclear but probably have much to do with the mentality and the political and economic climate then prevailing, the new government's attitude towards computers was negative. Computers were viewed not as productive tools for progress but as job-destructive machines that could be eliminated. The notion that new technology might lead to new kinds of jobs had not yet been realised by the newly elected government. Computers were also expensive both to purchase and maintain. Thus, computers did not exactly fit in with government's plans of job creation through industrialisation (including tourism which started to be developed in the previous decade and by now had already achieved remarkable success).[48] Additionally, the building of a sound infrastructure, then still lacking, was government's main priority. Another major concern was how to compensate for the eventual loss of revenue from the British government on achieving complete independence by decade's end, and how to absorb those employed by the British services into the new job schemes.[49]

---

[46] For an illuminating account of some of the problems of tabulating machines see Walker (1996).

[47] These problems were also discussed with Joe D'Amico in the interview of 4 May 2005. Additionally, an interesting report in connection with the water and electricity billing system drawn after an official enquiry into customer complaints regarding excessive bills, also comments on the "cramped" conditions in which the COS personnel had to operate. See Montebello, et al. (1963: p. 15).

[48] See, for example, Pollacco (2003: pp. 236-237).

[49] In 1971 the British Forces still employed about 7% of the Maltese labour force. Alternative employment had to be found for these workers by the beginning of 1979.

To achieve its objectives the new government regime adopted a policy of stringent economy and tightened spending.[50] In fact, in the 1970s the economy was essentially a directed or command economy. The spending curb negatively affected government departments, not least the COS, which effectively curbed its expansion. At one time, there were even plans—indeed arrangements had been made just prior to the 1971 election—to set up a government computer centre or "organization", as it was then referred to, but this project was eventually abandoned.[51, 52] So dismal was the situation at the time that, after 1970, even the COS's official annual reports which gave a wealth of information on the Office's functions ceased publication. Instead, this was relegated to a small section in *Reports on the Workings of Government Departments*.

The 1970s saw little in the way of computing technology, generally. A handful of private companies, amongst them Barclays Bank (Malta), did introduce some new equipment, but the lack of the introduction of computers was quite evident. As for the COS, the department remained stuck with the old machinery until the creation of the Government Computer Centre in the early 1980s when the Centre took over the machine division's work. For a number of years, the COS itself had reverted to full manual operation until, with the advent of the PC, networking, and decentralisation, it switched back to computers.

---

[50] The early 1970s also coincided with a worldwide economic depression as well as with a substantial increase in oil prices which caused a further economic depression.

[51] "Computer ghal l-Gvern", *Ir-Review*, 10 April 1971, p. 8.

[52] That the intention to go ahead with the setting up of this government computer organization was imminent (but never materialised until a decade later), may be inferred from this and other reports which mention that steps had been taken to train personnel on the operation and use of computers. A number of officers from the Efficiency Division branch actually followed courses in Systems Analysis leading to the British National Computing Centre certificate, and were sent abroad to gain practical experience. In March of 1971, a call for tender for the supply of computers also appeared in the government gazette. See the next chapter for more details.

Part II

Early Data Processing Services and Computer Installations, 1967-1982

Part II
Early Data Processing Services and Computer Installations, 1967-1982

In Chapter 1, reference was made to three major office equipment vendors operating in Malta, namely ICL, Olivetti, and NCR. With the exception of ICL, which closed its Malta office in the late 1990s,[53] the two local agents for Olivetti and NCR continued their business in Malta to this day and therefore played an important role in bringing computing within reach of the public and private enterprise.[54] For many years ICL accounted for the majority of local computer installations. The Olivetti and NCR Malta agents had more of the accounting and office machines sector, but by the late 1970s they, too, had moved into computing. ICL and NCR's local representative were also the first companies on the Island to offer data processing and programming courses.[55]

In Malta, the late 1960s may be considered as the period when the first signs of the computer's importance became visible. This was a time when government took steps to investigate efficiency in the civil service. Under the auspices of the United Nations Bureau of Technical Assistance Operations, a UN expert was appointed to survey the existing administrative structure and develop a training programme for civil service personnel. The aim was to achieve greater uniformity of performance in the field of Organization and Methods (O&M). Since O&M also covered Electronic Data Processing (EDP) development, an extensive study by the Efficiency Development Branch (EDB) of Establishments was undertaken on the possibility of computerization. In 1970, a cabinet decision was taken to centralise a number of departmental activities by purchasing a computer

---

[53] In 1984, ICL became a wholly owned subsidiary of the UK company Standard Telephones and Cable Ltd (STC). It closed its Malta office in the late-1990s after being taken over by Fujitsu.
[54] NCR's local representative is Philip Toledo Ltd, and that for Olivetti is Charles A. Micallef Ltd.
[55] At least as early as 1963, ICL was already organising data processing courses locally. See, for example, "Data Processing Techniques–Lectures at University", *Times of Malta*, 19 July 1963, p. 9.

sufficiently powerful to serve the needs of government departments, but the computer was never acquired after the then ruling Nationalist party lost to the opposition in the summer of 1971 (see Chapter 2).

The late 1960s also saw a handful of relatively short-lived small firms attempting to move into the punched-card data preparation and processing services field. Two companies, in particular, set up punched-card operations, acting as bureaux for overseas companies, importing blank cards and re-exporting them after punching. They were, in effect, among the first computing services companies in Malta. Very little is known about these companies, and the short account given in chapter 3 is based primarily on newspaper articles and company formation documents.

For reasons that will probably never be ascertained, few developments can be identified in the 1970s,[56] although at least two were sizeable undertakings. These include the computerization of Barclays Bank in 1973, followed by that of the Inland Revenue in 1976. Barclays Bank was the largest bank operating in Malta at the time, employing close to four hundred local workers. Its Malta division was sold in 1975 to the Maltese government when Mid-Med Bank (later privatised and purchased by HSBC) thus came into being. The introduction of computers by this Bank made big news in Malta, apparently more than when computerization was introduced at the Inland Revenue, which seemed to have gone almost unnoticed by the general public.[57] The Inland Revenue's computer installation is described in chapter 2, and that of Barclays Bank in chapter 3.

By 1980 a number of private computer firms began to appear, two set up specifically to provide time-sharing services, a few others specialising in minicomputer installations and custom software. These companies' founders had vision and realised the computer's potential and the many uses it could be put to even in a small market such as that of Malta. They knew that the Island could not possibly escape the information technology revolution. These companies may have appeared late internationally but were early enough on the local scene to establish themselves as technology leaders. Few, if any, who

---

[56] Chapter 3 attempts to give an explanation for the low level of computer installations throughout the 1970s.

[57] Apart from the COS's ICT 1004 computer, Barclays Bank's computer is generally considered to be the first mainframe to be installed in Malta.

started up in the late 1970s and early 1980s did not fare well; they went on to beat the masses of small computer firms that were eventually to proliferate as a result of the PC by just a few years, and in so doing acquire a reputation that effectively secured a stronghold for at least the next two decades. Part of their success also lay in the fact that they specialised in market niches in which, over a few years, they developed capabilities against which it was difficult for the newcomers to compete. Some of these companies have grown to a moderate size (employing over 50 persons) and now have revenues exceeding two million Euros. Chapter 3 discusses time-sharing and gives a description of one firm that specialised in teleprocessing.

The year 1981 was a watershed year for computing in Malta because, apart from the formation of a few computer companies, the government computer centre was officially inaugurated and, only weeks before, the first electronics fair (in which a handful of computers were displayed to the public) was organized. As such, the computer centre operated for almost exactly a decade before it was superseded by another organization called the Management Systems Unit.

The opening of the government computer centre and the first *Electronika* fair can probably be considered as the two events that more or less concluded one period of computing history in Malta and started another. Beginning from 1982, a business computer exhibition was held yearly, the number of computer suppliers and users multiplied, and governments' rather negative attitude to computers began, very slowly, to abate. That era is relegated to Part III.

2

The Civil Service's First Computer

Efficiency Development in the Civil Service and a Failed Attempt at Creating a Government Computer Organization

In 1967, just one year after the COS had introduced the 1004 data processor and three years after the publication of the Stolper report,[58] the Maltese government began investigating efficiency in the civil service.[59] An expert, working under the auspices of the UN Bureau of Technical Assistance Operations, was appointed for the task. The terms of reference were: (i) to survey the existing administrative structure and services common to all departments with a view to promoting greater efficiency and coordination; and (ii) to develop a training programme for civil service personnel to ensure greater uniformity of performance in the field of O&M (Westermark, 1969: p. 1; Westermark, 1970: p. 2). As mentioned, O&M covered EDP and therefore the latter also fell under the expert's remit. Of course, the investigation into government efficiency was nothing new, the field of O&M having received much attention in Britain all through the 1950s

---

[58] The Stolper report (entitled *Economic Adaptation and Development in Malta*) was the outcome of a UN mission that came to Malta on the Maltese government's invitation to advise on the economic policies that Malta should follow, given the British government intentions to run down the Services establishments on the Island.

[59] This period also coincided with the publication of the government's Second Development Plan, which had as its main aim industrialisation, efficiency and competitiveness. This plan also announced government's intentions to set up the Malta Development Corporation.

and 1960s (see, for example, Milward, 1967; Anderson, 1980; and Agar, 2000).

The expert, Gunnar Westermark, arrived in Malta in the spring of 1967 and left six months later, after his initial findings were published in a report to the Malta Government dated November 1967. The proposals made in this report dealt mainly with the organization for the Establishments Division, a division within the Office of the Prime Minister primarily responsible for personnel functions, and did not delve deeply into EDP. In the summer of 1969, however, Westermark was again asked to undertake a second assignment of six months in order to follow up the proposals made in the 1967 report (by which time some of the recommendations had already been implemented) and conclude the findings.

For some reason, the second assignment—started on 2 June 1969—was split in September of that year into two parts. A report was drawn up and presented to government in which the findings of that second visit were detailed (Second Report dated September 1969). Except for a brief visit in February 1970, Westermark did not return to complete his assignment until July 1970, when he spent another eight weeks in Malta. The full recommendations relating to EDP can be found in his third and final report, officially published the following year (Westermark, 1971). The second report, however, also contained a substantial chapter titled "Automatic Data Processing", where the need to computerise is explained (Westermark, 1969: pp. 32-43).

The sections of the report that concern EDP made recommendations about both the organizational structure of the proposed automatic data processing (ADP) system as well as its administration and planning, apart from the ADP functions. It was suggested that initially, at least, the ADP project fall under the Efficiency Development branch of Establishments and only later be taken over by a separate ADP department. The proposed organization structure envisaged the Efficiency Development branch as constituting four ADP sections, each accommodating a certain number of personnel (see Figure 2.1 which has been adapted from the final report). The Efficiency Development branch was to be headed by an Assistant Secretary whose task would have been to administer and co-ordinate the computer project.

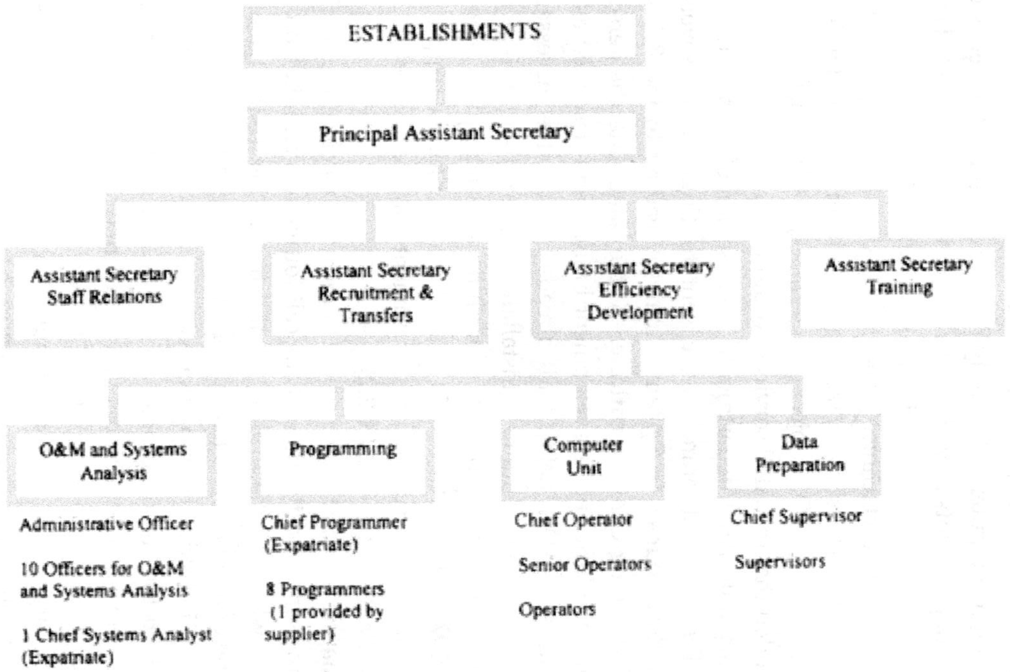

ESTABLISHMENTS

Principal Assistant Secretary

Assistant Secretary
Staff Relations

Assistant Secretary
Recruitment &
Transfers

Assistant Secretary
Efficiency
Development

Assistant Secretary
Training

O&M and Systems
Analysis

Administrative Officer

10 Officers for O&M
and Systems Analysis

1 Chief Systems Analyst
(Expatriate)

Programming

Chief Programmer
(Expatriate)

8 Programmers
(1 provided by
supplier)

Computer
Unit

Chief Operator

Senior Operators

Operators

Data
Preparation

Chief Supervisor

Supervisors

Figure 2.1
Proposed Organizational Structure of the Government Computer Organization

In 1970, as part of the recommendations, a cabinet decision was taken to go ahead and centralise a number of departmental activities by purchasing a computer sufficiently powerful to serve the needs of government departments as well as of state bodies like the Malta Dry-docks, the Central Bank, the Malta Development Corporation, the University and the Polytechnic.[60] The cabinet decision recognised the expert's advice by endorsing the fact that Establishment would indeed be responsible for the ADP project (Westermark, 1971: Appendix Aa). It was intended that the ADP services would at a later stage be taken over by a separate ADP department. Four senior officers from the Efficiency Development branch were sent to England for several weeks to follow courses in Systems Analysis leading to the British National Computing Centre certificate. At the same time, the person then heading the Efficiency Development branch, and described as a specialist in the ADP field, had already begun the necessary preparations for the computer installation, even though it was planned that the installation itself was unlikely to take place before the start of 1973.[61] In March of 1971, a call for tender for the supply of computers also appeared in the government gazette (*Gazzetta tal-Gvern ta' Malta*, 1971) (see Figure 2.2).

As it happened, 1971 was the year of the national elections. Only three months separated the date of the call for tenders and the voting date, so that when the then ruling administration lost to the Labour Party in June of that year, the EDP project was shelved off, never to be resuscitated. Indeed, no computer system was purchased and it would not be before almost exactly another decade that a government computer centre was set up, under very different circumstances.

Although never acted upon, it is nevertheless instructive to consider the arguments that were put forward for the proposed organizational structure shown in Figure 2.1. It was stated in the report that in other countries with government organizations about the same size as the Malta Government it had proved to be

---

[60] The Central Bank, the Malta Development Corporation and the Polytechnic (the former Malta College of Arts, Science and Technology) were relatively new enterprises, all having been established in the 1960s.

[61] This person is identified as Joseph Caruana. According to the report, he was at the time 'the only senior civil servant who specialised himself in the ADP field'. In reality, as pointed out in Chapter 1, personnel at the COS had already been sent to gain experience in computer data processing.

advantageous to concentrate ADP and other efficiency development work to the same unit. 'This concentration of resources', it was argued, 'is especially essential during the initial period [of the project]' (Westermark, 1971: Appendix Aa).

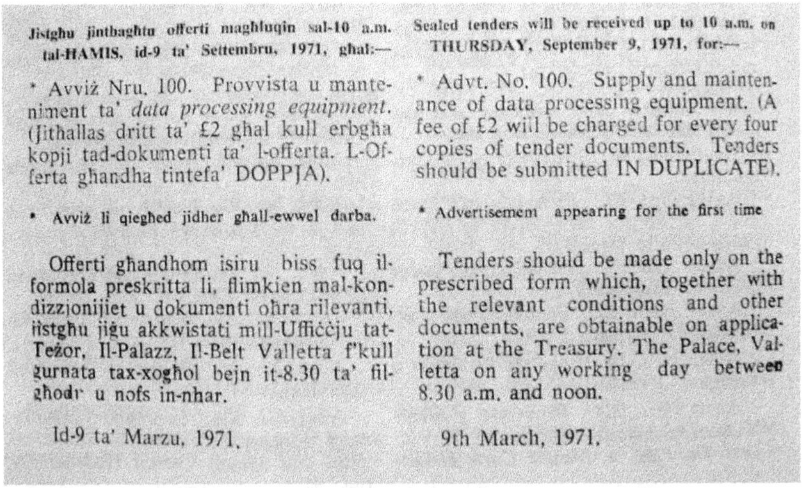

Jistghu jintbaghtu offerti maghluqin sal-10 a.m. tal-HAMIS, id-9 ta' Settembru, 1971, ghal:—

* Avviż Nru. 100. Provvista u manteniment ta' *data processing equipment*. (Jithallas dritt ta' £2 ghal kull erbgha kopji tad-dokumenti ta' l-offerta. L-Offerta ghandha tintefa' DOPPJA).

* Avviż li qieghed jidher ghall-ewwel darba.

Offerti ghandhom isiru biss fuq ilformola preskritta li, flimkien mal-kondizzjonijiet u dokumenti ohra rilevanti, iistghu jiġu akkwistati mill-Uffiċċju tat-Teżor, Il-Palazz, Il-Belt Valletta f'kull ġurnata tax-xoghol bejn it-8.30 ta' filghodr u nofs in-nhar.

Id-9 ta' Marzu, 1971.

Sealed tenders will be received up to 10 a.m. on THURSDAY, September 9, 1971, for:—

* Advt. No. 100. Supply and maintenance of data processing equipment. (A fee of £2 will be charged for every four copies of tender documents. Tenders should be submitted IN DUPLICATE).

* Advertisement appearing for the first time.

Tenders should be made only on the prescribed form which, together with the relevant conditions and other documents, are obtainable on application at the Treasury. The Palace, Valletta on any working day between 8.30 a.m. and noon.

9th March, 1971.

Figure 2.2
The call for tenders for the supply of a computer system for what should have been the first government computer centre.
Source: *Gazzetta tal-Gvern ta' Malta* (9 March 1971: p. 698).

It was further reasoned that Systems Analysis should not be separated from the Efficiency Development branch because the Systems Analysis would take over the main part of the O&M work in several fields. It was also recommended that the section for the data preparation would remain in the Department of Statistics until the computer's installation which was expected sometime in 1973. The report reveals that it was anticipated that the computer would be installed in new offices at the former Evans Laboratories in Merchants Street, Valletta.

It is also interesting to note that although this report does not specifically mention the role played by the Central Office of Statistics, except for the remark about the data preparation, an article in an issue of *Ir-Review* mentions that in carrying out their investigations for the purchase of a computer, the officers from the Efficiency Development branch were helped by COS personnel, who 'had considerable experience in the use and programming of tabulating machines'.[62]

In the previous chapter a reference was made to the two main Maltese political parties whose ideologies led them take specific measures on the adoption of computing technology. The cabinet decision that approved the purchase of a computer and the setting up of the said computer organization (which never materialised) was made under the Borg Olivier (Nationalist Party) administration, whose term of office had begun in 1962 and ended in 1971 (having won the 1966 general elections). The paradox here is that the Nationalist Party (PN) appeared to have been in favour of modernization whereas the subsequent Mintoff (Malta Labour Party) administration that followed—with its supposed progressive ideology—were against (see Chapter 1).

The Nationalists apparently had no problem with the proposed creation of a computer organization, possibly for the following two reasons. Firstly, in the period 1965-1970 Malta registered a moderately good economic performance overall, although it had not reached the stage of self sustaining growth, apart from the fact that the national debt increased significantly in that period (see, for example, Azzopardi Vella, 1973: pp. 14-15; Briguglio, 1988: pp. 190-200; and Spiteri, 1997: pp. 184-201). This overall good performance may have encouraged the PN to adopt modern office methods. Secondly, the envisaged computer organization formed part of a civil service restructuring process, an exercise in O&M that would tackle efficiency. Indeed, the Stolper report and the Second Development Plan 1964-1969 (which was modelled on the Stolper study) had stressed the importance of efficiency and competitiveness.

Therefore, why is it that the newly elected administration was uninterested in the computerization project? Later (in Chapter 3), I will attempt to give an explanation for the relatively low rate of IT diffusion in the 1970s and the Labour Party's apparent negative attitude towards computers. For now, however, it is important to note that the MLP—and its leader Dominic Mintoff, in particular—

---

[62] "Computer ghal l-Gvern", *Ir-Review*, 10 April 1971, p. 8. A few former COS employees did eventually go on to work for the government computer centre at Swatar, Dingli, in 1981 (see Chapter 4).

had very different political ambitions than those of the Nationalists. Apart from speeding up the tempo of economic diversification, beginning from 1971 the MLP took a stand of non-alignment (political neutrality) and began a process of obliterating every trace of British domination in the islands.

The MLP disagreed with the PN on many fundamental issues to the extent that it disregarded former (i.e., PN) administrative policy and tactics. To the MLP, for example, the mutual defence and financial agreements the Nationalists had reached with Britain were unacceptable and had to be revised in Malta's favour. The Third Development Plan devised by the PN in the late 1960s was short-lived: it was not followed through by the MLP which drew up its own in 1973. Likewise, for various reasons (see Pollaco, 1992; and Chapter 11 of this book), the 1970 EEC Association Agreement completed under the PN administration was allowed to lapse by the labour government. In brief, several initiatives started under the PN administration appeared to be incompatible with the beliefs of the subsequent MLP administration. The computerization project simply suffered the same fate.

Computerization at the Inland Revenue Department

The attempt to set up a government computer centre by the early 1970s, which had failed to materialise, could not have been completely in vain. That wish was expressed by personnel from three government departments, namely the COS, the Treasury, and the Inland Revenue. In all three departments accounting machines were employed for various tasks. Accounting machines provided a very cost-effective solution to modern accounting techniques, and cost only a very small fraction of a full-blown computer (see Box 2-1). By at least 1976, the Treasury even had its own "Machines Unit" section. In the *Reports on the Working of Government Departments* (henceforth, *GD Reports*) covering the period 1 April 1976 – 13 August 1977 (p. 67), the Accounts Section of Treasury reports that

> ... With the help of Electronic Accounting machines this
> Section keeps a record of all Government accounts and

effects payments for all supplies delivered and services rendered to the Government. In addition, the Machines Unit compiles the monthly salary paylists for all Government Departments, issues monthly pension drafts to ex-Government employees or their widows and to Personal Injuries Scheme beneficiaries and issues six-monthly dividend warrants to holders of Local Development Registered stocks.

At the Treasury Department, new electronic accounting machines were introduced in April 1972 in preparation for the Decimal Currency changeover, which came into effect later that year (*GD Reports*, 1972: p. 64). Some of the older accounting machines installed at the Treasury could be converted to conform with the decimal system, however a UK expert who inspected the old machines was of the opinion that new machines should be purchased. This expert was brought over on the recommendation of the Decimal Currency Committee, set up in 1970. Once the new accounting machines were installed, all accounting work had to be re-programmed.

Box 2-1
Electronic Accounting Machines

Although mainframe computers had become fairly popular by the late 1960s, they were still very expensive and therefore only used by large corporate companies and sizeable government departments. Small companies and government organizations that wished to adopt relatively new methods of accounting often resorted to accounting machines, of which different makes and models existed.

Initially, accounting machines were electro-mechanical, but by about 1970 electronic accounting machines began to appear which incorporated several of the key features found in their electro-mechanical counterparts. The latter consisted of the following important components: a register section to hold totals; an electric typewriter, a numeric keyboard; a printing unit, which had functions to set its size so that different-sized documents could be fed; and a programme bar, which was used to control each step in an accounting procedure.

The two important improvements of the electronic accounting machines on the electro-mechanical ones were the inclusion of a processor and a memory unit. The processor enabled calculations to be made much quicker, and the memory unit consisted of several hundred locations where the data and the program could be stored. The memory in these machines was of the core memory type, which was then appearing in many larger computers. Paper tape units and punched card units (for loading program and data) also formed part of the electronic accounting machine. Given that these machines were designed to replicate manual accounting methods, with the final output printed directly on ledger cards and other documents, they were known by the title of "visible record computers" (or VRCs). Occasionally, they were also referred to as mini-computers, office computers, or even as desk-top computers, terms that would take somewhat different connotations about one decade later.

VRCs were produced by several office equipment manufacturers (e.g. Philips, Olivetti, NCR, IBM, Burroughs, Nixdorf) and filled a niche that lay somewhere between the very small and the very large business sector. They were popular because they were considerably faster than their electro-mechanical counterparts and at the same time cost much less than even the smallest mainframe computer. They were used typically for sales accounting, purchasing, stock control and payroll.

By the mid-1970s, the amount of work at the Treasury, the Inland Revenue and the COS had increased to such an extent that executive officers there were putting pressure on government to purchase a computer. Why it was the Inland Revenue that secured its (the computer's) acquisition in 1976 is not entirely clear, but according to Godfrey Calleja,[63] now a retired ex-Inland Revenue Department employee, it could have been due to the fact that the Inland Revenue had the biggest amount of data and was the most in need of computerization.[64] At that time, the Inland Revenue Department frequently resorted to overtime in order to cope with the amount of work there. One argument put forward in the computer's favour was that overtime work would be reduced, if not eliminated, thus saving in personnel wages. However, any talk of computerization did not go

---

[63] Interviewed by author on 2 July 2009. Calleja was then internal auditor, and later an officer in charge of the computer centre at the Inland Revenue.

[64] By the end of 1976 the number of employees working for the Inland Revenue was 283, making the Inland Revenue a medium-sized, if not a large, department by Maltese standards.

down well with the many employees who felt threatened about the prospects of working shorter hours, if not being made redundant, so that those few officials in favour of computerization were in a rather uneasy situation of wanting to move forward but simultaneously being somewhat hindered and handicapped by their colleagues. The ministers concerned were also very reluctant to introduce a computer, doubting its true benefits. A second argument was that a computer would make it easier to trace tax evaders. The latter were apparently very numerous and not always easy to bring to justice. Indeed, some considerable time and effort was being expended to deal with these defaulters. The argument about the reduction of overtime work was turned on its head, as it were, by asserting that the hours saved in overtime as a result of computerization could still be utilised productively by concentrating on defaulting taxpayers. Additionally, some of the staff would be retrained on the more modern methods of office organization. Of course, whether or not it was these arguments that won the day is anybody's guess, however the government was ultimately lured into a computer's purchase on one condition, namely that—for all intents and purposes—the computer would be referred to as either a data processing machine or a sophisticated electronic machine.

It has not been possible to ascertain with precision the date when the computer system was installed. However, analysis of the Inland Revenue Department sections of the *Reports on the Workings of Government Departments* (for the periods 1 April 1975 to 31 March 1976 and 1 April 1976 to 31 March 1977) reveals that the computer must have been installed between the spring of 1976 and the winter of 1977. The computer was an ICL 1901A miniframe computer used in batch mode (see Figure 2.3). The batch mode of operation was still very common up to the late 1970s when interactive computing had also gained popularity (see Box 2-2).

Once operational and having been programmed for a number of Inland Revenue tasks including Income Tax Returns, Tax Assessments, and the creation of history and taxpayers' balance records to aid staff in dealing with the general public, the computer began to be utilised for non-Revenue tasks. By 1979, for example, the Inland Revenue's newly formed Data Processing Unit was offering services for the Treasury (Wages, Salaries and Pensions), the Department of Social Services, the COS, and the Department of

Agriculture (Pitkali Payments, formerly undertaken by the COS) (*GD Reports*, 1979: p. 69). With the exception of a limited amount of overtime expenditure, all costs for the large volume of work undertaken on behalf of other Departments were borne by the Inland Revenue. However, at least as far as the COS was concerned, the punching of data was done at source, i.e., the COS prepared the punched cards in advance and then passed them on to the Inland Revenue for processing.

Figure 2.3
The computer system at the Inland Revenue, c. 1978.
Source: Department of Information.

No archival documents have been found that give the organizational structure of the Data Processing Unit, however according to Calleja by about 1981 this Unit consisted of 3 operators and between 4 to 5 programmers working under the supervision of an Operations Manager who, in turn, reported to an "Officer in Charge" (the Unit Head). The senior officer of the three operators was known as the "Systems Administrator" and was primarily responsible for computer-time allocation, how the computer was to be used for the various jobs. The other two operators were mainly responsible for the actual running of the equipment (switching the system on and off, handling of disk packs, printing, etc.). Although other departments were not being billed, it is conceivable that the Inland Revenue Department also wanted to keep an internal record of the total monthly hours spent on external services for accounting purposes.

Staff training in programming and systems analyses was primarily provided by the computer supplier. Although ICL occasionally organized short courses in data preparation and programming in conjunction with the University (of Malta), the latter had not itself yet embarked on a computerization programme and did not offer any such courses (see Chapter 5). Hence up to at least the end of 1981 when the Swatar Computer Centre was opened (see Chapter 6), personnel wishing to learn programming either had to travel overseas or enrol on a distance-learning programme, often on their own initiative. Cobol was the preferred language for applications development although much later, at the Swatar Centre, Informix was also extensively used.

November 1981 saw the official opening of the Government Computer Centre at Swatar. Both the COS and the Inland Revenue played an important role in the Swatar's first years of operation; indeed experienced computer personnel at these departments, together with others from Mid-Med Bank were seconded to the Swatar Centre to help in its running. It would probably be true to say that one of the earliest manifestations of knowledge transfer in the computing field in Malta on some considerable scale took place at the Swatar Centre in this period.

Shortly after the Swatar Centre was set up, all the staff at the Inland Revenue Data Processing Unit was transferred enbloc to that Centre, with the exception of Calleja who was asked to head the newly set-up Computer Liaison Unit at the Department. The ICL equipment at the Inland Revenue was stored after the data and systems had been successfully transferred to the new Prime Computer System at Swatar. In due course, the equipment was dismantled and the disk packs were destroyed under the surveillance of a Board which was set up for the purpose.

At this point in time (c. 1983), top management at the Inland Revenue Department, mostly the Commissioner at the time, Vincent Galea and Calleja himself, was feeling that the Department needed a more sophisticated system to give more direct and online aid to the end user in order to offer a better and accurate service to the taxpayer. The Department had already embarked on the computerization of the Cash Office. Up to then, the issue of receipts was effected manually, which was laborious and time consuming. Following a tender, a computer system was set up by which cashiers issued receipts electronically to the taxpayer using dot matrix printers. This included those who called at the Cash counter and also those who sent cheques, the latter being referred to as the back office. The equipment consisted of three Televideo stations that used a CP/M operating system.[65] Each station was made up of a main PC with a 10MB hard drive and 5.25inch floppy drive, two dumb terminals and three printers. At the end of the day data was transferred from each station to one of the stations labelled as the main server. The software organized and gathered all the data and copied it on to a floppy disk. This data was subsequently transferred to update the Swatar Computer System.

Eventually the Department obtained approval to effect a feasibility study in order to find out if a more online and efficient system was possible. A tender was issued and awarded to a foreign company. The study not only backed the department's wishes but concluded that a more sophisticated on-line computer system was a must.

Consequently, requirements and specifications were drawn up in collaboration with the Swatar Technical Staff, and a new system was developed. The new replacement system catered for on-line inputting of data (tax assessments, payments, adjustments, refunds, etc.). Each Inland Revenue Department user was given a PC that was linked to the main server on which he/she was able to access all transactions effected to date and the resulting balance.

---

[65] The CP/M (Control Program for Micros) operating system was a popular, disk-based system designed by Gary Kildall between 1976 and 1977 for personal computers. By the mid-1980s, however, its days were numbered as Microsoft's MS-DOS became the PC's operating system of choice. For a brief history of CP/M and MS-DOS, and why MS-DOS was more successful than CP/M, see Ceruzzi (2003).

Box 2-2
Centralised Batch and Interactive, Time-Shared, Computing

Much of the business computing that was done in the 1960s and 1970s involved mainframe computer systems running in batch processing mode in which the computer could only execute one application at a time. By the early 1970s time-shared systems, allowing users to interact directly with the computer, were also becoming popular.

A centralised computer system consisted of one large computer (a mainframe or a miniframe) to which were connected several peripheral devices such as printers, plotters, magnetic disk drives, magnetic tape drives, teletypes and terminals (VDUs with keyboards, or consoles). Several input/output (I/O) communication channels handled the I/O requests. Other equipment such as key punches, punched paper tape readers, and punched card readers were also needed.

For batch processing, a program would be written on paper (often after a flowchart had been prepared), coded onto punched cards or punched paper tape (typically after standard coding sheets had been used), and read in (from the punched cards) and executed. In early systems—those that worked in batch mode—the user did not interact with the computer. Instead, programmers would hand in their computer programs on punched cards to a computer operator who would arrange for the processing of the cards. The results would be given back to the programmers in the form of printed output. The system was referred to as a batch processing system because it handled the cards in "batches": in order to speed up processing the operator would group (or "batch") together program jobs with similar needs and run them through the computer as a group. Also, in batch applications, the typical approach was for transactions to be accumulated and processed periodically (for example, a sorted group of inventory punched cards which were processed to produce a weekly inventory report). Interestingly, the batch mode of processing pretty much reflected the way data processing was carried out manually, i.e., it was effectively the manual method extended onto a computer.

Although batch-processing systems remained in use for decades, another mode of computing—interactive time-sharing—appeared in the 1960s. The idea of connecting several user terminals to a mainframe computer and allocate CPU time-slices (CPU cycles) to each of the terminals in turn (i.e., make each terminal have sole use of the computer for a short time interval in a "round-robin" fashion) can be traced to at least two persons, John McCarthy being one of those credited with the time-sharing concept. McCarthy was interested (and became a pioneer) in artificial intelligence and human-machine interaction and wanted computers to be used in an interactive manner. An experimental system was tried out at MIT (where McCarthy spent several years) in 1962. Running on an IBM 7090 this system evolved into the first proper time-sharing system called the Compatible Time-Sharing System (CTSS). CTSS was developed by IBM in conjunction with MIT.

CTSS, in turn, partly led to another related project called Project MAC. Funded almost entirely by the US Defense Advanced Research Programme Agency (DARPA), Project MAC was an ambitious undertaking that attempted to make computers more user friendly by also incorporating the basics of time-sharing. The man behind the concept was a psychologist and computer scientist, J. C. R. Licklider who, in 1960, published a classic paper entitled "Man-Computer Symbiosis" that essentially formulated a manifesto for human-computer interaction. The goal of Project MAC was to go beyond stimulating the spread of time-sharing, to achieve Licklider's (and his colleague Robert M. Fano's) dream of human-computer symbiosis. The latter goal was only partly realised, however. Project MAC was completed around 1966 when it ran on a General Electric 635 computer. The abbreviation MAC stood for "Machine-Aided Cognition" and "Multiple-Access Computer", but has also been translated as "Man and Computers".

Meanwhile, other groups of scientists were exploring the time-sharing concept. For example, at Bell Labs people like Kenneth Thompson, Dennis Ritchie and others who had been working on the MULTICS system, began writing software for what would become their time-sharing Unix operating system, which for many years almost became the *de facto* operating system used in many Universities worldwide. Unix also more or less began the move away from large centralised computer systems.

The other place where work on time-sharing evolved was Dartmouth College (in Hanover, New Hampshire). The idea there –proposed by John Kemeny, a mathematics professor—was to have a system intended for a broad spectrum of users. For example, it was felt that undergraduates, whilst not necessarily reading for a computer science degree, might still want to make use of, and benefit from, a computer. This led not only to the development of the Dartmouth time-sharing operating system itself but to the creation of BASIC, a programming language specifically designed (by Kemeny and his colleague, Thomas Kurtz) to be relatively easy to learn. The Dartmouth system was begun in 1962 and made operational two years later.

Although a number of time-shared computer systems had been developed by the late 1960s it was from roughly the beginning of the 1970s that these systems began to gain momentum. They also led to the use of a computer as a "utility" (much like electricity was a utility) when firms specialising as computer bureaus were purchasing powerful time-sharing computer systems and providing computing services to customers. With terminals in customers' offices, users could also be linked by means of telephone lines to a bureau's mainframe. On a rental payment basis, on-line interactive computing became another new mode of computing.

3

Early Private Initiatives

The First Bureau Services

In the 1960s when computers were so expensive that only large corporate companies could afford them, computer suppliers began offering computing services to their clients that did not necessarily involve the sale of a computer system. Additionally, in the late 1960s thousands of firms entered what could be termed the beginning of the software and services industry. In the main these services were of three types: local processing, facilities management, and teleprocessing.[66] Many of the major computer manufacturers, such as IBM, NCR, Honeywell, General Electric and Computer Data Corporation, developed extensive service-bureau operations, but independent firms with sufficient computer expertise and funding also began offering these "processing services" (see Box 3-1).

In Malta, processing services were not introduced until 1980 when Computime (followed shortly by Management Computer Systems and, some time later, by Intercomp) set up operations to offer local processing as well as teleprocessing (see later). However, many years before, at least two companies were already planning to offer computer-related services but chose to take a less risky route by initially offering a simpler type of service, namely that of data preparation. Combined with the knowledge that no other local firm

---

[66] For an explanation of these terms and the relevant history, see Chapter 3 of Campbell-Kelly (2004).

was offering this service,[67] the motivation for starting this type of business was cheap labour, since the companies involved had foreign links and their aim was to carry out the data services for overseas as well as Maltese clients. Following is a description of three related ventures.[68]

Trans-World Data Processing, Computers in Business and OCR Data Services

In the first half of 1967 two businessmen, Robert Greenshields and Maurice Henry Williams travelled to Malta from the UK to start what must probably have been the first private data processing company on the Island, after ICL. Called Trans-World Data Processing Ltd, the company was set up at a time when the global computer industry was expanding and in the belief that this growth would continue at a rapid pace. Malta, because of its strategic position and its British connection, was seen to offer certain advantages, particularly given that such services were new locally and labour was still extremely cheap.

An article in *The Malta Economist* states that the company initially employed 25 girls and had a staff of about 60 by mid-1969.[69] The company's main activity was the preparation of data on punched cards for shipment worldwide. It is not revealed—and it has not been possible to find out—which countries were the recipients, and no reference has been made regarding the amount of cards that were being punched and shipped. However, the UK was probably the prime (if not the only) recipient: an article in the *Times of Malta* reports that the company had just finished punching the cards for the British Medical Directory.[70]

Roughly a year after Trans-World Data Processing was formed, another company, Computers in Business (Malta) Ltd (henceforth,

---

[67] ICL was then primarily in the business of building and selling computer hardware, although it frequently offered training to its customers, whether they purchased or leased.

[68] Apart from the companies mentioned in this section, American Data Preparation Corporation (Malta) Ltd, set up by Frank V. Fenech in 1973, offered similar services.

[69] "Malta: a computer centre", *The Malta Economist*, June 1969, p. 2.

[70] "It costs less to operate in Malta", *Times of Malta*, 21 August 1968, p. 9.

CIB) (see Figure 3.1), was set up by different directors, seeking probably even greater ambitions. According to the company's Memorandum of Association (Veglio & Duncan, 1968), the company's objectives were (amongst others):

- to carry out computer data preparation
- to carry out software development
- to provide computer programming and consulting services
- to undertake sales of computer systems and computer bureau services
- to act as importers, wholesalers and retailers of computers, machinery, furniture and fittings, office equipment, electrical goods and ancillary computer goods and appliances

The Memorandum was signed by John Veglio of London and John Leslie Duncan of St Julian's, Malta. The first appointed directors were Lionel Louis Jacobs and Arnold Shaw. John Veglio, the major shareholder who visited Malta in September 1968 to investigate the possibility of selling computer services to industrial concerns was appointed managing director on 23 September 1968.[71] A second director, Alexander Frederick Wilson, was appointed on 16 December of the same year.

Shortly after CIB was set up, CIB purchased 50% of the shares of Trans-World Data Processing, following which Trans-World formed another company called Optical Character Recognition Data Services Ltd (henceforth OCR). The same article that appeared in The *Malta Economist* (see note 4) reveals that once optical character reading and verifying was performed it was stored on magnetic tape and then flown to the UK (from whence the raw data originated) for further processing. The motivation for setting up this type of service in Malta was cost, which in the UK had become prohibitive. However, it was also planned to attempt to capture a share of the Libyan market which was seen as offering potential in view of the computer equipment (primarily from the US) that was already installed there but nevertheless lacked data preparation services.

---

[71] "Computer Services", *Times of Malta*, 25 September 1968, p. 20.

C.I.B. (MALTA) LTD.

(INTERNATIONAL DATA PREPARATION SERVICE)

Sunvalley Flats

Msida Road, BIRKIRKARA

REQUIRE

TRAINEE Punch Operators (Female)

Starting Wage. — £4. 15 per week and progress increases available. When trained minimum guaranteed over £6. with possibility to earn further qualification increments. Overtime available

Apply in writing to

THE MANAGER

Figure 3.1
A 1970 advert by Computers in Business (Malta) Ltd. Like typists, punch operators were invariably women.
Source: *Times of Malta* (19 February 1970: p. 16).

Again it is not clear whether CIB and OCR were competing with each other. The *Times of Malta* (of 21 August 1968) reports that both CIB and the former Trans-World Data Processing had submitted a joint application for aid to the Malta Development Corporation to expand their data preparation bureau. The article also states that the intention was for CIB to extend its business to Italy if funds were forthcoming. However, it would appear that the response from the MDC was unfavourable, since CIB was dissolved on 31 December 1970. The relatively short operating time span of CIB is somewhat of a mystery, especially given that less than a year before it was still advertising for personnel (Figure 3.1). What is more, by October 1969 it had employed 104 female workers and was punching 130,000 cards per week.[72] Company documents reveal, however, that in its short period of existence, four directors resigned from their posts.

Box 3-1
Service Bureaus and the rise of Software Firms

Before the advent of computers when organizations used punched-card tabulating equipment for data processing (such as that used by Malta's former Central Office of Statistics), service bureaus were already in existence. These bureaus specialised in providing data processing services to companies that could not afford to own expensive equipment or did not have the time or expertise to operate the equipment which required trained personnel. The service bureaus effectively turned data into machine-readable form and produced reports for clients, sometimes also making data processing equipment available to its customers.*

When comptuers began to be used by businesses from about the late 1950s onwards some of these bureaus, and many others founded later, purchased (or leased) computers to continue offering the same type of service to its customers, this time on a computer. It was the beginning of what has been termed the "processing services industry", the first sector of what later would become the software industry. The client reports produced by the bureaus were typically sent by post or delivered physically to the client's premises, but developments in telecommunications soon made it possible for the bureau to send this information via a telecommunications line, an approach pioneered by the Massachusetts Institute of Technology (MIT), among others, as early as 1961.

---

[72] "General Manager at 23", *Times of Malta*, 10 October 1969, p. 2.

In the decade between 1960 and 1970 the number of computers produced in the United States rose from about 4000 in 1960 to about 50,000 in 1970. The applications to which computers were put also increased proportionately, and at one time in that period (c. 1966) a shortage of programmers was even reported (the first software crisis). This shortage was not merely the result of the quantities of computers being marketed; it was also due to the nature of the machines. Computers and their operating systems were becoming much more sophisticated, with the large mainframes (e.g. IBM's System/360) requiring considerable human effort to develop the necessary operating systems.

Initially, when a computer manufacturer sold its products it supplied its software as part of the hardware, the software not being billed separately. Applications were also sometimes supplied by the hardware vendor as software packages "bundled" with the cost of the computer. In 1969, IBM—the world leader in computers—decided to "unbundle", meaning it would start offering software packages separately from the hardware, instead of supplying both for one price. This move led some service bureaus and many new firms to enter the software producing world. Effectively, following 1969, software had become a commodity, a product that could be produced (and priced) by individual firms not necessarily involved in the manufacture of computer hardware. It was the start of a major sector of the software industry—the software products industry—one that in the 1970s experienced massive growth.

* A services bureau did not itself necessarily purchase equipment but may have leased it from the equipment manufacturer.

Barclays Bank's Computerization

Barclays Bank (Malta)—formerly a subsidiary of Barclays Bank DCO and Barclays International—was, for many years, one of Malta's main commercial banks. In Malta since 1882 but operating initially as the Anglo-Egyptian Bank and later (beginning from 1952) as Barclays Bank Dominion, Colonial and Overseas (after mergers with two other banks), Barclays Malta expanded rapidly after the Second World War from a handful of offices to as much as seventeen branches by 1956 (Consiglio, 1979).[73] Its workforce also grew quickly, with much of it

[73] A comprehensive history of banking in Malta is given in Consiglio (2005), although this work fails to mention Barclays' computerisation project.

comprised of local personnel: in 1973, 390 Maltese worked for the Bank.[74] Thus, apart from the services it offered, the Bank was important for Malta for the opportunities and training it provided to local personnel.

In 1973, Barclays Bank (Malta) installed its first computer in Malta. The decision to computerise was not spontaneous: Barclays Bank as a corporate entity had embarked on a computerisation exercise of several overseas divisions not much earlier. Among its latest computer installations, for example, were those of Trinidad and Jamaica.[75] Although implementation of the computer system did not take place until the summer of 1973, the order was won by ICL in the spring of 1970.[76] The computer system—an ICL 1901A with six magnetic tape units and a high speed line printer—cost about GBP125,000 and was to be installed in 1971. In reality, the system that was delivered two years later was the more advanced ICL 1902A (see Figure 3.2). The software system for Malta was the same as that for Trinidad and Jamaica, all three, naturally for that time, using the same hardware platform. Two contributing factors for the delay in the actual system installation were the delays in building and finishing the bespoke, state of the art computer centre in Mill Street, Qormi, and the fact that the software had to be amended to cater for the three decimal places associated with the Maltese lira, a change which came about in 1972. Previously, Malta used Sterling (with pounds, shillings and pence), the latter having been decimalised in 1971.

To house the equipment, a purpose-built centre—designed by the well-known local architects England and England—was erected at Qormi (Figure 3.3). Later, this building was extended to serve as the bank's administrative headquarters (and, later still, that of Mid-Med and HSBC banks, respectively). Shortly before the actual installation, some publicity was given to the project by way of a few short articles in the local press. These press reports referred to the project as Barclays Qormi Computer Centre, or simply as the Computer Centre.[77] The air conditioning installation was entrusted to Medairco,

---

[74] "Conciliation meeting", *Times of Malta*, 3 September 1973, p. 2.

[75] "Barclays to build computer centre at Qormi", *Times of Malta*, 21 July 1972, p. 24.

[76] "First Malta computer comes from ICL", *The Malta Economist*, 15 May 1970, p. 6.

[77] See, for example, "Barclays to build computer centre at Qormi", *Times of Malta*, 21 July 1972, p. 24.

at that time a prospering company and a leader in the air conditioning field.

Figure 3.2
Barclays Bank Computer Centre: The Computer Room
Source: *The Sunday Times of Malta* (2 June 1974).

This computer system made news in Malta since it was the first of its kind to involve the use of a true computer (unlike the equipment at the COS which comprised of tabulating data processors). So much had been written about the computer in other countries, that it is as if the Maltese community was looking forward to the day when such a machine—almost considered alien in Malta—would make its "debut" locally; and Barclays' event provided just that, an historic milestone in Maltese computing history. In June 1974, two special reports, appearing as supplements, were even prepared by the Bank, one in English for *The Sunday Times of Malta*, and another in Maltese for *It-Torca*.

Figure 3.3
Barclays Bank Computer Centre: The purpose-built building at Mill Street, Qormi.
Source: *The Sunday Times of Malta* (2 June 1974).

Much later, addressing IDPM members at the Malta Chamber of Commerce in 1988, David Pullicino—then Senior Manager at the Central Bank of Malta—would say this about Barclays' computer centre:

> Looking back Malta can be thankful to that bank for what was a solid foundation for our computer industry and many faces in this room can I think vouch for that. It provided us not only with what was the most impressive collection of hardware in Malta at the time, but more important with a disciplined team of managers, analysts, and programmers most of whom form the corner-stone of our industry today (Pullicino, 1988).

Thus, more than the hardware itself, the Centre served as a place where computer professionals were bred, akin to the previous situation at the COS, only this time in a different environment (one that provided modern facilities) and a different sector. It should be mentioned that the other banks were at that time using mechanical accounting machines (later replaced by electronic ones) and continued doing so well into the 1980s.

The persons chosen to manage and operate the Computer Centre were all Barclays employees, no call for applications to fill the new posts that would be created as a result of the computerisation project having been made. Cecil Busuttil was chosen as manager and Sammy Nichols as assistant manager. According to David Grech,[78] another bank employee who was trained as a programmer and formed part of the Centre's small programming team, Busuttil was chosen as manager partly because of his experience with tabulating equipment systems and because he had also formed part of the national decimalisation committee. Before computerisation, the Bank had made use of NCR accounting machines and Busuttil, apart from being an experienced banker, was well versed in their use: he had designed a partially mechanised system that spread the interest calculation workload.

The first team of software developers included Robin Beck, David Grech, and Joe Vella. Harry Restall was chosen as operations manager after being sent on a three-month intensive course in London, which included practical work on a computerised banking system.[79] Restall had joined Barclays in 1956 when he was only 18. Much later, he went on to set up his own computing firm, Intercomp Ltd (still in existence) but, sadly, died relatively young. Beck, Grech and Vella also underwent training with ICL and Barclays in London.

The main accounting application used by the Bank was that adopted already by the Trinidad and Jamaica branches and modified for Malta. Subsequent to successful implementation of the "Barclays" package in 1973 the local development team adapted the system to cater for savings accounting, produced a small CBM package, and designed and developed a Standing Orders system. These applications were written in COBOL with some PLAN routines that

---

[78] Interviewed by author on 9 April 2009.
[79] "Computer Training", *Times of Malta*, 5 October 1972, p. 2.

would have strained the 16K computer memory available. PLAN was the assembly language then used on ICL machines.

It has to be noted at this point that when Barclays Malta ceased to function as such and was sold to the Maltese government in 1976 (when Mid-Med Bank was created), the computer staff initially stayed on. However, especially following the industrial disputes of the summer of 1977 and the advent of a more affordable generation of mini-computers, a number of employees moved to pastures new. Hence David Pullicino's comments reproduced earlier in this section. At that time, the state of computing in Malta was dismal, so that these computer professionals found it hard to find alternative jobs in the data processing field. Apparently, however, only one emigrated, the rest taking up different jobs, and—like Restall—started their own computing business. The remaining staff was integrated with government IT personnel to form the Swatar Computer Centre when it opened in 1981 (see Chapter 6).

Timesharing, Software Houses, and Turnkey Solutions

Excluding ICL and NCR (represented locally by Philip Toledo Ltd), which were predominantly equipment manufacturers and suppliers (although they later also specialised in software development), computer services bureaux and software houses first appeared on the local scene in the years 1979-1981, indisputably late by international standards. The companies that started up in this period are (in alphabetical order) Business Development Systems (BDS), Computime, Intercomp, Management Computer Services (MCS), and Megabyte (see Table 3.1). Three of these companies initially had some foreign (overseas) connection, and all five companies went on to become major players, although one of them—MCS—stopped operating in 2005. BDS was taken over in the 1990s by the Gasan Group of Companies, a major car importer and insurance broker and, after a further merger with another established office equipment firm (V. J. Salomone Equipment) in 2004, was renamed SG Solutions Ltd.

What follows are brief profiles of Computime and Megabyte, the first of the five companies listed above to be created. The emphasis of both accounts is on the early years of their formation. Although one of these two firms was a spin-off and the other a start-up, both started from scratch as far as computing is concerned. One specialised in computer time-sharing and data communications and eventually in computer systems, networks and software, the other in custom software development and turnkey solutions. Likewise, the background of the founding directors are different, coming from management and accountancy in one case, and management, computer science, and electrical engineering in the other.[80]

TABLE 3.1
Computer companies and agents operating in Malta in, or before, 1982[a]

Company	When Established	Type of Business	Make Represented
Charles A. Micallef	1882	oe, tk	Olivetti
ICL (Malta Branch)	1947[b]	tk, c&t, m	ICL
Philip Toledo	1949	oe, tk, c&t	NCR, H-P
Computime	1979	tsb, tk, c&t	DEC
Megabyte	1979	tk, c&t	DEC, Altos
BDS	1981	tk, c&t	Apple, Honeywell
Intercomp Data System	1981	tk, c&t	Data General
MCS	1981	b, c&t	ICL
Panta Computers	1982	b, c&t	Prime

Key: c&t = consulting and training
      b = bureau
      m = manufacturing
      oe = office equipment vendor
      tk = turnkey
      tsb = timesharing bureau
Notes: a. Only the major players are listed.
        b. This is the date when the company opened its Malta office.
Source: Compiled by author from local newspaper articles and *Informatics* magazine.

Computime

Computime Ltd, the first (and only) company in Malta to have offered a true, online, interactive time-sharing service came into being in December 1979, after being spawned from the local accountancy and

---

[80] The choice of these two companies is arbitrary, but Computime was the major computer time-sharing company in Malta, and Megabyte the first to offer complete turnkey solutions.

audit firm of Diamantino, Manfré & Co. Recognising the need for a computer time-sharing service in Malta, the founding directors decided that the best way to go about the new venture would be to involve a foreign computer firm for support. After forming a small, specialist team of systems analysts and making arrangements with the UK firm Systime to provide and support the equipment—a DEC-based PDP-11/34 system running the RSTS/E operating system—and simultaneously act as their consultants, the company was ready to start offering its services to customers in early 1980.[81]

The business model behind the time-sharing service was that by pooling the very limited manpower that was available at the time, and with ready access to a powerful remote computer and software, customers could start to implement computerised systems; besides, they would be saving on capital expenditure by paying only for what they needed in monthly rentals.[82] Connection from users' premises to Computime was accomplished either via a normal telephone exchange line or—more typically—a private dedicated wire directly to the computer centre (i.e., a leased line). In fact, for several years Computime pioneered data communications in Malta and widely used modems and multiplexors for multiple network connections both locally and internationally.

According to Mario Mizzi,[83] the only founding company director still alive, the first few years were difficult, with the company at one time even running at a loss, so that were it not for the backing of the original accountancy firm from which Computime was spun off, it is conceivable that the whole enterprise would have been called off. However, perseverance and overcoming the initial hurdles paid off, because about four years after the company was formed, an event happened that was to give some breathing space to the company and change its course. Interestingly, this happened by chance.

---

[81] "Time-sharing in Computing Resources for Firms", *Times of Malta*, 22 April 1980, p. 3.

[82] For a detailed and insightful account of computer time-sharing, emphasising the economic perspective, see Campbell-Kelly & Garcia-Swartz (2008). For Dartmouth College's Time-Sharing System see Kemeny & Kurtz (1968); for computer time-sharing at MIT see Lee (1992a and 1992b). See also O'Neill (1992).

[83] Interviewed on 24 July 2008.

Systime, a UK company and Computime's original consultants, was an Original Equipment Manufacturer (OEM) and a computer consultancy firm, importing and modifying computer and peripheral equipment produced by the American company Digital Equipment Corporation (DEC) and Control Data Corporation (CDC), and then selling them mainly in the UK and Europe. Systime's and Computime's company logo closely resembled that of DEC (see Figure 3.4). Coming across one of Computime's adverts in the newspapers, Reuters, the famous English news reporting and financial services group, contacted Computime from their offices in Cairo, their HQ in the region, to enquire about the possibility of doing business with them. At the time, Reuters were looking for someone to support their first financial services client in Malta,[84] the Central Bank. Since they were also using similar DEC computers and Racal-Milgo communications equipment, Reuters asked Computime to provide support to their clients in Malta. At the time (mid-1980s), Reuters were expanding their operations moving into, and investing heavily in, the financial information services field. Some basic statistics from the period reveal the extent of their success: in 1987 Reuters' turnover reached 1200 million ECU, with profits standing at 254 million ECU; and in that year about 141,000 video terminals throughout the world had been installed (see, for example, Ungerer & Costello, 1990: p. 60). A deal was eventually struck between Reuters and the Maltese firm, giving the latter a boost that helped keep the company going.

As so often happens in business, and with the company specialising more and more in data communications and networks, one contract led to another and some years later Computime secured another important contract, this time involving SWIFT and all the main local banks which wanted to introduce a national system of secure inter-bank financial transactions linked to the international SWIFT banking system (established in 1973).[85]

---

[84] The first Reuters client in Malta (since the mid-1940s) was the Times of Malta. Interview with Mario Mizzi on 24 July 2008.

[85] In February 1989, Mid-Med Bank signed a Lm1.5 million (= c. US$4.5 m.) agreement with ICL and Kindle Software Ltd for a computerised banking system making use of a resilient dual processor ICL series 39 mainframe (that would be installed at the Bank's Computer Centre in Qormi) and Kindle's Bankmaster application. See: "Bank signs Lm1.5 m. computer agreement", *The Times*, 17 February, 1989, p. 2.

Figure 3.4
A popular Computime advert of the mid-1980s. Note the similarity of
the company logo with that of DEC.
Source: *Informatics* (June 1985, No. 14).

What about Computime's other Maltese customers, who and what
type of customers were they? Most of them were medium-to-large
sized firms that included both manufacturing and services companies
like De La Rue, KPH, Malta Insurance Brokers, Medserv, Sea Malta,
and SGS-Ates (now ST Microelectronics). In the majority of cases, the

desired applications requested by users were accounts and payroll, but also word-processing and bespoke systems. Some of these applications (like payroll) were developed in-house by Computime, others purchased and customised to user's requirements. Depending on the number of installed terminals at the customer's premises and the sophistication of the application and service offered, an agreed fixed monthly rental that varied from about Lm300 (c. US$900) to Lm900 (c. US$2,700) was charged. The contract would typically be for a minimum of three years, following which the same contract would be renewed or a new one designed.

Interestingly (and surprisingly for the author) two customers continued using the by-then aging computer time-sharing system until the late 1990s, before they were finally persuaded by Computime itself to switch to modern technology. It is another concrete example of the resistance to change, and of the trauma that companies perceive (and often go through) when changing their existing (and correctly functioning) computerised system with a completely new one.

With a workforce of over eighty and a turnover in 2008 of over five million Euros, Computime is today one of the largest local and wholly Maltese-owned computer company.

Megabyte Ltd

Another Maltese-owned company, Megabyte may be considered a success story of the Maltese software industry. Set up by Thomas and Carmel Galea—two computer graduate brothers—in 1979 at a time when computing in Malta was still in its infancy, the company grew to become one of Malta's leading software firms, employing over fifty people and having a turnover in 2008 in excess of 2 million Euros. Its office at the Mosta Techno Park lies alongside a number of foreign firms of international repute.

With just one technician and a part-time salesman and secretary (excluding the company founding directors), the company started very modestly importing computers for the local market. Brand names like Osborne, Altos, Epson and, later, Digital, were among the early makes of computers represented. From the very beginning the company's aim was to provide "total business solutions", meaning that with every computer system sold, the client was to get the required software, training and after-sales support (hence, a turnkey system). Initially, the company's main target was the small businessman, but within less than a decade, it was already catering for larger concerns. During its first two years of operation, progress was modest, if not slow, with only a few sales having been secured.

It will be recalled that in the late 1970s only a handful of Maltese firms owned a computer. These were large business firms, which also had their own small data processing department. The computers installed at these companies were mainframe or miniframe systems, typically used for tasks such as accounting, payroll, costings, inventory control and production management (see Table 3.2). The introduction of microcomputers and their promotion in Malta by Megabyte (and some years afterwards by other start-ups) opened up the possibility for small businesses to computerise at an affordable price. Moreover, and importantly, those businesses contemplating computerisation could now do so in the knowledge that they would get the required professional support.

The company did not take long to realise that the market for computers (especially turnkey systems) in certain niche areas was still very much untapped, and therefore immediately concentrated its energy on developing software for the vertical market, in particular the hospitality industry (e.g. front office systems for the many hotels on the Island—see Figure 3.5). Identifying key areas was important because it meant that the effort spent designing software for one customer was time well-spent: that same software could—with some modifications—be used for other clients who were in the same line of business.

A distinguishing feature which undoubtedly gave the company a name was the latest, state-of-the-art, equipment the company continuously invested in. For example, no sooner had the DEC Alpha RISC processor been announced in 1991 than a server based on that processor was purchased and added to the company's small cluster of minicomputers.[86] This meant that young programmers looked at the company with respect, often preferring it to others because of the exposure to the latest technology (hardware and programming tools) the company gave its new recruits. The company's policy generally

---

[86] The author used to work with this company at the time.

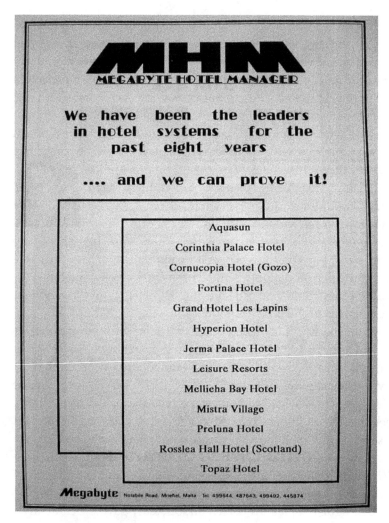

Figure 3.5
A 1989 advert by Megabyte. Hotel Management Systems was one
application in which the company specialised in the early years of its
formation.
Source: *Informatics* (November 1989).

was either to recruit qualified and experienced personnel (for senior
positions and often whenever a major contract had been won) or take
on young, trainee-programmers and "home-brew" them, training
them in-house and simultaneously encouraging them to further their

studies (e.g. obtaining professional qualifications) on a part-time basis. Much of this—the company's reputation regarding employee training—was public knowledge, therefore further enhancing the company's image, if not giving it a competitive advantage.

In 1988, the Company was reinforced (by an injection of capital) with the introduction of a Maltese holding company, Farrugia Investments Ltd, which became a fifty-percent shareholder of Megabyte. The synergy between the two companies further strengthened Megabyte and accelerated its growth.

That same year, the company also won its first major government-related contract. By this time, the former labour government was no longer in power, and the government of the day, elected in 1987, had just announced its intentions to reform the public service which, among other things, would involve a programme of computerisation. Educational reforms were also on the newly elected government's agenda. In that period, the Swatar Computer Centre (see Chapter 6) had just begun to implement a policy of procurement whereby new computer systems for the public sector would be developed by private companies. One of the earliest projects, the public lotto system, was awarded to Megabyte by public tender. The winning of this contract was an important milestone for the company, giving it that much needed capital. The successful implementation of this system, although not without its sceptics and critics, enabled the company to win other important government contracts, such as the Identity Card system for the Electoral Commission. In the spring of 1989, in collaboration with the Education Department, and after having been appointed sole distributors and representatives of the UK-based Research Machines company, Megabyte also got involved in training schoolteachers in the use of computers and basic networking.[87] Research Machines Ltd was a company that produced quality computers for educational purposes, and Maltese shools (both private and state schools) had chosen that company's Nimbus microcomputers (which could be networked together) for installation in their laboratories.

In 1990 Megabyte celebrated its ten-year anniversary and used this opportunity to launch a massive advertising campaign. By this

---

[87] See, for example, "New Computer Systems for Maltese Schools", *The Sunday Times*, 16 April 1989, p. 23.

time, the company had already acquired the rights to sell renowned software products like those from Oracle, and therefore these brand names also featured prominently in the campaign. One of its flagship products at the time was its Hotel Management System, which had been implemented in several hotels. With a reasonably sized customer base to its credit, it could therefore boast of its achievements.

Megabyte has been one of the most successful ventures on the Island. The reason for this must be a combination of factors, but it is worth quoting an economist who—referring to the economy of increasing returns—argued that, for success, 'what counts to some degree—but only to some degree—is technical expertise, deep pockets, will and courage' and that 'above all, the rewards go to the players who are first to make sense of the new games looming out of the technological fog, to see their shape, to cognize them' (Arthur, 1996).[88] This quote fits Megabyte well, but one must also emphasise hard work and perseverance, without which it is doubtful if the company would have achieved the success it did.

Data Processing Installations: an Analysis

The previous sections looked at the few significant computer-related events spanning the period 1967-1982. This section concludes this chapter with an analysis of the low number of computers installed in this same period, and (i) suggests possible reasons for this slow take up; (ii) compares the monetary value of imported computers as a percentage of GNP with typical global figures for the period in question, in order to show that the number of installed computers throughout the 1970's was indeed small in comparison to many European countries in the same period; and (iii) makes some observations about the type of installations, the vendors and the customers.

A list of data processing and computer installations in Malta for the period 1947-1982 is shown in Table 3.2.[89] A similar list done for many developed countries for only part of the period considered

---

[88] As quoted in Campbell-Kelly (2004: p. 242).
[89] ICL, which was the major computer supplier in Malta at the time is excluded from the list of companies shown in Table 3.2 This table also does not show companies that used specially-designed computers or terminal equipment for very specific

TABLE 3.2
Data Processing Installations in Malta, 1947-1982

Year	Where Installed (User)	Type of Business	System	What Used For (Application)
1947	Simonds Farsons	Brewery	Tabulating[a]	Costings; Payroll
1950	COS	Government	Tabulating	Statistics
1960	Dockyard	Ship repair	Tabulating	Costings; Payroll
1962	Archbishop's Curia	Ecclesiastical	Tabulating	Accounting
1966	COS	Government	ICT Univac 1004	Statistics; Billing
1970	COS	Government	ICT Univac 1004[b]	Statistics; Billing
1973	Barclays Bank	Banking	ICL 1902A	Accounting
1973	Dockyard	Ship repair	ICL 1901A	Costings
1976	Inland Revenue	Government	ICL 1901A	Payroll; Tax Returns
1977	Mid-Med Bank	Banking	ICL EDS 60	Accounting
1978	Foster Clark	Manufacturing	ICL 1501-43	Payroll
1979	Philip Toledo Ltd	Agent	NCR 8250 Series	Various
1979	Drydocks	Ship repair	NCR 8250/70	Costings
1979	Dowty (Malta) Ltd[c]	Manufacturing	ICL 2903	Process Control
1979	Computime Ltd	Bureau	DEC PDP Series	Time-sharing
1980	University of Malta	Education	MINC-11	Scientific/Engineering
1981	MCS Bureau Ltd	Bureau	ICL 2903	Time-sharing
1981	Panta Computer	Agent/Bureau	Prime 50 Series	Time-sharing
1981	Intercomp Ltd	Agent/Bureau	DG Nova Series	Time-sharing
1981	Mira Motor Sales	Auto Dealer	DG Nova 3	Inventory
1981	Swatar Centre	Government	Prime 750	Various
1982	Farsons	Brewery	ICL ME29	Inventory
1982	Gasan Group Ltd	Auto Dealer	ICL ME29	Inventory
1982	Miaco Int. Aviation	Aviation	ICL ME29	Inventory

Notes: a. Conventional tabulating punched card equipment supplied by BTM
b. Later removed and reinstalled at GIE
c. Formerly, Malta Rubber Ltd
Source: Compiled by the author from local newspaper articles and various issues of *Informatics* magazine.

would run into hundreds or thousands,[90] but for a tiny place like Malta having a population of under half a million and, at that time,

---

applications. For example, in the summer of 1979, the Libyan Airlines Malta office introduced the first computer reservations system in Malta by linking computer terminals to British Airways' "BABS" system. In 1972, another company, Andrews Feeds (Malta) Ltd, also installed a computer aas part of its plant to control the production of 32 different feeds.

[90] According to a study by the Diebold Group, for example, there were almost twelve thousand computers installed in 1966 in the UK, France, Germany and the Benelux countries, split up as follows: 5000 in Germany, 3000 in Britain, 2600 in France and 1400 in Belgium and the Netherlands. See "Electronics Industry", *Times of Malta*, 21 March 1967, p. 11; and Table 5-1 of Flamm (1988: p. 135).

few firms large enough to afford a computer, one expects the numbers to be small. The question is, how small?

Some observations can be made from Table 3.2. Firstly, it will be noted that ICL had the largest share of the market. As mentioned elsewhere, this was the first computer company to set up operations in Malta. Distinctively missing from the list is Olivetti, even though this company has been represented locally for at least as long. However, Olivetti has traditionally concentrated more on office equipment such as typewriters and accounting machines. Until the late 1960s when the Olivetti Programma P101 was produced in quantities, the company did not offer any commercially inexpensive computer. Often, accounting machines such as the Auditronic 730 served most businesses' needs well enough for the businesses to not have to spend a fortune on a computer system.

The second point to note is that, excluding the Univac 1004, which was more of a punched-card data processor, albeit programmable and with a small core memory, the first true computer system was not implemented until 1973. This would seem to be—and is by international standards—rather late, but it must be recalled that in the preceding decade, few commercial computers at a price that was within reach of small-to-medium sized companies (e.g. employing between 10 and 50 persons) were available. In Malta, where wages were miserably low in comparison to most developed countries, a typical entry-level cost price of, say, US$100,000 for a 1970 computer represented the equivalent of the combined yearly income of about 50 workers.[91] Few companies therefore could afford to install a computer system, even if they actually needed one. For illustrative purposes only and in order to gain an idea of the "economies of scale", Tables 3.3 and 3.4 give, respectively, the Maltese population and GDP, and Maltese company sizes in the manufacturing sector, vis-à-vis the UK.

---

[91] In the mid-1960s, the American company Digital Equipment Corporation (DEC) introduced its PDP-8 minicomputer at the relatively cheap price of US$18,000. This computer was very popular for scientific and dedicated applications such as factory process automation, and its success essentially started the minicomputer era. However, larger business computers such as those typically used in Banks and Insurance companies cost much more, and US$60,000 for a small, entry-level mainframe computer of the mid- to late-1960s (e.g. IBM's System 360, and Honeywell's Model 200) was not atypical.

TABLE 3.3
Population and Gross Domestic Product, 1981

	MALTA	**U.K.**	**(ratio)**
Population:	0.32 m.	55.9 m.	(1 : 174)
GDP:	£M347 m.	£211,792 m.	(1 : 469)
Per Capita GDP:	£M1,084	£3,789	(1 : 2.8)[a]

[a] Based on an exchange rate of £1.26 to £M1.0.
Source: National Statistics Office, Malta; and Stanlake (1983: p. 148).

TABLE 3.4
Manufacturing establishments by size of employment

Numbers Employed	**Number of Firms MALTA (1978)**	**UK (1979)**
fewer than 10	1377	59,783
10 – 49	222	30,302
50 – 99	58	6,683
100 – 499	50[a]	8,284
500 and above	-	2,341
All firms	*1728*	*107,393*

[a] It should be noted that this figure (= 50) may include some firms that employed in excess of 499 persons.
Source: Malta 1978 figures compiled from Table 6 of *Census of Production 1978 – Summary Tables*, COS (1980: p. 62); UK figures from Stanlake (1983: p. 87).

Worth noting is the small number of computer systems implemented all through the 1970s. Even given Malta's size one would have expected—at least from about the mid-1970s onwards when minicomputers had become popular worldwide (see also Box 3-2), and the price of computers in general had fallen significantly compared to a decade earlier—to find a similar proportion of computer installations to other developed countries. Is it possible to account for this bleak picture? The answer is yes and no: yes, because of then-government's disinterest in technology; no, because even if government had shown enthusiasm, there is no way of knowing with certainty if the outcome would have been any different.[92] The 1970s coincided with an oil crisis and a world recession, which affected Malta too, although—it has been pointed out—not as severely as some other countries.[93] Additionally, global fears of mass unemployment as a result of computerisation—also promoted by the cybernetics pioneer Norbert Wiener as early as 1950—were widespread in the 1970s.[94] Although there is little evidence to suggest that these fears were reverberated also in Malta, it is conceivable that Maltese politicians were cognisant of the supposed negative impact new technology might have on unemployment and the still developing Maltese economy. Given that the government of the day had the added problem of the British Forces run down on its hands, whereby alternative employment had to be found for the thousands of Maltese workers engaged with the British Services, government's concern about unemployment was warranted. The unemployment problem was further exacerbated when, following the oil crisis, Britain and Australia—two countries to which the majority of the Maltese emigrated (the other being Canada)—introduced tight immigration control, and consequently from 1975 onwards Maltese emigration slumped well below the projected targets (Delia, 2002: p. 100).

---

[92] Malta's premier throughout the 1970s, Dom Mintoff, is generally known to have been against the introduction of computers. Previously, Mintoff tried hard to obtain funds from the Marshall Plan, which Britain denied Malta (see Chapter 1, note 16). In some countries (e.g. the Netherlands), Marshall Plan funds were used to import novel means of production (including machinery and expertise) which, in turn, created a climate favourable for office automation and domestic development of experimental computers. See Alberts (2010).

[93] Actually, it was fortunate for Malta that West Germany—one of the few countries that turned out to be the most resilient to the upheaval to which the industrial world was subjected—invested heavily in Malta during this period. See, for example, Mizzi (1995: pp. 186-187); and Pollacco (1992: pp. 66-67).

[94] Wiener's concern was about the improper use of new technology, for example, by the military and by profit-conscious industrialists who could use the technology to lay off workers and increase production (Wiener, 1950). In 1963, the dangers of automation on the American economy was also being warned by a group of distinguished scientists and economists led by J. Robert Oppenheimer, following which a Commission on Automation, Technology, and Economic Progress was officially established by Congress (Rifkin, 1995: Chapter 4). With the introduction of the first microprocessor in 1971 and the advent of microelectronics, the technology-work debate intensified further. See, for example, Forester (1980); and Gill (1985).

Apart from the very limited size of the local market, a determining factor for the slow take-up of computers in the period considered is—as already noted—the high purchase price, or rental fee of the machines. The price factor is confirmed by Table 3.2, which reveals that the majority of computer users were either large private companies or the government. Farsons is a large brewery employing hundreds of workers; Foster Clark is another large manufacturing concern, a food producer targeting both the local and export markets; and Gasan is a group of companies dealing in insurance and the importation of automobiles. These companies could justify the high initial expense of installing and running a computer and, equally as important, they could also afford to have their own small data processing team to develop in-house software.

That the number of computer installations in the 1970s in Malta was nevertheless miniscule may be gauged from the value of installed computers as percent of Gross National Product (GNP). In 1973, for example, this value was between 1% and 2% for the industrialised nations and considerably less for developing countries, but still above 0.1% for the rest of the world (Cortada, 1996: p. 76). Throughout the 1970s, Malta's computer installation base was still so small as to be insignificant. In 1980, for example, the estimated value of imported "data processing" machines, including their peripherals, was Lm255,000 or 0.07% of GNP. By contrast, a decade later, the picture is very different: in 1990, the estimated value of imported computing equipment stood at Lm2,017,000, which works out at 0.3% of GNP. By 1995 the percentage value was closer to 0.6%.[95]

Referring again to Table 3.2, this shows how difficult it can be for even well established companies to capture the computer market when that market is small and has already been exploited by another competitor. In Malta, this seems to have been the case with NCR. Although NCR was the number one player in Malta when it came to cash register sales,[96] its sales of computers was certainly unimpressive, their first local computer sale not being secured until 1979. This, in spite of some aggressive marketing such as when the Century series of

---

[95] Percentage figures estimated from data found in the *National Abstract of Statistics* for 1980, 1990 and 1995, respectively.

[96] One account states that by 1968 NCR machine population (accounting and adding machines and cash registers) [in Malta] exceeded one thousand. See, for example, "NCR plans for Malta", *Times of Malta*, 3 April 1968, p. 5.

computers was launched in 1968, when full-page adverts appeared in local newspapers, and no less a key figure than NCR's Vice President and Group Executive International Operations—George Haynes—visited Malta to discuss NCR's future. Yet, not one Century model was sold. Of course—and this is an important point to note—NCR's original speciality lay in office accounting machines, and many organizations (both local and overseas) were happy to invest in accounting machines instead of the more expensive and sophisticated computers.[97] For example, in 1960 the Treasury made precisely this choice when it purchased a number of National Class 31/32 Accounting Machines.[98] Patrick Pullicino, who worked with the company (Philip Toledo) during the 1960s and 1970s and is now CEO of STC Training, also confirmed that at the time NCR concentrated more on selling accounting machines than computers, since the former were cheaper and easier to maintain.[99] In addition, customers required less training on them. Government organizations, the banks and hotels were all heavy users of these machines, and Philip Toledo Ltd had a good chunk of the local market. In Pullicino's words, the 1960s and 1970s could be considered as the 'accounting machine era, and an important one which is often neglected'.

Finally, one notes that, beginning from 1980, computer makes other than ICL and NCR start appearing. In fact, from this date onwards, the two leading computer and office accounting firms no longer enjoyed a duopoly, although their sales continued to rise steadily in the 1980s.

---

[97] Anderson (1978) gives a list of advantages of accounting machines (both electromechanical and electronic) over computers.

[98] See "Mechanized Accounting at the Treasury", *The Review*, 6 April 1960, p. 1.

[99] Interview with Pullicino on 9 September 2009.

Box 3-2
The Minicomputer Era

Beginning from about the late-1960s, companies such as IBM, DEC, Honeywell, Data General, Hewlett-Packard, Texas Instruments, Motorola, ICL, Bull, and other lesser-known companies started manufacturing minicomputer systems that cost a fraction of the larger mainframes but served the needs of small groups of users equally well. The production of these minicomputers came about as a result of the integrated circuit (IC), also known as the semiconductor chip, or microchip. The IC effectively contained an entire electrical circuit on a single wafer of silicon and therefore truly commenced the era of electronic miniaturisation. Importantly, the IC allowed many electronics firms to enter the computer market because of the ready supply of inexpensive chips from which computers could now be built. The IC was developed independently by two researchers (Jack Kilby working at Texas Instruments and Robert Noyce of Fairchild Corporation) in 1959. Computers based on the microchip came to be categorised as third-generation computers, to distinguish them from earlier second-generation computers which did not contain ICs.*

Rather than rent a mainframe, small businesses and research establishments could now afford to purchase much smaller systems and upgrade them according to their needs. These systems typically supported anything from a handful to a few dozens of users and, whilst they still worked on the time-sharing principle, the costs associated with large time-shared systems (such as expensive communications for remote access and an hourly rate for processor use) could be avoided. Minicomputers remained popular well into the 1990s, by which time powerful networked PCs and the client/server model of computing had become widely adopted.

In Malta, it was not until the late 1970s that several businesses—particularly manufacturing concerns, wholesalers, and insurance agencies—began investing in minicomputer systems. In doing so, they invariably created their own small data processing departments, employing a small team of IT personnel for administering their systems and developing in-house software. These firms, in addition to the early local software companies, thus provided the first generation of Maltese data processing professionals.

---

* In the 1970s computers began to make use of the microprocessor, the first of which was produced by Intel (Robert Noyce's new company) in 1971 under the direction of Ted Hoff.

Part III

Affordable and Widespread Computing:
Developments in the 1980s and 1990s

Part III
Affordable and Widespread Computing: Developments in the 1980s and 1990s

Just as the closing years of the 1960s is remembered for the United States' Apollo missions, so the end of the 1970s is remembered—in computing history—for America's introduction of microcomputers, also known as personal computers.[100] In Malta, as in Europe, these mass-market machines began to appear shortly afterwards, around 1980-1981. Within a short span of time, they became very popular as a number of existing local importers and newly created businesses began importing these products and, in some cases, also offering ancillary services such as introductory programming courses (typically in BASIC).

Thanks to the early home computers, the first of which also came in kit form (for example, the American Altair 8800 and the later British products such as the Tangerine and Acorn), a hobbyist community emerged which, to a certain extent, played a role in locally promoting the home computer's popularity and furthering basic computer skills. These enthusiasts, unwittingly, have helped the diffusion of the home computer: by offering advice, encouragement and practical support, they likely encouraged more sophisticated and extensive ownership and use. As in Britain, from where most of the home computers were imported, computer clubs were formed which increased the rate at which knowhow about these machines was acquired. Whilst some of the home computers were

---

[100] Based on Intel's newly introduced 8080 microprocessor, the Altair 8800 was among the first personal computers for the serious hobbyist. It was announced in the January 1975 issue of *Popular Electronics* as the 'world's first minicomputer kit' that could be purchased for under $400. In 1977, Radio Shack began offering its TRS-80 at roughly the same price, and because the company had stores all over the US, the TRS-80 first model allowed the personal computer to find a mass audience. The Apple II, based on the 6502 architecture, was introduced at the same time; but the IBM PC, which was meant for serious business use, did not appear until 1981. From then on, IBM PC clones would flood the world markets. See Chapters 7 and 8 of Ceruzzi (2003); and Chapters 10 and 11 of Campbell-Kelly & Aspray (2004). For an interesting account of the PC clone industry see Chapter 9 of Cringley (1996).

used as toys for playing games, others were put to more practical, albeit very limited, use. Interestingly, a number of these "hobbyists"—whom the author came to know personally at that time (1983-1984)—turned themselves into "self-made" professionals. Some started their own computer business, and others went on to occupy middle-management, if not more senior, positions in the IT field.

During the 1980s, as the IBM-compatible PC started replacing the more humble home computer, Malta witnessed an explosive growth in the use of computing equipment. The Maltese information technology fair, first held in Naxxar's then popular trade fair grounds in October 1981, became an annual event that attracted a great deal of interest among the public. Within a few years, as minicomputers and desktop business machines became more affordable and popular, the fair was being targeted for the serious business user. On a number of occasions, it was held at the Phoenicia Hotel in Floriana, next to Valletta (the capital city). This was a prestigious venue and centrally located. A trade fair magazine called *Informatix* was also produced for every occasion of the event. It gave information about the participants and included short articles and brief news about the latest IT scene. A small entrance fee was typically charged, and the IT magazine could be purchased for an additional nominal price on entrance.

One sector that stood to gain from the relatively cheap PC prices was education. In the early-to-mid 1980s, church schools began introducing computers and offered computer studies as part of their curriculum. State schools, however, would take longer to adopt computers. Contemporaneously, a number of start-up firms also began exploiting the computer training business, expanding later into consultancy. Like the early software houses, these "first movers" had a competitive lead on later firms and managed to secure a small niche in the computer services market (see also Chapter 7 on the software industry).

As the decade wore on, software companies were becoming more demanding when it came to recruitment. These software houses, of which a number existed by the end of the 1980s, would either expect applicants to be both qualified and experienced, or employ young college leavers and train them, sometimes also helping them to gain formal qualifications such as the UK's (then popular)

Institute of Data Processing Management (IDPM) diploma. By the early 1990s a growing number of Maltese IT personnel had become full IDPM members and, about this time, an IDPM Malta branch was opened. This branch regularly organized talks on various IT topics, and in so doing served to bring together what was otherwise a loosely-knit IT community. By this time also, the University of Malta had formally introduced diploma and degree courses in computing, the need for which had long been felt by prospective students and industrialists.

As for the public sector, the major computer-related institution dominating the 1980s was the government computer centre. Known also as the Swatar Centre, the computer centre brought together groups of people from various government departments and for almost a decade influenced the way computing was done in the civil service.[101] The government computer centre ceased to exist in 1992 when its functions were taken over by a new entity, the Management Systems Unit (MSU), created following a civil service reform exercise. The MSU was itself subsequently to take a differnt form when it was replaced by the Malta Information Technology and Training Services.

---

[101] By this time (early 1980s), a number of countries had long established their own national computer centres. Some examples include: the UK's NCC (established in 1966); New Zealand's Government Computer Centre (est. 1970); the Philippines NCC (est. 1971); India's Computer Centre (set up as an attached office of the Department of Statistics in 1967 but used by other Departments and Ministries) and its National Informatics Centre (est. 1977); and Nepal's NCC (est. 1974).

4

The Personal Computer: From a Hobbyist Culture to Small Business Computing

Hobbyist Culture

A cursory look at some of the computer and electronics magazines (e.g. *PC World, Computing, Micro Decision, Practical Computing, Byte, Electronics Today,* and *Popular Electronics*) of the early-to-mid 1980s will indicate the extent to which the personal computer explosion occurred. Articles and adverts about a vast range of microcomputers appear in profusion. Undoubtedly, this was the era of the microcomputer, the beginnings of which go to some years before with the introduction of such brand names as the Apple I, the Commodore PET, and the Radio Shack TRS-80, among others (see also Box 4-1).

In Malta, the explosion of the personal computer followed a trend which is similar to that which occurred in most developed countries, perhaps lagging behind by a year or two (also, as we shall see later, Malta did lag behind in the introduction of computers in state schools). The pattern of the microcomputer's initial take-up in Malta is akin to the same phenomenon that led to the evolution of the microcomputer itself; the latter was the result of the experimentation by electronics hobbyists on readily available, relatively cheap microprocessor and supporting chips bundled together into a working, sometimes crude, computer. The microcomputer revolution has been likened to the way wireless telegraphy and radio broadcasting evolved half a century or so previously (Campbell-Kelly

& Aspray, 2004: pp. 208-213) in the sense that just as it was the electronics hobbyist who delighted in building radio receiver circuits and communicating with other radio amateurs and in so doing popularised the new technology, so it was the same type of person (the "enthusiast") who gave the microcomputer that important boost.

It has been pointed out (Murdock, Hartmann & Gray, 1995: p. 275) that for many enthusiasts, these early machines offered pleasures that derived not from particular applications but from possession of the technology itself and from solving the problems involved in getting them to perform. For this reason, the early microcomputers have also been dubbed as "self-referring". In Malta, where at least two small microcomputer clubs are known to have existed, many of the earlier microcomputer users delighted, more than anything else, in writing short programs (sometimes in pure machine code) to do whatever clever things they conceived of. Their pleasure certainly derived from the challenges the machine offered: they showed little interest in applications, which in any case were initially very limited in functionality.[102] As club members, however, they not only shared their interest between themselves, but imparted knowlege to others by, for example, organising public lectures and encouraging people to attend. Indeed, Malta's BBC Users Club even organized exhibitions, especially to instil computer interest in children and the young (see Figure 4.1).

The "self-referring" practice is one of four major discourses that have been identified with home computers. The other three include the discourse of the serious applications (related to the use of computers in schools and in business); that of games-playing; and finally the discourse of righteous concern for the welfare of the young (Murdock, Hartmann & Gray, 1995: p. 279). Whereas the topic of computers in schools (and to a lesser extent that of computer games) had their fair share of discourse, the effect of computers on the young received little, if any, attention in Malta. This is somewhat surprising given that Maltese society is predominantly catholic and family-based.

---

[102] A number of PC magazines from that period (early-to-mid 1980s) used to publish BASIC and machine code programs written by enthusiasts for the microcomputers of the day. They include, among others, *Personal Computer World* and *Practical Computing*.

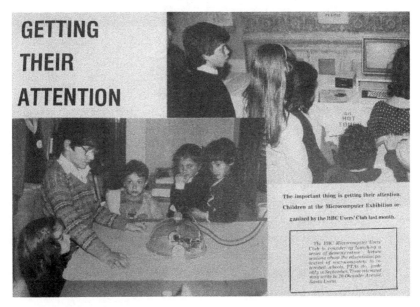

Figure 4.1
An exhibition organized by Malta's BBC Users Club in 1985.
Source: *The Times Electronika Fair Supplement* (25 April 1985)

Microcomputers in Schools

The introduction of computers in Maltese schools began very slowly in 1980 when Stella Maris College of Gzira purchased its first computers for educational purposes.[103] However, whereas within a few years some private schools had established proper computer laboratories and introduced computer courses as part of their school curricula, it was not until at least another decade that more serious attention began to be given to computer studies in state schools. A survey-based study by Girodmaina in 1987 and another carried out a year later by Cassar & Dimech (1988) give us an insight into the state of computer education in Malta in the 1980s. Giordmaina's study concentrated primarily on microcomputers in schools, whereas Cassar & Dimech—apart from building on Giordmainia's work—also

---

[103] See, for example, "Stella Maris College faces the computer challenge", *The Sunday Times Computers Supplement*, 3 July 1983, p. XI.

investigated the computer's potential in the home. The salient points that came out of these two studies might be summarised as follows:

- Up to 1987, very few schools made use of computers. In 1986, c. 10% of government schools owned at least one computer, compared to c. 33% for private schools. However, the total number of installed computers in schools was minimal: the estimated number being under 40 for 1986.[104]

- The computer's introduction in schools was sporadic and often depended on the headteacher's initiative. Moreover, student fund raising and donations were the primary means of funding for their purchase.

- The computer's use in the school was primarily for learning the basics of programming and for computer awareness courses. Although some of the computers were also used for administrative purposes, few were utilised for other educational applications.

- Only a handful of schools (4 out of a total of 120 schools that responded to the 1986 survey by Giordmaina) had a computer room/lab.

- The two most popular makes of computer in schools were the BBC and the Olivetti M24, followed closely by Research Machines and the Apple IIe.

- The most popular make of computer found in homes was the Sinclair Spectrum, followed by the Amstrad. Since Sinclair Research, the manufacturers of the Spectrum, was at the time (1987) owned by Amstrad, the latter dominated the local computer sales scene (c. 42% of the computers sold for home use). Other popular makes included the Atari and the Commodore 64.

---

[104] Unfortunately, we have no statistics for the number of computers in schools following Giordmaina's and Cassar & Dimech's surveys (except for recent NSO data). By the early 1990s, however, it is likely that this number stood in the few hundreds after government announced in 1989 its intention to a commence a programme of educational reform that would include computer education and computerisation in schools. See "New Computer Systems for Maltese Schools", *The Sunday Times*, 16 April 1989, p. 23. 1989.

- 19% of girls and 5% of boys had used a computer at school, but at home the percentage of boys that made use of a computer was higher than that for girls (presumably because boys spent more time playing computer games).

Given that by the late 1980s many countries had not only introduced computers in schools in quantities but had already established some basic form of computer studies curricula, one must conclude from the above that Malta was trailing behind in computer education by a number of years.[105] This, in spite of the fact that by the mid-1980s, microcomputers had already infiltrated the local market (see Table 4.1). Politics and the lack of government initiatives can only be to blame for this situation. However, the general public also failed to voice their concern about the lack of state incentives regarding computer education. Throughout almost the entire 1980s, for example, the local media reported surprisingly little about computer education: indeed, with one or two exceptions (e.g., Cachia Zammit, 1985), it was only in the late 1980s and early 1990s—when the subject of computers in education began to be officially addressed—that related articles started appearing in the local press.[106, 107]

---

[105] In Britain, the government launched a scheme to put a microcomputer in every secondary school in 1981, and extended this scheme for primary schools a year later. The subject of "computer studies" could already be taken in 1978 as an elective by fifth formers (school-leaving students) (Miles, 1990). In Australia, the first national seminar about the role of computers in schools (across Australia) was held in Adelaide in 1969. By the 1970s, a number of secondary schools were running experimental programming courses and offering accredited Computer Studies subjects; and in the early 1980s, Education Departments in different Australian states had adopted computer education policies for schools (see Pirie, 1994). In New Zealand, the acquisition of microcomputers by schools was marked by controversy and confusion but by 1985 96% of secondary schools had at least one computer (Potter, 1985).

[106] It should be noted that even important works such as those of Zammit Mangion (1992) and Caruana (1992) have failed to treat the topic of computing in education.

[107] The Department of Education in New Zealand has also been criticised for being slow to respond to the needs for computer education and training in the late 1970s and early 1980s, however it has been pointed out that the private sector did little to ameliorate the situation, having 'consistently avoided the expense of the initial training role, preferring instead to employ staff with experience gained elsewhere' (Potter, 1985: p. 124).

TABLE 4.1
Imported makes of microcomputers and supermicros, 1980-1986.[a]

Computer Make/Model	Home/ Business	Year Released	Year Imported	Importer (Agent)
Apple II	B	1977	1981	BDS
Commodore PET	H/B	1977	1980	Economicard
Altos ACS-8000	B	1978	1981	Megabyte
NewBrain	H	1980	1982	Megabyte
Commodore VIC-20	H	1981	1982	Economicard
ICL PC	B	1981	1983	ICL
Osborne 1	B	1981	1982	Megabyte
Sinclair ZX81 & Spectrum	H	1981	1983	F Borda & Sons
Ai Electronics (Ai-M16)	B	1982	1983	Megabyte
Commodore 64 & 8096	H/B	1982	1983	Economicard
Franklin ACE Pro/1000	B	1982	1983	DMA Micro Serv.
Morrow Micro Decision 1	B	1982	1983	Megabyte
Olivetti M20	B	1982	1983	Charles A Micallef
Apricot PC	B	1983	1984	Professional Computing
Aquarius	H	1983	1984	Qualitex Co. Ltd.
Atari 800XL	H	1983	1984	V Petroni Ltd
BBC	H/B	1983	1984	Teleray Hi-Fi
British Micro MIMI 805	B	1983	1985	DMA Micro Services
Dragon 32/64	H	1983	1984	Datatech
Facit DTC	B	1983	1984	Office Electronics
LSI Octopus	B	1983	1984	DMA Micro Serv.
Lynx	H	1983	1984	Telectron Co. Ltd.
Memotech	H/B	1983	1984	Microtech
Multitech MPF III	H/B	1983	1985	Micro Computers
Spectravideo SV-318/328	H/B	1983	1985	C & G Eurocomp
TeleVideo TS803	B	1983	1984	Panta Computers
Texas Instruments PC	H/B	1983	1984	Tip Top
Xerox 820	B	1983	1984	Image Systems
Advance 86	B	1984	1985	C & G Eurocomp
Alpha Micro	H/B	1984	1985	Economicard
Bondwell 14	B	1984	1985	C & G Eurocomp
Ceedata	B	1984	1985	Computer Systems
Imtec 256	B	1984	1985	Intercomp
Laser	H/B	1984	1985	V J Salomone
NCR Decision Mate	B	1984	1985	Philip Toledo
North Star	B/B	1984	1985	Charles A Micallef
Amstrad PC1512	H/B	1985	1986	DATALINK
Apple Macintosh	B	1985	1986	BDS
Honeywell X-Superteam	B	1985	1986	BDS
ICL PC Quattro	B	1985	1986	ICL
NCR Tower	B	1985	1986	Philip Toledo
SPRITE	B	1985	1986	DMA Micro Services
Tandy 1000 EX	H/B	1985	1986	Microtech

[a] The year in columns 3 and 4 may vary by plus or minus one.
Source: Compiled by author from local newspapers, Internet sources, and various issues of *Informatix* magazine.

Private Initiatives: Small Business Computing

The schools were not the only institutions where computer education was being imparted. Small businesses, cognisant of the more professional IBM-compatible PC's potential,[108] soon began offering computer courses for adults and children. The companies that took this initiative were typically office-equipment retailers who had started importing computers both for their own use and to sell them. However, the solitary "entreprenuers" who had sufficient home space and funds, also were quick to establish this type of business. Some converted their large garages into computer classrooms and part of their home into an office. In a relatively short time, as was to be expected in view of the success these early start-ups were having, other firms were doing the same; some companies (like Shireburn[109]) even had specific training in mind, targeting, for example, the business executive.[110]

Initially, the type of courses offered by these private companies were of a general nature, courses about the computer itself and computing in general, and about BASIC or COBOL programming and the fundamentals of office applications (mainly, word processing and spreadsheets) (see Figure 4.2). However, in time, the range of courses offered was expanded to include the full "Ordinary-level" (school-leaving) computing syllabus,[111] and courses aimed at a special class of students such as computer technicians. Courses on the use of databases and others for network administrators were also occasionally offered, according to the demand. The emphasis of these, often short but intensive, courses was on practical ("hands-on")

---

[108] The "high-end" business PC was by no means the only type available at that time (mid-1980s). Computers like the Amiga were a considerable improvement over the hobbyist machines such as the ZX Spectrum or the Commodore 64. They could be used for some serious work, yet cost only a fraction of the top-end business equivalents.

[109] Shireburn Co. Ltd., a successful venture set up by John Degiorgio that initially specialised in business consultancy and computer training, had as its motto: 'The last thing you want to do is buy a Computer' (with "last" underlined for emphasis).

[110] See "Courses on how to make full use of computers in business", *The Times*, 29 April 1985, p. 2.

[111] The local SEC computer studies syllabus had not yet been introduced, so students had to follow the British syllabi.

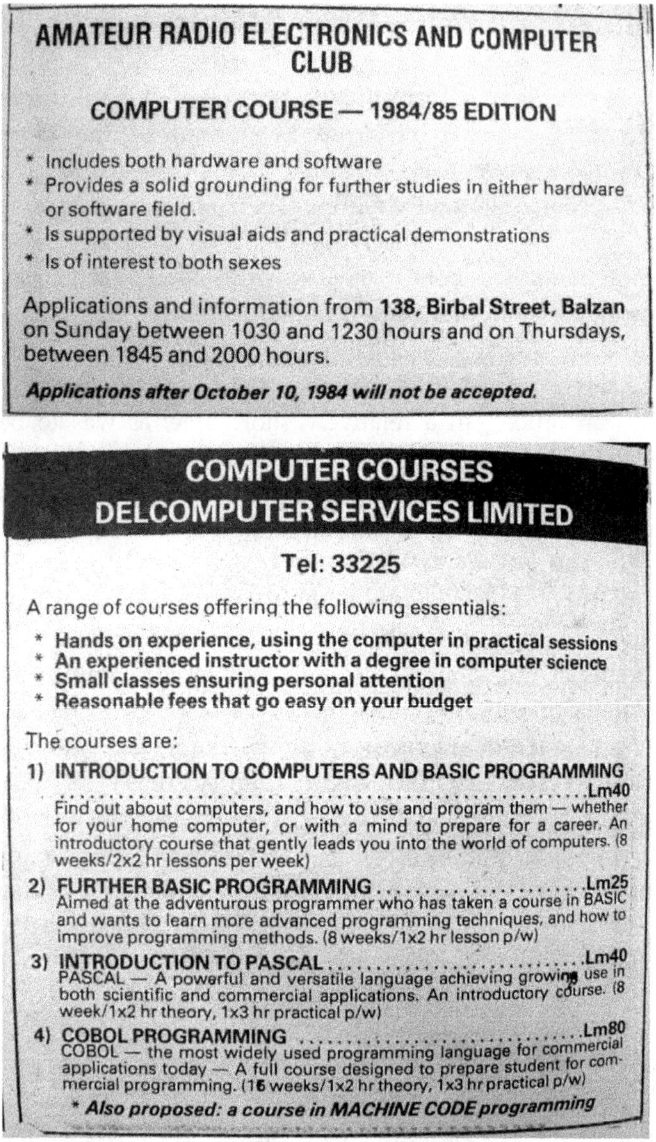

AMATEUR RADIO ELECTRONICS AND COMPUTER CLUB

COMPUTER COURSE — 1984/85 EDITION

* Includes both hardware and software
* Provides a solid grounding for further studies in either hardware or software field.
* Is supported by visual aids and practical demonstrations
* Is of interest to both sexes

Applications and information from **138, Birbal Street, Balzan** on Sunday between 1030 and 1230 hours and on Thursdays, between 1845 and 2000 hours.

Applications after October 10, 1984 will not be accepted.

COMPUTER COURSES
DELCOMPUTER SERVICES LIMITED

Tel: 33225

A range of courses offering the following essentials:

* **Hands on experience, using the computer in practical sessions**
* **An experienced instructor with a degree in computer science**
* **Small classes ensuring personal attention**
* **Reasonable fees that go easy on your budget**

The courses are:

1) **INTRODUCTION TO COMPUTERS AND BASIC PROGRAMMING** Lm40
Find out about computers, and how to use and program them — whether for your home computer, or with a mind to prepare for a career. An introductory course that gently leads you into the world of computers. (8 weeks/2x2 hr lessons per week)

2) **FURTHER BASIC PROGRAMMING** Lm25
Aimed at the adventurous programmer who has taken a course in BASIC and wants to learn more advanced programming techniques, and how to improve programming methods. (8 weeks/1x2 hr lesson p/w)

3) **INTRODUCTION TO PASCAL** Lm40
PASCAL — A powerful and versatile language achieving growing use in both scientific and commercial applications. An introductory course. (8 week/1x2 hr theory, 1x3 hr practical p/w)

4) **COBOL PROGRAMMING** Lm80
COBOL — the most widely used programming language for commercial applications today — A full course designed to prepare student for commercial programming. (16 weeks/1x2 hr theory, 1x3 hr practical p/w)

**** Also proposed: a course in MACHINE CODE programming***

Figure 4.2
Adverts by two organizations for computer introduction and programming courses. By 1985, such courses had become very popular in Malta as a number of (mainly small) local private firms (and societies) specialised in computer training.
Source: *The Times* (3 October 1984, p. 11; 22 March 1985, p. 12)

training. Much later, around the late-1990s accreditation of courses (by companies such as CISCO) had also become the norm.

The use of computers for private education was a tiny niche exploited by small businesses. By the mid-to-late 1980s, microcomputers and multi-user super-micros were being used in many areas of the private sector and were beginning to change the way business was being undertaken. Unfortunately, no statistics are available for the amount of computers used throughout the 1980s by either the private sector or government, however Tables 4.1 and 4.2 show that the take up of computers in this period was significant. The government was a late adopter, with computerisation in the various government departments not having been initiated until the late 1980s and early 1990s. This means that the private sector was the prime user of computer technology in the 1980s, generating modest revenues.

TABLE 4.2
Imported value of computers as percentage of GDP, 1980-1995.

Year:	1980	1985	1990	1995
Value of imported computers (including peripherals) (in LM million):	0.25	1.50	2.02	5.81
Value as percent of GDP (nominal):	0.07	0.35	0.31	0.59

Source: Compiled from NSO data

One needs to exercise caution in the interpretation of Table 4.2 which has been included primarily as a proxy for computer usage. It would be hazardous, for example, to try to explain the drop in imports (as percentage of GDP) for 1990. On the other hand, the increase in imports by 1995 is not difficult to account for. In fact, this value reflects the massive computerisation programme that was being undertaken across the entire public service at the time (early-to-mid 1990s), the setting up of computer laboratories in state schools, and the continued adoption of computers by the private sector.[112] Moreover, given that computer hardware has constantly and significantly fallen in price over the years, and that the per capita GDP (not shown) almost trebled in the ten year period between 1985 and 1995 (with approximately a 9% increase in population), the value of imported computers for 1995 is the more significant.[113]

Box 4-1
Origins of the Personal Computer

...When the developers of the first xerographic copying machine put their toe in the water with a market survey, they were told that there was no need for such a thing—people didn't want to do that much copying. It took imagination and conviction to defy this now laughable analysis. Similarly, during the middle-ages, when a wide variety of currents and cross-currents swept back and forth across the conceptual space as a host of now long-forgotten architectural experiments took place, it took especially keen insight to decide that the thing to do was to try to build a personal computer.

SEVERO M. ORNSTEIN, *Computing in the Middle Ages: A View From the Trenches 1955-1983* (2002)

The personal computer (PC) is often associated with famous persons such as Bill Gates and Steve Jobs. Although these persons and a few others working close with them played a key role in the development of the PC they were by no means the only ones involved. In fact, several factors and a number of organizations and people contributed to the shaping of the PC. What follows is a brief account of the developments that eventually led to the personal computer as we know it.

The development of the personal computer is often likened to that of radio. As with the development of radio, there have been at least three key points in the making of the PC. The first is an enabling technology whose long-term importance—perhaps not unlike that of radio—was probably not immediately recognised. This technology was the microprocessor. The microprocessor

---

[112] The local banks, for example, were undertaking massive computerisation during the early 1990s.

[113] According to the 1985 and 1995 population censuses, the population for those respective years was 345,418 and 378,132. This represents an increase of approximately 9%. As for GDP per capita, this stood at US$2959 in 1985 and US$8587 in 1995.

continued the era of miniaturisation started earlier by the introduction of the integrated circuit. Developed by Intel around 1970, the microprocessor soon began to be manufactured in fairly large quantities by a handful of other semiconductor firms. The first microprocessor originally designed by Intel, and announced in 1971, was a 4-bit device to be used in scientific calculators. An 8-bit version, an upgraded design perfectly suited for the first microcomputers, was out by April 1974.

The second key point in the shaping of the PC involved the electronics hobbyist. Amateur electronics technicians go back to the radio days when construction of radio equipment, purchased in kit form often through mail-order advertisements, was a popular passtime. This passtime continued following the second world war with the building of equipment such as TV's and Hi-Fi's, and was similarly extended to the microcomputer with the onset of the microprocessor. The early-to-mid 1970s was the time when the electronics *dilettanti*—now turned into computer buffs—experimented with putting together a functioning microcomputer, initially using individual integrated circuit components and then the microprocessor.

Up until then, not much could be done with these machines, however, because they lacked two very important ingredients to make the computer usable. Firstly, the hardware was at the bare minimum with no proper keyboard, screen, or magnetic tape from which to load (and on which to save) programs. Secondly, there was no operating software for the machines: the barebones of a microcomputer operating system still lay in the (not too distant) future. These features constituted the third key point.

No computer is very useful without an operating system. Moreover, even with such system software, a computer's practical use would still be very limited unless a programming language is designed to run on it. A programming language enables applications to be written and then to be executed on the machine. These requirements is what led to one person and one company (Digital Research) to create and promote the CP/M operating system, and another company (Microsoft) to develop a flavour of the BASIC language—originally created for use on time-shared mainframes—for the personal computer.* With an operating system and a relatively easy-to-learn programming language specially designed for the PC, the beginning of personal computing was completed.

The above account captures in a nutshell the main events that led to the development and introduction of the PC. The story is somewhat more complicated, however. For example, in the 1960s a team of computer engineers who had worked at the Massachusetts Institute of Technology and its Lincoln Laboratories on the Whirlwind—considered the first real-time flight computer simulator—had developed a computer called the LINC (short for Laboratory Instrument Computer), a stand-alone system and sufficiently small to be used much like one uses a PC (although it looked more like a laboratory instrument than a 1980s PC). The LINC was designed to be used for neurophysiological research, the idea being for the researcher to have sole access to a portable computer for extended periods. Just as visionary was Doug Engelbert's idea of interactive computing using the mouse, a successful demonstration of which was given as early as December 1968.

It has been argued that the hand-held programmable electronic calculator that became widespread by the mid-1970s created a community of people very passionate towards programming. When the more general-purpose PC made its appearance very shortly afterwards, those engaged in the calculator's use were only too eager to replace it by the new, more powerful, machine and in so doing exploit and popularise it.

Finally, towards the end of the 1960s and the beginning of the 1970s, there was a drive by some—particularly in California—for the "liberation" of the computer, to bring computing to the ordinary people. Computer liberation was a phenomenon associated with the young American hippie culture and civil rights movement that was against, for example, political and social orthodoxy. Computers were then very expensive, within the reach and control of only government entities and large private organizations. These liberal movements felt computers should be made accessable to the average person. In publicising their belief, these counterculture movements may have helped the personal computer gather momentum.

---

* The person behind the creation of CP/M was Gary Kildall who had consulted (and wrote PL/M for system development) for Intel. Kildall was also familiar with IBM and DEC computers and his CP/M operating system was the fruit of his experience with software to manage magnetic disk drives, software that IBM had called a disk operating system (DOS). As for Microsoft BASIC, the prominent figures were Bill Gates and Paul Allen, who before setting up thier own company (initially called "Micro Soft" and later "Micro-Soft") developed their BASIC interpreter primarily for use on MITS's Altair 8800 computer.

The Role of Professional Bodies

The Malta Chamber of Commerce and The IDPM Malta Branch

Computer (and data processing) societies in many parts of the world have generally played an important and active role in promoting computing. They have done this in a number of ways, including:

passing on computer knowledge to the public through the organization of public lectures and seminars; designing and offering accredited qualifications, thereby enabling industry practitioners to obtain professional status; and publishing journals and newsletters about the latest developments in the field. Some computer societies (e.g. the New Zealand Computer Society – see Potter, 1985: pp. 124-125), conscious of the early problems those engaged in computer education once faced, also formed Education Committees and published position papers on the subject, going so far as advising governments on computer education matters.

In Malta, where there was still a dearth of knowledge in computing matters in the early 1980s, the local branch of the UK's Institute of Data Processing Management (IDPM) was also instrumental in publicising computing. Formed in 1983 through the initiatives of industry practitioners and the computer section of the Malta Chamber of Commerce (itself set up that year), IDPM (Malta) initially was a centre where its members could meet and share their experiences.[114] Meetings were often held at the Malta Chamber of Commerce premises in Valletta. Local industry speakers and, occasionally, foreign experts would be invited to give talks about a specific theme of data processing (see Figure 4.3).[115] These talks usually attracted a good audience.

Since its inception the Malta Branch of the IDPM was concerned about the lack of appropriate computer education in Malta, and immediately took initiatives to partly remedy this situation by beginning to offer the UK IDPM courses locally. In collaboration with the Education Department, it was arranged for examinations to also be held locally twice yearly under the control and supervision of the Examinations section of the Education Department.

Initially, study had to be undertaken by the distance-learning method which, apart from being expensive, required self-discipline on

---

[114] The Maltese IDPM members who got together on 29 June 1983 for an inaugural meeting to form the IDPM Malta branch included (in alphabetical order): Pierre Azzopardi, Carmel Cachia, Harry Restall (deceased), Joe Ross, Joe Vella, David Wallbank, and Tony Zahra. See *The Sunday Times Computers Supplement*, 3 July 1983, p. VI.

[115] In May 1984, for example, Edward G. Cluff of the London's IDPM branch was invited to Malta as a guest speaker for a forum entitled "Computers in Business: The Changing Times". See *The Times*, 24 May 1984, p. 6.

the part of the Maltese student who had to adhere to strict work schedules. Additionally, the student was greatly disadvantaged in not benefitting from the presence of a tutor to help with difficulties. In 1986, in an effort to improve this situation, the IDPM local committee launched an "Approved Tutors Scheme" whereby appropriately qualified personnel interested in teaching IDPM modules would get in touch with the IDPM so that the latter could draw up a list of approved tutors (Vella, 1989).

In the summer of 1988, IDPM (Malta) personnel and officers from the Information Technology Trade Section of the Chamber of Commerce got together to draft a policy proposal about formal computer education, the final version of which was submitted to the Education Minister in December. Up till then, computer education received little attention and was hardly ever discussed even at the ministerial level. The following summer, however, the Education Minister officially announced plans for a three-stream educational policy (starting at secondary level and going to tertiary level) that, according to the IDPM seemed 'to dovetail perfectly' with the IDPM policy document submitted to the Minister (ibid.).

Another area where this time the Chamber of Commerce felt it could not remain silent relates to import controls. In the 1970s, Customs Tariffs conformed to the 1964 Import Duties Act and the 1976 Import Duties Act (Act No. XXV of 1976) which replaced the 1964 Act. According to the Import Duties Act (1976), Automatic Data Processing Equipment (essentially computers), although needing an import licence, was exempt from tax.[116]

In 1985 Parliament passed a bill (Bill No. 100 of 1985) which required every imported computer to be subjected to a customs duty of 20% if manufactured outside the (then) EEC area, and 12% if produced within the EEC. The motivation behind this bill is not clear but, given the rapid increase in computer imports, the likely reason

---

[116] Interestingly, most other office equipment such as typewriters, calculators, cash registers and accounting machines (falling under Tariff headings 84.51 and 84.52) were liable to a 25% import duty if their place of origin were outside the (then) EEC, or a 16.2% duty if manufactured in the EEC.

Figure 4.3
An advert by the IDPM Malta Branch showing a list of activities for 1989-1990.

Source: *Informatics* (November 1989).

was the collection of revenue.[117] Apart from causing aggravation and frustration to both suppliers (importers) and users, particularly owing to the lengthy bureaucratic procedures involved, it did not deter new and existing businesses from continuing to import all types of computer make, as Tables 4.1 and 4.2 show.[118]

In a bid to explain the repercussions the new bill would have on the local industry, the then recently-formed Computer Section of the Chamber of Commerce, wrote a letter to all members of the House of Representatives. The letter essentially voiced the Chamber's concern and argued that whilst the imposition of customs duty may be financially benficial to government in the short term, it will have 'disastrous long term effects' (de Domenico, 1985).[119] At a time when Malta had a price freeze and a wage freeze, such a bill would increase the eventual computer selling price and make it especially difficult for the larger businesses, which required the use of already expensive computers. The bill was also incommensurate with government's then policy statement encouraging the uptake of computer science by the young generation. In spite of the Chamber's efforts, the government did not reverse its decision and computers remained subject to import duty.

Other Professional Institutions

By the early 1990s a number of local computing professionals were either IDPM or British Computer Society (BCS) members, sometimes even belonging to both institutions. BCS members felt that it was perhaps time to also set up a BCS Malta Branch and began moving forward that idea. Others were of the opinion that Malta could have its own computer society, independent of the two British societies. In the event, the 1990s saw two more professional bodies being formed

[117] In 1975, New Zealand's Labour Government imposed a 45% tax on office machinery, according to Bell (1985: p. 83) largely for fear of job erosion. Bell explains that this decision prevented small businesses from taking advantage of computerisation for several vital years.

[118] In spite of the import controls, no statistics have been published of the actual number of imported computers for a given period. Although intended only as a guide, Tables 4.1 and 4.2 do indicate the extent to which computers proliferated the local market in the 1980s.

[119] This Chamber of Commerce letter, signed by Andrew de Domenico, is reproduced in full in Appendix E.

domestically: The Computer Society of Malta and the BCS Malta Branch, respectively. The former, initially called simply "The Computer Society" was created in 1994, while the latter formally came into being in 1997, although talks about setting it up began some years before. During the first few years of their formation both societies were very active, but after the initial enthusiasm their activities became less regular over time. That said, both societies still occasionally organize informative and educational events. Typically their talks and seminars are sponsored by local institutions including the banks and ICT companies, and attract a wide audience.

In the earlier days of data processing, some members of the Malta Institute of Bankers (MIB) and the Malta Institute of Management (MIM) also played a minor role in bringing up computing issues for the attention of the public (e.g. through newspaper articles). The (Malta) Chamber of Engineers (set up in 1978) also contributed significantly to the Maltese computing profession, particularly at the technical level and in areas related to data communications and computer networking. Through efforts of some of its members and others who belonged to the Institute of Electrical and Electronic Engineers (IEEE), Malta now has an IEEE Malta Section (IEEE Region 8).

5

Computing at the University of Malta

By any measure, the introduction of computers and computing courses at the University of Malta (henceforth, UOM or the University) came late. Although at least as early as 1963 the University was already hosting short courses in data handling in collaboration with (and possibly on the initiative of) the ICT company,[120] and similar courses were also being organized by the Extension Studies Board by 1977, the study of computing as an academic discipline in its own right did not commence until after the acquisition of the University's first computer in 1980.[121] The first diploma course in computing was launched in 1983, to be followed three years later by a higher diploma course, which then developed into a degree. These courses were being offered by the Mathematics Department before the two separate departments of Information Systems and Computer Science were set up in 1993.

Following the formation of these departments and the setting up of The Board of Studies for Information Technology to oversee them, a Bachelor's honours degree was designed to meet industry requirements, and computer courses at the masters level also began to

---

[120] See, for example, "Data Processing Techniques–Lectures at University", *Times of Malta*, 19 July 1963, p. 9.

[121] Many North American and British Universities had already established computer science departments by the 1960s, and a number of European universities also introduced computers well before 1980. Short histories about the creation of Computer Science departments have appeared from time to time in the *IEEE Annals of the History of Computing*. See, for example, Rice & Rosen (2004); and Minker (2007). See also Box 5-1.

be offered. In 2007, in line with government policy but also partly because these departments (together with that of computer engineering) had expanded and partly because of the expertise gained over the years, the need was felt to upgrade the Board of Studies for IT to a full-fletched faculty. Set up in May 2007, the new faculty was given the title of "Information and Communication Technology". From that year onwards, this Faculty started accepting applications for doctorate degrees.[122]

The Beginnings

The first computer introduced at the UOM was a MINC-11 (see Figure 5.1). This computer was acquired by the Department of Mathematics and Science at the request of the late Charles J. Camilleri, a former Dockyard engineer who in the late 1970s was professor and head of the Mathematics and Science Department. According to Paul Micallef—then lecturer and later professor and dean of the Engineering faculty—Camilleri was the driving force behind the introduction of this computer.[123] In collaboration with a handful of other lecturers that included Micallef himself, Camilleri was also instrumental in introducing a microcomputer engineering module. The *UOM Annual Report* for 1980 (p. 19) had this to say about the purchase of the University's first computer:

> With the acquisition of the MINC 11 Small Computer System, the Department of Mathematics and Science[124] has become a focal point for the development of mini computer techniques in the University. Students from the Faculties of Management Studies and Education as well as Engineering and Architecture have been introduced to the computer and its applications, thereby

---

[122] The Faculty of Engineering and Architecture, like some other Faculties, had long been issuing doctorate degrees, however.

[123] Interview with Micallef on 15 September 2009.

[124] Formerly, Mathematics was a separate department falling under the Faculty of Science. In 1979 it fell under the Faculty of Engineering and Architecture. In 1987 it became again a part of the Faculty of Science.

strengthening the mathematical basis of their respective studies.

The MINC-11 was essentially a PDP-11 computer and at the time very popular with the scientific and engineering communities. At the UOM, those that benefited mostly from the introduction of the MINC-11 were the staff and students of the Electrical Engineering department, since in the period 1979-1986, following very radical (and unpopular) educational reforms,[125] the Faculty of Science had ceased to exist and a "Mathematics and Science Department" was created which, for many years, fell under the Faculty of Engineering and Architecure. The MINC-11 computer was installed in what is currently (2009) the Physics boardroom.[126]

During the early 1980s a number of study units were introduced on microelectronics, microprocessors and microcomputers by the Department of Electrical Engineering.[127] This department also organized related lectures and seminars for the public, some of the lectures having been delivered by staff from the Polytechnic of Central London with whom Camilleri probably had contacts. The *UOM Gazette* of March 1982 (Vol. 14, No. 1: p. 12) states that attendance for these seminars was high, the participants coming from academia, business, and the industrial engineering sector. Up till then, students graduating with a Bachelor in Electrical Engineering did not qualify with computing as a main speciality, although specialisation had just begun to be offered in Electronics, Microprocessors and Telecommunications. By 1982, an examinable microprocessors and

---

[125] These controversial reforms are discussed in Zammit-Mangion (1992). The address delivered on 15 December 1978 by the former UOM Rector, Borg Costanzi—which can be found in The UOM Annual Report 1978/1979—expresses the concern by that Rector of the negative consequences the proposed reforms would have on tertiary education. The reforms—in particular, the extent to which Government began controlling all aspects of University life—eventually led Prof. Ralph Dahrendorf to resign from the chairmanship of the Commission for the Development of Higher Education in Malta, set up in 1975.

[126] Interview with Micallef on 15 September 2009.

[127] This department was formed in 1975 (*The Royal University of Malta Gazette*, 1975). The other two departments that predated Electrical were those of Mechanical and Civil Engineering, which fell under the Faculty of Engineering and Architecture.

microcomputer technology module had been established which
appears to have been fairly popular with students.[128]

Figure 5.1
Students using the MINC-11, the first computer introduced at the University
of Malta in 1980.
Source: *University of Malta Annual Report 1981.*

Meanwhile, staff at the mathematics department were also interested
in certain areas of computer science. Computing-related research
interests of the mathematics department included topics like Groups,
Graphs, Boolean Algebra, Gamma and Zeta functions, Topological
Spaces, and Numerical Techniques (*Royal Univeristy of Malta Annual
Report 1968-69*; *Royal Univeristy of Malta Annual Report 1971-72*; and
Old University Gazette, 1979).

By the late 1970s, the Mathematics Department was also
organising introductory, computer-related courses for the public. In
1977, for example, two evening courses were given under the auspices
of the Extension Studies Board (*University of Malta Gazzette, 1978*).

---

[128] The *UOM Annual Report 1982* (p. 25) lists a number of student projects involving
microprocessors and microcomputers.

One course was called "Introduction to Modern Mathematics" and included the main topics of Groups, Linear Algebra and Analysis. According to the *UOM Gazette* (*ibid.*) this course was of particular interest to secondary school teachers who had been 'brought up in the traditional mathematics'. The late Professor J. V. Pulè and Stanley Fiorini (later also a professor) delivered the lectures. The second course was called "Data Processing and Computation", which covered Data Processing, Computation, and Operational Research. This course was aimed at programmers and systems analysts, and other personnel involved in large amounts of data gathering and analysis. The course lecturers were Albert Leone Ganado (now also a professor) and Carmel Galea, who would later start (and direct with his brother Thomas) the Megabyte company.

Box 5-1
Early Computer Science at American Universities and the development of a Computer Science Curriculum

Computer Science is a relatively young discipline. Although several universities in the United States and elsewhere were involved in designing and building their first computers, often in collaboration with industry, government, and the military, it was not before the 1960s that computer science as an academic discipline began to gain popularity. In part, this is because many areas of computing were maturing in that period and various departments in different faculties were becoming exposed to the computer. To mention a few examples: in the 1960s, a lot of work was being done on the theory of programming languages and some of the first high-level language compilers were developed and improved upon in that period. Many university engineering faculties had gained considerable expertise in computer architecture and although a computer might typically be built for a specific use, researchers in other departments would often find different applications for it. For example, the artificial intelligence community, which consisted of researchers from differing disciplines, made heavy use of computers, as did engineers, mathematicians and physicists. It was also in the 1960s that the computer began to be widely used for business applications, and that the ARPANET was conceived and started to be developed. Moreover, by about 1960 a variety of educational programmes—some in the form of summer schools—were organised for the international community. Conferences dealing with university computing education were also becoming popular.

Although by the early 1960s, many universities had been offering computer courses, there was still no formal computer-course curriculum in place. In 1962, on the initiative of a small group of educators that included Louis Fein (a fervent education promoter and at one time chairman of the ACM Education Committee), the Association of Computing Machinery (ACM, established in 1947) formed a Curriculum Committee on Computer Science. The ACM believed that in order to be a legitimate discipline, computer science required a computer curriculum. In 1963, the ACM organised a National Conference (held at Denver, Colorado) during which a number of academics presented papers describing courses that could form the basis of a computer science curriculum. The ball was set rolling for universities to form departments that would be distinct from the Mathematics, Engineering and Physics departments where computing was typically taught and practised. Later, in 1968, a report was published by the ACM entitled "Computer 68: Recommendations for the Undergraduate Program in Computer Science". This report, which is often considered as the seminal document on computer science curriculum development was finalised following numerous consultations with academia in order to take into account the rapid developments that had taken place in computing education. Drawing from previous reports and on the basis of the numerous courses that had by then become popular, the 1968 report made recommendations for course curricula at different academic levels, for example what should be covered in an undergraduate course and what would typically constitute a master's course.

Interestingly, although the ACM had agreed to the name "computer science" as a new discipline, not all academics were in favour of this title; indeed, some were even unsure as to a proper definition for it. For some considerable time misconceptions about computer science abounded: the National Academy of Sciences and other US government bodies, for example, believed in the 1970s that it was still immature to have computer science programmes. Even the National Science Foundation (NSF), which had supported computer education workshops, was late in officially designating computer science as a distinct discipline, doing so only in 1982.

Amongst American universities that made seminal contributions to computer engineering and science, and established early computer centres (or equivalent) we find: the University of California at Los Angeles (UCLA, known for its work on numerical analysis, its use of two large analogue computers, the building of the National Bureau of Standards' SWAC computer, research in computer architecture and parallel processing, and involvement in the ARPANET); Carnegie-Mellon University (CMU, famous for its work on artificial intelligence and language interpreters, and also involved with the ARPANET project); Columbia University (established the

Watson Scientific Computer Lab with IBM in 1945, and formed the ACM two years later); Harvard University (worked on the development of the Harvard Mark I computer in 1945 in conjunction with IBM); Universtiy of Illinois (where the ILLIAC supercomputer was built); the University of Maryland (used early computers for high energy Physics, and was involved in CS curriculum development with the ACM); Massachusetts Institute of Technology (MIT, famous for its Whirlwind real-time, flight-simulator computer project, development of core-memory, the SAGE Air Defence System, and the first computer time-sharing system); Universtiy of Pennsylvannia (famous for the development of ENIAC in 1946 and the summer school lectures in computing at its Moore School of Electrical Engineering that same year); Princeton University (where the Institute for Advanced Studies was established in the late 1940s, and the IAS computer was built and served as a model for other machines); Stanford University (famous for AI work and robotics); and the University of Utah (famous for work on computer graphics, and where one of the first ARPANET nodes was also installed).*

* This list is far from exhaustive and there are other universities, including several European ones, that have made equally important contributions to computing.

The First Diploma and Degree Courses in Computing

In December 1982, the Department of Education announced that the University would be offering Diploma courses, on a three-semester basis,[129] in a number of subject areas including Mathematics (*UOM Annual Report 1985*).[130] For the latter, students were given a choice of pursuing their studies in Pure Mathematics or in Computing. The first group of students thus completed their diploma in computing or mathematics in the summer of 1984. In September 1984, the mathematics course was reorganized to include Mathematics,

[129] At the time, one semester was of approximately six months' duration, and courses were based on the "student-worker scheme", whereby students alternated between spending periods in industry and periods at the University (somewhat similar to sandwich courses in Britain in the late 1970s and 1980s involving industrial training). The student-worker scheme was introduced in 1979 as part of the mentioned educational reforms. It is treated in some detail in Caruana (1992).

[130] These diploma courses were aimed at students who did not wish, or did not have the requisite qualifications, to pursue the more demanding and lengthy Bachelor's degrees, offered in the pure sciences but did not include computing.

Computing and Logic, and began to be offered by that title. This was shortly followed (in March 1985) by a Higher Diploma course in computing.

At about this time, an ad hoc Computer Steering Committee was set up to identify the needs of the University and the direction computing would take. Members of this committee included Paul Micallef from the Electrical Engineering department, and Albert Leone Ganado from the Mathematics department. One of the recommendations was that, as University staff in these departments had by now acquired sufficient computing experience, a Bachelor's course in Mathematics and Computing could be offered. It was also felt that a Bachelor's degree would meet the needs of many industry professionals who had hands-on experience but lacked formal qualifications in the subject. For this reason, the entry requirements were relaxed, mature students without the prerequisite qualifications but with some years of relevant experience having been allowed to apply. Following approval of Senate, this course was announced in the winter of 1987 (see Figure 5.2). Commencing the following September and running on a part-time, evening, basis and spread over nine consecutive semesters, the course attracted a record 160 students (*UOM Gazette*, 1987). The first group of students graduated from this course in the summer of 1992.

Meanwhile, in that period (second half of 1980 and early 1990s) further developments took place that would put computer studies on a stronger footing. Coinciding roughly with the 1987 general elections held in May, the University acquired its second—but what may be considered its first major—computer system, a Prime 750 computer, similar to the one already installed at the Swatar Computer Centre. The call for tenders for the purchase of a computer was issued some months before the election and—perhaps owing to the uncertainties associated with political elections—only three companies tendered, Panta Computers having won the bid.[131] The newly acquired computer, installed in the Autumn of 1987, could cater for about a dozen users. Important software that was ordered as part of the computer system included a VLSI tool called SOLO, which is CAD

---

[131] Interview with Micallef.

software that produces VLSI layouts from optimised MOS circuit schematics; and a NAG Fortran compiler.[132]

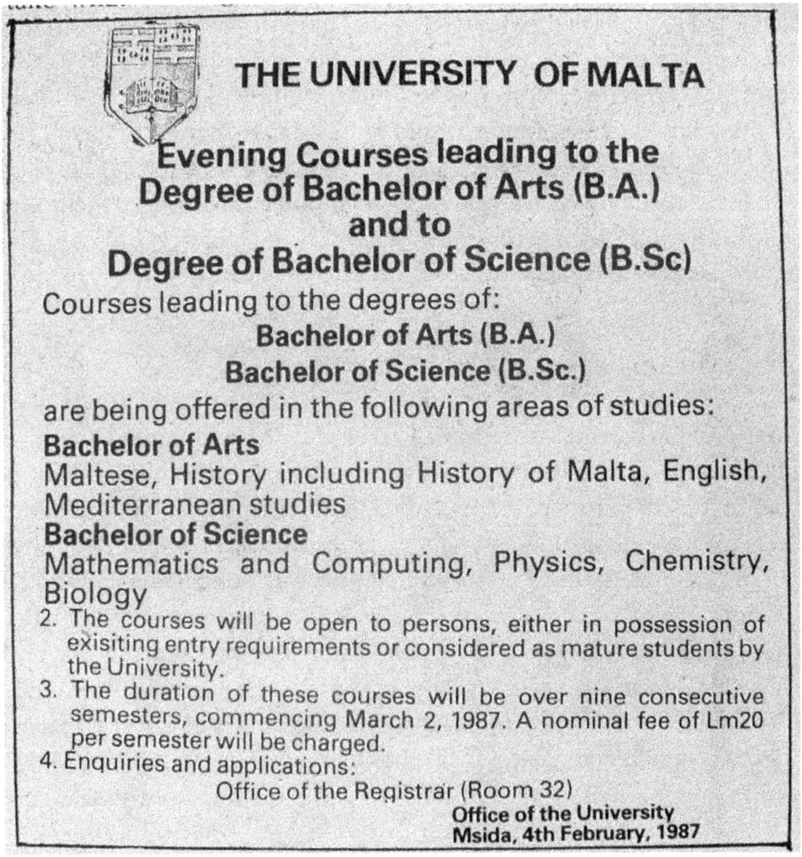

THE UNIVERSITY OF MALTA

Evening Courses leading to the Degree of Bachelor of Arts (B.A.) and to Degree of Bachelor of Science (B.Sc)

Courses leading to the degrees of:

Bachelor of Arts (B.A.)

Bachelor of Science (B.Sc.)

are being offered in the following areas of studies:

Bachelor of Arts

Maltese, History including History of Malta, English, Mediterranean studies

Bachelor of Science

Mathematics and Computing, Physics, Chemistry, Biology

2. The courses will be open to persons, either in possession of exisiting entry requirements or considered as mature students by the University.
3. The duration of these courses will be over nine consecutive semesters, commencing March 2, 1987. A nominal fee of Lm20 per semester will be charged.
4. Enquiries and applications:

Office of the Registrar (Room 32)

Office of the University
Msida, 4th February, 1987

Figure 5.2
A University of Malta call for applications for undergraduate degree courses. This advert is of historic importance because it announces for the first time the Bachelor's course in Computing (see text).
Source: *The Times* (6 February 1987: p. 17)

[132] NAG stands for Numerical Algorithms Group, a specialist group of mathematicians and computer scientists formed in 1970 to develop mathematical software. See the NAG homepage at *www.nag.co.uk*.

Some years before the Prime installation, a number of BBC microcomputers were purchased for the Electrical Engineering Department to be used solely by engineering students. Some students utilised these computers for their bachelor's thesis project, for example by interfacing them to electronic circuits designed for data acquisition and control.[133] Several years later, in the early 1990s, the existing computer equipment was complemented by SUN Microsystems workstations running UNIX. Up till then, the Computer Services Centre (now IT Services) had not yet been established and therefore the entire computer installation including cable runs for the networking had to be carried out by the departmental staff themselves.

Creation of new IT Departments

In 1993 a fundamental restructuring was effected within the Faculty of Engineering and the Faculty of Science. In the Faculty of Engineering, the original department of Electrical Engineering was split up into three separate departments, namely, an Electrical Power and Control Engineering department; a Microelectronics department; and a Communications and Computer Engineering department. The latter was created to cater primarily for the emerging information and communications technologies, which Malta had to embrace to remain internationally competitive. This department would ensure that its students would be trained in the use of the latest technology, equipping them with the right skills required for the rapidly-changing ICT field.

The restructuring exercise also coincided with, but was not directly related to, the publication of the *National Strategy for Information Technology* (see Chapters 11 and 14). In fact, that same year the Communications and Computer Engineering department participated in a number of NSIT working groups, apart from involving itself in the establishment of the University Radio Station and the setting up of the high-speed data network across the

---

[133] See, for example, the Electrical Engineering thesis by Camilleri (1990).

University campus (*UOM Annual Report 1993*: p. 51). Collaboration with several British Universities was also pursued.[134]

In the Faculty of Science, two IT-related departments were created: the first—which emerged from a restructuring of an earlier Department of Computer Studies (itself established in 1987)—was the Department of Computer Information Systems; and the second was a completely new Department of Computer Science and Artificial Intelligence. Again, both departments were involved in the NSIT project, amongst others. Fundamental research interests of these departments included Formal Methods, and Distributed and Concurrent Systems. In September 1994 the Computer Science & AI department hosted the seventh International Conference on Higher-Order Logic Theorem Proving and its Applications; the latter was sponsored by the local Bank of Valletta and held in Valletta. Of the 30 papers presented, and subsequently published as part of the Springer Verlag Lecture Notes in Computer Science series, one paper was jointly authored by one Maltese researcher (see Melham & Camilleri, 2004).

As for the Computer Information Systems department, this department initially continued to coordinate the original BSc degree course in computing for a few years until the different BSc (Hons) courses (the first offered in October 1994) with specialised areas were introduced (see also Chapters 7 and 13). This department's main interests were in information processing and management, and in management issues in IT. This department was also heavily involved in the Bachelor's degree in Business and Computing, a popular course run jointly with the Faculty of Economics, Management and Accountancy (FEMA). Especially in the early years, FEMA also played a leading role in the promulgation of computing by, for example, organising business computing-related short courses and

---

[134] Universities with whom contacts were made included the Loughborough University of Technology, the University of Surrey, Aston University, Edinburgh University, the University of Manchester, and the University of Sheffield. At the time, the main research interests of the newly set up department were in cursive script recognition, text-to-speech (for Maltese), image processing, and CASE tools development for parallel systems (*UOM Annual Report 1993*: p. 5).

seminars, apart from collaborating with the Mathematics Department in the design of the Business and Computing degree.[135]

In order to effect the structural changes mentioned above, a Board of Studies for IT was set up in 1993 that would be responsible for all matters relating to information technology, including the running of all IT-related courses. The introduction of the BSc (Hons) degree course in IT (and, later, the masters IT conversion and research courses) came about directly as a result of the setting up of this Board of Studies. The latter continued operating unitl May 2007 when it was superseded by the new ICT faculty.

The restructuring process involving the Board of Studies for IT and the creation of the new departments was carried out following a planned expansion programme that involved the recruitment of new graduates in different disciplines, many of whom were awarded scholarships to continue Master and Doctorate programmes of study abroad. Thus, by the mid-to-late 1990s, the IT-related departments had a core number of enthusiastic Maltese academics engaged in teaching and research. The undertaking of doctoral courses overseas by Maltese lecturers further led to collaboration with more foreign (mainly British, and some German) universities.

Complementing the restructuring process, a new computer building was completed in 1994: it included three new computer laboratories and housed the three departments of Mathematics, Computer Information Systems, and Computer Science & AI, and— for a brief period—the Electrical Engineering department. Another new building—the Engineering Building—was completed and officially inaugurated in December 1995. The engineering laboratories were equipped with some of the latest state-of-the-art instrumentation and machinery on the Island, enabling researchers to engage in varied areas of engineering.

By the turn of the new millennium, an estimated 500 students were following IT-related courses. Between 1999 and 2003 inclusive the average number of students that graduated with a first degree

---

[135] Some members of the Faculty of Economics had shown an early interest in computers. For example, when Barclays Bank introduced its first computer in Malta in 1973 (see Chapter 3), students from the Economics Department led by Prof. Salvino Busuttil made a study visit to the Bank's Centre where they were shown around by the Centre's Manager and Operations Controller. See "Tour of Barclays Computer Centre", *Times of Malta* , 8 March 1974, p. 9.

having a substantial IT component was 106 (see Table 7.7 of Chapter 7). Departmental staff numbers for the 2001-2002 academic year are given in Table 5.1. For that academic year, the lecturer to student ratio for students undertaking IT-related courses was therefore of the order of 1:17.

ICT as a new Faculty

Already by the year 2000, the Faculty of Engineering alone consisted of six departments and had been running the four-year undergraduate Bachelor of Engineering Honours degree for several years.[136] In keeping with general University policy to become more entrepreneurial, the Faculty had established close links with local industry: various projects were being developed in collaboration with major (mainly electronics) firms.[137]

TABLE 5.1
University of Malta lecturing staff numbers in the different IT-related departments, 2001-2002

Department Name	Academic Post							
	P	AP	SL	L	AL	RA	TA	*Totals*
Computer Science & AI	0	1	3	2	3	3	2	*14*
Computer Information Systems	0	1	1	0	3	0	0	*5*
Communications and Computer Eng.	1	0	3	1	2	1	0	*8*
Microelectronics	1	0	0	2	1	1	0	*5*

Key: P = Professor; AP = Associate Professor; SL = Senior Lecturer; L = Lecturer;
    AL = Assistant Lecturer; RA = Research Assistant; TA = Teaching Assistant
Source: Compiled by the author from the *University of Malta Calendar 2001/2002* handbook.

---

[136] The six departments are: Communications and Computer Engineering; Electrical Power and Control Engineering; Manufacturing Engineering; Mechanical Engineering; Metallurgy and Materials Engineering; and Microelectronics.

[137] For an insight into some of the joint projects carried out in collaboration with industry see Micallef (2001) and Cilia (2002).

The Faculty of Science also constituted six departments, two of which were computer-related. Within this faculty, the Department of Computer Science and Artificial Intelligence (CS&AI) and the Department of Computer Information Systems took initiatives to further strengthen their collaboration with industry. For example, beginning from 2003, the CS&AI department began to organize the Computer Science Annual Research Workshop, a workshop aimed at presenting current research being carried out locally. Typically, this workshop (which has been running annually since) has been of two days' duration, with the first day devoted to R&D presentations and reports, and the second day dedicated to industry research, during which companies present problems for discussion. This event has been sponsored by ICT companies, the banks, the Malta Council for Science and Technology, and the Ministry for Investment, Industry and IT. In 2007, 24 papers were read at the workshop.

Various factors, amongst them the increase in the number of students choosing IT courses, the growth of ICT nationally which was also being encouraged by government, and the recognition that ICT is one of the most substantial economic enablers moved forward the idea of setting up an ICT faculty (which could be seen as effectively upgrading the Board of Studies for ICT). Following months of internal consultations, the new faculty was officially established by the University Council in May 2007.

The establishment of the new ICT faculty necessitated some further reorganization within the faculties of Science and Engineering, respectively. The two former departments of Computer Information Systems and Computer Science & Artificial Intelligence were transferred to the new ICT faculty; moreover, the Computer Science & Artificial Intelligence department was split up into two departments, respectively called Department of Artificial Intelligence (and further renamed the Department of Intelligent Computer Systems), and Department of Computer Science. The former department of Microelectronics, formerly under the Engineering Faculty, now became the Department of Micro and Nanotechnology under the new ICT faculty; and finally, the Department of Communications and Computer Engineering was transferred to the new ICT faculty. This reorganization was done to reflect the needs of industry which now requires practitioners to be broadly knowledgeable in ICT apart from being proficient in a particular field.

More lecturing staff were also recruited to meet the increase in student numbers. A total of 40 academics constituted the ICT faculty as at 2007-2008 (Table 5.2).[138] Undergraduate courses were also restructured and a new, part-time, evening undergraduate programme in ICT was created to cater for those in employment. At the master's level, too, a conversion course was created that focused on giving graduates in other disciplines an entry point into the ICT field.

TABLE 5.2
University of Malta lecturing staff numbers in the ICT Faculty, 2007-2008

Department Name	Academic Post							
	P	AP	SL	L	AL	RA	TA	*Totals*
Artificial Intelligence	0	0	3	1	3	3	0	*10*
Computer Science	1	0	3	1	4	0	1	*10*
Computer Information Systems	0	1	1	0	6	0	0	*8*
Communications and Computer Eng.	1	0	4	2	0	1	0	*8*
Microelectronics	1	0	1	1	0	0	1	*4*

Key: P = Professor; AP = Associate Professor; SL = Senior Lecturer; L = Lecturer;
    AL = Assistant Lecturer; RA = Research Assistant; TA = Teaching Assistant
Source: Compiled by the author from the *University of Malta Calendar 2007-2008*.

That year (2007) the University submitted requests for funding under the European Regional Development Fund (ERDF) and the European Science Foundation (ERS) programmes of a value of c. 30 million Euros to be used for various projects including the construction of an extension of the Junior College, the construction of an IT services centre, the construction of a building to house the new Faculty of ICT, and the furnishing and equipping of the science and engineering laboratories. Approximately two years later, in May 2009, the sum of

---

[138] The first appointed ICT Faculty Dean was Ernest Cachia, a long-serving University of Malta computer science senior lecturer. Prior to the Faculty's creation, the computer science department was headed by Mike Rosner.

17.3 million Euros was awarded to the University from the ERDF for a three-year project to construct a state-of-the-art building for the new ICT Faculty that would be located at the tal-Qroqq campus.[139] Construction works started shortly thereafter. A space of over 7000 square metres will be occupied by the new building. Table 5.3 summarises the main computing "milestones" at the University. Appendix D gives further information about undergraduate IT-related courses as at 2008-2009.

TABLE 5.3
Chronology of computing milestones at the University of Malta

Year	Event
1975	Electrical Engineering Department formation.
1977	Maths department organizes introductory and non-examinable, computer-related courses.
1980	Purchase of first computer, a MINC-11 system.
1982	Examinable microprocessors and microcomputer technology module is established.
1983	Diploma course in Computing is launched.
1984	Diploma course re-organized and offered as a Maths, Computing & Logic course.
1985	Higher Diploma course in Maths, Computing & Logic course is launched.
1987	Purchase of a Prime 750 computer and several stand-alone microcomputers. A Department of Computer Studies is established.
1988	Part-time evening, BSc in Computing is introduced.
1992	Several Unix-based SUN Microsystems workstations are installed in the Engineering labs.
1993	Board of Studies for Information Technology is set up, responsible for the running of undergraduate (and later, postgraduate) IT courses. Major restructuring of the Faculty of Engineering: Electrical Engineering Department is split up into three separate departments. Also, in the Faculty of Science, the former Department of Computer Studies is restructured and renamed Information Systems, and a new Department of CS & AI is created. A high-speed data network using a fibre-optic backbone is installed across the University campus.

---

[139] In total, the University was awarded over € 42 million in ERDF and ESF funds to be utilised for fifteen projects ranging from research analysis and training for enhancing library services to a super computing laboratory.

TABLE 5.3 (continued)
Chronology of computing milestones at the University of Malta

Year	Event
1994	New computer building is opened. BSc (Hons) IT course is offered to students for the first time, commences in October.
1995	New Engineering building is completed and officially inauguraated in December.
1999	Applications are accepted for the first postgraduate (master's) degree in IT.
2003	Department of Computer Science and Artificial Intelligence, Faculty of Science, begins to organize the Computer Science Annual Research Workshop.
2007	New Faculty of ICT is set up. This necessitates a restructuring of the Faculties of Science and Engineering, respectively.
2009	Work on the construction of a building to house the new ICT faculty commences.

6

Government Computer Organizations: Deployment of I.T. across the Public Sector

The Government Computer Centre

The Government Computer Centre at Tas-Swatar (henceforth, the Swatar Centre, or Computer Centre), limits of Dingli, was a labour party initiative, with a project manager chosen by the same party. After exactly two terms in office and ten years of almost total neglect in computing matters, the labour government of the late 1970s was under pressure to introduce more modern methods of data processing. With the exception of the Inland Revenue, all government departments still used antiquated computational procedures and equipment, and some departments had long requested government to introduce computers. Moreover, the computer installed at the Inland Revenue had shown its worth, in addition to being utilised for tasks external to that department. A computer centre was therefore government's response to those requests.

The Swatar Centre was officially inaugurated by the then Minister of Finance, Customs and People's Financial Investments, Dr. Joseph Cassar, on 18 November 1981, a few weeks following the organization of the first Maltese electronics fair (in which a handful of computers were displayed for the first time to the public). The contract for the equipment was awarded to Interdata of Greece representing Prime Computers and to Philip Toledo Ltd representing Hewlett Packard on 15 March 1981, the equipment and software being delivered the following September. Data entry clerks were initially "borrowed" from various government departments, advertisements in the local press for recruiting computer personnel having appeared much later.

In his inaugural speech, Dr. Cassar is reported to have stated that 'the Computer Centre can contribute substantially to the development of these Islands so that the rapid progress achieved during the last few years in the economic and social sectors could be increased and improved'.[140] In view of the Malta Labour Party's attitude towards computers up till then, this was an acknowledgement by a labour party minister of the computer's worth.

Housed in a complex which used to form part of NATO's Western Telegraphy Network (see Figure 6.1), the Swatar Centre was set up 'to provide a service for all government departments, banks, and established parastatal organizations on a sound business basis' (*Reports on the Working of Government Departments*, 1981: p. 30).

The Centre's project manager, Emanuel Camilleri, was an Australian of Maltese origin seconded to the Malta Government specifically to set it up (and subsequently to run it). Camilleri's Gozitan parents were staunch labourites and had emigrated to Australia in 1957 to settle in Melbourne. In Australia, Emanuel studied business accountancy and computing, and had subsequently headed the Computer Services in the Australian Department of Productivity.[141]

Apart from expert assistance provided by the equipment vendors, the coordination of a number of government departments was sought in the initial stages of the project, and computer staff users at Mid-Med Bank (formerly, Barclays Malta which was purchased by the Maltese government and nationalised), the Inland Revenue Department, and the Central Office of Statistics (now the National Statistics Office) were therefore seconded for the task. Initially, the Centre's scope was rather narrow, carrying out government-related data processing activities, but training and consultancy services later also formed part of its business functions. Eventually, the Swatar Centre also started commissioning software from local computer

[140] "The Government Computer Centre", *Informatix*, 1982, p. 20.
[141] "Formidable assignment for Maltese-Australian expert", *The Times Government Computer Supplement*, 18 November 1981, p. V.

services firms (e.g., the outsourcing of the public lotto computerization to a private firm). The heart of the Swatar Centre was a Prime 750 minicomputer with Hazeltine terminals and a number of Hewlett-Packard peripherals (see Table 6.1 for the technical specifications). The system configuration ran under the PRIMOS operating system, which included PRIMENET as the network communications software, the latter capable of remote connections. Programming languages included FORTRAN, COBOL, BASIC, and RPG. Initially, the Centre operated on a double shift of six days a week, but this was eventually extended to an uninterrupted round-the-clock service of seven days a week.

Figure 6.1
The former Government Computer Centre. In the 1960s and early 1970s, this building formed part of NATO's Western Telegraphy Network.
Source: Author's collection

The Centre's main responsibility was the development of application programs for use by all government departments and parastatal bodies.[142] With something like thirty government departments and parastatal entities that included The Malta Development Corporation, Bank of Valletta (which did not fully computerize until the late 1980s) and Telemalta Corporation (later Maltacom, now GO) amongst others, the number of software applications developed by the Centre during its eleven years of existence amounted to 104 (see *Reports on the Working of Government Departments*, 1992).

TABLE 6.1
Technical Specifications of the Prime 750 Computer System at the former Government Computer Centre (as at 1982)

Unit	Quantity	Description
Processors:	2	Prime 750 processors
Internal Memory:	1 (per processor)	1.5 Megabytes (expandable to 8 MB)
Storage Devices:	6	300 MB Disk Drives
	2	Magnetic Tape Units
Input Devices:	?	Card Readers
	?	Paper Tape Readers
	20	Hazeltine Video Terminals
	15	HP-85 Terminals
Output:	3	Line Printers (1200 lines per minute)
	1	Drafting and Graph Plotter

Source: Informatix (No. 2, 1982: p. 21).

Although not a single official detailed report from the Swatar Centre is available, we can gain some insight into the type and scope of the programs written in the 1980s from the annual *Reports on the Working of Government Departments*, which contain a small section dedicated to the Centre's work. The 1981 report (i.e., the report published in 1982

---

[142] The development of application programs for use in government departments has been a function of a number of computer centres around the globe.

for the previous year) gives the organization structure of the Centre. It claimed 30 programmers, 6 systems analysts and 3 project managers (apart from many data entry clerks), by far the largest concentration of computer personnel in any organization at the time.

The 1984 report reveals that by the close of that year as many as ten different "systems" had been fully implemented. During the first few years of its operation, the Centre concentrated on what it considered to be priority tasks, application areas deemed vital to the progress and well-being of a nation. The key application areas initially envisaged included:

- Statistical applications
- Invoicing of public accounts and records in different government departments
- Computerization of identity cards
- Computerization of the health system
- Banking applications
- Payroll
- Manpower Planning System

The target date for the full-implementation of the above systems was (probably too ambitiously) set to mid-1983. However, only the statistical, invoicing and payroll systems had been completed by that date, and some applications were either never completed, or eventually subcontracted, much later, to private firms. This was the result of a lean team of senior personnel (experienced project managers, systems analysts and senior programmers) and severe lack of government funding. The annual budget for the computer centre was typically of the order of Lm400,000 (c. US$1,200,000) (see Spiteri, 1982; and Bonello Du Puis, 1987). This budget represented under 0.1% of GDP, very tiny even by Maltese standards. Government also spent little on computer equipment, generally: for example, in five years between 1981 and 1986 only an estimated Lm350,000 worth of computers and peripherals were purchased for different government departments.

The 1984 report also mentions that computer training, mainly in the form of systems analysis and programming (in BASIC, COBOL and FORTRAN), was organized for government employees and those of parastatal organizations. These courses were run by lecturers from the UK sent under the Commonwealth Secretariat Training Scheme with arrangements made by the Ministry of Foreign Affairs. The 1983 report makes a reference to the fact that university students following engineering and business management courses were also being sponsored, the aim being to 'make Malta self-reliant without the need to import foreign expertise and software products which are normally very expensive' (*Reports on the Working of Government Departments*, 1983: p. 27).

Apart from acknowledging the high fees normally associated with computer training, the above remark hints to the tight budget that the Centre had to contend with, and which contrasts starkly with the excessive funds the MSU expended a decade later (see next section). The Swatar Centre was a government entity set up by a socialist labour regime at a time when a wage freeze was being enforced, so that the government of the day could not afford (and certainly did not want to appear) to be extravagant. The lean nationwide budgets of the late 1970s and 1980s hit many sectors badly, including education and the University, which in that period registered an all-time low in student numbers.[143]

On 13 October 1984 the Computer Centre made news again when it became the target of a bomb attack. The bomb, which exploded in the early hours of the morning and did moderate damage, was placed on the sill of one of the main computer room's windows.[144] The motive behind this act of cowardace is not clear, but the intention was obviously to cause severe disruption, particularly given that the pay slips for all government employees and pensioners were issued from this centre. Luckily, no one was hurt.[145]

---

[143] This, in turn, may have had an indirect effect on the evolution of the software industry, perhaps retarding it owing to the lack of suitably qualified IT personnel (see Chapter 7).

[144] "Bomb damages Dingli Computer Centre", *The Sunday Times*, 14 October 1984, p. 1.

[145] In the second part of 1984, the nation was undergoing a very tension period. In a span of 16 weeks between 25 September and 31 December 1984 no less than 19 bombs were planted. On every occasion the excuse has been very flimsy, but motivated by political reasons, and possibly a tit-for-tat tactic. Persons and organizations belonging to both of the two main political parties were subjected to such violence.

The Management Systems Unit

By 1990, after almost a decade of existence, the Government Computer Centre had become very stretched, carrying out functions for which it was probably not fit. Managing the many computer projects that had been started earlier, particularly with the limited resources—financial and human—at its disposal, was proving difficult, if not impossible. Its role as a trainer of IT personnel and simultaneously as a consultancy agency only made matters worse.

By this time (c. 1990), management information systems were being advocated as the technological methodology by which business problems should be analysed and solved, by which management functions should be carried out. Some private companies had also moved into the computer consultancy business, offering management and consultancy services. Partly to mimic what was happening in private industry and partly to relieve the Computer Centre of some of its burden, the Management Systems Unit (MSU) was created which initially complemented the Computer Centre's work, but subsequently took over its functions; 1992 was in fact the last operating year of the Computer Centre.

The setting up of the MSU, however, went beyond that of merely acknowledging private industry practice or replacing the Computer Centre's work, and its creation therefore merits explanation. The MSU's formation had more to do with a perceived change in the civil service, combined with a recognition that information technology and information systems in the public sector needed revamping.

In 1987, the Malta Labour Party (MLP) lost the elections to the Nationalist Party (PN). The newly elected government was of the opinion that the public service needed a general shake-up and a re-organization,[146] so that in May 1989 a Public Service Reform Commission (henceforth, the Commission) was set up by order of the Prime Minister to investigate and report on the status of the civil

---

[146] It was not only the newly elected government that was of this opinion. The general public, including former senior civil servants had voiced their concern on a number of occasions about the civil service's state. See, for example, "State of the Civil Service", *The Times*, 11 March 1989, p. 3; and "Civil Service Reform", *The Times*, 27 March 1989, p. 18.

service and how the latter may be improved.[147]   In July 1989, the Commission drew up a report in which the Commission's findings were highlighted and recommendations put forward (see Chapter 11).

The Commission's report, entitled "A New Public Service for Malta – A Report on the Organization of the Public Service" tackled a number of issues, including the development of administrative structures, the establishment of a new employee grading scheme and employee training, human resources management, accountability, and the adoption of national empolyment legislation and international conventions as standards for public service regulations.   It also pointed out matters that, in its opinion, were lacking or very limited in the civil service (e.g. the capacity for planning, policy analysis and design – see *Public Service Reform Commission*, 1989).   The PSRC identified three so-called "change agencies" to be responsible for the reform in the public service, of which one was the Management Systems Unit.[148]   Complementing the Commission's work, an Operations Review body was also set up, tasked with the designing of a five-year Information System Strategic Plan (ISSP).   The MSU's internal organization was detailed in a project plan prepared by the Operations Review team as part of the ISSP, the latter presented to the Cabinet in the summer of 1990, some months before the official creation of the MSU.

The MSU was thus set up as a limited commercial company under the Commercial Partnership Ordinance on 30 November 1990. Fully government owned, it was given an initial capital of Lm100,000 (about US$300,000) for the short period to December 1990, and Lm800,000 for the following year, raised to over two million in subsequent years.   The limited liability commercial company model was chosen for its supposed ease of execution and 'to allow the organsation greater freedom in the recruitment and renumeration of

---

[147] The broad-ranging terms of reference were 'to examine the organization of the public service and to recommend means by which the Service can effectively respond to the changing needs for effective Government' (Public Service Reform Commission, 1989: p. (i)).

[148] The other two were called the Management and Personnel Office (MPO), responsible for human resource management strategies; and the Staff Development Organization (SDO), responsible for training, and later integrated into the MPO. All three change agencies fell under the responsibility of the Office of the Prime Minister, thus emphasising the importance of the reform exercise.

human resources and in determining procurement processes' (Mifsud, 1997: p. 5).

The main objective of the MSU was

> ... to investigate, define, evaluate, develop and implement guidelines and procedures in the field of general management, financial management, human resources management, technology management, with the aim of promoting the effectiveness and efficiency, financially and otherwise, of institutions and organizations, including, but not limited to, Government Ministries, Departments of Governments, agencies of the Government and other Government owned or controlled bodies (ibid.).

The MSU's mission was

> ...to facilitate change programmes to transform the public sector in terms of its leadership, range and quality of services, quality of work life and its role in contributing to the achievement of the Government's vision (i.e., to have a public service that provides quality of infrastructure and public services to improve the economic well being and quality of life of the Maltese citizens, and enables Malta to compete successfully in EC and global markets) (ibid.).

Following the approval of the Information System Strategic Plan, the MSU was then charged with its execution embracing the Computer Centre, so that development and support were also added to its other main management consultancy role. Under the chairmanship of Joseph V Tabone, another Maltese expatriate, this time hailing from Canada, the MSU was given a beautifully refurbished Villa in Cospicua from where to operate, away from the bustling business centre of the capital city where most government departments are located (see Figure 6.2).[149] Starting with a dozen or

---

[149] The MSU's occupation of lush premises (for which a huge rental sum was being paid annually) that contrasted starkly with the often poor ambience in government

so personnel, this number soon shot up to over 300 within five years of the company's operation (see Table 6.2). In 1995, some 50% of the country's IT expertise lay within the MSU workforce, much of it relatively young (Figure 6.3).

Figure 6.2
Villa Portelli in Kalkara, the building that once housed the offices of the former MSU.
Source: Author's collection

Almost from the beginning, the MSU was seen as a white elephant by many, and could not avoid public scrutiny. The MSU came under fire on a number of occasions, although the criticism was often made by the opposition party which saw this entity as another government

office buildings was also seen by some as not auguring well with a company that supposedly had very close ties with government departments and civil service personnel.

failed endeavour and having achieved little in practice.[150] Just over two years after the MSU's creation, its Business Plan for 1993 was tabled in parliament for members to examine its contents. By this time the MSU had already acquired a reputation of squandering public funds, particularly since a considerable number of foreign consultants were being hired at phenomenal salaries.[151] The business plan therefore offered a good opportunity for the MLP, then opposition party, to have its say and, in February 1993, the MLP drew up a report to constructively analyse its contents (Malta Labour Party, 1993).

TABLE 6.2
MSU Employee Breakdown by position, 1994-1995

Position	Number of Employees
Senior Consultants	20
Junior Consultants	20
Group Managers	9
Programme Managers	8
IT Professionals	99
Technical Support	104
Business Support	18
Administrative Support	45
Total	*323*

Source: MSU 1994/1995 Annual Report

---

[150] As opposition party, the Malta Labour Party also saw the MSU as something worth attacking and in the process gain political sympathy from party members and non-members alike.

[151] In spite of the fact that the MSU's pay scales (listed in Mifsud, 1997) were never made public for fear of an inflationary spiral that would have ensued as a result, common knowledge of the abnormally high salaries the MSU was offering did in fact lead to some private software firms revising their own salary scales in order not to lose some of their more able IT staff to the MSU (which, in fact, did happen to a certain extent). In that same period, the signing of a contract binding the employee for at least three years of service was becoming increasingly common in view of the high mobility that was taking place in the software industry.

The overall conclusions of the MLP report were negative. Major criticisms included:

- lack of transparency: the Business Plan apparently did not provide information regarding the costs of projects;
- poor performance: a number of projects planned for implementation by a target date were far from being completed; and
- little or no technology transfer: the business plan did not encourage the concept of technology transfer since most projects were controlled by non-permanent Maltese nationals.

The 1993 Business Plan was described in the MLP report as 'disgraceful and dishonest', and as 'nothing more than a costly propaganda exercise' (ibid.).

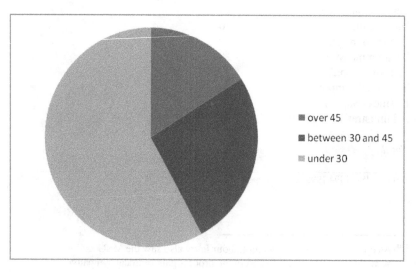

Figure 6.3
MSU Age Structure as at 1994
Source: MSU 1994/1995 Annual Report

Interestingly, the MSU's 1994/95 Annual Report acknowledges that in 1994-95 its work had shifted in focus, from managing and consolidating its earlier work to an emphasis on information systems services (*Management Systems Unit*, 2005: p. 7). Additionally, the MSU was to provide an independent, systematic review and appraisal of all the company's operations by appointing an internal auditor who, with the chairman's assistance was to provide assurance that operations were well managed and improvements identified (*ibid.*: p. 7). It is possible that the above were being contemplated in response to the MLP's criticism and in order for the MSU to appear to be more transparent.

In 1996, after two terms in office, the Nationalist Party lost to Labour. Once in power, the new government was quick to pick-up on the MSU again. A consultant was appointed to conduct a strategic resource audit with the view of identifying key areas that needed change. Once more, the findings—drawn up in a thirty-one page report—did not project a good overall image of the MSU (see Mifsud, 1997). Major criticisms were not very different from the 1993 report (absence of commercial accountability, excessive spending, abnormally high salaries, abnormally high percentage of expatriate workforce, lack of policy regarding skills transfer, and not meeting deadlines were some of the points mentioned), but unlike the 1993 report, this study did include a number of recommendations, of which perhaps an important one was for the IT budget to be allocated to the respective Government Departments with strict instructions to be spent through MSU rather than being allocated to MSU directly (i.e., in effect MSU would have 'sold' its services). This would have enabled Departments to foster a better IT culture and narrow the knowledge gap between them and outside suppliers. Eventually, it could have led to a full commercial environment where MSU would even have had to compete with private suppliers for Government IT projects.

Despite the criticism and the scepticism that surrounded the MSU, some good did come out of this organization which achieved more than has otherwise publicly been led to believe. First, the MSU had the very ambitious task of propelling the entire civil service into the information age, no mean feat after the stark neglect of the 1980s. A number of sorely needed operational changes in the civil service were instigated, and numerous well-designed IT systems were managed, developed and deployed. At a management level it promoted concepts like strategic planning, quantitative management, human resource management, and financial management; at a technical level, competencies were enhanced and specialisation ensured. The MSU also oversaw the wholesale training of swathes of civil servants at all levels in basic IT competence. Additionally, as an unofficial trainer of young Maltese graduates, the MSU had created a situation where, if these graduates moved on from the company, their skills would be employed in Malta's then nascent but growing consultancy and IT sectors.

The level of sophistication of the IT infrastructure that had been developed by the mid-1990s—also thanks largely to MSU—may be judged by the type and quantity of software and equipment installed: it included some 200 information systems, and a Wide Area Network which connected about 200 servers and 7000 PCs. This Wide Area Network formed part of MAGNET, the Malta Government Network (see Box 6-1).

The Malta Information Technology and Training Services[152]

Partly as a result of the strategic audit study of the MSU's operation, the MSU was restructured in 1997 into the Malta Information Technology and Training Services (MITTS) Ltd. This name was chosen to better reflect the company's new emphasis on information technology. The newly formed company had to make the transition from management consultancy for the public service to a technical IT agency (with an emphasis on project implementation) for the Government of Malta. This resulted in a radical change in organizational structure, corporate strategy, and funding. Consultancy services would still be carried out, but they would now be integrated into the Civil Service. A body called the Management Efficiency Unit (MEU) at the Office of the Prime Minister was created for this purpose.

---

[152] Since MITTS essentially continued on the work of the MSU, this account of MITTS is necessarily brief. In 2000, to celebrate its tenth anniversary, MITTS produced a 30-page brochure that gave some history about the company (MITTS, 2000). The company's Annual Reports also give a wealth of information about ongoing projects.

By the time MITTS was formed, the local workforce had matured in terms of skills, experience and exposure, and thus, the dependency on foreign expatriates was incrementally reduced. Many Maltese with the necessary skills to take over had by now been trained, both within the former MSU and outside. The transition of having Maltese employees replacing foreign expatriates thus proved to be a natural process.

In 1997 company funding was altered. All funds formerly allocated to the company were devolved to the various government departments instead. This effectively meant that responsibility for IT now rested with the Ministries, and the MITTS Ltd role became, primarily, that of a service provider—providing 'end to end' IT services directly to government entities, in competition with other IT companies in the private arena. Financial allocation for 1997 amounted to Lm1.961 million, almost as much as the budget voted to the Ministry of Economic Affairs and Finance which received the highest sum (MITTS, 1998). The sum of Lm1.961 million represented 22.4% of the total budget voted for all Ministries.

Apart from the changes mentioned above, MITTS continued on the work started by the former MSU. Projects carried between 2000-2003 include the commissioning of the Government's common on-line payment mechanism, known as the Electronic Payment Gateway (EPG); eXAMS On-Line, a project in collaboration with the Department of Examinations for offering related on-line services; the official CHOGM (Commonwealth Heads of Government Meeting) website, effectively a dynamic online information portal on Commonwealth member states; and a host of services added to the Electronic Government Mail (EGM), includng Securemail which uses the industry standard Public Key Exchange (PKE) and is based on the concept of Secure Digital Certificates (see MITTS, 2003).

From the beginning significant emphasis was also placed on IT training, particularly courses that would lead to recognised qualifications. To this end, a branch of MITTS called Swatar Training Centre (STC) was formed in the late 1990s which specialised in IT education. Initially, STC concentrated its efforts in offering certificate and diploma courses in IT and management, but strategic alliances with industry players such as CISCO and ORACLE were later sought and reached. This alliance allowed STC to also offer short and intensive, industry-oriented, programmes. STC is now a leading training centre and its courses—which can be taken by anyone with the right aptitude and qualifications—are highly recognised by the local ICT industry.

In the summer of 2008, it was decided by the Ministry for Infrastructure, Transport and Communications to replace MITTS with a new organization, this time called Malta Information Technology Agency (MITA). One of the reasons put forward for the creation of MITA was that there were still some important functions, such as IT policy, that were the responsibility of, and carried out directly by, the Ministry. Under the new setup, MITA took over such Ministerial functions, apart from having absorbed into it the operations of MITTS. In effect, MITA is now the only agency (excluding the MCA) completely responsible for all IT-related matters and the execution of long-term IT policy programmes.

Box 6-1
MAGNET: The Malta Government Network

The Malta Government Network (MAGNET) was one of the first major projects undertaken by government in the 1990s. Started as an MSU initiative to initially link a handful of key government ministries, it developed into a nationwide data network interconnecting all government entities.

Prior to MAGNET's inception, government computing consisted of small and disparate computer systems at a few government departments and parastatal bodies, and a centralised, batch-processing system at the Government Computer Centre. As late as 1990 most of the computers in use by government did not form part of a local area network. As LANs started to become popular worldwide, the traditional centralised (and generally secure and reliable) mainframe computer systems started to be replaced, or complemented by, network systems involving inteconnected personal computers and servers, a model of computing that would be termed client/server computing. Within a few years a number of local government departments adopted this client/server model, installing small computer networks and applications relevant to their type of work. These networks were still isolated systems, however, and it was with the creation of MAGNET that they were turned into one large, interconnected system, effectively a wide area network.

The MAGNET infrastructure and the technologies used to build it were quite sophisticated even for its time. A major component of the infrastructure was the Wide Area Backbone to which many subnetworks were attached. Originally, this Backbone was envisaged as an FDDI network, but because ATM (Asynchronous Transfer Mode) technology was at that time (mid-1990s) gathering pace it was decided to implement the underlying fibre optic network using ATM switches. ATM has the advantage over some other switching technologies (such as frame relay) in that the packet size (referred to as a "cell") is small and of fixed length, and hence the ATM switches can be very fast (more instructions are typically included in firmware and hardware). Also, ATM is the ideal technology for voice and video transmission, hence it could cater for integrated (multimedia) services. The fibre network was layed underground and spanned the Valletta, Floriana and Blata l-Bajda area. Interestingly, the network configuration was a combination of ring and star topologies: the main backbone was layed in the form of a ring to which, at various points, attachment devices (switches) were placed to connect several sites in a star fashion. Given the different requirements of the various sites, network connections consisted of a mix of technlogies including ATM, FDDI (used at the former St Luke's Hospital), Point to Point, Frame Relay and Channelised E1.

As for the network devices and software platforms, it was decided early on in the project to standardise, as far as possible, on major brands such as Intel-based servers, UNIX SVR4, TCP/IP, and Microsoft Windows. Informix (for UNIX) and SQL (for Microsoft) was used as the database software. Whist offering certain advantages, this strategy also risked remaining static on the chosen brands, perhaps being unable to adopt newer and more advanced products from other suppliers.

Depending on a given site, interconnectivity was achieved using various techniques and technologies. For example, 64K and 2Mbps leased circuits (from the former Telemalta) were commonly employed, as was ADSL and dialup access for situations which did not require high transmission rates (e.g. electronic mail). Microwave links (using spread-spectrum technology) were also accomplished by installing pairs of antennas on government building rooftops.

In 1998, at the time when MSU was being restructured into MITTS and was already operating from Gattard House in Blata l-Bajda, a number of Maltese Embassies had their LANs configured for connection to the MAGNET system. The Brussels, London, Rome, Toronto, Washington and New York sites were linked to the Corporate Data Centre at Blata l-Bajda a year later via the network at the Foreign Affairs site in Valletta. The then popular international X.25 standard was used as the underlying network protocol. Internet access was initially via a service provider in Holland, where Internet gateways and servers were installed. In 1999, facilities for connecting directly to the Internet from Malta were installed as part of the Malta Internet Exchange (see also Chapter 9).

The development of MAGNET occurred over a number of years and involved the participation of many entities, all of whom played crucial roles in making it possible. As at 2000, MAGNET consisted of approximately 200 Structured Cabled LANs, connected several Government Ministries and Departments, and extended to at least 68 local councils, 20 police stations, 8 health centres (all linked to St Luke's, the old state hospital), 21 social service district offices, 8 public libraries, and 7 embassies abroad. The state schools, about 180 in all, were connected a few years later.

In 2005, as part of an initiative to develop further e-government, MITTS, in partnership with Maltacom and Melita Cable launched what was termed MAGNET II, which provided enhanced badwidth per site, better reliability (through strict service level agreements) and better security. Voice over IP calls were another benefit of the enhanced wide area network. Each site was dual linked for increased resiliency, with the backup circuits at each site providing redundancy.

Part IV

Emergence and Development of the Software Industry

Part IV
Emergence and Development of the Software Industry

In the late 1980s, faced with the prospect of foreign competition and the 'new global economy' based on advanced technology, Maltese politicians and policy makers set out to devise a strategic plan that would propel Malta into the information age, transforming the Island's economy from merely depending on manufacturing and tourism into a service-oriented market. At that time, attention was therefore focused on at least two key areas, namely, offshore banking and financial services; and high-technology, value-added industries such as those of the pharmaceuticals and informatics. At the same time, a series of measures were taken to continue to promote investment by attracting foreign companies to Malta's shores. In particular, the emphasis was on foreign investment that aimed principally to increase the export market but simultaneously did not compete with sectors that were already well served by local businesses. In this vein, a Technopark was built; an Industry Development Act was enacted offering excellent tax incentives for foreign, export-oriented, firms; the Malta Council for Science and Technology (MCST) was set up; and an overhaul of the telecommunications infrastructure was undertaken to enable organizations to conduct business more effectively.

Concurrently with the above initiatives, a policy to promote the sciences and provide IT education at all levels was actively pursued because it was recognized that without a good supply of IT graduates there was no way that the vision for turning Malta into a centre of ICT excellence would be realised. Apart from making the teaching of basic IT skills compulsory in primary and secondary schools and encouraging young people to study ICT by providing valuable bursaries, a number of IT courses targeted for adults were offered in the hope to win the battle against the digital divide. The latter courses were either offered free or were heavily subsidised. Additionally, in the late 1990s and early 2000s strategic alliances with IT market leaders such as Microsoft, Hewlett-Packard, Cisco, Oracle and SAP were also sought as a way of boosting the local ICT sector.

The above policies, coupled with a well defined IT strategic plan, and other factors such as a stable political environment, had a positive effect on information technology which began to expand rapidly. This led to a corresponding substantial growth in software development and firm formation. New niche markets began to appear which software companies could tap into. Opportunities for companies— both local and foreign—to do IT business seemed optimal, particularly at the turn of the millennium when it began to emerge that the likelihood of Malta becoming an EU member, which therefore would open a vast market, appeared more imminent. Indeed, in the decade 1995-2005, close to one hundred new ICT firms were formed, most still operating. Many of these include software developers offering services from small custom applications to fully integrated systems. A software industry was in the making.

Whilst the aforementioned government initiatives have undoubtedly been conducive to the growth of software development, they have by no means been the only contributing factors for the software industry's emergence. Even before the first IT Strategic Plan was finalised in 1993, in which for the first time software was mentioned as a potential economic growth sector, a number of local firms had already firmly established themselves, although Malta-based foreign software firms were almost unheard of. Additionally, although the 1993 IT Plan made reference to software development, the Maltese government never set out with the express intention of developing an indigenous software industry. The latter thus emerged initially on private initiative, as a result of professional entrepreneurship. It was helped by the diffusion and acceptance of computer technology in the mid- to late-1980s and, only later, by the generation of the right input factors in the form of public policies.

7

Malta's Nascent Software Industry

Origins of Software Development in Malta

Software development in Malta did not see its humble beginnings until the late 1970s when a handful of computer services companies were set up to offer time-sharing and turnkey solutions (see Chapter 3). As happened elsewhere, small powerful computers began to infiltrate the local market, leading to a great demand for software. This accelerated the software development process and within less than a decade programming had become an important business activity. New advances in information technology including the Internet, telecommunications, and mobile telephony, created a further need for new applications, and software production therefore showed no sign of abating. With market liberalisation in the late 1990s, foreign software firms were also attracted to Malta's shores, adding further to the software scene. Other than the fact that Malta initially lacked the technical capabilities and was slow, if not late, in adopting computers, the need for (and the development of) software in Malta from about 1980 therefore followed much the same general pattern as that in many other countries.

To speak of a software industry in Malta may seem perhaps somewhat inappropriate in view of Malta's extremely small size, but the increase in software output in recent years—compounded by an investment in Malta of a number of foreign software firms—has been significant, so that software is now justly becoming another industry, even if tiny by international standards. Apart from the reasons already given, this rise in software production in Malta is the result of a number of factors: the creation of the Government Computer Centre in the early 1980s, followed by the establishment of the Management Systems Unit and the Malta Information Technology and Training Services, both of which provided training opportunities for aspiring civil servants as well as spearheading the procurement of IT projects to private companies; the liberalisation process started in the late 1990s; government incentives for small to medium sized enterprises (SMEs) which also attracted a number of foreign firms and promoted interest in local company start-ups (see later); the building of an advanced telecommunications infrastructure (the lack of which previously had put off companies doing computing business); the development in the early 1990s of the Malta Government Network (MAGNET); the more recent emphasis on tertiary education in the sciences; and the continuing demand for software not only by organizations who have come to understand the importance of computerization for efficiency and competitiveness, but also by new markets such as web and database hosting and I-gaming. In terms of global production, therefore, software output in Malta is small, but in terms of national output (e.g., as percentage of GDP) software development is beginning to be measurable. In 2005, for example, output was estimated at 49 million Euros (approximately US$63 m.), or about 1.1% of GDP and 1.5% of all services activities.[153] The software industry in Malta is still in its infancy but is bound to become a major source of economic growth in forthcoming years as government's vision to place Malta at the forefront of technology and make the Island the number one place for ICT business is beginning to be realised.[154]

---

[153] For an explanation of how the Maltese software industry revenue was calculated, see Appendix F.

[154] In 2006, an agreement was signed with the Dubai-based company Tecom Investments for the setting up of a "Smart City" in Malta akin to that of Dubai. The project is estimated to create in the region of five thousand IT jobs, with Tecom investing about Lm 110 million. See, for example, Zammit (2006); and Balzan (2006).

ICT and Software Firms: Statistical Profile

Unfortunately, software-related statistics such as the number of software companies operating in Malta in any given year, the number of workers employed in software-related jobs, and software revenues have not been available for Malta.[155] Obtaining accurate figures for any of these parameters—particularly for past years—is therefore problematic since no detailed statistics were ever kept either by government departments or industry analysts. However, the number of ICT firms in the last two decades has increased by about a tenfold, from about twenty firms in 1985 to circa two hundred in 2005 (Aloisio, 2010: Appendix H). As one might expect of a small island, the vast majority of these enterprises are small: about 80% employ under 10 persons and therefore have low turnovers. The small firms are often set up by IT professionals who leave other private companies, or by new computer graduates. Spin-offs—companies spawned from bigger ones—also account for some of these firms.

It has been estimated that the two hundred or so ICT firms operating in 2005 together employed around 4500 people.[156] Malta's population is 400,000, of which, about 139,000 were economically active in 2005. This means that the ICT workforce in 2005 accounted for roughly 3.2% of total employment. Similar statistics for some other countries, shown in Table 7.1, reveal that Malta's ICT sector as a percentage of total employment compares favourably with other countries, even if we assume that Malta's ICT employment figure for

---

[155] The National Statistics Office (NSO) has been producing "Information Society Statistics" for a number of years but these are mainly concerned with the use of ICT technology as such (e.g. use of ISDN, broadband, mobile telephony, etc.), and obtained for the purpose of knowing to what extent technology has penetrated society. See the NSO website at *http://www.nso.gov.mt*.

[156] A 2006 Malta Enterprise document states that Malta has over 200 ICT firms employing about 6000 people. The number of firms agrees well with a list of firms that the author has independently drawn up (given in Appendix H of Aloisio, 2010), but the figure for the number of employees could not be verified. In a meeting with Malta Enterprise officials (held at their office on 18 May 2007), it was revealed that the figure of 6000 includes workers employed in IT departments of non-ICT firms, and that the actual figure for all ICT firms is probably nearer 4500. It was also revealed that as at the end of 2006, the number of employees doing software-related jobs as estimated by the Employment and Training Corporation stood at 1250; and at 1500 as estimated by the NSO.

the year 2002 (for which other country figures are mainly given) was about 20% less than that for 2005.

Whilst it is difficult to attempt to categorise the business activity of each ICT company, a broad categorisation into one of four main sectors was nevertheless made in order to gain an insight into the type of business the ICT firms are involved in.[157] According to this scheme, it is found that about 37% are involved in software development and services. It also emerges that the ICT sector in Malta is roughly equally split-up into companies that are predominantly involved in the sales of hardware, and those offering solutions.

TABLE 7.1
ICT workforce for various countries as percentage of gainfully employed

Country	Working Population (in millions)*	Total ICT Workforce**	%	Employees in Software Sector**	%
Brazil	83.34	>160,000 [2002]	>0.2	83,300 [2003]	0.1
China	778.50	>330,000 [2002]	>0.4	160,000 [2002]	0.2
Germany	40.57	550,000 [2002]	1.4	300,000 [2002]	0.7
India	480.00	1,300,000 [2003]	0.3	500,000 [2003]	0.1
Ireland	1.73	90,000 [2003]	5.2	24,000 [2003]	1.4
Israel	2.99	55,800 [2000]	1.9	14,500 [2000]	0.5
UK	29.81	902,000 [2001]	3.0	326,000 [2001]	1.1
US	150.99	2,922,000 [2002]	1.9	1,024,000 [2002]	0.7
Malta	*0.14*	*4,500 [2005]*	*3.2*	*1,000 [2005]*	*0.7*

*Figures are for 2004.
**Figures are for the year indicated in square brackets.
Note: The figures for both the ICT workforce and the number of software employees are only approximate, as there is often disagreement in the figures quoted by different sources.
Source: Working population figures are from World Bank; others were compiled by author from various sources, including Arora & Gambardella (2005), and Commander (2005).

---

[157] The four broad categories are: Hardware Supply and Configuration including Computer Repairs, with little or no software development; Software Development and Services including Systems Integrators and Web Designers; Business Consultancy and IT Training, with little or no software development and including Call Centers; and Voice and Data Communications Providers and ISPs.

Table 7.1 also lists the number of employees in the software sector. It shows that, at about one thousand for 2005, the number of Maltese software jobs (as percentage of working population) also compares favourably with some other countries although there is scope for further growth in this sector. Nationally, the number of employees in software-related jobs for 2005 becomes more meaningful if it is compared with the number of workers employed that same year in other domestic jobs. This data is presented in Table 7.2 below. It will be noted that the employment figure for agriculture accounts for about three times that of software-related jobs, but it should be remembered that the agricultural sector has been dwindling over the years.

TABLE 7.2
Selected sectorial employment figures, 2005*

Direct Production	
Manufacturing	24,635
Construction	10,524
Agriculture, Hunting and Forestry	3,107
Fishing	436
Market Services	
Education	12,042
Public Administration and Defence	10,850
Hotels and Restaurants	9,166
Health and Social Work	9,158

*Total of private and public, but excluding temporary employees.
Source: Employment and Training Corporation.

Finally, Figure 7.1—which shows a histogram of (predominently software) firm formation between the years 1979 and 2005—reveals that somewhat more firms were set up at the turn of the millennium than at any other time. Although this may be purely coincidental, it is conceivable that the higher rate of firm formation in this period is related to Malta's then preparations to join the European Union as well as to the dot-com boom.

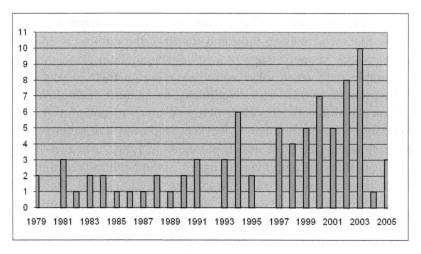

Figure 7.1
Formation of software companies for the period 1979-2005.
Source: Generated from data collected by author from various sources.

Software Industry Structure and Characteristics

Table 7.3 shows the top twenty software firms operating in Malta in 2005. A number of observations can be made from this table, namely:

(i)   In comparison to the top software firms of many other countries, the top software firms operating in Malta are small. This is to be expected in view of Malta's small size and the relatively young age of the industry.

(ii)   As with other countries, however, firm size decreases rapidly. For example, the top five or so Brazilian, Irish and Chinese software companies employ well in excess of one hundred workers, but most companies ranked below the tenth place employ considerably fewer workers. To take one example: in 2002, only 13% of all indigenous Irish firms employed more than fifty workers (Sands, 2005).

(iii)   Apart from a few foreign firms, most of the top twenty firms operating in Malta in 2005 were Maltese. This contrasts with some places (like Brazil) where many of the larger software firms are foreign. Some countries (like

Ireland) have had a very successful indigenous software industry (although again multinationals there played an important role in the development of the software industry). Malta's success in creating its own indigenous software sector is notable.

(iv)   Most of the well-established companies are start-ups, only a handful being spin-offs.

From Table 7.3 it also emerges that—with the exception of a few firms—it takes a relatively long time for indigenous software firms to grow in size. For example, it has taken anything between twenty to thirty years for companies the like of Computime, Megabyte, and Shireburn to grow to employing between twenty and fifty persons. On the other hand, foreign firms (e.g. Crimsonwing) or those that have had an overseas connection (e.g. 6pm) appear to have grown more rapidly than their Maltese counterparts. This may be explained by the fact that these companies will have targeted a bigger market and were therefore able to expand more rapidly. Thus, whilst the software industry has traditionally been seen as fertile ground for innovation and small-scale entrepreneurship—as may also be gathered from the numerous Maltese firms that have been created in the last fifteen years or so—the data in Table 7.3 appears to confirm a 1989 OECD report that cautioned that 'it is not easy to develop an activity [referring to software] to a meaningful size' (UNIDO, 1993: p. 10). It has also been pointed out that whilst niche firms are typically stable and profitable businesses, a key to growth is breaking out of niche markets and focusing on large projects. This, however, requires considerable expertise at both the managerial and technical level.

It should be remarked that just because a company is not listed among those shown in Table 7.3, or happens to be at the bottom of the list, does not imply bad performance on the part of the company. There are a number of software firms that have been in existence for a number of years and have done well, but have nevertheless chosen to remain relatively small. These firms have often targeted the local market, and specialised in niche (vertical) applications. Their survival stems from the fact that they have successfully designed, developed, and implemented a few good products and managed to support and enhance them over the years; or specialised in customising off-the-shelf products or in providing some type of IT consultancy. Thus, for these firms, software maintenance and support activities—including product enhancement—have provided sufficient income to sustain them. Examples of such firms include Dakar Software (established in 1994) and specialising in people management systems, particularly payroll; NLA Systems (established in 1988) and specialising in management and accounting software and point of sale systems; Kinetix IT solutions (established in 1995), specialising in business consultancy; and Technosoft Ltd (established in 1991), specialising in software for the hospitality sector.[158] There are also relatively new entrants like Ascent, CCBill, Ixaris and Uniblue that are expanding rapidly and may soon join the list of the top software firms.

As noted, Malta has a relatively high percentage of indigenous software companies, many of whom have been very successful having dominated the list of the leading ten software firms for many years. Remarkably, most of these firms are start-ups: they were created in the late 1970s and early 1980s when the industry was non-existent. In many cases, the founding directors were either computer science/engineering graduates (e.g. founders of Megabyte), or persons with previous computer and management experience which was often gained by having worked in data processing departments of large organizations (e.g., founders of Intercomp and Computime). Some founding directors (e.g., Shireburn's and BDS's, respectively) had qualifications unrelated to computers, yet have been highly successful in their ventures.

Table 7.3 shows that although the majority of firms are indigenously owned, exports are dominated by the foreign firms. The targeting of the export sector by local firms, however, may be on the increase as local firms are beginning to realise that this route may be the only one left for them to expand. Indeed, some indigenous firms have already begun to sell products or outsource work for overseas companies (see later).

---

[158] The respective company websites are: *www.dakarsoftware.com*; *www.nlasystems.com*; *www.kinetix.com.mt*; and *www.technosoft.com.mt*.

TABLE 7.3
Leading (top twenty) Maltese Software Companies, 2005

Company Name	Year Estab.	Owner- ship	Employ- ment	Grad- uates	Specialization	Origin	Exports
Crimsonwing	1996 (1998)	F	89	52	e-business ; data management; logis- tics; supply chain	S	100%
GFI Software	1993	F	76	?	messaging; content and network security	S	100%
Intercomp	1980	M	65	?	systems integration; networking	S	?
Philip Toledo	1946	M	60	?	legacy applications; network design & implementation; banking/financial services; training	S	?
Megabyte	1979	M	49	?	gaming/lotto systems; Human resource man- agement; airline route profitability	S	?
Computime	1979	M	45	27	accounting; network & facilities management; server hosting; e-business	S	56%
6pm	1996 (2000)	M	43	?	RAD/prototyping; accountin & business intelligence; telecommunications	S	?
RS2	1989	F	36	?	e-card payment; services for financial industry	S	?
Hob Software	1990	F	27	21	connectivity/security; software; systems software; kernel drivers	S	100%
Computer Solutions	1986	M	26	?	information strategy; planning & integration; data communications	S	?
Shireburn	1983	M	24	12	financial manage-; ment collaborative & messaging solutions	S	30%

TABLE 7.3 (*continued*)
Leading (top twenty) Maltese Software Companies, 2005

Company Name	Year Estab.	Owner-ship	Employ-ment	Grad-uates	Specialization	Origin	Exports
Tenovar	1999	M	20	2	telecommunications; CRM; web application	S	65%
Anvil	1986 (2001)	F	15	?	front- & middle-software for financial markets; trading & risk management	S	?
Alert	1998	M	15	4	web applications; e-procurement management systems	S	?
Cursor	1991	P	14	4	customised POS; electronics; interfacing/control; handheld applications	S	10%
IT Services	1993	M	14	?	accounting & business applications; manufacturing applica-tions; e-commerce	S	?
Dakar	1994	M	12	5	payroll and other people management solutions	S	25%
Acrosslimits	2001	M	10	?	e-commerce/e-business; knowledge management & collaboration; remote online data backup	S	?
Ascent	2002	M	10	9	Telecommunications; Billing; Scientific Applications; Retailing	S	80%
Icon Studios	2000	M	9	2	web applications; content management systems; e-business	S	7%

Notes:
2nd Column: A year in parentheses refers to the year when the company set up a base in Malta.
3rd Column: M = Maltese, F = Foreign, P = partly Maltese, partly Foreign.
8th Column: The exports are expressed as a percentage of revenues for 2005.
Source: Compiled by author from a company profile e-survey and other sources, including *The Malta Business Directory*; *Malta Enterprise ICT Online Directory*; *The Malta Business Weekly*; *Malta Economic Update*; and *The Commercial Courier*.

This table also reveals how far software companies have gone from the early days when relatively small vertical applications such as insurance billing and retail software were the norm. While the development of custom vertical applications for local niche markets continues to be an important source of income for small companies, many local firms have had to diversify and specialise in certain application areas. The type of specialised work that is carried out by some firms and the technology tools that are used for some of the projects may also be inferred from the adverts for software engineers that regularly appear in the local press, describing not only the prerequisite qualifications but also some of the projects companies are involved in. Relatively young companies like Ixaris and Ascent—both set up by current and former full-time University of Malta lecturers— are examples where the theory of computer science from neural networks and fuzzy logic to distributed transactional systems and computer security are also being put into practice. With a base in London and an R&D office in Malta, Ixaris specialises in secure web-based services; whilst Ascent is more applications oriented, having produced software packages such as vehicle routing and production process optimization. Specialization is, of course, one strategy for survival: it is a way of deepening competencies and differentiating oneself from other firms that cannot do so.

Classification of Software Development Activities

The author's company profile e-survey from which Table 7.3 was compiled (see Aloisio, 2010: Appendix F) includes a section on the type of software development activity companies are engaged in. The results for this section of the survey are reproduced in Table 7.4.

Not surprisingly, custom software development is pursued by many indigenous companies, whereas product development is carried out primarily by the larger foreign firms. However, a number of companies have reported their engagement in customisation. An independent survey carried out by Bonello (2006) as part of an MBA dissertation on outsourcing also reveals that customisation is a common activity: 16 out of 20 respondents indicated that they did customisation of software products. However, how much of the total software effort is actually spent on customisation (i.e., as percentage of

TABLE 7.4
Software Development Activity, 2005

	Local Firms	Foreign Firms	Combined
Custom software development (tailor-made):	41%	18%	30%
Customisation of off-the-shelf software:	25%	8%	16%
Packaged software development (mass-market):	8%	52%	30%
Other (e.g., embedded):	26%	22%	24%

other business activities) is not known. The results of Bonello's survey regarding products and services offerings are reproduced below as Table 7.5. Note that the percentages of the subcategories are with respect to each of the four main types of products and services offerings. Taken globally, the percentage split-up of the four main categories given in Table 7.5 work out roughly as follows: 14% for Software Product Development/Sales; 42% for Software Services; 14% for Outsourcing Services; and 30% for Other Services.

From these results, it appears that software product development is still a relatively minor activity, carried out by the larger established firms. Generally, software companies start out by producing custom (tailor-made) programs for the domestic market and only later venture into packaged (product) software production. As the Maltese software industry is still relatively young, product development—which entails aggressive and costly marketing as well as the careful addressing of issues such as genuine user need, extensive documentation, thorough testing for quality, and major after sales support—is still beyond the reach of many indigenous companies, particularly the smaller ones.[159] Software products are also launched as a result of greater innovative intensity, a characteristic that nations strive to achieve, but one that is not easily attainable (Carmel & Tija, 2005: p. 204). Indeed, Carmel & Tija (2005) have pointed out that, with few exceptions, none of the new offshore nations has made a mark on this sector. That said, some Maltese firms, amongst them Shireburn and 6pm, did expand their original bespoke or custom services into

---

[159] For issues related to software product development, including the main attributes that characterise product software, see Kittlaus & Clough (2009), Condon (2002), and Kopetz (1993). See also Messerschmitt & Szyperski (2003).

consultancy and products which they now also export. The few foreign Malta-based software firms, on the other hand, specialise predominantly in product development.

TABLE 7.5
Local Suppliers IT Product Offerings

Products Offering/Activity	Count	Percentage
Software Product Development/Sales		
Shrink Wrapped Software/Off the Shelf Packages	9	36%
Customisable Software	16	64%
Software Services		
Installation including configuration (no code changes)	11	15%
Customisation (including code changes)	15	20%
Developing bespoke applications	16	22%
Maintenance	17	23%
24 x 7 – 1st Line Support	11	15%
*Other	4	5%
R&D, Technical Support, Consultancy & Training, 2nd & 3rd Line Support		
Outsourcing Services		
Web hosting	7	27%
Application Hosting	9	35%
Facilities Management	5	19%
Full Outsourcing	4	15%
**Other	1	4%
**Co-branded prepaid payment service*		
Other Services		
Business Consultancy	9	17%
IT Security Services	9	17%
Support Management	10	19%
Contract Resources (body-shopping)	5	8%
Training	11	21%
Networking/HW Configuration Services	9	17%

Source: Bonello (2006).

Industry Constraints and Factors Affecting Growth

In this section I will highlight some of the factors that have contributed to the indigenous firms' initial success, and then consider others that—if not directly responsible for the software industry's slow growth—have worked against and disadvantaged Maltese software firms. I will start with the former.

Contributing Factors

There is no doubt that part of the reason for the initial success of many of the top indigenous companies stems from the lack of any competition from foreign software companies, which had no presence in Malta in the 1980s and early 1990s when a number of the indigenous firms were formed. Although the market was not protected as such by policies that specifically aimed at discouraging foreign competition, the early situation was akin to a protected market. At that time, IT in Malta was still in its infancy with many businesses still not having computerised. There was thus much scope for the new software firms to do business by exploiting the hitherto untapped local market. The advent of the PC and the fall in price of computer hardware led to an increase in computer installations that translated to more business for the software companies.

Government procurement—although initially not a policy specifically adopted to boost the software industry, as in China's case, for example—was another stimulus for growth. A handful of start-up companies strengthened their position when they were capable of winning government contracts by tendering. Megabyte's first substantial government contract won in 1989 and involving the computerisation of the public lotto system is a point in case. This project provided an opportunity for the company to expand its workforce and simultaneously use some of the project contract funds for research and development, building on its expertise. Often, one government contract would lead to another as when, shortly afterward, Megabyte was entrusted with another government project, that involving the national identity card system.

The overhaul of the telecommunications system by the Maltese government in the 1990s also opened up opportunities for aspiring software companies (again, as happened in Ireland in the 1980s and in Brazil and China in the 1990s) (Sands, 2005: p. 50).[160] The number of

---

[160] Brazil has a highly networked economy with a sound telecommunications infrastructure that has enabled a number of software companies to specialise in e-commerce. See, for example, Behrens (2005).

Internet Service Providers (ISPs) and companies offering web services shot up in this period. With a good telecommunications infrastructure in place, companies could now be in direct contact with their clients and transact their business online, and those seeking to expand their line of business could also promote their products and services on the web. For example, a recent NSO "ICT-Usage of Enterprises Survey" has revealed that in 2003 as many as 90% of the enterprises surveyed marketed their products on their own website (although other facilities made available on the website such as access to product catalogues and providing after sales support rank much lower) (NSO, 2006, Table 1.14: p. 9 and Table 2.13: p. 31). Now, although designing and launching one's own website can be a relatively trivial task, professionally looking, highly-interactive and intelligent-based websites require more than just a basic knowledge of web design, particularly if this entails large database access involving security features. Procurement thus became important, evident from the relatively high number of new entrants in the late 1990s specialising in web design and hosting. Mobile telephony and its associated technology also created opportunities for new software firms. While not a prerequisite for software growth, the new telecommunications infrastructure has undoubtedly been conducive to the growth of the IT industry. Companies like Alert Communications, which specialise in multimedia, e-commerce systems and other interactive marketing tools, and have recently won contracts worth over a million Euros (see later) in addition to several quality awards, would not have come this far were it not for the robust telecommunications system. It is also doubtful if companies like Ixaris and RS2, both of which specialise in the development of electronic card payment and transaction systems, would have set up a base in Malta. Government's e-vision initiative has also been a contributing factor in furthering the opportunities for software firms.

Traditionally, local companies have tended to concentrate their effort in the local arena, producing software tailor-made for local customers' needs, and only later ventured into the global marketplace, if at all. The Internet has changed a lot of that, partly (if not chiefly) because a company with its own web page has immediate global presence, lessening some of the problems associated with both marketing and distribution. Thus, whereas the older firms had practically no choice but to tackle the local market, newer firms (some of them at least) have been more adventurous and ambitious in attempting to immediately target the open global market. One of Malta Enterprise's roles has been to provide new firms access to contacts abroad. Some of these new entrants have reportedly quoted Malta Enterprise as being instrumental in their initial success. The recently set up Business Incubation Facility at Kordin (operated by this same agency) also appears to be bearing fruit. Through it, entrepreneurial start-ups are provided with the necessary economic development tools (e.g., business premises at cheap rates, a collaborative environment, ready access to advice and business development services, and educational and networking opportunities) to enable them to grow successfully.

Finally, Malta's accession to the EU in 2004 — whilst bringing with it new challenges to local industry — has also now made it possible for firms, particularly SMEs, to benefit from the many EU initiatives such as bilateral trade treaties (concluded by the EU with the rest of the global market) and access to funding and the means to participate in EU funded research projects. Some companies, for example Icon Studios, have already made use of these funds: this company's SNAP system — a .NET web application providing advanced tools for building websites and networked applications — was partly sponsored by the European Regional Development Fund (ERDF) Grant Scheme for Enterprise Structural Funds Programme for Malta 2004-2006. Of course, in order for these benefits to be reaped to their fullest, government should play a proactive role in supporting SMEs by adopting the ten key areas of the European Charter for Small Enterprise.[161] The Malta Federation of Industries (FOI) has often stated that small firms cannot work in isolation and should receive governments backing where possible.[162] The tapping of EU

---

[161] These include: Education and Training for Entrepreneurship; Cheaper and faster start-up; Better Legislation and Regulation; Availability of skills; Improving online access; Getting more out of the Single Market; Taxation and financial matters; Strengthening the technological capacity of small enterprises; Making use of successful e-business models and developing top-class small business support; and Developing stronger, more effective representation of small enterprises' interests in the Union and national level. See http://ec.europa.eu/enterprise/enterprise_policy/ charter/index_en.htm.

[162] See, for example, *Industry Today* (No. 46, September 2001; and No. 54, September 2004).

opportunities therefore needs to be facilitated if the industry is to attain comparative advantage.

Constraints

In discussing India's software industry, Heeks (1996: p. 272) identified four main constraints that the Indian software industry experienced:

- access to finance and skills
- low level of research and development
- access to markets and information about markets
- low demand and high piracy in domestic market

Although the above constraints referred specifically to the Indian software industry, they have also been the same kind of constraints experienced elsewhere.

In Malta, these constraints were experienced just as strongly by local companies, particularly in the early years of their operation. Additionally, other factors may have retarded the development of software in Malta, including the very small domestic market, and the lack (in the early years) of an informatics or computer industry policy.[163]

As Heeks (1996: p. 273) notes, working capital finances software development, market entry and maintenance work (in the form of labour costs).   Finance is particularly important to software companies, which have a lot of capital invested in incomplete projects. If financial institutions are unwilling to provide the necessary financial support, then these companies will find it difficult to operate. New entrants, in particular, will need financial aid to help them start up; lack of financial incentives may well put off prospective companies, therefore missing opportunities for new businesses.

Securing a loan or obtaining a significant overdraft has traditionally proved difficult in Malta, although in recent years this has become somewhat easier, with the main banks now regularly advertising "soft loan" schemes for start-up companies.   Brincat (2001a) has reported, for example, that as recently as 2001 start-ups

---

[163] For a list of constraints that typically retard the development of a software industry, see UNIDO (1993: pp. 135-136, 166-167).

were still finding it difficult to obtain bank loans because of lack of security. Government incentives for small business enterprises in general have also been minimal: local software firms have not been treated any differently, i.e., they have not been granted special status or incentives. Again, however, government aid has tended to improve over the years. In 2004 a national agency called Malta Enterprise was set up specifically to promote trade, investment and industrial development, and to help new companies. This agency caters for all types of companies but, owing to the importance now attached to the ICT sector, it also has an ICT section geared at supporting computer firms.[164]

Marketing and market size play an important role in the success or otherwise of a new product, and for companies operating in a small country like Malta they are crucial. Reference has already been made to the large number of small firms operating in Malta. This situation, of course, is not confined only to the computer or software industry but also to other types of businesses (see, for example, Bonnici, 2000); nor is it unique to Malta. Studies of the software industries of other countries show that a number of countries (e.g. Romania, Ireland, Scotland, and China) also have many "micro-enterprises" (Heeks & Grundey, 2004: p. 332; and McFall, et al., 2006: p. 3). In the case of Malta, the fragmented market and lack of economies of scale are the result of a micro local market and weak exposure to foreign contract work. Software companies (and, indeed, other SMEs) therefore need to consolidate their position through a combination of strategic vision, better management, higher standards and increased efficiency. Again, up to quite recently, incentives and the stimuli needed to help the small enterprises to realise this vision were practically non-existent.

As well as the small size, the immaturity of the business market makes it difficult for Maltese software firms to develop new products or achieve scale economies. After the government, the largest domestic customers for software in Malta are the state-owned enterprises, most of which have now been privatised. Additionally, not all of them choose to go for solutions offered by local software

---

[164] Malta Enterprise now assumes the roles previously held by IPSE (Institute for the Promotion of Small Enterprises), the MDC (Malta Development Corporation), and METCO (Malta External Trade Corporation). See the Malta Enterprise website at *http://www.maltaenterprise.com.*

firms: for example, Malta Freeport's state-of-the-art, real-time, NAVIS computer system is a sophisticated, ready-made imported system customised to some extent (Freeport Terminal (Malta) plc., 1999). As for the large private companies, whilst some have tended to outsource software to indigenous firms, others—probably the majority—have preferred to develop software internally. The reason for this may stem from a traditional lack of belief in outsourcing, or it could be technical, but it is also likely that Maltese users have not matured as much in other countries, where ERP (enterprise resource planning) became dominant in the 1990s.

Apart from the problem of scale economies, Malta's small size negatively affects the software industry in other ways. For example, unlike those countries where the native language is not English, Maltese software companies do not enjoy what has been termed a continuing "natural protection" arising from the nation's language, for while there is sometimes a need to configure software for the native Maltese language this requirement is only very limited: not only is Malta small, but English is widely understood.

A second example is that of legacy systems. Again, owing to the small market few companies have had big computer installation typical of mainframe (or large miniframe) systems, and therefore the opportunities to specialise in providing services for legacy systems are extremely limited. In fact, the one Maltese company that offers such a service is Philip Toledo Ltd, the oldest IT provider and systems house on the Island.

An injustice local software (and other) firms faced for many years when competing with foreign firms operating locally is the fiscal incentives foreign firms enjoyed which Maltese-owned companies did not. In order to attract foreign investment, the Industrial Development Act of 1988, for example, granted all foreign companies setting up a base in Malta and meeting certain criteria a ten-year tax holiday in which no tax was paid on any profits arising during ten consecutive years of operation (Fenech, 2002). This placed local companies—which typically had to contribute 35% of their eligible profits to the Inland Revenue—at a gross disadvantage. Partly (but not exclusively) for this reason this act was significantly revised and broadened in 2001 and renamed the Business Promotion Act. Under this new act, no distinction is made between foreign-owned companies and Maltese firms, and the export-linked incentives for foreign firms have been removed, thus placing Maltese firms at a level playing field.[165]

The Business Promotion Act 2001 classifies ICT as a priority sector and accordingly includes a number of incentives ICT companies can benefit from. They include: reduced rates of income tax (as low as 5%) on company profits; tax credits of up to 65% on expenditure on investment of a capital nature; competitive rates of rent for company premises; low interest loan financing; loan guarantees; and financial assistance for training of employees (e.g. up to 80% of the costs involved).[166]

Manpower, Education and Training

Up to 1987 when the University of Malta (the only university on the Island) began offering information systems (and, later, computer science and computer engineering) diploma and degree courses, the technical capability of programmers and systems analysts were acquired mainly through knowledge transfer and experience, by following long-distance courses, or by attending overseas institutions. Entities like the government's former Swatar computer centre and the Management Systems Unit (MSU) were instrumental in this respect, although the MSU was criticised for the way it handled knowledge transfer (see Chapter 6). The Malta Information Technology and Training Services (MITTS) also offered a number of computer-related courses at various levels, some specifically aimed at management and others more suited to programmers. By the turn of the millennium the NCC international diploma course run by MITTS had become a very popular course,[167] particularly as it was offered on a part-time (in addition to full-time), evening basis, but partly also because the

---

[165] Another reason for removing the export-linked incentives (and revising the 1988 Act) was to make the new Act more "EU-friendly", since preferential treatment towards export-oriented companies is considered discriminatory by such organizations as the OECD and the EU. At the time, Malta was also preparing to join the EU.

[166] See also Malta Enterprise (2006b) for the salient points of the Business Promotion Act.

[167] NCC is the UK's National Computing Centre, the leading UK corporate IT body set up in 1966. See: http://www.ncc.co.uk.

Employment and Training Corporation (ETC) was offering 'traineeships', as it called them, for those interested in following this course (see Figure 7.2).

Table 7.6 lists the major bodies that have organized computer programming and systems analysis courses over the years and prior to 1996 when computer studies was introduced as a subject in secondary schools. Of these, the University remains the primary institution offering the most comprehensive (both in depth and breadth of the subjects offered) range of IT-related courses. It was also the first on the Island to offer courses leading to qualifications of professional bodies such as the British Computer Society (BCS) and the Institute of Data Processing and Management (IDPM).[168] More recently, the new Malta College of Arts, Science and Technology (MCAST) has also been actively engaged in tailoring certificate and diploma courses to suit industry's needs, especially in the field of ICT.

It is to be noted that a number of private training centres (as well as other educational institutions) have played a crucial role in providing computer education, particularly when it comes to programming and the use of software applications. These private centres have often specialised in key areas of training, usually by type of product. Thus, for example, if one wanted to specifically obtain first-hand experience in the use of Oracle products and database programming, a relatively short but intensive course at one of these private training centres was likely to prove more beneficial than perhaps the more general (and probably more theoretical) module offered by the University as part of an undergraduate course. Also,

---

[168] Interestingly, most of these courses' earlier lecturers were part-timers, software and management professionals working for private software firms.

Diploma in Computer Studies

Malta Information Technology and Training Services Limited and the Employment and Training Corporation are pleased to announce that an agreement has been reached with the National Computing Centre of the United Kingdom to hold specialised Diploma and Higher Diploma courses in Computer studies which will lead to international qualifications recognised by the National Computer Centre (NCC).

International Diploma in Computer Studies
(Full / Part time)

• Basic Computing Principles • Computer Programming • Modelling for Computing with Mathematics • Human Communications & Information Systems • Business Systems Development • Computerised Accounting • Practical Project

Entry Requirements:

Δ 16 years of age or over
Δ Four 'O' levels including
English & Mathematics
Δ A pass in the NCC entry Tests

International Higher Diploma in Computer Studies
(Part time)

• The Network Environment • System Analysis and Design • The Software Environment • Project Management •Business Management •Object Oriented Techniques • Practical Project

Entry Requirements:

Δ Entry Requirements for Diploma
PLUS
Δ NCC Diploma or equivalent

Details of the syllabus together with more information can be viewed on
http://www.mitts.net/ncc/

ETC is offering a part-sponsorship to the best rated 30 Maltese applicants for the Diploma course and to the best rated 15 Maltese applicants for the Higher Diploma course.

Persons interested in enrolling in one of the above-mentioned courses may complete an application form at the ETC Job Centre in Valletta or at the ETC Information Centre in Victoria, Gozo by not later than *Friday 14th August 1998*. Envelopes should be marked NCC/98.

This program may fall (depending on individual circumstances) under the Mid-Med bank YES scheme. Contact your nearest Branch for more information about obtaining a soft loan to cover the course expense.

MISSION STATEMENT
To provide and ensure an equitable access to training programmes and employment services to contribute towards the social and economic development of the community.

General Member of

Figure 7.2
A 1998 advert by the Employment and Training Corporation for the NCC Diploma and Higher Diploma in Computer Studies. These diploma courses were initially offered by the Malta Information Technology and Training Services and later by the Swatar Training Centre.

Source: *The Times* (11 August 1998: p. 37)

some of these centres and a number of private and church schools were instrumental in being among the first educational institutions to offer computer studies at secondary and post-secondary level in the 1980s at a time when computer studies as a subject was far from having been made compulsory in schools. Finally, apart from the Engineering Faculty of the University, the former Fellenberg Institute and the former neighbouring Technical Institute (now both incorporated into MCAST) were among the first to specialise in electronics and microprocessor-based courses (e.g. City and Guilds International Certificate and Higher Technicians Diploma). Between them, they produced, yearly, about twenty or so high-calibre graduates for the IT hardware industry.

TABLE 7.6
Major Educational Institutions and Training Centres offering IT-related courses, pre 1996

Name of Institution	Course(s) Offered	Year Introduced*
State, Post Secondary:		
Fellenberg School of Electronics	Microcomputer Technology	1980
G. F. Abela Junior College	I.T.; Computing	1992
Mikiel-Ang Sapiano Technical Inst.	Microcomputer Technology	1992
University of Malta	I.T.; Computer Science; Computer Engineering; Information Systems	1987
Private and Church Schools:		
De La Salle College	Computer Studies	1983
St. Aloysius's College	Computer Studies	1982
St. Edward's College	Computer Studies	1983
Stella Maris College	Computer Studies	1981
The Archbishop's Seminary	Computer Studies	1987
Training Centres:		
Compex Training Centre	I.T. awareness; Programming	1986
Datatech Computer Centre	I.T. awareness; Programming	1984
Delcomputer Services Ltd	I.T. awareness; Programming	1984
Malta University Services	Programming; Management	1987
Office Electronics Ltd	Programming	1983
Philip Toledo Ltd	Programming; Management	1982
Shireburn Ltd	Programming; Management	1984

* For institutions where a number of courses are now available, the year refers to that when the first of these courses was offered.
Source: Compiled by author from various sources including e-mail correspondence, the local *Informatics* magazine, and annual reports.

Student Numbers

Although on the increase, the output of ICT graduates from recognised academic and vocational institutes appears to be progressing at a slower rate than government officials have been hoping for, and the gap between e-skills supply and demand has been a major concern for the government, which is striving to develop Malta into a high-tech information centre (*Information Society Review*, 2006). In this vein, the Maltese government has, in the last few years, directed its efforts to enhance the ICT skills base via the establishment of specialised IT Training Academies. These academies provide the opportunity for anyone with basic IT skills to attain industry specific ICT certification. This initiative, started in 2002 and called "myPotential", involved partnership agreement between the IT Ministry and industry players like Cisco Systems, Microsoft, and Oracle to offer a number of certified courses. Delivery of these courses is through accredited bodies that include the University of Malta, MCAST, Swatar Training Centre (STC) and the ETC. In addition, new tax schemes aimed at funding advanced specialist studies in science and engineering have also been introduced. These incentives essentially pay back for money spent by employers to train their staff, or that paid by individuals pursuing post-graduate studies. Austin Gatt, the Minister once responsible for Investment, Industry and Information Technology, believes that 'if human capital is the key to a successful ICT future for Malta, then [as a result of these initiatives] government is many steps closer to finding it' (*Information Society Review*, 2005).

Table 7.7 lists the number of students that have graduated in IT-related courses from the University of Malta and from MCAST in the period 1997-2007. Since the "new" MCAST came into being in 2002, the first group of HND graduates was that for 2005, hence only statistics for two years are shown for MCAST courses.

One notes that whilst the number of B.Eng. (Hons.) graduates has remained roughly the same, there has been a steady increase in the number of University graduates of the other (B.Sc.) courses. It must be remembered, however, that the University student population has increased significantly in this same period, so that the percentage increase of University IT graduates needs also to be seen in context of the total student population. Thus, in 1997, the student population was 5800 and IT graduates amounted to 71, or 1.2% of the student population; in 2007 student population stood at 9600 and the number of IT graduates were 187, or 1.9% of the student population. Thus, the real increase in IT graduates relative to the student population has been of the order of 60% over a ten-year period, corresponding to a mean annual growth rate of 6%.

TABLE 7.7
IT Graduates, 1997-2007

(a) University of Malta

Course	Year										
	1997	1998	1999	2000	2001	2002	2003	2004	2005	2006	2007
B.Eng.	1	-	-	-	-	-	-	-	-	-	-
B.Eng. (Hons.)	54	40	54	51	48	64	48	54	57	90	76
B.Sc. (Business & Comp.)	16	14	19	14	19	21	29	36	59	37	46
B.Sc. (Hons.) IT	-	1	27	39	26	28	30	42	43	32	46
B.Sc. IT	-	-	3	5	4	3	-	4	7	1	2
MBA (e-Business)	-	-	-	-	-	-	-	28	11	-	17
Total	*71*	*55*	*103*	*109*	*97*	*116*	*107*	*164*	*177*	*160*	*187*

(b) Malta College of Arts Science and Technology

Course	Year										
	1997	1998	1999	2000	2001	2002	2003	2004	2005	2006	2007
HND (Software Dev.)	-	-	-	-	-	-	-	-	17	20	14
HND (Systems Support)	-	-	-	-	-	-	-	-	19	15	24
Total									*36*	*35*	*38*

Source: University of Malta; MCAST

The figures shown in Table 7.7 far from tell the whole story about tertiary IT education in Malta since other (relatively new) educational institutions have, in this same period, offered a number of degree or degree equivalent courses in IT. Many vocational courses at roughly the HND level have also become common in the last five to ten years, and a number of training centres are now affiliated to foreign universities and are able to offer the foreign universities' courses locally. In addition, a number of Maltese regularly follow graduate courses abroad. This means that for the last few years, the total number of persons who have graduated in IT has been much higher than the counts shown in Table 7.7, which only include UOM and MCAST graduates. For comparison purposes, Table 7.8 lists the number of IT graduates for selected countries. The value quoted for Malta is a minimum count: it could well be higher by a factor of fifty percent, if not more.

TABLE 7.8
IT graduates as percentage of total employment for selected countries

Country	Working Population (in million)*	IT Graduates**	Percentage
Brazil	83.34	18,000 [2000]	0.02
China	778.50	89,000 [2002]	0.01
Germany	40.57	5,000 [2000]	0.01
India	480.00	300,000 [2002]	0.06
Ireland	1.73	8,000 [2003]	0.46
Israel	2.99	10,000 [1999]	0.33
UK	29.81	22,000 [2000]	0.07
US	150.99	53,000 [2000]	0.04
Malta	0.14	>163 [2004]	> 0.12

*Figures are for 2004
**Figures are for the year indicated in square brackets
Source: Working population figures are from World Bank; others were compiled by author from various sources, including Arora & Gambaderlla (2005), and Commander (2005).

Business Linkages, Offshoring and Outsourcing

Malta's strategic geographical position in the middle of the Mediterranean combined with a mild, sunny, climate are natural advantages that have attracted a number of foreign companies to either locate in Malta or start joint ventures with Maltese companies. More important reasons for choosing Malta include the Island's historical ties and trade relations with North Africa and the Middle

East, a stable political environment, the widely spoken English language, a legal framework that is very much based on the European system, and—more recently—a supply of suitably qualified manpower. As already noted, the advanced telecommunication system now makes it possible for all types of businesses to make heavy use of this infrastructure. The technology penetration rate (Internet use, etc.) is high, and telecommunications access costs are now beginning to be comparable to those of many advanced European countries.[169] It has also been pointed out that this robust infrastructure and Malta's small size make the Island an ideal test-bed for new projects such as e-commerce and applications involving secure data transfer.

A frequently quoted reason for outsourcing and offshore work is low wages in countries where offshoring and outsourcing is done. Although companies contemplating of offshore outsourcing are often cautioned to weigh any potential benefits carefully because of hidden costs, a change of government policy, or a rapid upward trend in the outsourcing country's economy that could result in a substantial increase in local personal income, it is rarely the case that companies have had to give up offshore work. As regards Malta, low income has always been a main factor in attracting foreign investors, and it seems likely that this will continue to be the prime motive. Although salaries in Malta have consistently increased from about the late 1980s onwards after a long period of wage freeze, the increases have often been marginal, rarely exceeding three percent per annum of average yearly salaries. While salary increases in IT-related jobs have generally tended to be slightly higher than in other sectors, the present salary scales are still far behind developed American or European states, but at the same time higher than those in a number of other countries including China, India, the Philippines and Russia to name a few. Table 7.9 highlights the typical remuneration earned by IT personnel in Malta in 2005. Assuming that a typical systems

---

[169] See the NSO's *News Release* dated 16 February 2007 at *http://nso.gov.mt/statdoc/document_file.aspx?id=1935*; and the World Economic Forum's *Global Information Technology Report 2006-2007* at *http://www.weforum.org/en/initiatives/gcp/Global%20Information%20Technolog y%20Report/index.htm*. According to this report, Malta's ranking in "Network Readiness" is 27 out of 122 (countries). Country details may be found at *www.insead.edu/v1/gitr/wef/main/analysis/showcountrydetails.cfm*.

analyst earns €27,000 (= c. US$35,000) then the average hourly rate based on a 37-hour week works out at about €13 (= c. US$17). For comparison, two tables are presented which give the wages of software professionals for selected countries (Tables 7.10(a) and 7.10(b)). These tables are given only as a rough indication of wage

TABLE 7.9
Typical IT Salary Scales for Malta for 2005*

Software/IT Manager	27,800 – 42,000	(*US$ 36,026 – 54,428*)
Systems Analyst	18,600 – 34,750	(*US$ 24,104 – 45,032*)
Senior Programmer	18,600 – 27,800	(*US$ 24,104 – 36,026*)
Programmer	9,300 – 16,300	(*US$ 12,052 – 21,123*)
Technician	11,600 – 20,900	(*US$ 15,032 – 27,084*)

*All figures in Euros.
Source: *ICT Malta*, Malta Enterprise, 2006.

TABLE 7.10(a)
Annual salaries for software professionals, 2001-2004*

UK	77,000
USA	63,000
Australia	62,000
Japan	44,000
Singapore	43,000
Israel	40,000
Ireland	29,000
Romania	23,000
Brazil	20,000
India	7,000
Mexico	7,000
China	7,000

*All figures are in US dollars and rounded to the nearest thousand.
Source: After Carmel and Tjia (2005: p.32).

differentials since, as pointed out by Carmel and Tjia, wage data need to be treated carefully and can vary by as much as 50% (Carmel & Tjia, 2005: p. 32). For example, Siemens' estimates of the hourly labour costs for software engineers for a number of countries may well include benefits, therefore inflating the actual basic salaries. Additionally, those given in Table 7.10(a) cover various years ranging from 2001 to 2004, so that absolute comparisons cannot be made with confidence.

TABLE 5.10(b)
Siemens' Estimates of the Average Labour costs per Hour for Software Engineers in 2001

Germany	€ 56.5	(US$ 73.2)
USA	€ 52.1	(US$ 67.5)
Austria	€ 41.9	(US$ 54.3)
UK	€ 30.4	(US$ 39.4)
Hungary	€ 28.9	(US$ 37.4)
Singapore	€ 26.9	(US$ 34.9)
Israel	€ 24.8	(US$ 32.1)
Argentina	€ 21.7	(US$ 28.1)
Brazil	€ 15.5	(US$ 20.1)
Romania	€ 13.0	(US$ 16.8)
India	€ 6.8	(US$ 8.8)

Source: *Intereconomics*, March/April 2005, p. 108.

In Malta, offshoring in general has been going on for many years but it is only in the past decade or so that international software companies have used Malta as an offshore site. The reasons why software companies have chosen to do business in Malta have already been noted. Of these, human capital remains an important attraction: local talent is high, Maltese employees are considered to be hard working and flexible, and IT graduates have been on the increase. Malta's leading foreign software company, Crimsonwing—which in October 2007 decided to go for a listing on the Malta Stock Exchange because of rapid growth—has always maintained that a key to its success has been its predominantly Maltese staff: 'a young-at-heart, dynamic and professional workforce with a wealth of experience'.[170]

[170] "Crimsonwing to go for local listing", *The Malta Independent on Sunday*, 21 October 2007, p. 46. See also "Q & A with David Walsh", *Information Society Review*, November 2005.

A similar sentiment has been stated by Anvil Software, another prominent global company, which remarked that a motivation for choosing to have a subsidiary base in Malta was 'a rich team of technical talent coupled with the typical hardworking Maltese ethic and standard of education'.[171] Anvil is also proud to pronounce that its staff retention rate is high.

Outsourcing work for foreign clients has also become part of the business of some local software firms. Unfortunately, Malta is small and therefore economies of scale are difficult to achieve. Thus, even if Maltese companies have been successful locally, the domestic market is much too limited to enable them to expand. Maltese firms have lately therefore either: (i) collaborated with foreign firms to tap the overseas market; or (ii) outsourced work for foreign clients. Strategic partnership with a foreign firm can give local companies the opportunity to enter into the export of software development and at the same time show the local company's full potential, as was the case with Makeezi—a Maltese firm specialising in RAD deployment using Magic Software eDevelopment—which partnered with a UK firm to develop a learner management and administration software for use in sixth form colleges in the UK.

Outsourcing directly to foreign clients provides essentially the same opportunities, namely, exposure and growth. In October 2007, for example, Alert Communications won two foreign contracts: a project involving online gaming for a German firm and worth over a million Euros, and another twelve-month outsourcing contract to develop a content management system for a Milan-based IT company. As a result of these contracts, the company—which started up in 1998 practically from nothing and now (2008) already employs close to 30 people—is again seeking to expand its business by recruiting dozens of employees that will be needed to cope with the extra work.

Over the years, in addition to diversifying in their product or service offerings, companies have also sought to expand by engaging in mergers, the prime reason being the integration of different capabilities or technologies. Mergers need not necessarily involve foreign firms: for example, two notable companies, Megabyte and the former BDS (Apple's former sole representatives) have long merged

[171] "Malta – A Good Place to do Business", *The Commercial Courier*, August-September, 2006, p. 38.

with larger, well-established local firms as a means of strengthening their positions. Following these mergers, both companies experienced rapid growth.

Finally, accessing and using higher skill levels in developing countries and emerging economies has been one of the more recent trends of, and fundamental approaches to, offshoring. The establishment of research centres in multiple countries—because of global competition in computer research that has resulted from the higher skill levels worldwide—is something multinational companies are now addressing (see, for example, Aspray, et al., 2006: p. 3). In recent years global industry players such as IBM, HP, Oracle, Cisco and Microsoft have shown interest in doing business in Malta. Although they do not have research facilities in Malta as yet, it is conceivable that some of these companies will eventually set up an R&D base there. Presently their main role has been to form strategic alliances with leading local ICT firms. These alliances can benefit all parties involved: thus, in 2001, Enemalta—Malta's government owned and operated electricity authority—and Microsoft Eastern Mediterranean, together with Computer Solutions who are Microsoft technology partners signed an agreement which will enable Enemalta to standardise all its IT requirements on a single and unified Microsoft platform. Hailed as one of the largest Enterprise-scale agreements of its kind in Malta (it involved about five hundred networked PCs), the move was part of Enemalta's overall business strategy to identify the right technological framework in order to expand its operations.

Apart from opportunities such as the aforementioned example, these multinational companies are also heavily involved in training support. As part of an agreement with the Maltese government, these multinationals are now working closely with government departments on various projects, including e-learning, the training of post-secondary and tertiary level students and an e-payment gateway. A particular initiative has been the sponsorship by these MNCs to set up Community Technology and Learning Centres aimed at providing local personnel with the necessary tools and training to enhance their ICT skills. These Centres also offer programmes such as HP's Micro Enterprise Acceleration Programme (MAP) with a curriculum that focuses on helping micro-entrepreneurs gain awareness and comfort in the use of ICT and its use to improve efficiency and growth.

Conclusion

The Maltese software industry constitutes perhaps the first example of a successful high-tech indigenous industry in Malta. Tracing its roots to the mid-1980s, the industry grew steadily since then, and now is a sizeable employer of manufacturing and services. Critical mass may have been achieved in the early 2000s or more recently, but it is conceivable that the industry will continue to grow further in the coming years. Lack of accurate time-series statistics precludes one from measuring (let alone forecasting) the industry's performance and growth rate; in terms of personnel, the author's estimate is that there was a ten-fold increase in a twenty-year period starting from c. 1985. In 2005, revenue per employee worked out at about €40,000 per annum, and the industry's share of GDP stood at about 1.1%.

The reasons for the industry's expansion have been noted. Important contributing factors include the overhaul of the telecommunications infrastructure, a reasonably good supply of qualified workforce, incentives for attracting foreign firms, a stable political environment and, of course, the demand for software for emergent applications. In absolute terms, the industry is tiny in comparison to that in other countries (owing to Malta's micro size and the limitations of scale economies), but taken as a percentage (e.g., IT graduates or software employees per working population) it compares favourably even with some of the more advanced nations.

In terms of industry structure and characteristics, Malta's software industry probably comes closer to that of Ireland (and possibly also Scotland) than any other country. That said, some differences can be identified: for example, whereas in Ireland the indigenous industry developed side by side with multinationals and the latter were very important for the indigenous industry's development there, in Malta the indigenous industry essentially developed independently, foreign companies having appeared on the scene well after the industry had been born. There are also interesting contrasts with other countries. For example, whereas the Brazilian's protectionist policy of the early Brazilian government regime in the 1980s worked in favour of the industry's growth, the Maltese government's market reserve policy and protectionism in roughly that same period had the opposite effect: a rather negative attitude towards computers coupled with restrictions on import quotas and the requirement of a licence for every imported computer were an impediment to growth. By comparison, the liberalisation process begun in the early 1990s had a positive effect. Malta's endeavours in joining the Common Market also very likely helped push forward the IT business and proved to be conducive to the software industry.

Government's latest initiative in trying to place Malta on the international ICT map has been the widely publicised Smart City project in collaboration with Tecom Investments of Dubai. Some members of the opposition party have occasionally criticised this project as no more than a grotesque construction industry exercise disguised under the umbrella of ICT. However, most have generally welcomed it. At the same time, concerns about the scale of the project have raised fears of a possible brain drain whereby highly qualified and experienced professionals would be lured away from local firms to their bigger multinational counterparts, simultaneously pushing up salaries and further disadvantaging small indigenous firms. Some have indeed argued that foreign workers would also be required as there is no way that sufficient local skilled personnel will be trained in time for the project's initial operating years.

Finally, whilst it is too early to assess which of the main export policy approaches have been, or are being, followed, it appears that the focus so far has been primarily on "generic" and "IT-enabled" services.[172] Both of these are typically easier to target than software products or attracting foreign R&D activities, and a number of emerging economies (such as the Philippines and Sri Lanka) have focused their attention on providing generic services and even migrated away for software to concentrate on IT-enabled services. Currently, Malta is probably experimenting with all possible strategies. The opening of a number of call centres in recent years and the increase in the IT consultancy field (including those of accountancy and law), however, leaves no doubt as to the importance attached to the easier options.

---

[172] Carmel and Tjia (2005: pp. 200-207) have identified four main policy decisions (or 'foci', as they call them) that governments can opt for: (i) Generic IT services; (ii) Attracting foreign R&D; (iii) Software products; (iv) IT-enabled services. Reasons why developing nations should invest in building a software export industry are also given in this text.

Part V

Telecommunications

Part V
Telecommunications

The history of telecommunications in Malta may be divided into three periods or "phases":

(i)   a long period when the traditional telegraph and telephone networks were established and expanded, from about 1860 to 1974, and during which time telecommunications was under foreign hands;

(ii)   a period when telecommunications was nationalised and continued to enjoy a monopoly, this time under local (Maltese) government. This covers the period from 1975 to 1996;

(iii)   a recent period of telecommunications liberalisation and privatisation, from 1997 onwards.

Since this study treats the development of computing and information technology in Malta, and since applications involving data communications have only matured in the last two to three decades, this part of the book is primarily devoted to the last two phases (discussed in Chapters 9 and 10). They cover a period when the telecommunications industry—not only domestically but globally— underwent rapid technological, structural and organizational change, when the evolution of data communications and computer networks, as well as market forces and the global economy were dictating the way the telecommunications sector would evolve.

Following roughly the above chronological periods, Part V therefore logically consists of three chapters. Chapter 8, included for completeness but also to put the next two related chapters into context, is a brief history of telecommunications in Malta from early times. The telegraph, telephone and radio were introduced in Malta under British colonial rule and, as with a number of other countries, the militia played an important role in the use and spread of these early forms of communication. The following chapter (Chapter 9) deals primarily with the expansion of the telecommunications sector under the former national monopoly of Telemalta Corporation. The importance of the telecommunications industry was recognised by the Maltese government from the 1970s—coinciding with Telemalta's creation—when a substantial sum (for those times) of twelve million Maltese pounds (c. US$32 m.) was budgeted for this sector, to be spent over a seven-year period. This section discusses briefly government's long-term plan in this area, and the technical and financial aid that was sought from the International Telecommunications Union (ITU), highlighting its modest success in obtaining the required help that was much needed. The period corresponding to the early to late 1990s is also examined in some detail because in this time events happened that directly affected, and indeed shaped, the evolution of ICT in Malta: this period, for example, saw the first independent, private cable television company set up in Malta and competing directly with Telemalta; the creation of a handful of internet service providers (ISPs); the beginning of mobile telephony; and the implementation of the Malta Government Network (MAGNET) which physically involved the laying of a fibre optic backbone and the networking of thousands of computers. Finally, Chapter 10 treats liberalisation and regulatory reform, how, in line with EU directives as well as in common with many other European countries, Malta first partly privitised the national telecommunications provider and then went on to take measures that eventually led to full liberalisation.

8

Early Telegraphy, Telephony, and Radio

The Electric Telegraph

Excluding the early forms of communication not utilizing electricity, telecommunications in Malta goes back to the late 1850s and early 1860s when the first experiments involving the electric telegraph were conducted locally. As a key fortress, Malta—then under British colonial rule—was accorded operational priority in the installation of the telegraph: in November 1859, when the first telegraph station at numbers 6-7 Marsamscetto Road, Valletta, was established by the Mediterranean Extension Telegraph Company, a proposal for the connection of the various Forts with the Palace (also in Valletta) was made by the then Governor of Malta, John Gaspart Le Marchant, to the Duke of Newcastle in England, Henry Pelham-Clinton, who was then Secretary of State for the Colonies (*Despatch to the Secretary of State*, 1859).[173] Approval for this request came within months and work began in earnest in the summer of 1860. By the following year, each Fort and defensive work had been directly linked to the Commander in Chief's headquarters at the Palace in Valletta (Samut-Tagliaferro, 1979). The use of the telegraph continued well into the middle of the twentieth century by which time the telephone started taking over.

---

[173] See also Samut-Tagliaferro (1979), which gives a brief introduction to the early British Military Communications on Malta and Gozo.

Figure 8.1
The first telegraph station in Malta at 6-7 Marsamcetto Road,
Valletta.
Source: http://atlantic-cable.com/CableCos/CandW/Eastern/Malta/index.htm.
Photo by R. Ellis.

The installation of the overhead telegraph cables proceeded roughly
in parallel with the laying of the submarine cables, the first of which
were completed in 1857 and connected Malta to Sardinia and Corfu
(*Despatch to the Secretary of State*, 1857). These cables—whose cores
were supplied by the Gutta Percha Company—were laid by the
Mediterranean Extension Telegraph Company, John Watkin Brett's

firm that would later be incorporated as part of the British company Cable and Wireless (Glover, 2005). Since a link between Cagliari (in Sardinia) and the UK had already been established, the Malta-Sardinia link enabled Malta to communicate telegraphically with London for the first time and simultaneously connect London to Corfu via Malta. Another important milestone in the early history of long distance telecommunications involving Malta occurred between 1868 and 1870. In 1868 the first direct cable from Malta to Alexandria was completed after John Pender formed his first telegraphic company, the Anglo-Mediterranean Telegraph Company, specifically for this purpose (Glover, 2005; Bruford, 1954). This cable put Malta on the telegraphic map because it was to become the central link in the system connecting Britain and India (see also Box 8-1). The British newspaper *The Times* of 17 September 1868 reported:[174]

> The progress of the expedition which has left England to lay the Anglo-Mediterranean cable cannot fail to be watched with considerable interest, inasmuch as the completion of the line will duplicate our means of communication with Egypt, and will also constitute a most important adjunct to our agencies for corresponding with our Indian empire.

Like Valletta, the port of Alexandria was another strategic location and served as an important relaying link to the Far East.

In 1869 Pender formed his second telegraphic company, The Falmouth, Gibraltar and Malta Telegraph Company, with the aim of completing the link between Britain and India (also a British colony) by laying a cable from Malta to England via Gibraltar (see also Box 8-1). The original intention was to land the cable at Falmouth (hence the company name), but the high risk of damage from ships' anchors at the busy port led Pender to choose Porthcurno instead. At Malta, cable laying started on 14 May 1870, and within a month the entire stretch of cable connecting Porthcurno, Carcavelos (Portugal), Gibraltar, and St. George's (Malta) had been completed (Glover, 2005).

---

[174] As quoted in Glover (2005).

Box 8-1
Submarine Cables and the Importance of the 1868 Malta-Alexandria and the 1870 Malta-Gibraltar Cables for the British Government.

The first experiments with underwater cables for the transmission of Morse code started around 1842-1844 when people like Samuel Morse and Ezra Cornell in the United States and Charles Wheatstone in the UK tried to send messages via weakly insulated cables laid across rivers, small sea channels, or harbours. These initial attempts often proved unsuccessful for various reasons. For example, the mass of water changed the cable characteristics drastically and the cable needed some very proper insulation material. The instruments used to generate, transmit and receive signals were still rather primitive. Additionally, the theory of electromagnetism was still not well understood: for example, scientists were not sure as to the optimal thickness of wire to use and whether low-voltage signals were preferable to high-voltage signals. However, by 1850 a number of submarine cables several kilometers in length had been successfully laid and made operational. In August 1858 Cyrus Field's (short-lived) transatlantic cable, laid by the young engineer Charles Bright, made news when the first transatlantic telegraph messages were transmitted between Valentia Bay in Ireland and Trinity Bay in Newfoundland. Before long, submarine cabling became a booming business.

In view of its world dominance, Britain had telegraphic connections with many major places around the globe, primarily via land cables. By the late 1860s, for example, it had already established alternative routes to India. However, because these long-distance telegraph cables passed at some point through foreign countries, the British government felt uncomfortable with their continued availability since any of the foreign countries could potentially block transmission in the event of war or times of stress (see, for example, Beauchamp, 2001: p. 167). For this reason, the need was felt to use a route—an all-sea route—that would be controlled solely by Britain (and also operated without the payment of way-leaves to foreign states). Given that in 1868 a deep-sea cable already joined Malta with Alexandria, there remained just one more submarine cable link from Britain to Malta (the latter then a British colony) to complete the all-sea UK-India connection. This resulted in the installation of the Falmouth-Gibraltar-Malta cable spanning a distance of about 3800km. This cable was paid out in just over two months in the spring of 1870.

The Telephone

It is generally held that Edwardo Rosenbusch, the knight who first established electricity in Malta, was also the first to have obtained a magneto type telephone set in 1882 (Bezzina, 1962: p. 49). On 30 March of that year, Rosenbusch was ordered by the government to install the telephone in a few Police Stations (Birgu, Bormla, Isla, Sliema and Valletta), at the Prison, at the Palace in Valletta, at the Customs House, and at Pinto Warehouse. A small telephone exchange was put into service in Valletta. The company Compagnie Générale des Téléphone (a subsidiary of Société Internationale des Téléphones) operated the service. This company later amalgamated with Melita Telephone Company, which had an office in Valletta, at 288 Kingsway (now Republic Street).

On 1 February 1897, the government allowed the public to make use of the telephones at the Police Stations against a payment of 3d (three British pence) for calls between Valletta, Floriana, Bormla, Sliema and Hamrun; and 6d for other places (*Malta Government Gazzette*, 1897; and Attard, 2003: pp. 45-46).[175] Only urgent calls were allowed between five and nine in the evening, during which time calls cost twice as much. According to a government notice that appeared in the Malta Government Gazette of 1 February 1897,[176] the procedure for effecting a call was as follows. Having called in person at the local police station, a person (the "caller") would give the police the details of the recipient with whom he or she (the caller) wished to speak. The police would then phone the station of the town or village where the person to be contacted lived, provided this person's address was close (within reasonable distance and therefore easily reachable) to that of the police station, whence he/she would be contacted in person and asked to call (walk) to the station. The police had to levy a fee, issue a receipt, and make an entry of the call details in a register kept for this purpose. The police continued carrying out this duty until 1915 when the Melita Telephone Exchange company was established.

[175] That same year the public was also permitted to make use of the military electric telegraph (by Government Notice 194 of 26 October) to send messages between Malta and Gozo.
[176] Government Notice No. 30 dated 1 February 1897. See Malta Government Gazzette, No. 3889, 1 February 1897, p. 73.

In 1933 the telephone service, which up till then had been run privately by Melita Telephone, was taken over by government, and a public telephone system started operating (Bezzina, 1962: p. 50; *The Malta Chronicle*, 3 January 1933; and *Reports on the Working of Government Departments for the Financial Year 1933-1934*). About 1000 telephones were in use. Between 1933 and 1936, the exchange capacity and system network was expanded, especially with the setting up of the Sliema exchange. Gozo was served by a small switchboard with a single junction line to Valletta. In 1936, a 14-pair submarine cable was installed which allowed up to 14 voice channels. The entire telephone system needed operator service.

Around 1937 telephone booths started appearing, and a 24-hour service commenced. Four stations were also added at St. Paul's Bay, Rabat, Sliema, and Gozo.

The impending war slowed down the overall development of this network however. In 1942 the Valletta exchange was completely destroyed by bombing, although the underground system used by the military was unaffected. The latter was wired in such a way that up to ten police stations could be informed about air attacks simultaneously.

Following the war, the public quickly began to realize the social value of the telephone service and its demand grew rapidly. The Valletta exchange having been rebuilt, the national network then consisted of two main exchanges (Valletta and Sliema) and three satellite exchanges (St. Paul's Bay, Rabat, and Gozo). In 1955 an order from Standard Telephones and Cable (ST&C) of England for an automatic exchange was placed (*Report on the Working of the Posts and Telephone Department for the Years 1949-56*: p. IX). A premises to house the new exchange was purposely built at Blata l-Bajda. The new automatic exchange was inaugurated in October 1957, but the process of conversion to fully automatic working was not completed until 1965 (Briffa, 1981: p. 4; and Bezzina, 1962: p. 50). In 1957, the number of subscribers stood at 7,000, and by the end of 1959 an estimated 12,000 telephones were in use. In 1969, the demand for the telephone rose to 26,000, but only 20,000 were operating (Briffa, 1981: p. 4).

International Exchange and Communication with Gozo

Communication with Gozo was originally via a submarine cable. In 1962 a 24 voice channel radio communication system between Malta and Gozo was established. The capacity of this network was extended to 60 voice channels in 1971.

As regards international calls, the first telephone circuits were not established until 1957, two years after the NATO submarine cable and its associated repeater had been installed.[177] This cable provided sufficient bandwidth for the optimum operation of 36 voice channels (Briffa, 1981: p. 50). Initially the circuits were reserved for NATO usage, but that same year two public telephone circuits were also established with Rome and Catania. Direct communication with the UK by phone took place in April 1964.

The Telex

Apart from the telephone, the telex was the main type of communication by which business was conducted in the 1960s and the 1970s, with many companies still using it even in the early 1990s. In Malta, the first small telex circuit was established in 1962 on a manual basis with only 6 subscribers (Briffa, 1981: p. 2).[178] An automatic electro-mechanical exchange was introduced in 1976 which provided 300 local telex subscribers direct access to foreign subscribers. A second extension was completed in 1978, which was then followed by the last fully automatic and electronic exchange. The telex began to be replaced by the modern electronic fax machine in the late 1980s, by which time the estimated number of local telex machines stood at over 1000.

Radio (Wireless) Communication

Although the first early experiments to establish a wireless station (a "Marconi Station" as it was then known) in Malta go back to the

---

[177] NATO's Mediterranean Headquarters, under the command of Lord Admiral Louis Mountbatten, was established in Malta in early 1953 and became operational on 15 March of that year. See Pirotta (1987, Vol. I: pp. 386-387).

[178] See also: "Arrival of Telex", *Times of Malta*, 5 October 1962, p. 3.

summer of 1900, it was not until 1914 that the architect Robert Galea, a retired Maltese Royal Engineer Officer, succeeded in building a receiver/transmitter set, which he used to communicate with an American Merchant Naval vessel in February of that year (Samut-Tagliaferro, 1979: pp. 8-9; and Bezzina, 1962: p. 51). Unfortunately for him, his set was confiscated the following August when he was ordered by government to hand it in to the police on account of the impending Great War.

On 10 March 1922 the Governor issued an Ordinance (Wireless Telegraphy Ordinance of 1922) by which the public was allowed the use of a radio set provided they obtained a licence for it. The number of radio sets soon ran into the thousands following this act.[179]

High frequency carrier wave Morse Code telegraphy was operated at least as early as 1 January 1931 when a 24-hour circuit was established with Rugby in England (Briffa, 1981: p. 85). Public correspondence circuits utilizing Frequency Shift Keying (FSK) were later established with Ongar (UK) in 1934, Tripoli in 1940 and Rome in 1955.

High frequency (radio) public telephony was operated shortly after the end of World War II, first with the UK, subsequently with Tripoli, Rome and Benghazi. This service was operated by Cable & Wireless Ltd (Malta Wireless, as it was then known) from its telegraph office at St George's (see Figure 8.2) and later also from a newly constructed receiving station at Ta' Wied Rini (limits of Rabat). FSK press transmissions were established with a number of countries in the 1950s and 1960s. Between 1963 and 1964, new high frequency SSB/PSK transmitters were introduced to operate the radio telephone and radio telegraph service. This equipment was made obsolete when a Malta-Sicily microwave system was introduced in 1989.

As for facsimile transmission (fax) this was introduced in Malta in the late 1940s by Cable & Wireless using a Muirhead D628 radio picture transmitter (Briffa, 1981: p. 102).

---

[179] The first licence to operate a wired broadcasting system (cable radio) was issued in 1933 and granted to commander Mansfield Robinson who set up a small Broadcasting Station. Two years later the licence was transferred to Broadcasting Relay Services (Malta) Ltd, known locally as Rediffusion, which continued to operate their broadcasting service until 1975. See, for example, Cutajar (2001: pp. 9-14).

Figure 8.2
Electra House, later renamed Mercury House, at St George's. For many
decades this building served as the main telegraph, telephone, and telex office
of Cable & Wireless Ltd and, subsequently, of Telemalta Corporation.
Source: *Sunday Times of Malta* (15 April 1956: p. 12)

9

Telecommunications Nationalisation, Private Competition, and the New Forms of Data Communication

The Formation of Telemalta

In 1964, under the Nationalist government, Malta officially became independent, and ten years later, under the socialist labour regime, Malta was made a republic. Independence did not imply that all things British would automatically become Maltese, or that the British forces would immediately pull out: indeed, the British naval basis continued to operate from Malta for several years following Independence; and the running of the external telecommunications system likewise remained under foreign hands for a number of years. When the Labour party won the 1971 elections (see also Chapters 1 and 2) talks were negotiated with the British government to run down the armed forces by 1979, and for the telecommunications sector to be handed to the Maltese government. The transfer of the telecommunications facilities to Maltese hands happened at the end of 1974 when the Malta subsidiary of Cable & Wireless was sold to the Maltese government, and shortly afterwards the wholly state-owned Telemalta Corporation was set up by Act of Parliament on 24 June 1975 (*Telemalta Corporation Act*, 1975).[180] Thus came into being what

---

[180] This Act established Telemalta Corporation as the new Operator and Regulator.

for over two decades would be Malta's sole telecommunications monopoly, the 'exclusive authority to provide for the transmission of messages for money or other consideration by telephony, telegraphy, telex or other means of telecommunications' (*ibid.*, section 3(2)). The newly set up company was also to be responsible for Broadcasting. In addition, with the setting up of this parastatal company, telephony no longer remained a government department (that used to form part of the postal service) although for all intent and purposes government still played a key role in its control.

Apart from the Act itself, Telemalta Corporation, managed by a Board of Directors appointed by Government, was bound in execution of its duties as a public Service by the *Telegraphs and Telephones Ordinance – Telephone Service Regulations 1972* (CAP. 125) and the *Broadcasting Ordinance* (Ord. No. 20) of 28 July 1961. The *Telegraphs and Telephones Ordinance* was the first primary legislation that introduced some form of government control over the telecommunications sector, although the *Wireless Telegraphy Ordinance* of 1922 (CAP. 49) was another legislation which established a government department (under the same name) to perform the role of vetting any transmission apparatus and issue the relevant location permit for it. The *Broadcasting Ordinance* (1961) set up the Broadcasting Authority and in the process removed all forms of control the local government previously enjoyed in the broadcasting sector (Cutajar, 2001: p. 42).[181]

What was the state of affairs of telecommunications when Telemalta was created? Like many other countries the telecommunications system in that period was still underdeveloped, and the services offered rather limited. All the exchanges were analogue, and international subscriber dialling had not been introduced (this had to wait until the 1980s), meaning that to effect an overseas call one had to visit a Telemalta office. For telegrams, the same procedure had to be followed; and as for telex, a service was

---

[181] The main motive behind the establishment of the broadcasting authority was to have an independent body that would ensure that broadcasting would not fall victim to politics. The years leading to the Broadcasting Ordinance were fraught with trouble over broadcasting issues, and this led to the new legislation. In practice, the legislation favoured the colonial government since the Broadcasting Authority was made directly responsible to the (British) Governor who could recruit its members as he deemed fit.

offered primarily to large companies who, at the time (mid-1970s), conducted their business by this means of communication. A phototelegraph service was also available. Table 9.1 gives some statistics of the basic telecommunications supply and demand as at 1974. It should be mentioned that just one year later (in 1975) the international telephone network capacity was more than quadrupled after an Italo-Maltese telecommunications agreement established a radio link which connected a newly constructed international communication centre at Birkirkara.

TABLE 9.1
Basic Telecommunications Statistics as at 1974

National Telephone Network
Exchange Lines in Service:	c. 28,000
Exchange Capacity:	c. 33,000
Exchange Demand:	c. 41,000
Telephone Sets:	c. 48,000 (c. 15 per 100 population)

International Telephone Network
Exchange Capacity:	48
Operational Voice Channels:	33

Telex Network
Capacity:	c. 500
Sub Connections:	c. 230

Source: Briffa (1981); and NSO.

The telecommunications facilities that were handed over to the local authorities at the end of 1974, following agreements with Cable & Wireless (Malta) Ltd and with NATO included:[182]

• the Submarine Coaxial Cable System between St. George's (Malta) and Pozzallo (Sicily) together with its associated repeater equipment. This system provided sufficient bandwidth for 36 voice channels.

[182] See Briffa (1981), from which this list has been compiled.

- the Telegraph System which included a phototelegraph service.
- a small manual Telex Network, established in 1962, which had under 300 subscribers in 1974.
- a radio link between Malta and Gozo, also established in 1962. The radio link was equipped with two 7400 MHz transmitter/receiver cubicles and the associated waveguide and antenna system. The transmission system consisted of STC type channelling equipment of ultimate capacity of 120 voice channels used by 1971.

The above shows that the state of telecommunications in Malta in the early 1970s, particularly with regards to public services, was still relatively primitive and needed to be upgraded considerably.[183]

Expansion of the Telephone Service, ITU Membership and Involvement

Shortly before Telemalta was formed, the Maltese government in 1973 allocated £M12 million (c. US$32 m.) to an expansion programme in the telecommunications sector, with the majority of the budget to be spent on the National Telephone Service. This allocation of funds was part of the 1973-1980 Seven Year Development Plan which the Labour government devised shortly after it won the 1971 elections.

---

[183] Although one might get the impression that little was done in the telecommunications sector before Telemalta's formation in 1975, this is not the case. In fact, during the second half of the sixties the telephone network had been built up substantially, one prime reason being to help with the development of the tourism industry (e.g. by extending the telephone network to reach remote places where new hotels were being built). For example, whereas in 1964 there were only two cable trunk lines to Rome and one to Catania, by 1971 the capacity had been increased to nine cable lines to London, six to Rome, one to Catania, one to Palermo, two to Milan and one to Libya. Notwithstanding these improvements, the increase in demand for telephones was more than had been anticipated, with over 2,500 new applications per annum being processed between 1965 and 1970. See *Report on the Working of the Telephone Department* (for the years 1966-1972); *Development Plan for the Maltese Islands, 1969-1974*; *Ir-Review*, 2 March 1966; *Ir-Review*, 5 April 1969.

In the seven year period between March 1973 and March 1980, the telephone exchange capacity was increased from 32,120 to 63,850 lines (*Malta Guidelines for Progress: Development Plan 1981-1985*, 1981: p. 212). The expansion involved the building of a number of new exchanges in various localities. The number of subscribers now stood at 51,142 against 26,653 in March 1973. Notwithstanding the new installations, the number of applicants on the waiting list by March 1980 rose to 24,417 compared to 14,058 in 1973. The apparent paradox of having so many applicants when there were almost 13,000 spare lines was due (at least partly) to unsatisfied demand that existed in areas where the limiting factor was cable capacity which could not take more than the connections already installed.

Although in the period 1973-1980 Malta's capacity for overseas telephone links had been increased, it needed to be strengthened further, particularly if tourism was to be exploited to the full.[184] A satellite earth station was one way of increasing international telephone traffic. With a view to install the first of these, expert technical advice was sought from the ITU in order to determine the type of Earth Station most suitable for Malta's needs. The first satellite earth station—a standard B type—was successfully installed in 1986 (*The Year Book 1987*). Initially operating on twelve voice channels, this earth station provided direct circuits with Algeria and North America, and later with other countries that included Canada, Germany, the Netherlands, the Nordic Countries, Switzerland and the UK. In 1989, a second standard F2 Earth Station was made operational, this time providing direct links to Australia (*The Year Book 1990*) (see Figure 9.1).

Malta joined the ITU in 1965. Membership of the ITU proved fruitful because it meant that Malta could take part in a number of ITU projects—which it did—and later also seek financial assistance. Initially Malta's role was passive, attending various seminars and meetings, but it later became more proactive when it became directly responsible for certain key areas, as with the EUROTELDEV project, for example. The EUROTELDEV (European Telecommunications

---

[184] As early as 1967, the Robens Mission had warned that if industrial and tourist development was to take place as rapidly as possible, programmes related to the telecommunications sector had to be completed immediately, and forward planning should prevent shortage of supply in the future. See Spiteri (1997: p. 170); and Robens (1967: p. 17).

Development) Project was initiated by the UNDP in 1983 (as Project Code RER/83/8004), and had as its prime objective the development of an advanced, Europewide, telecommunications network by involving twelve developing countries.[185] The project had several phases to it. The first phase (RER/83/8004) aimed at fostering close relations between the participating countries. It involved various meetings

Figure 9.1
The telecommunications satellite earth station at Maghtab. Two of the first large dishes to be made operational were Telemalta's Intelsat standard 'B' and 'F' types, respectively installed in 1986 and 1989. The first of these was donated by the Algerian government.
Note the parabolic wall structure (behind the dishes) known locally as "il-Widna" (meaning the "ear") which was used during World War II as an early warning system (acoustic radar) to help detect approaching enemy aircraft. In the distance (at right) can be seen one of the several 18th century coastal watch towers.
Source: Author's collection.

---

[185] The countries involved in the EUROTELDEV project were Albania, Bulgaria, Cyprus, Czechoslovakia, Greece, Hungary, Malta, Poland, Portugal, Romania, Turkey, and Yugoslavia.

made possible by UNDP and ITU support as well as by non-IPF countries, which provided the required expertise.[186]   The second phase, coded RER/87/025, commenced in 1987 and had as its objective staff training in computer-aided network planning and other areas such as data communications so that   the   participating countries would be able to use this experience to introduce new techniques and technologies in their telecommunications network.[187, 188] Following a Steering Committee meeting held in Geneva in January 1988, it was decided to initiate networking activities so that the Regional (European) Backbone Telecommunication Network that was to be developed to serve the traffic requirements of the region could be better implemented. Seven of the twelve countries involved in the EUROTELDEV project were therefore assigned specific tasks, with Malta made responsible for the Economic and Financial Aspect of the project.

Master Plan for Telecommunications

In 1986 Telemalta embarked on a long-term ambitious programme of expansion and modernization. Although by this time the local telephone capacity had been increased substantially, most of the equipment consisted of electro-mechanical exchanges and a central international exchange where traffic had become congested. The ever increasing public demand for the use of the telephone and other services was placing stress on the system; delays for processing applications for telephone installations were common as the prospective customer waiting list became ever longer. The new expansion programme aimed to address these basic needs, and more.

Advocating high technology, the programme took into consideration government's plans in the economic sector that sought to create employment by promoting the productive and market sectors including an offshore financial and trading centre. A

---

[186] IPF stands for indicative planning figure. IPFs are funds a country could expect to receive (e.g. from the UN or an international organization) over a five-year time frame to assist with long-term development planning.

[187] The EUROTELDEV project and Malta's involvement in it is discussed in Debono (1989: pp. 38-44).

[188] For a concise account of the state of telecommunications in Central and Eastern Europe in the late 1980s and early 1990s see US Congress (1993: Chapter 6).

programme of this nature, especially in those times of scarce resources and human expertise, could not have been undertaken without outside help, and assistance was immediately sought for this project.

The ITU and the UNDP were the obvious candidates to turn to for help for a number of reasons: firstly, Malta was a full member of the ITU; secondly ties with both the ITU and the UNDP had already been established; and, thirdly, the ITU, only four years before, at the Nairobi Plenipotentiary Conference of 1982, announced its intention to step up telecommunications development by promoting and offering technical assistance to developing countries in the field of telecommunications, and also by promoting the mobilization of the material and financial resources needed for implementation.[189] It was a good time for Malta to seek assistance. Moreover, Malta was then still considered a developing country.

In 1986 a request for financial assistance through the European Investment Bank (EIB) was therefore made in order to cover the intended expansion programme. This necessitated the drawing up of the Long Term Development Plan, soon to become known simply as the Master Plan. In order to formulate the Master Plan the ITU was officially asked for expert assistance. The initial request was for a short term evaluation mission by ITU technical staff to appraise the state of the telecommunications network, identify the needs, and prepare a work plan from which the Master Plan could be formulated up to the year 2000. Through its Technical Cooperation Department, the ITU responded favourably to the request, and in October 1986 a group of ITU experts were sent to Malta to carry out their task.

The evaluation mission being completed, the next step was to seek funds for the preparation of the Master Plan itself. This proved difficult as it resulted that funds were not forthcoming from either the ITU's Technical Corporation regular budget, or the ITU's then newly set up Centre for Telecommunications Development (CTD).[190] Eventually, it was agreed that 30% of the Master Plan costs would be

---

[189] See, for example, Walden & Angel (2001: p. 360). The ITU's priority to telecommunications development is laid down in Art. 1(1)(b) of its Constitution.

[190] The ITU Centre for Telecommunications Development was set up in 1985 with the aim of co-ordinating the development of telecommunications worldwide. It has since been superseded by the Telecommunication Development Sector (ITU-D), a merger between the former Technical Cooperation Department and the Centre for Telecommunications Development. See *ITU Newsletter 7/94*.

met by the CTD and the rest financed under a funds-in-trust agreement from UNDP funds allocated to Malta for 1987 (Debono, 1989: pp. 47-48).

By the end of May 1987, a Project Document, which essentially set out the framework for the formulation and implementation of the Master Plan was signed by the Maltese Government, the ITU and the UNDP. The time limit set by the EIB for the submission of the final Master Plan document was the end of 1987, however arrangements were made with the EIB to present the report by the first quarter of 1988 instead. In the meantime, immediately following the signing of the Project Document, twelve ITU and UNDP experts were recruited who, together with Telemalta officials, drew up the Master Plan. The final report—*The Long Term Development Plan for Telecommunications in Malta*—was officially presented to the Prime Minister of Malta, then Dr. Eddie Fenech Adami, on 18 April 1988 by the then ITU Secretary General, R. E. Butler (Debono, 1989: p. 51).

The Master Plan was very ambitious in its intentions seeking to radically transform the telecommunications sector by completely modernising it by adopting the latest state-of-the-art technology. This, it succeeded in doing. Most of the services introduced from the beginning of the 1990s are a result of direct implementation of the Master Plan. Figure 9.2(a) shows the extent to which expansion in the basic telephone service has occurred, while Figure 9.2(b) shows Malta's fixed line teledensity against four advanced European nations for different periods. Although not shown, the teledensity of most Easter European countries for the period under consideration (1977 through 1993) are well below those of Malta, typically ranging from about 8 to about 22 for the year 1991 (see Steinfield, Bauer & Caby, 1994: p. 259). Indeed, the number of telephone connections per 100 of population for Malta compares well with the other four countries indicated in Figure 9.2(b) and by 1993 even surpassed them. Figure 9.3 also indicates Malta's position vis-à-vis other countries as regards fixed line teledensity but includes the GDP.

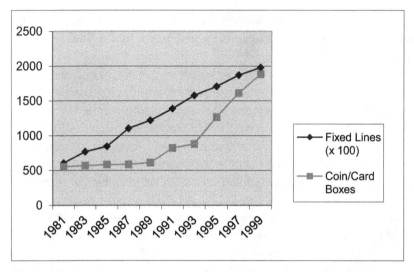

Figure 9.2 (a)
Development of the Maltese telephone service, 1981-1999.
Source: Generated from NSO data.

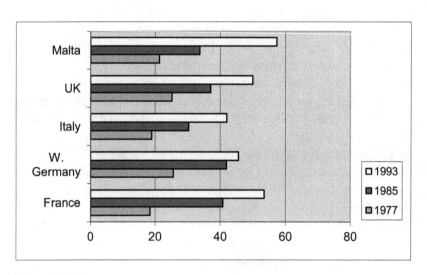

Figure 9.2 (b)
Telephone lines per 100 population for France, Germany, Italy, Malta, and
the UK for the years 1977, 1985, 1993.
Source: ITU (1992, 1995)

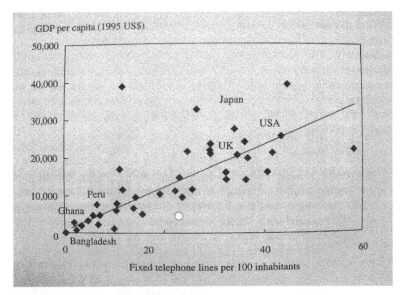

Figure 9.3 (a)
Fixed telephone lines and per capita gross domestic product, 1980. Malta's
inclusion in this graph is shown as a filled white circle (added by the author).
Source: Torero & von Braun (2006: p. 34).

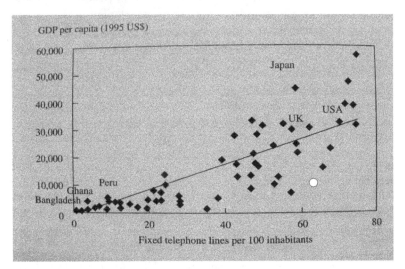

Figure 9.3 (b)
Fixed telephone lines and per capita gross domestic product, 2000. Malta's
inclusion in this graph is shown as a filled white circle (added by the author).
Source: Torero & von Braun (2006: p. 34).

Mobile Telephony, Cable TV, Data Services and Networks

Mobile Telephony

On 22 February 1989 Telemalta signed a memorandum of understanding with Racal Vodafone of Britain for the setting up of a Cellular Mobile Telephone System (*The Year Book 1990*, p. 250). Racal, at that time the largest operator in the UK and one of the fastest growing electronic giants in Europe, had been seeking to expand its overseas cellular mobile expertise outside the UK. In 1988 its Telecom arm joined the French company COFIRA, whose wholly-owned subsidiary SFR subsequently opened a cellular network in France. In 1989 Racal joined another goods producer consortium headed by the Greek telecommunications authority QTE to establish a cellular network in Greece; and in the same period it also became part of a third consortium involving the German companies BMW and Veba, which bid for the second digital cellular licence in Germany.

Initially aimed to invest Lm3 million (c. US$9 m.) over the first two and a half years, Racal was given a twenty year licence to operate the mobile cellular telephone system, with Racal paying Telemalta Lm15,000 (c. US$45,000) annually in licence fees for the duration of the licence. The joint venture was initially implemented by the setting up of a limited liability company, called Telecell Limited (later to become Vodafone (Malta)), with Telemalta having an initial share capital of 20% which, in terms of the agreement, were free of charge. Racal was to wholly finance the paid-up share capital.[191]

For the purpose of operating the service, nine base stations were installed around Malta and Gozo. These were linked to a Switching Centre at B'Kara so that both local and overseas calls could be effected. Nine base stations were considered sufficient in view of Malta's small size and the system's specifications, which required the distance between each station to be not greater than 16 km. The ETACS 900 standard was adopted to make the Maltese network fully compatible with the Vodafone service in the UK. Analogue in nature,

---

[191] "Cellular Mobile Telephone System for Malta and Gozo – Racal Vodafone Bell Rings to the Tune of LM3 million", *Informatics*, April-May 1989, p. 8.

this standard was first introduced in the UK and Hong Kong in 1985.[192]

Racal's operating licence did not preclude the possible overlaying of a GSM pan-European digital cellular network. It also did not give the British operator exclusivity as regards type of subscriber equipment, which meant that local and foreign subscribers could provide their own equipment provided they were system compatible.

According to the then Parliamentary Secretary for Posts and Telecommunications, Pierre Muscat, the reasons for the granting of this licence were that Telemalta had no direct experience in this field. Neither did it have the necessary human and financial resources to establish and operate the service itself. Moreover, Racal's offer was the most advantageous out of the twenty-two proposals that were submitted (*ibid.*: p. 8). For almost a decade mobile telephony in Malta was very expensive compared to some European countries. In 1999, for example, a person in Malta who used an hour of airtime each month, with most of the calls during the day, paid an average 32c (32 Maltese cents) per minute, whereas a similar user in Italy (with one of the leading service providers) paid only 18c per minute (Scarlett, 1999). Prices eventually dropped following Maltacom's entry as a competitor to Vodafone in 2000.

Data Services and GSM

Before Telemalta inaugurated its first packet switching node in 1993, users who wanted to transmit and receive data had three options: either use the existing (analogue) public switched telephone network (PSTN, sometimes also referred to as POTS, for plain old telephone system), or dedicated (i.e., leased) point-to-point data circuits, or a trial service of a limited packet switching facility called Maltapac introduced in 1988. The first option required the use of a dial-up modem, and transmission rates rarely exceeded 9.6 Kbps (Kilobits per second). The second option meant one could use either an analogue or a digital system. Telemalta introduced its point-to-point digital data transmission network in 1991; this was more reliable than the local and international PSTN, faster (typically operating at about 64

[192] For some of the major cellular and cordless systems used up to 1994 see Englund (1999: pp. 218-237); and Muller & Toker (1994: pp. 182-203).

Kbps), but also more costly, charge being worked on a line rental only basis. Maltapac was an experimental system, slow, and therefore not very popular.

Significant headway in the data communications area was made after the first Packet Switched Data Network (PSDN) node was installed and made fully operational in 1993. Apart from enabling faster access to remote (non-local) data because the PSDN node could be linked to other PSDNs overseas, the packet switching exchange brought certain advantages with it, such as flexibility, reliability and cost. Since a PSDN system allocates transmission capacity dynamically according to demand and, by virtue of it being a switched service, also enables facilities to be shared (hence maximising the available capacity), it is more cost effective. Tariff structure is in fact based more on volume than duration, and call charges are independent of distance. PSDN also has the advantage that it is based on an established international standard, that of X.25, hence guaranteeing equipment compatibility and—to a cetain extent—obsolescence.

Telemalta's first PSDN node was followed by other similar nodes and digitial exchanges, so that by the turn of the millennium its telecommunication system consisted of the following main items:[193]

- 12 AXE10 Ericsson digital exchanges and 1 Siemens EWSD Exchange
- Common channel signalling & ISDN
- Packet switching, frame relay, high speed leased lines
- Optic fibre backbone based on SDH technology
- 2 digital gateways
- 2 satellite standard B earth stations
- Optic fibre submarine cable to Sicily, extended terrestrially to Palermo (where a hub of submarine cabling is located)
- SDH Malta-Sicily microwave link

Apart from the above equipment, the company also owns IRUs on several international submarine cables and on FLAG, the Fibre Optic Link Around the Globe, which has a landing point at Palermo.

---

[193] This list is compiled from the jubilee edition of the *Malta Year Book 2002*, pp. 253-254, and various local newspaper and magazine articles.

As for wireless data communication, before the widespread use of GSM in the mid-1990s, wireless data could be transmitted over the ETACS mobile channel (and other early types of analogue systems) using an analogue wireless modem. Data rates seldom exceeded 9.6 Kbps because of the adverse nature of the radio mobile channel. The cost of the service was also expensive, often as much as a voice call (Zammit, 1997).

In Malta, GSM was introduced by Vodafone (formerly Telecell Ltd) for voice telephony in 1998. Before its introduction, the use of mobile phones in Malta was still very low: in 1999 only about 50,000 persons (13% of the population) had access to a mobile phone. By 2006, the mobile telephone penetration rate had reached 86 per 100 of population (see Tables 9.2 and 9.3). However, this was still below the EU average, although some countries—notably France—lagged Malta in the period 2002-2006.

In 1998 Vodafone applied for, and was granted a licence, to provide data services. This meant that the company could now offer customers the ability to send and receive fax as well as e-mail over its GSM network, a service which it actually introduced that same year. For almost a decade, Vodfone was completely alone in the local mobile communications field, without competitors. In late 2000, a second mobile communications license was issued to Mobisle Communications Limited, a subsidiary of Maltacom specifically set up a year previously to offer mobile services (under the "Go Mobile" brand name). The license was issued on the condition that Maltacom divests itself of the shares it held (20%) in Vodafone within six months from the commencement of operations of its subsidiary. This had set the scene for competition in mobile telephony, although a third license has not, to date (2009), been issued. Cable services and fixed line telephony would follow suit, when they were liberalised on 1 June 2001 and 1 January 2003, respectively (see later).

Cable TV

The story of Cable TV—or, rather, of data services over the cable TV infrastructure—is an interesting, if not a turbulent, one: it involves politics and rivalry between Malta's then telecommunications incumbent and a new entrant in the data communications field, as well as the internet service providers. It also highlights the difficulties involved in the interpretation of technical jargon, in this case the term "data services". It begins with Melita Cable Television Ltd in the early 1990s when it was set up to offer Maltese customers cable television for the first time (see Figure 9.4).

The Maltese registered Melita Cable Television Ltd company (henceforth Melita Cable TV, or simply Melita) was formed in December 1989, following a public call for applications for the provision of cable TV in January that year (Government of Malta, 1989).[194] Melita Cable TV then consisted of a consortium of companies that included American and Maltese interests, and was one of 9 companies that bid for the call.[195] The decision by Government to choose Melita Cable TV was taken on 5 June 1990, the final agreement between the Maltese Government and the company being signed on 3 June 1991. That agreement gave Melita a monopoly on cable TV for a period of 15 years.

On 1 June 1992, a separate agreement was also signed with Telemalta to allow Melita to access Telemalta's structures, buildings and buried conduits for the laying of the fibre optic cable and the installation of other TV (coaxial) cables.[196] The agreement established the conditions, tariffs, and cost apportionment procedures applicable to the shared use of the structures, and covered a period of 15 years. The understanding was that the cabling would only be used for TV broadcasting, barring it from providing telephony over the infrastructure. The laying of the fibre optic cable started shortly after this agreement was signed (see also *Reports on the Working of Government Departments*, 1992).

Melita's TV service was officially launched in the autumn of 1992, when its customer base was a few hundreds. Subscriptions increased steadily, as new programme packages were introduced and an advertising campaign carried out. By 1999 cable TV users stood at about 70,000 (Samsone, 1999: p. 6), equivalent to about 18% of total population (see also Table 9.2).

---

[194] The companies involved were the Cleveland (Ohio) based North Coastal Cable International (NCCT), United Communications International (UCI) of Denver (Colorado), and GH Communication Ltd and Stefanotis Co. Ltd, both Maltese.
[195] "Il-Cable TV jinsab wara l-bieb", *It-Torca*, 17 May 1992.
[196] "Cable TV firm to use Telemalta ducts", *The Times*, 2 June 1992, p. 19.

Figure 9.4
One of the first adverts by Melita Cable TV following the testing of their cable TV service in Malta in the summer of 1992.
Source: *The Times* [of Malta] (14 July 1992: p. 16).

Part of the reason for the company's success in attracting new customers was the number of English programmes that were being offered, including documentary channels such as "Discovery" and

"National Geographic".[197] Hitherto, Maltese viewers were accustomed to only tune to Maltese or Italian channels; now, in addition, they had a wider choice and in a language that they could also easily understand.[198] Of course, this choice came at a price since, at Lm6 (c. US$18) monthly for what was termed "basic reception", the entry-level programme package, it was not cheap.

In the summer of 1999, a clash broke out between Telemalta (by now renamed Maltacom) and Melita Cable when the latter announced that it would enter the Internet field, a tussle which developed into a legal battle between the two rivals. The battle persisted for several months partly because the law in this telecommunications area was unclear.

The battle started with Maltacom filing two judicial protests on 23 June 1999: one against Melita; and another against the then Acting Regulator of Telecommunications, the Attorney General, and the permanent secretaries at the Office of the Prime Minister, the Finance Ministry, and the Ministry for Economic Services.[199] Maltacom was saying that, according to the 1992 interconnection agreement, Melita was given permission (a licence) to use Maltacom's infrastructure for cable television transmission purposes only, and not to provide internet access through this infrastructure. Moreover, Maltacom was claiming that Melita had approached Maltacom's clients informing them that it would soon start providing data services. Unless Melita honoured the agreement, Maltacom declared it would take action to terminate the contract itself.

The second protest against the Regulator revolved around a January 1998 licence which Maltacom had been granted by the Regulator that, according to Maltacom, gave it exclusive permission to provide data and internet services. Although, on 3 June 1991 the

---

[197] By December 1993, Melita had also started televising local football matches. This led to dwindling crowds at Malta's only national football stadium, and was a matter of concern to the Malta Football Association. "Televised football major cause of dwindling crowds", *The Sunday Times*, 25 December 1994, p. 69.

[198] Satellite TV was, in this period (mid-1990s), still very expensive with a typical installation (dish, receiver, and installation fee) costing in excess of Lm300 (c. US$900). Also, an annual licence fee of Lm25 was charged. The licence fee was later dropped, making satellite TV an attractive proposition and commonplace as equipment and installation costs came down.

[199] "Maltacom files two protests against Melita Cable", *The Times*, 24 June 1999, p.22.

Regulator also issued Melita a licence allowing it to provide data services (at least according to Melita), in March 1998 the Regulator had decided that the only services Melita was licensed to offer were those for radio and television broadcasting. That same year, however, Melita had requested the Regulator to reconsider its decision about data services and internet provision, a request that (according to Maltacom) was apparently about to be granted.

Melita was quick to react to the two Maltacom protests by filing its own counter-protests in the Civil Court on 28 June 1999.[200] Melita argued that Maltacom's allegations were unfounded and that it had no right to terminate its contract. After several more protests and counter-protests that lasted some months, it was decided by the Court on 9 November 1999 that Melita should only use Maltacom's infrastructure for cable TV transmission.[201] This was not the end of the story since the following October (2000) new amendments were made to Chapter 81 of the Laws of Malta,[202] following which Maltacom was ordered by the telecommunications minister to allow Melita to use its ducts even for data services.[203] That order post-dated the Court's decision of 28 June 1999, giving Maltacom no choice but to accede.[204] In November 2000 Melita launched its Internet package for the first time on the Island.[205]

Internet Services

In October 1995 when Telemalta still had the dual role of operator and regulator, the first two licences to provide Internet services were issued to Video-on-Line of Santa Venera and Electronic Systems Ltd of San Gwann (see Figure 9.5).[206]

---

[200] "Melita Cable replies to Maltacom protests", *The Times*, 29 June 1999, p. 16.

[201] "Court decides against Melita", *The Times*, 10 November 1999, pp. 1 and 21.

[202] Chapter 81 is the "Utilities and Services (Regulation of Certain Works) Act" (substituted by Act XXIII of 2000).

[203] "Maltacom ordered to allow Melita to use its ducts", *The Times*, 7 October 2000, p. 14.

[204] The communications minister's order was meant to enforce the sharing of facilities as stipulated by the new Utilities and Services Act (see previous note).

[205] "Melita Cable offers internet access", *The Times*, 9 November 2000, p. 6.

[206] "Internet licenses given", *The Malta Business Weekly*, No. 54, 2-8 November 1995, p. 5.

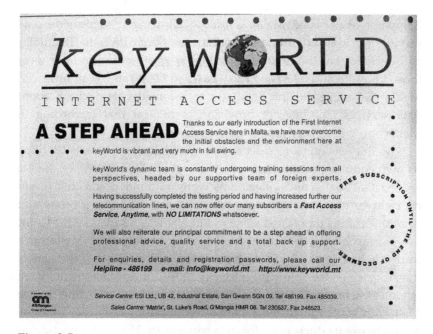

Figure 9.5
An early advert of one of the first Internet Service Providers in Malta. The first licences for Internet provision in Malta were issued in October 1995.
Source: *The Malta Business Weekly* (30 November – 6 December, 1995: p. 22).

From the beginning, this sector was pluralistic, with no single provider dominating a disproportionate section of the market, since it had been decided that Internet provision should be totally liberalised. By the end of 1999, the number of licensed providers amounted to ten, with the number of Internet subscribers probably not exceeding 15,000 (Aloisio, 1999; Kelleher, 1999). Three of these providers were government institutions, namely, Terranet Ltd—Telemalta's subsidiary set up in 1995 specifically to provide Internet services under the brand name of Maltanet; the Management Systems Unit (see Chapter 6); and the University of Malta.[207] As in all major industrial nations, Internet in Malta saw an explosive growth in users as Tables 9.2 and 9.3 illustrate.

---

[207] Both the MSU and the University of Malta were not ISPs as such: they did not provide internet services to the public, but only to their employees.

Note from Table 9.3 that whereas in 2005 Malta was trailing behind Europe in the use of Internet, from 2006 onwards it had reached and surpassed a number of EU countries.

TABLE 9.2
Information Society Indicators for Malta, 1999-2009

	1999	2001	2003	2005	2007	2009
Fixed Telephone Lines	197,764	197,745	208,271	209,305	?	?
Fixed Line Subscriptions	?	?	206,500	205,500	228,000	245,852
Public Phones	1,883	?	1,764	1,275	?	?
Mobile Tel. Subscriptions c.	50,000	220,545	289,902	324,787	371,530	422,083
Cable TV Subscriptions	c. 80,000	90,091	99,732	107,771	119,552	110,659
Internet Subscriptions	c. 12,000	51,343	78,260	88,771	99,947	111,290
Narrowband	?	?	?	46,601	18,735	631
Broadband	?	?	?	42,170	81,212	110,659
VOIP (minutes consumed[a])	?	?	3.82	12.93	?	?

[a] in millions
Note:
1) Mobile Tel. Subscriptions figure of 422,083 (2009) is equivalent to 101.3 per 100 population.
2) Cable TV Subscriptions figure of 110,659 (2009) is equivalent to 26.5 per 100 population.
3) Internet Subscriptions figure of 111,290 (2009) is equivalent to 26.7 per 100 population, or 78.2 per 100 households.
Source: National Statistics Office

Apart from outlining the rights and obligations of the Internet Service Provider (ISP), the ISP licence, as it was originally worded, bound all ISPs to deliver their services to their subscribers over Telemalta's telecommunications infrastructure only. This meant that all local connections with subscribers had to be established via Telemalta's public switched telephone network (PSTN), and to connect internationally ISPs had to use Telemalta's fibre optic link to Palermo in Sicily where an international gateway was in place. Thus, ISPs were also precluded from connecting internationally via a satellite link.

TABLE 9.3
Mobile Phone and Internet Use for Selected European Countries, 1998-2009

| | Mobile Tel. Subscription[a] | | | | Internet Access[b] | | | |
	1998	2002	2006	2004	2005	2006	2007	2009
Finland	55	87	108	51	54	65	69	78
France	19	63	82	34	-	41	49	63
Germany	17	72	104	60	62	67	71	79
Greece	19	85	99	17	22	23	25	38
Ireland	26	77	112	40	47	50	57	67
Italy	36	95	134	34	39	40	43	53
Portugal	30	83	116	26	31	35	40	48
UK	25	84	115	56	60	63	67	77
Malta	*5*	*70*	*86*	*-*	*41*	*53*	*54*	*64*
EU[c]	20	71	106	40	48	49	54	65

[a] Mobile Phone Subscriptions per 100 population
[b] Level of Internet Access: Percentage of households having Internet access at home
[c] 27 countries
Source: Eurostat

Telemalta's entry into the Internet field in 1996 combined with the terms of the ISP licence soon raised questions about the well being of a free market. Terranent was initially a joint venture company, but it became a fully owned subsidiary of Maltacom (formerly Telemalta) in 1998.[208] By this time the ISPs were feeling threatened by the prospects of a new monopoly (Samsone, 1999: p. 8). It further led to some heated debates when, as noted, in the summer of 1999 Melita Cable announced that it would be providing Internet access over its cable infrastructure which up to now had been used only for television transmission.

Arguing that not only will they be disadvantaged by such a move, but that this went against the licence conditions and an EU directive that required network operators to be separate from service

---

[208] Before it was acquired by Maltacom, Terranet was a joint venture company between Telemalta (25% holding), the Bianchi Group of Companies (20%), Terracom (40%), and Megabyte (15%). See Micallef Trigona (1995: p. 6).

providers (see also later), the ISPs requested the Telecommunications Regulator and the then Minister, Censu Galea, to alter the licence conditions so that an ISP could connect to any licensed network operator (Thake, 1999: p. 11).[209] They even considered legal action over the services planned by Melita Cable, which they alleged would push their telephone line-based systems out of business. This situation was further complicated by the fact that if Melita were to enter the cable internet field, it was not known whether it would simultaneously grant the ISPs access to its cable link facilities. Thus, the ISPs were not even sure whether legal steps would be taken against Melita, Maltacom, or the Regulator (Aloisio, 1999) (see also Figure 9.6).

In spite of the ISPs stand, which was understandable, many users did not sympathise with the ISPs who were seen as charging excessive fees for their service, and were considered expensive when compared to the same type of service being offered in the UK and the USA. They were in favour of Meltia Cable's entry into the field which, they hoped, would push prices down.[210]

The Internet Foundation and the Malta Internet Exchange

In 1992 authority over the top level domain (TLD) for the Republic of Malta was delegated to the University of Malta (UOM) by the Internet Assigned Names Authority (IANA), the global authority for Internet domain name service (Mifsud, 2000: p. 266; http://www.nic.org.mt). Three years later, when Internet in Malta was just beginning to take off—see also Box 9-1—the Domain Name Registration Committee was set up within the University to manage the domain name service for MT, the TLD for Malta. This was followed in June 1998 with the establishment of the Malta Internet Foundation, also known as NIC (Malta). The task of administering the TLD for Malta now fell to NIC (Malta), but the latter's objective was also 'to seek, identify and engage in other activities related to the general development of the Internet in Malta'.[211]

---

[209] By 1998 Telemalta had become Maltacom and was no longer the regulator.
[210] "Malta Internet Exchange", *The Sunday Times*, 26 September 1999, p. 57.
[211] "Malta Internet Exchange", *The Sunday Times*, 26 September 1999, p. 57. See also the website at http://www.nic.org.mt.

Figure 9.6
A cartoon sketch capturing the turbulent atmosphere of 1999 in connection
with the provision of data services that involved disputes between Melita
Cable TV, Maltacom, and the ISPs.
Source: *The Times* (11 October 1999: p. 9)

An important outgrowth of the Malta Internet Foundation was the
development and operation of the Malta Internet Exchange, a facility
that connected all major local ISPs. This project, initiated in 1999
involved the University's Computer Services Centre (CSC) and the
ISPs. It was an important initiative, which benefited both users and
ISPs as will now be explained.

Up to that time, Malta lacked a proper integrated services
backbone. A service provider, having obtained the required licence to
operate, would set up its own internal network to allow users access
to the Internet via Maltacom's telecommunications infrastructure. As
more providers appeared on the local scene, a situation developed
whereby a handful of local independent networks were being used, all
connected to Maltacom's network infrastructure. This presented an

irregular network scenario when it came to local traffic (i.e., traffic originating at a local network and destined to another local network): instead of remaining within Malta's shores, traffic would go out onto the Internet (outside Malta) using expensive international bandwidth. A traceroute carried out by Terranet Ltd in 1996 showed that data sent from Terranet's office in Balzan to the University of Malta at Tal-Qroqq only a few kilometres away, ended up crossing the Atlantic Ocean twice, detouring through Scandinavia in the process (Cassar, 1997). In order to remedy this situation the CSC, in collaboration with the ISPs and Maltacom, set up a national "backbone" specifically to handle local traffic, thereby increasing efficiency and also potentially lowering expenses and tariffs. This backbone was operated as The Malta Internet Exchange.[212]

The initial Internet Exchange set-up made use of a Frame Relay infrastructure to connect the ISPs to the Exchange, and was one of the earliest experiments in Malta involving Frame Relay. More recently Asynchronous Transfer Mode (ATM) Private Virtual Circuits (PVCs) and leased lines have been employed.

Box 9-1
Data Services and the Internet before the World Wide Web

The Internet's rapid growth in popularity at the start of the 1990s is generally attributed to the World Wide Web which, apart from allowing multimedia presentations, made it relatively easy to search for, and navigate through, large amounts of data. This rapid growth was accompanied by a corresponding explosion in the number of Internet Service Providers. Service providers, however, predated Tim Berners-Lee's World Wide Web, since the Internet existed well before, albeit in a somewhat different form than how we know it today. Moreover, apart from the Internet, a few independent "data" networks were created in the late 1970s which users could tap into. This box briefly describes these early network developments.

---

[212] Among the key persons involved in the setting up of the Malta Internet Exchange was Dr. Alex Mifsud, a former University of Malta lecturer, later CEO of the software company Ixaris (see Chapter 7 about the software industry). In essence, a router was configured at University which connected the local ISPs. The connection was still made through Maltacom's infrastructure (as a paid service) but in such a way that each ISP now had a direct link to the University-installed router (Sultana, 2008). Information provided by Robert Sultana (UOM CSC director) during a brief meeting with the author on 16 May 2008.

As many readers are aware, the Internet owes its origins to a project on wide area networking that was conceived in the mid-1960s (by scientists at MIT and the RAND Corporation, amongst others) and involved the United States Department of Defence's Advanced Research Projects Agency (ARPA). The latter was interested in the networking project—particularly the suggested use of packet switching—because it appeared to support a secure form of communications, useful in the case of war. For this reason, ARPA funded a number of computer network-related projects, some of which eventually led to the development of ARPANET. A small network connecting just a few nodes (sites containing computers linked to each other), ARPANET grew quickly in the 1970s. Electronic mail was invented in the early 1970s as part of ARPANET's research effort in order for the scientists to have a quick means of communicating together. E-mail proved to be the "killer application" becoming considerably more common than its inventors ever imagined: it popularised the network. For many years, however, most ARPANET users were those employed by institutions involved, in some way or other, in military-related work.

An important event that was to make the less well-known Internet (essentially still the ARPANET) of the early 1980s more accessible to a large community of people occurred in 1984 when the National Science Foundation (NSF) initiated a project whose goal was to bring information technology to *all* academic and professional institutions, not just those that had some relationship with the Department of Defence. NSF designed and built a national network called NSFnet which acted as a "backbone" network to which regional computer networks such as those at universities, government agencies, museums, libraries and medical centres could attach. This took place in America, but beginning from roughly the same period (earlier in some countries) other nations developed similar backbone networks. As these national networks were created, they were progressively linked to form one large network of networks, what would become today's Internet.

Meanwhile, the popularity of computer networks and e-mail led to many existing computer services companies to restructure and respond to users needs. Computer time-sharing companies such as Telecomp and Tymshare relaunched themselves as Telnet and Tymenet, respectively, both establishing numerous network nodes in American cities (and later elsewhere outside the US) and providing e-mail and other information-related services. As explained above, the same was happening in other sectors. Thus, Universities and Colleges formed educational consortia and developed their own networks and software that allowed users access to these networks. So-called bulletin-board systems (where users could post brief notes for all to see) and newsgroups—which were mainly specialised type of groups—developed from these efforts. The big communications companies likewise set up subsidiaries to offer similar services.

By roughly the beginning of the 1990s, apart from mainframe computers which one could access via communications software such as TELNET, the result was to have different categories of information servers—computers that stored large amounts of text-based information and that were now linked to the Internet—which users could access provided they were subscribed to an appropriate provider. Telnet, Gopher, WAIS (wide area information services), and USENET are examples of such information servers that could be accessed using the appropriate software protocols. BITNET and LISTSERV were others that typically used IBM mainframe computers.

One must also mention that, apart from the Internet itself, beginning from about the mid-1970s, a number of computer network schemes were devised that allowed users to remotely access various databases. The information could be viewed either on a monitor screen that formed part of the user's computer system, or on the TV set that contained a decoder (often as part of the receiver) to decode the "data" signals (typically transmitted as part of the vertical blanking interval lines). Known by their generic names of Teletext and Videotex, two such systems first appeared in Europe in the mid-1970s. They both sought to provide a range of business and consumer services through the use of a television or a computer. These services provided multiple screens ("pages") of text and very limited "block" graphics. Whereas Teletext was a one way system, Videotex was a two-way interactive system designed with the small business user in mind. Indeed, Videotex could be used for financial transactions, such as banking and shopping. Travel agents also made use of this system. Because of its interactive nature, Videotex required the use of a computer (at home or in the office) equipped with the right software and connected to the telephone lines via a dial-up modem. Examples of Teletext include Britain's Ceefax ("see facts"— pioneered by the BBC) and Oracle (by ITV); and France's Antiope. Examples of Videotex are British Telecom's Prestel and France Telecom's Teletel and Minitel. In Europe Videotex lasted until the 1990s, and teletext is still transmitted on top of many European TV channels. In the United States both systems never caught up.

10

Telecommunications Privatisation, Regulatory Reform, and Liberalisation

International Background

The history of the privatisation of national telecommunication organizations, of the breaking up of large private monopolistic companies, and of regulatory reform and eventual liberalisation of both telecommunications services and equipment does not go back very far. In the US, the beginnings of the telecommunications revolution is generally considered to have started by the divestiture of the private telecommunications giant American Telephone and Telegraph (AT&T), when this company was ordered by the Justice Department to be split up into one long-distance company and the five Baby Bells in 1982 (Eliassen & Sjovaag, 1999: p. 9; Goldman, 1998).[213] The divestiture was actually the result of a 1974 anti-trust lawsuit by Microwave Communications, Incorporated (MCI) claiming unfair dealings, so that although the US Federal Communications Commission (FCC), a federal regulatory agency, ruled in 1971 that MCI could compete with AT&T for long-distance service, it was the lawsuit that led to the actual break-up of the American

---

[213] For the history of AT&T see Temin & Galambos (1989). See also the Bell System Memorial Home Page at *http://www.porticus.org.bell/bell.htm.*

telecommunications monopoly (see also Box 10-1).[214]   In Europe, the UK is recognised as having been at the forefront of liberalisation when, in 1983, under the conservative Thatcher government, the national company of British Telecom (BT) was privatised and a second competitor, Mercury, was helped to be established and allowed to enter the same market (Thatcher, 1999: pp. 93-109; Tunstall & Palmer, 1990: pp. 262-281). Since then many European countries have, more or less, followed in the footsteps of the UK.

Although a number of forces have been noted as potentially giving rise to regulatory reform and liberalisation, the ultimate rationale for liberalisation is mainly economic.   The impact of globalisation of economies and increased world trade necessitates liberal measures: in the case of telecommunications, the liberalisation process also involves a framework for its regulation whose main aim is to secure fair and effective competition in all segments of the telecommunications sector (Eliassen & Sjovaag, 1999: p. 9). Encouraging fair competition means lowering the barriers for entry, making it easier for new companies to enter the telecommunications field. In turn, this competition has the effect of lowering overall costs.

The liberalisation process in Europe has been accelerated in the last two decades thanks to direct European Union (EU) involvement. The EU feared in the 1980s that unless action was taken at the EU level, Europe's telecommunications market would not remain competitive against that of the US. The EU's concerns of becoming uncompetitive were raised when, following the US's liberalisation decision, AT&T quickly entered into joint ventures with European companies, whilst IBM also announced its intention to diversify into telecommunications by purchasing stakes in European companies. At the same time, however, the US government also began to press the EU to open up its (the European) protected telecommunications markets (Braun & Capito, 2002: p. 51). These two factors gave the European Commission the legitimacy it sought to become involved in telecommunications policy, and in 1984 the first EU action programme involving telecommunications was begun. This was followed in 1987

---

[214] For a brief history of US telecommunications and key regulatory developments see Lee & Prime (2001: pp. 314-345). A chronological summary in point form is also given in Ungerer & Costello (1990: pp. 104-107). See also Brock (1994).

by a Green Paper, which is now often considered the first EU blueprint that aimed at increasing deregulation and competition.[215]

Box 10-1
The Beginnings of Telecommunications Regulation in the USA

Although the words regulation and liberalisation have almost become buzzwords in the last two decades or so, the idea of having government intervene in the economy and in certain crucial industries (for whatever reasons), and then liberalise markets in the hope of creating competition goes back to over a century. As with everything else, public regulation has its proponents as well as its opponents. Even so, regulation has been applied (successfully and unsuccessfully) to a number of industries, the utilities in particular. This precis takes a look at the early developments of telecommunications regulation (and deregulation) in the United States.

One of the first United States telephone companies, set up in 1877, was that of Alexander Graham Bell and his associates, called the Bell Telephone Company. During its initial years this company was struggling for survival, but as luck would have it Bell's small concern would soon turn into a giant. One firm that had a sizeable presence at that time was the telegraphic company of Western Union. The latter had also entered the telephony sector when the Bell company filed a judicial process accusing Western Union of infringing Bell's telephone patents. Reluctantly, Western Union chose to settle matters outside court, and as a result decided to give up the telephone business. An agreement was signed in 1879 whereby Western Union allowed Bell to use its right of way for long-distance pole lines, at the same time selling to Bell its many telephone exchanges. Two years later, the Bell company also purchased Western Union's manufacturing unit—the Western Electric Manufacturing Company—which eventually became Bell's manufacturing arm. Then, in 1885, the new firm of American Telephone and Telegraph Company (AT&T) was formed to concentrate on long distance telephony; it was initially a subsidiary of American Bell, but later (in 1900) became the parent company. The idea was to have AT&T serve as a holding company, providing finance, accepting stock in return and taking over the franchises of the Bell operating companies as they expired. Within a span of less than two decades, AT&T had become what today we would call a vertically integrated company.

---

[215] *Green Paper on the Development of a Common Market for Telecommunications Services and Equipment*, COM (87) 290 final, 30 June 1987. The Regulatory Framework of this Green Paper is discussed in a number of textbooks, including, for example, Koenig, Bartosch & Braun (2002); and Kamall (1996).

Although there were initially several other independent companies that provided a telephone service (especially after the fundamental Bell patents expired in 1894), many of these were relatively small firms that maintained isolated exchanges for local (mainly urban) connections. Moreover, these companies were unable to form a nationwide network as did AT&T. The only way these independent companies could provide a long-distance service to their customers was to make arrangements with bigger companies (such as AT&T, Western Union and Postal Telegraph) to interconnect with their networks. Often, the big companies would refuse to interconnect with these small local providers. This led to protests by the smaller players. In 1913, in response to the threat of federal antitrust litigation, AT&T agreed to abide by a federal legislation known as the Kingsbury Commitment, requiring AT&T to allow the use of its long-distance lines by the smaller firms. The Kingsbury Commitment was one of the earliest form of legislation relating to regulation, where the government intervened in order to promote fair practices. Even so, this legislation did not stop AT&T from growing by acquiring local phone systems and eliminate competition. By the 1930s AT&T had become a monopoly.

At that time, the idea of a natural monopoly—where a utility (such as telecommunications) was best served by a single firm for economic reasons—was still very much an accepted and unchallenged view. To the US government, AT&T appeared to be the natural monopolist. Rather than trying to nationalise it—as most European countries did with the Post, Telegraph and Telephone Companies (the "PTTs")—the federal government chose to let AT&T operate and retain its monopoly but simultaneously monitor closely its activities. Partly, if not chiefly, for this purpose, the first Communications Act was enacted in 1934 which establishsed the Federal Communications Commission (FCC) as the primary communications regulator. This Act essentially consolidated already existing legislation, for example that relating to the assignment of radio frequencies and another existing act concerning the common regulation for railroads. Under the 1934 Act, the FCC's primary duty was to secure universal service.

For several decades the FCC allowed AT&T to operate as a monopoly. In time the view that the provision of telecommunications services was a natural monopoly was being challenged by many economists, and the FCC also gradually began to consider introducing competition in various aspects of telecommunications. Other telecommunications companies began challenging AT&T and the FCC for lack of fair competition, particularly in the area of long-distance telephony in which AT&T clearly was the major player. One company that made this challenge was the Microwave Communications, Incorporated (MCI), which filed a lawsuit in 1974 against AT&T, Western Electric, and Bell Telephone Laboratories, alleging that the monopoly held by these companies in several telecommunications service areas and equipment manufaturing violated the Sherman Antitrust Act. The latter, enacted in 1890, sought to prevent monopolistic or any other practices that could potentially harm competition.

Eight years later, AT&T was ordered by the Supreme Court to divest itself of its twenty-two Regional Bell Operating Companies (called RBOCs), resulting in the separation of local and interexchange markets. This ruling is known as the Modified Final Judgement (MFJ). Accordingly, the RBOCs, which were reorganised into seven holding companies, would provide communications in "exchange areas", i.e., geographical areas that encompassed one or more contiguous local exchanges. Essentially, the RBOCs would originate and teminate calls within the exchange areas, whereas AT&T, MCI and other long-distance providers would carry calls between exchange areas.

Apart from regulation, a certain amount of deregulation was also being applied. For example, by the 1980s phone companies had been allowed to compete in an unrestricted manner in other industries such as the computer and information systems fields, the idea being to encourage a market-driven, customer-dictated economy. The divestiture, regulation and deregulation activities enabled telecommunications companies to sell long-distance services on a level playing field. For the end user, it also meant more choice of long-distance carriers and lower prices for related services.

Regulatory Development: the EU and Malta

When Telemalta was created in the mid-1970s, it was not only made responsible for the operation of the telecommunications networks and services, but it was also vested with the legal regulatory functions. The powers to make regulations are specified in Part VII (Miscellaneous Provisions) of the 1975 Telemalta Corporation Act under section 37 (Telemalta Corporation Act, 1975). Section 39 of this Act goes on to state that

> No person shall in Malta, except for or on behalf of Telemalta or under a licence from Telemalta, contract, install, extend or operate any telephone or telegraph, or do any work or install any apparatus or other thing intended for the transmission of messages by telephony or telegraphy or in any other manner encroach upon the

exclusive rights vested in the Corporation by section 3 of this Act.

This meant that the company was both the regulator and service provider responsible for issuing licences as it deemed fit to other operators who wanted to enter the telecommunications field. This dual role persisted up to the end of 1997 when a new Telecommunications Regulation Act was enacted which came into force in January 1998 (see below).

Up to the 1980s public telecommunications monopolies were still common, worldwide, a number of reasons being attributed to this monopolistic "model". For example, by having a monopoly, governments could restrict new technologies in order to avoid harming existing investments (Steinfield et al., 1994: p. 5). The nationalisation of telecommunications was often justified on the basis of a disappointing experience with private providers who charged exorbitant prices and provided poor services. Another reason was the view that a telecommunications monopoly could be a secure form of tax-like revenues. Likewise, a state monopoly often had control not only over the basic telephone and telegraph networks, but also on the supply of telecommunications equipment, to the extent that, in some countries, the manufacturing of such equipment became a tool of industrial policy whereby the equipment was provided by only one or a very few domestic suppliers (*ibid.*, p. 6). Finally—particularly for the European case—a private telecommunications system was seen as posing a threat to national security.

Given the above, it is hardly surprising, therefore, that following Malta's independence and the election in 1971 of a political party that was known for its socialistic attitude, the telecommunications sector should be made a national affair under the umbrella of a fully state-owned corporation.

As noted above, the EU 1987 Green Paper is often considered to be the starting point for the European-wide liberalisation process. Following this paper, the EU Council adopted a resolution approving the main conclusions of the Green Paper (Kamall, 1996: p. 29; Koenig et al., 2002: p. 53). This resolution laid out several objectives to be achieved by 1992, including full liberalisation of the telecommunications equipment market, and the separation of regulation and operations of telecommunications services in all

Member States. To implement the main recommendations, subsequent legislation was required, and this came in the form of a number of Directives which the European Commission issued and which bound by law all Member States to carry out the reforms set out for them (Kamall, 1996: p. 55; see also Box 10-2).

As for non-EU countries then contemplating becoming full members — like Malta — these had to show commitment to follow the reforms. These commitments were typically the result of formal agreements signed with the EU (e.g. Association Agreements in preparation for full membership) (*ibid.*). Since the Maltese Nationalist government of the late 1980s had long been in favour of Malta joining the EU, this government officially applied for EU membership in July 1990. In the early 1990s, following the EU's assessment on Malta's eligibility (the *avis*) and in conformance with the *avis*, Malta began implementing major financial and legal reforms, reforms that were much needed anyway (Busuttil et al., 1999: p. 85).

In the meantime, in 1996, the opposition labour party was elected which, being unsympathetic with the EU, decided to freeze (suspend) Malta's application in November of that year. As it turned out, this government remained in office for only two years, following which the re-elected Nationalist government again immediately reactivated its membership application in September 1998. It was not long before the EU Commission replied in favour of Malta's accession, so that negotiation agreements in preparation for full membership had started by 2000.

Thus, commencing from the early 1990s, a number of measures were taken by the Maltese government in a bid to join the EU and as part of the liberalisation process, not only in telecommunications but also in other sectors of the industry. The telecommunications-related measures, explained below, were in line with the EU directives and recommendations. By July 2000, Malta had closed the negotiations on eight chapters of the existing corpus of EU laws (the *Acquis Communautaire*). One of these chapters was that of telecommunications.

Box 10-2
Some Early EU Liberalisation and Harmonisation Directives

The process of telecommunications liberalisation in Europe has been underpinned by concepts involving terms such as "special or exclusive rights" and "essential requirements".

In a nutshell, "special or exclusive rights" refer to certain rights which Member States grant to public or other organizations ("undertakings") through any legislative, regulatory or administrative instrument. Further, a distinction is made between exclusive rights and special rights. For example, an exclusive right reserves a right for an undertaking to provide a telecommunication service or undertake an activity within a given geographical area. On the other hand, a special right can be given to more than one undertaking and may include conferring to the undertakings legal or regulatory advantages which substantially affect the ability of any other undertaking to provide the same telecommunications service or to undertake the same activity. Examples of special rights include powers of compulsory purchase and derogations from laws on town and country planning.

"Essential requirements" refer to a set of requirements deemed essential as either part of a telecommunications service (e.g. security of network operations, and maintenance of network integrity) or a telecommunications equipment (e.g. health and safety of user, and effective use of the radio frequency spectrum).

The EU Directives required Member States to withdraw the grant of the aforementioned special or exclusive rights as well as conform with the essential requirements. The prime motives behind the Directives were to open up national markets to competition and at the same time provide harmonisation measures whereby all Member States adopt the same laws. Four examples of EU Directives are listed below.

Directive 88/301/EEC – Terminal Equipment Directive

A liberalisation directive, this directive opened the terminal equipment market for competition and introduced the principle of full mutual recognition of type approval for terminal equipment. In other words, according to this Directive, special or exclusive rights for the importation, marketing, and connection of telecommunications equipment had to be withdrawn by the Member States.

Directive 90/387/EEC – Open Network Provision (ONP) Framework Directive

This was a very important harmonisation directive adopted on the same day as the Services Directive (see below). The regulation, based on Article 95 EC,* aimed at facilitating access by private companies to public telecommunications networks and services. It also sought to achieve harmonisation of technical interfaces and to eliminate discrepancies in conditions of use and tariffs. A timetable for legislative action was set whereby the need for a series of harmonization Directives and Recommendations were identified.

Following a step by step strategy, the Community then went on and applied ONP principles to other fields of the telecommunications sector, for example to leased line and voice and telephony (Leased Line Directive 92/44/EEC and Voice Telephony Directive 95/62/EC).

Directive 90/388/EEC – Services Directive

This liberalisation directive aimed to rapidly liberalise the telecommunications services markets. All exclusive rights except for voice telephony had to be withdrawn. The Directive also obliged Member States to separate regulatory and entrepreneurial functions, and to establish a transparent and non-discriminatory procedure in the admission of new telecomunications services.

This Directive was limited in scope: it did not include the abolishment of exclusive rights regarding telex, mobile radiotelephony, paging and satellite services. Therefore further Directives amending Directive 90/388/EEC were later adopted to liberalise other services (e.g. Directive 94/46/EC re Satellite communications, and Directive 95/51/EEC re Cable TV networks).

Directive 96/19/EC – Full Competition Directive

This was an important Directive because it led to the abolition of special and exclusive rights regarding voice telephony as from 1 January 1998. Directive 96/19/EC required Member States to withdraw 'all exclusive rights for the provision of telecommunications services, including the establishment and the provision of telecommunications network required for the provision of such services'. In other words, this Directive removed the so-called "reserved service" exception made for the provision of voice telephony, which was seen as forming an integral part in the provision of network infrastructure. Certain Member States (e.g. those considered less developed) were granted transitional periods during which to comply.

* **Article 95** of the **EC Treaty** is the basis for acts aimed at establishing the internal market and securing its proper functioning. It empowers the Community institutions (the European Parliament and the Council) to adopt legislation intended to improve the conditions for the establishment and functioning of the internal market, i.e., remove barriers to the economic freedoms provided for by the Treaty (free circulation of goods, freedom of establishment, freedom to provide services, free movement of capital).

Regulatory Development: the Maltese General Legal Framework

Liberalisation in Malta may be considered to have begun in 1990 when terminal equipment was fully liberalised following a government legal notice that year (Legal Notice, 1990).[216] This came less than two years from the date when the EU issued the terminal equipment directive (88/301/EEC), which made use of Article 86(3) EC (former Article 90(3) of the Treaty of Rome) (Eliassen & Sjovagg, 1999: p. 32).[217] This EU directive opened up the market for terminal equipment such as telephone handsets, modems, and all other attachments to the network. In many countries, Malta included, this equipment could only be obtained from the Post, Telegraph and Telephone Department (the 'PTT') and often could only be rented and not purchased.[218]

---

[216] In 1988 licences were granted (under the Wireless Telegraphy Ordinance) for the first time to a particular sector of the industry that included hotels, holiday complexes, offices of daily newspapers and radio/TV stations, making it possible for this sector to have in its possession satellite terminal receiving equipment which previously was under the exclusive possession and control of Telemalta. Legal Notice No. 6 of 1990 extended this to the entire population.

[217] Article 90 of the Treaty of Rome reinforces the EU's rules on competition and permits the Commission to address directives or decisions to Member States in order to ensure compliance. Article 90(3) states that 'The Commission shall ensure the application of the provisions of this Article and shall, where necessary, address appropriate directives or decisions to Member States'. See also Kamall (2000: p. 88).

[218] PTTs typically purchased their equipment from preferred national suppliers and used national standards and type approval processes to keep foreign equipment providers from entering the market. Such a policy foreclosed national equipment providers from capitalizing on economies of scale, hence often resulting in higher equipment costs, which were passed on to the user. See Steinfield et al. (1994: p. 39).

In 1993, roughly three years after the EU Commission published its Green Paper on satellite communications with the aim of fostering growth in satellite services, Very Small Aperture Terminals (VSATs) which were not connected to the public telecommunications network were liberalised by an Order of the Prime Minister. VSATs make use of small satellite antennas with apertures (diameters) of about 60cm or less. The appearance in the 1990s of high-powered direct broadcasting satellites (DBSs)—such as the French TDF1, the German TV-SAT2, and the UK's BSB—suited for directly beaming down television programmes, played a major role in the European market, accelerating the building of the Europe-wide information services. Foreseeing the growth in satellite services, the EU therefore quickly sought to liberalise this area.[219, 220]

In March 1994, Telepage Ltd—a subsidiary of Telemalta established that year—was given an exclusive licence to operate a National Radio Paging Service on the 931.735 MHz band, valid for a period of ten years. It was also allowed to operate voice messaging, telemarketing and wireless messaging services on a non-exclusive basis, as a result of which the company also started operating a call centre in 2001. Thus, by 1994, data modems, telefax machines, telephone sets, PABXs, telex equipment, and voice facilities over private satellite links not connected to the Public Switched Telephone Network (PSTN) were all liberalised.

In 1995, another order was issued by the Prime Minister making it possible for Data Network Operators to be licensed to provide access to the Internet and other global data networks (Government Notice, 1995). Licenses for the Data Network Operators (service providers) were initially issued by the Department of Wireless Telegraphy (*ibid.*). The regulatory functions relating to the Internet was initially granted to the Department of Wireless Telegraphy and the Ministry responsible for telecommunications, but the Malta Communications Authority was later created for this purpose.

---

[219] In the US, an open-sky policy for satellite communications has been introduced progressively since the 1970s, as a consequence of which its satellite communications market expanded rapidly. See Ungerer & Costello (1990: p. 70).

[220] Maltacom regained its exclusive rights over VSATs in the license granted to it in 1998. VSATs licensed prior to 1998 were allowed to continue to operate in virtue of their licenses.

An important step in the liberalisation process was the enactment in 1997 of a new Telecommunications (Regulation) Act (Act XXXIII of 1997, CAP. 399), which legally separated the regulatory functions from those of operations. This law, which came into force on 1 January 1998, established the Office of the Telecommunications Regulator (OTR) responsible for a number of principal areas, including: (i) the supervision of the telecommunications sector; (ii) the issuing of licences for the provision of telecommunications services; (iii) the establishment of a numbering plan; and (iv) the monitoring of interconnection agreements. The Regulator was also responsible for establishing technical standards in the telecommunications sector and to ensure compliance with law.

An important facet of the 1997 legislation was that of user protection. Section 4(1) of the original Telecommunications (Regulation) Act, stipulated that the Regulator had to ensure that

> ...telecommunications services are provided for the benefit of the users...[whilst giving]...due consideration...to the commercial viability of authorised providers.

Consumer protection was further expanded in Section 23(2), which empowered the Regulator to investigate any complaints that could be lodged by customers. Other important functions, falling within the above mentioned areas of responsibilities, include the approval of tariffs charged by service providers, ensuring fair competition amongst the telecommunications players, monitoring local and international developments with a view to advising the relevant ministry about telecommunications policy, and identifying means of improving efficiency and standards in this field. Notwithstanding these measures, the Telecommunications Act did not immediately remove Telemalta's monopoly in this sector, although later measures did address this situation. The 1997 Telecommunications Act was amended a number of times since its enactment, for example in November 2004 the title was changed to "Electronic Communications (Regulation) Act", by which it is currently known. This was done following the EU's reform of the entire regulatory framework, the "cornerstone" of which was the Framework Directive of March 2002 (Directive 2002/21/EC).[221]

At the same time as the Telecommunications Act removed Telemalta as regulator, Telemalta was succeeded by (i.e., changed to) a public limited company (again as happened much elsewhere in Europe). Set up in December 1997 and named Maltacom plc, the new company was originally granted a twenty-five year operating licence with exclusivity to provide fixed line voice telephony, data services, DCS 1800 (a derivative of GSM), UMTS (Universal Mobile Telecommuncations System – a standard system developed by the European Telecommunication Standards Institute), and other services.[222] Maltacom's licence also carried with it the obligation to provide voice telephony services within a reasonable time to all applicants, as well as to provide interconnection to its network to other authorised providers.

Up until then, the OTR and Maltacom both reported to one Ministry—that of Transport, Communications and Technology—but in 1998, to further emphasise the distinction between Regulator and Operator, the government placed their respective responsibility under different Ministries. The Regulator fell under the Ministry of Transport and Communications, while the Operator fell under the Ministry for Economic Services.[223] It should be mentioned that whereas in many countries the Office of the Regulaor is a department or an institution made up of several employees some of whom are experts in a particular field, in Malta the regular was a one-person entity with a political connection and a former Maltacom Board Director who often had to consult with Maltacom experts on matters beyond his competence, not an ideal situation and one that has met with some criticism (see last section below).

---

[221] Chapter 7 of Koenig et al. (2002) is devoted to this directive.

[222] It should be pointed out that in order to preserve the telecommunications network infrastructure one had to safeguard the telecommunications incumbent's revenues, which primarily derived from voice telephony, hence these services were not initially subject to the process of liberalisation. See Walden et al. (2001: p. 280); and Koenig et al. (2002: p. 107).

[223] The UK is one of the few countries where regulation was assigned to a private body (Oftel), which is completely independent of government although, as Thatcher points out, regulatory decisions in the 1980s and 1990s were dominated by three actors, namely, the government, Oftel, and BT. See Thatcher (1999: p. 96).

In June of that year, as part of the liberalisation and privatisation process, forty percent of Maltacom was also sold. This was done through an International Public Offering, whereby twenty percent of the shares were sold on the domestic market and another twenty percent offered to institutional investors on the international market in the form of Global Depository Receipts (GDRs) (EU-ESIS, 1999).[224] The Company's shares were traded for the first time on the London Stock Exchange and the Malta Stock Exchange. The share offer in Malta was oversubscribed, and nearly 8000 shareholders were accommodated, of which, sixty percent were private individuals (*ibid.*).

Between 1998 and 2000, a number of legal notices were introduced in order to set up the necessary regulatory framework and technicalities relating to telecommunications. The 1998 regulations include:

- Telecommunications (Universal Service Obligations) Regulations, 1998 (L.N. 216/1998)
- Telecommunications Appeals Board (Jurisdiction) Regulations, 1998 (L.N. 217/1998)
- Telecommunications Appeals Board (Rules of Procedure) Regulations, 1998 (L.N. 218/1998)
- Telecommunications Apparatus (Standards) Regulations, 1998 (L.N. 219/1998)
- Fees for Type Approval of Telecommunications Equipment Regulations, 1998 (L.N. 220/1998)
- Authorised Providers (Provisions of Information) Regulations, 1998 (L.N. 278/1998)
- Rate Mechanism to be Applied to Certain Telecommunications Services (L.N. 332/1998)

---

[224] A Global Depository Receipt (also known as a European Depository Receipt or an Internatioanl Depository Receipt) is a negotiable certificate issued by one country's bank against a certain number of shares held in its custody but traded on the stock exchange of another country. GDRs facilitate trade of shares, and are commonly used to invest in companies from developing or emerging markets. A prime reason for issuing a GDR is to increase a company's visibility in the world market. For further explanations see Prior-Willeard (n.d.), and the website at *http://thismatter.com/money/stocks/global-depositary-receipts.htm*.

As amended a month later (by Notice No. 425), legal notice 332 established a rate mechanism, which came into force on 1 January 2000, whereby telecommunication services such as fixed line telephony and national and international leased lines, are stipulated by the Regulator and published in the Government Gazette after an authorised provider will have submitted to the Regulator the rates it proposed to charge.

As noted already in the previous chapter, the provision of data services and networks was a thorny issue in 1999. In an attempt to address this, a document entitled "Internet and Other Data Networks (Service Providers) Regulations, 1999", was published on 8 October of that year (EU-ESIS, 2001). This document included regulations that aimed to resolve the issue of whether Melita Cable, then the sole cable TV provider was breaking the law by not allowing the ISPs to make use of its network for Internet access. These regulations, however, failed to solve the issue, and Melita continued to refuse to open its network to other ISPs by not launching its own Internet access over cable.[225]

On 29 April 2000, the Government published its Policy for the Liberalisation for the Telecommunications Sector as part of a draft bill that would set up the Malta Communications Authority (MCA) (L.N. 280 of 2000). The bill itself, titled "The Malta Communications Authority Act, 2000", was approved in July (EU-ESIS, 2001). With the enactment of this Act, the OTR stopped functioning when the MCA inherited all the powers and duties of the OTR, and assumed further reponsibilities in accordance with the new Act.

The MCA and post-MCA developments

Given the relatively fast pace at which communications technology was being adopted in Malta in the mid-to-late 1990s, and the rapid developments that took place in the liberalisation arena at the EU level in that same period, the 1997 Telecommunications (Regulation) Act, which created the OTR, was a timely measure and a step in the

---

[225] Melita Cable did however introduce an Internet service in November 2000 (following the setting up of the Malta Communictions Authority in July 2000 and after having purchased Video-on-Line, a former ISP). This was a broadband service using cable modems. See also Chapter 9.

right direction. However, in the short period of its existence, the OTR was criticised mainly on the grounds of efficiency, since a sole regulator could not possibly cope with the sheer volume of work involved. Neither could a single person — the regulator — be expected to be knowledgeable in the vast field of telecommunications policy and law, not to mention technical matters. Therefore, the setting up of the MCA was the natural way forward, probably inevitable given the circumstances. It could be seen as the product of a process of dialogue and the progress being made in the ICT sector in Malta at that time.

The role of the MCA is spelled out in the Malta Communications Authority Act itself, but it is not the intention here to list the MCA's functions and powers. According to Joseph V. Tabone, the first MCA chairman (and formerly the MSU chairman), the MCA sees its role as largely strategic, serving to bring about competition and creating an environment that is conducive to sector investment and innovation (Tabone, 2007). The three main sectors for which it was made responsible since its inception are electronic communications, postal services and eCommerce, sectors that together accounted for approximately 5% of GDP in 2006 (*ibid.*).

When the MCA was set up there were still some areas of telecommunications that had not been fully liberalised (see Table 10.1), so that in the early years of its formation, the MCA concentrated on liberalisation issues. At the same time, it started investing heavily in human capital, building up a team of experts in different fields, including telecommunications law, policy and technology. With a staff complement in December 2004 of 27 (excluding 5 board members), the MCA had then reached critical mass (Malta Communications Authority, 2005). The number of employees increased to 50 by the end of 2006.

During its formative years, the MCA published a number of consultative papers on different aspects of telecommunications. In 2002 alone, for example, no fewer than eight papers were published (see Table 10.2). The purpose of publishing such documents is to provide certain guidelines about proposed changes and obtain feedback from the telecommunications industry before actually effecting the intended changes or executing a new project. To mention one example: in July 2006 a consultative paper entitled "A National Internet eXchange" was made publicly available, in which a number of suggestions were put forward regarding ways of achieving interconnection. Interested parties were asked to respond to "consultative questions" (included in the document) by a fixed date, so that the project would be subsequently implemented based on the received feedback and within the legal framework and proposed timeframe (see also Figure 10.1).

TABLE 10.1
Liberalisation dates of the Maltese telecommunications sector

Service/Infrastructure	Operator/ Owner	When Started*	When Liberalised
Fixed telephony (service)/ Public telecommunications network including local networks for voice telephony	Maltacom	1975	1 Jan 2003
Leased lines (infrastruct.)	Maltacom	-	1 June 2000
Pay TV; Radio (service)/ Broadcasting (infrastruct.)	various	1991	1991 2000 (Broadcasting Act)
Cable TV (service & infrastruct.)	Melita Cable	1990	1 June 2001
Paging (service & infrastruct.)	Telepage Vodafone (Malta)	1995 2000	1 June 2000
Mobile telephony (service)	Vodafone (Malta) Mobisle[a]	1989 2000	1 June 2000
Satellite communications (service & infrastruct.) (including satellite TV)	various	mid-1990s	1 June 2000
Internet and data services	various	1995	1 June 2000

*refers to the year when the service was introduced by the operator
[a] Go Mobile, now GO plc
Source: EU-ESIS (2001); and MCA Annual Reports (2002, 2003, 2004)

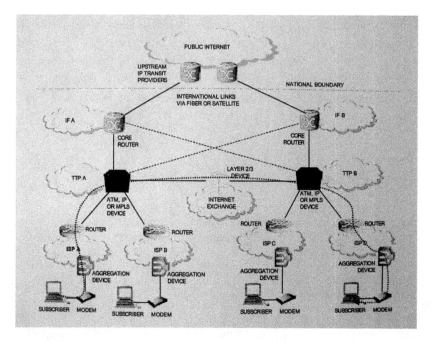

Figure 10.1
A proposed national internet infrastructure put forward in a consultative document by the MCA in 2002. Consultative documents are aimed at generating dialogue between interested parties and obtaining important feedback before a project is actually implemented.
Source: Malta Communications Authority (2002: p. 12)

Regulatory functions are any communications authority's major involvement, and the MCA has spent a great deal of its efforts in the promotion of competition (and ensuring ease of entry to new undertakings) via regulatory instruments. The EU has a regulatory framework for electronic communications that involve a number of competition policy tools and, since Malta became an EU member in 2004, the MCA is required to adopt the EU policy guidelines. A key exercise that forms part of the regulatory process, for example, is the carrying out of market reviews (aimed to verify whether or not relative markets are effectively competitive, i.e., determining if an operator has a dominant market power), which the MCA was obliged to undertake (and has undertaken on a regular basis since 2006) and report its findings to the EU. Other MCA tasks, together with major telecommunications-related developments in Malta covering the period 2001-2007, are summarised in Table 10.2.

TABLE 10.2
Major telecommunications-related developments in Malta, 2001-2007

2001 - MCA commences operations on 1 January
   - Ministry for Justice and Local Government announces intentions for the design and implementation of the e-Government project
   - Liberalisation of cable services.
   - Enactment of Data Protection and Electronic Commerce Acts
2002 - Numbering Plan, previously managed by Maltacom is taken over by MCA
   - Publication by MCA of consultation papers on:
      The implementation of Cost-based Accounting
      Accounting Separation and Publication of Financial Information
         for Telecommunications Operators
      Dominent Market Position
      Price Control Review
      Carrier Selection/Carrier pre-Selection
      Universal Service Obligation
      The Malta Internet Exchange
      Voice over IP (VoIP)
   - Electronic Commerce (eCommerce) Legislation comes into force in May
   - Vodafone is granted a licence to provide International Gateway Services beginning from 1 January 2003. (Commencing from this date, operators other than Maltacom could establish and maintain communications systems between Malta and other countries. The liberalisation process was completed by this date when data services and the fixed telephony sector were opened to new entrants.)
   - Introduction of Multimedia Messaging Service (MMS)
2003 - Emergence of Internet Protocol voice services (VoIP)
   - MCA updates its register of operators having DMP in the relevant telecommunications market
   - Divestment of Maltacom's share in Vodafone. (When Maltacom launched its "go Mobile" service it was obliged by law – for competition reasons – to divest itself of the shares it held in Vodafone.)
   - Fixed line telephony is liberalised (as of 1 January)
2004 - Maltacom reduces its international fixed-line telephone charges by about 50%
   - Government publishes a white paper proposing significant amendments to the Malta Communications Act 2000. The modified Act is brought into force the following September.
2005 - Introduction of Digital Terrestrial Television (DTTV) by Multiplus

TABLE 10.2 (continued)
Major telecommunications-related developments in Malta, 2001-2007

_____

2006 - A carrier pre-selection service operator (CPSO), Sky Telecom, starts
          operating under the brand name of "Sky"
        - Melita Cable launches its VoIP telephony service (called "Hello")
        - Go Mobile and Vodafone Malta roll out their Third Generation (3G)
          network. Vodafone also adopts the High-Speed Download Packet Access
          (HSDPA) protocol.
        - MCA undertakes a number of market reviews with a view to measure the
          competition in a given communications sector
2007 - Broadband Wireless Access (BWA) service is introduced by Vodafone
          (WiMAX). In June Vodafone starts providing fixed telephony service via
          its wireless broadband network. (The entry of Vodafone brings the number
          of nationwide broadband networks to three.)
        - Go acquires Multiplus, making it the first quadruple play operator in Malta
        - Melita Cable secures access to 3G spectrum after taking over 3G
          Telecommunications Ltd. (This makes Melita the second operator capable
          of offering quad-play services.)
        - New roaming tariffs are introduced according to the new EU roaming
          regulation

_____

Source: Compiled by author from various MCA Annual Reports and newspaper articles

Part VI

Government I.T. Policy and Initiatives

Part VI
Government I.T. Policy and Initiatives

In computing history, the 1990s must at least be remembered for the Internet's take-up and the convergence of computer and communication technologies. Spurred partly by the U.S. Vice President Al Gore's vision of a 'National Information Infrastructure' in 1993, many countries—for example, Japan, Singapore, Barbados and Hong Kong—launched initiatives that reflected their economy, political environment, and other national circumstances (Kahin & Wilson, 1997).[226] Malta was one of those that followed a similar path, announcing in that same period its vision for the information society. Like these countries, it too managed to successfully implement a national information infrastructure that has since borne fruit.

Unlike those countries that had an indigenous computer industry (for example, the USA, the UK, Germany, the Netherlands, France and Italy) Malta—for many years an underdeveloped country—could not have had an early IT policy, as did those countries where the computer was invented or created. Additionally, Malta's take up of computers was slow and late by international standards (see Parts II and III), and neither industry nor the University (of Malta) were in a position to undertake research and development until the late 1990s. This meant that when it came to initiatives like the European Strategic Program for Research in Information Technologies (ESPRIT), launched by the European Commission in 1984 in response to US and Japanese domination in information technology, Malta could not but stand back and watch.[227] In fact, it was only with the Fifth Framework Program (covering the period 1998-2002), initiating the European Information Society Technology Program, that Malta began to participate in research and innovation.

---

[226] Singapore's *The IT2000 Report: Vision of an Intelligent Island* by the National Computer Board (of Singapore) predated the United States' National Information Infrastructure Report.
[227] For a brief account of ESPRIT see Assimakopulos, et al. (2004). Jowett & Rothwell (1986) has a good section on ESPRIT and the Alvey programme.

That said, by the mid-1980s it had become clear in Malta that computers would play a very significant role in the Island's economy, and the social and cultural formation. Were it not for the particular circumstance and the political climate then prevailing, it is conceivable that some sort of IT policy—for example developing a software industry, or investing in IT education—would have been contrived in that period, years before ministers began thinking of including IT as part of their policy agenda.   Even in the microelectronics field there are those who believe that Malta missed the boat in the late 1970s by not investing sufficiently in this technology (Aquilina, 1984).

The chapters that make up Part VI focus on recent developments concerning Malta's IT policy. Chapter 11 gives an introductory overview of industrial and economic policy generally, and then moves on to discuss the early IT policies. A section about the 1999-2001 information system strategic plan and other initiatives are also discussed. Chapter 12 is dedicated to IT legislation and intellectual property, in particular copyrights and patents; and Chapter 13 treats IT education policy, and research and development initiatives.

11

Towards a Policy for I.T.

Overview of Industrial and Economic Policy up to c. 1987

Before we take up the issue of IT policy, which in Malta was non-existent before the 1990s, it will be instructive to outline briefly the industrial and economic policies of the 1970s and 1980s in order to get a feel for the political and economic climate then prevailing, before computer and IT-related policy begins to be mentioned for the first time. This will help us to understand why IT policy was neglected by politicians even as late as the second half of the 1980s when—as a result of the proliferation of the PC in the local market—it had become clear that Malta could not escape the IT transformation.

It will be recalled from earlier chapters that in 1971 the Malta Labour Party (MLP) defeated the Nationalist Party (PN) then in power, and was subsequently twice re-elected to govern for three consecutive terms up to May 1987. Essentially a socialist party—but not extremist as some opposition supporters sometimes paint it to be—the MLP's political ideologies and aspirations differ from those of its major political rival, the PN. The individual parties' approach to solving disputes, be they industrial or political, have also been— especially in the past—very different: whereas, for example, the PN would typically tackle a problem diplomatically, the MLP might resort to forceful measures in order to have its way.[228]

---

[228] The MLP's sometimes-arrogant attitudes of the 1970s and 1980s have somewhat changed since, recognising that diplomatic efforts and dialogue can be just as effective in winning arguments or solving disputes.

For reasons that will immediately become obvious, the economic policy that was generally adopted beginning from the 1970s all through the 1980s was one of protectionism, a policy of central planning involving a high degree of state intervention. A former British colony and, until quite recently, an underdeveloped republic, for many years Malta derived its income from the British military and naval base. At the peak of military activities, during World War II and for some considerable time after, nearly 30% of all gainfully occupied were employed by HM Services. Following Malta's independence in 1964 and the start of the process of the British forces run-down thereafter, plans were drawn up to develop tourism and boost industrialisation, measures that aimed to not only replace the income traditionally derived from the presence of the UK's (and NATO's) military base that eventually was to close down, but also make Malta self-supporting.[229] During the years that followed, a number of industrial estates were built, and foreign firms were encouraged to set up operations in Malta, which they did. However, most firms, for example the textile industry and those in electronics, employed unskilled or semi-skilled labour, which meant that technology transfer remained very limited. Official statistics clearly indicate that both the tourism sector and manufacturing industry registered rapid growth in the decade 1971-1981. In this period, a process of nationalisation also occurred: the state-owned companies (mostly now privatised) Air Malta (the national airline), Telemalta (telecommunications), Enemalta (water and electricity supply), and Mid-Med Bank were all set up in the mid-1970s.

Why was it necessary to nationalise certain key industries and adopt a policy of protectionism? Put simply, and economic reasons apart, the rationale for nationalisation is that although Malta was granted independence, all of these key utilities remained under foreign (British) hands, something the MLP disapproved of. In fact, the MLP never accepted the political settlement negotiation by the PN that led to Malta's independence, arguing that for a country to be truly independent, it must also have control of its own major

---

[229] The industrialisation drive was actually launched with the *First Development Plan* in 1959. By the time of Independence in 1964, the percentage of those working with the British Services had fallen down to 14%, the remainder (16%) having been absorbed by the Malta Government and the Private Industry.

infrastructure utilities (see, for example, Pirotta, 2005). Indeed, at the time of independence, the Maltese constitution (as established in 1964) still recognised a monarchical form of government, with the Head of State of Malta remaining Britain's Queen.[230]

As for protectionism, it was reasoned that it would be almost impossible to build new industries without providing direct aid, especially in the initial stages of industrialisation. When an Association Agreement with the then European Economic Community (EEC) was concluded by the PN in 1970, with the aim of eventually taking Malta in the EEC, that agreement was allowed to lapse by the MLP government precisely on those grounds: because it believed that what Malta required was preferential treatment for its exports and aid to help it reach its development targets, not a customs union.[231] Apart from aid, state intervention was necessary to ensure economic stability, for example to counter the effect of a general depression. Indeed, there are cases where economics allows for the possibility of state intervention, for example instances of market-failure (goods and services required by individuals in a society which are unable to be exchanged through the market) and the "natural monopolies", which predominantly refer to the public utilities.

Since Malta has no natural resources, the Island is heavily dependent on imports of raw material for manufacturing, so that the import-content of the total final expenditure has tended to be high, but decreased over the years as a policy of import substitution and strict import controls were eventually adopted (in the late 1970s). Import substitution, because it is usually accompanied by import controls and restrictions, has the disadvantage of sheltering local producers against competition which could result in inferior quality products and inefficient production, but according to Briguglio (1988: p. 134) it was a necessary measure that promoted domestic value added and employment.

How does the above relate to computing, in so far as policy is concerned? Although there is no direct link as such, the inability to consider IT policy—or, rather, the refusal to discuss IT policy—has to

---

[230] This arrangement was amended on 13th December 1974, when the highest executive authority was vested in a President who had to be a Maltese national.
[231] For a good introduction on the early Malta-EEC relations, including the improved Malta-EEC Association Agreement of 1976, see Pollacco (1992).

be seen in the context of those particular conditions of that time. In a nutshell, the MLP's view of computers as job-destructive machines did not fit the general framework of industrialisation, particularly in the early phases, of which a primary aim was job creation. Under the circumstances, it is therefore hard to see how there could have been an IT policy: any formulation of it by the then ruling MLP would have meant going against the MLP's fundamental belief that computer technology could, far from solving the economic and political problems of the time, exacerbate the unemployment crisis.

Of course, those decisions also had repercussions as far as information technology on a national scale was concerned; for although in November 1981 the MLP government opened its computer centre, hence partially acknowledging the computer's importance as a tool, if not as an economic benefit, it still viewed computers with scepticism. Thus, every computer purchase required a government licence, causing much resentment from suppliers and consumers alike (because of the bureaucratic procedures and, at times, preferential treatments and corrupt practices). Far from encouraging the use of technology, therefore, the government of the day kept postponing its widespread diffusion to the public. Indeed, as late as the mid-1980s, few schools had made use of a computer and the ones that did were private (mainly Church schools). They decided to offer computer studies completely on their own initiative. The University itself did not introduce its first computer until 1980, and run its first computing diploma course until years later. In brief, Malta had fallen behind many European neighbours in informatics.

IT Policy Beginnings

In the advanced and industrialised countries computer policy goes back to more or less the time when the computer was created in the 1940s, and IT-related policy to perhaps a decade or two later (see Box 11-1 at the end of this chapter). In many countries that did not have an indigenous computer hardware industry, official policy regarding IT came much later, often during the 1980s or after. Malta was a latecomer in policy matters, and the beginnings of IT policy is partly related to the change in the public service perceived by the newly elected nationalist government in 1987.

Public Service Reform and the first ISSP

Although the Nationalist Party 1987 electoral manifesto, titled "Xoghol, Gustizzja, Liberta", dedicates a very small section on IT (Partit Nazzjonalista, 1987),[232] it is nevertheless probably true to say that the PN—elected again in 1987 after a long span in opposition— was (and has been) both more open to, and a believer in, technology. The PN also was envisaging a restructuring of the civil service, hoping to make it more transparent and efficient, so that within two years of winning the election, the newly elected government appointed a Public Service Reform Commission (PSRC) to examine the organization of the Public Service. The Commission's findings were published in 1989 as a report titled "A New Public Service for Malta" (Public Service Reform Commission, 1989).

The PSRC's Report, instead of making definite recommendations, was a 'statement of findings' which, according to Pirotta (1992), therefore made an analysis and a discussion of the Report more difficult. A general criticism of the Report has been that it gave inadequate attention to the political environment, which—according to Pirotta—ultimately shapes and dictates public service behaviour. The Report expounded on thirteen goals which the Commission saw as necessary for the public service reform to be successfully implemented. In spite of the criticism, many of the Report's goals made sense, with most of the recommendations advanced in it having actually been introduced. One of the goals (goal number 8) was to invest in technology and plant, effectively providing government departments with the resources required for their better management and execution.

The PSRC was complemented by a so-called Operations Review (OR) exercise. The OR essentially entailed the setting up of a task group which was charged to devise a five-year strategic plan for the Malta Government. This plan—an attempt that included the establishment of an ICT infrastructure within the Public Service—was a combined initiative of the OR, the PSRC, and government. The program of reform ranged from institutional re-design and the re-

---

[232] The only section related to IT is in Part III(11), section 1.7 ("Jitfassal pjan nazzjonali ta' l-Informazzjoni"), a page-length brief mention of an anticipated national information plan that would be based on UNESCO recommendations.

skilling of public officers to the adoption of management techniques in the public service.

In the summer of 1990 government took the first concrete steps to formulate an IT policy and thus place IT on a strong footing. That summer, the Government of Malta established the first "blueprint" for the introduction of information systems across the Public Service by presenting to the Cabinet an Information System Strategic Plan (ISSP) (Government of Malta, 1990). The ISSP was officially presented to the Cabinet by the OR team. Envisaging a preliminary investment of Lm20 million (= c. US$60 m.) over a five-year period, the ISSP was endorsed, and implementation initiated in early 1991.

In order to implement the ISSP—which aimed to comprehensively revive the entire public service—a new organizational entity called Management System Unit (MSU) was constituted. An Information Systems Division and a Consultancy Division (the designated agent responsible for institutional and organizational reform) were created within the MSU that between them would implement the ISSP policy goals. As explained in Chapter 6, funding for IT in Government was routed directly through MSU over the period 1991-1996, but was subsequently routed to Government Ministries. Also, in 1997, MSU evolved into two organizations: the Malta Information Technology and Training Services (MITTS)—previously the Information Systems Division of MSU—and the Management Efficiency Unit, which was previously MSU's Consultancy Division. Table 11.1 summarises these key events.

The three main policy goals of the 1991 ISSP were the distribution of personal computers, the development of applications, and networking. All three goals were achieved. For example, in 1990 the number of PCs in the Maltese public service amounted to a few hundreds, whereas in 1998 this number had increased to around 8000, half of which were in state schools (MITTS, 1999: p. 15 & 28). In that period, a number of substantial applications had been developed by the MSU team, foremost among them being corporate projects throughout various departments (e.g. Departmental Accounting Systems), ministry specific systems (e.g. Law Courts Computerisation; Vehicle Licensing) and the Common Data Base (public domain personal "tombstone" information which would later be used as a single source of data by all government software applications).

Computer networking had also been introduced in many government departments: 95 sites had been connected by 1996 as part of the Government of Malta Wide Area Network (MAGNET).

TABLE 11.1
Key events that led to the establishment of the first ISSP, the NSIT, and the MSU

Year	Description of Event
1987	PN's 1987 Electoral Manifesto makes a very brief mention of a proposed national plan for Information Technology, based on UNESCO recommendations.
1989	PN Government appoints PSRC to examine the organization of the Public Service. PSRC is also complemented by an OR task group to device a 5-year strategic plan. PSRC's findings is published as a report entitled "A New Public Service for Malta".
1990	OR team presents to Cabinet its strategic report entitled "Information Systems Strategic Plan 1991-1996". It is a policy framework that addresses IT for the Public Service.
1991	The ISSP begins to be implemented. A new entity called Management Systems Unit (MSU) is set up for this task.
1993	Government announces its plan to establish a nationwide framework for IT. The Malta Council for Science and Technology is entrusted to commission the study.
1994	MCST's study is published as the NSIT, called "A National Strategy for Information Technology for Malta".

By the end of 1996, the MSU—which employed some 476 staff—also began to be involved in projects such as the Automated Systems for Customs Data (ASYCUDA) training project in a partnership agreement with the United Nations Conference on Trade and Development (UNCTAD) (Management Systems Unit, 1997).[233] This

---

[233] ASYCUDA is a computerised customs management system which covers most foreign trade procedures. The system handles manifests and customs declarations, accounting procedures, transit and suspense procedures. It also generates trade

involved the setting up of a training centre so that training on the ASYCUDA system and related subjects could be provided. In 1996 foreign delegations received training. The ASYCUDA project essentially supported the Maltese Government's agenda to expand its co-operation with UNCTAD.

The National Strategy for Information Technology

The 1991 ISSP was a policy framework that primarily addressed information technology in the Public Service: it was not a nationwide framework for IT. The latter came about later when, in 1993, the Malta Council for Science and Technology (MCST) was entrusted to commission an autonomous and independent study to formulate what came to be called a National Strategy for Information Technology (NSIT). Set up in 1988, the MCST had already gained some experience in producing a number of policy documents, so that it was perhaps natural to involve the MCST in carrying out the NSIT study. It should be pointed out that during this period (early-to-mid 1990s) many countries were in the process of drafting (or had just developed) their national IT strategies. These policy strategies have typically been oriented to economic and innovation strategies, linking them to a broad concerted drive to evolve as regional or global hubs for various types of electronic services (Cassingena-Harper, 1998: p. 275).[234]

The onus of coordinating the NSIT fell on Juanito Camilleri who, at the time, had just returned with a doctorate in computer science from the University of Cambridge (and would later hold key positions in Industry and more recently become University Rector). With the help of a Steering Committee and several expert working groups, Camilleri essentially directed the project and edited the final report. The latter, a 200-page document entitled "A National Strategy for Information Technology for Malta", was published by the University of Malta in October 1994.

In the preface to this strategic plan (see Figures 11.1 and 11.2),

data useful for statistical economic analysis. See
http://www.asycuda.org/aboutas.asp.
[234] See also Kahin & Wilson (1997) in which several case studies of national information infrastructure initiatives are analysed.

Camilleri explains that

> [the strategic plan] conveys the vision of a small island
> in the centre of the Mediterranean at the cross roads
> between cultures, and its aspiration to become a
> regional hub of activity through the strategic
> deployment of Information Technology (Camilleri, 1994:
> p. xi).

Further on in the report, it is stated that

> the purpose of the strategy is to establish what
> functions, capabilities and resources are required of I.T.
> so that the resulting strategic thrusts may embed I.T.
> within Malta's business, industry, and society, and
> provide strong support for the desired growth and
> welfare of the Maltese economy and society (*ibid.*, p. 7).

The NSIT identified ten "strategic directions", and recommended complementary actions for each direction with the aim of integrating IT considerations into Malta's socio-economic growth.[235]

Coming from an academic and professional body of experts that included University lecturers, professors and experienced industry practitioners, one of the highlights of this document was an emphasis on human development and socio-economic aspects, where topics like IT education, the opportunities for developing an export-oriented ICT sector (including a software industry) and the infrastructural requirements to support IT were discussed at length. The strategic plan was well received by the government of the day and was also welcomed generally by the opposition. It has undoubtedly served as a model upon which later decisions would be taken with many of the recommendations having actually been implemented. The brief of the strategic plan did not include the issues related to the introduction

---

[235] The ten strategic directions are: 1. An Information Technology Culture; 2. I.T. as a means for Education and In-Career Training; 3. I.T. Human Resources; 4. Assistance for I.T. RTD and Business Ventures; 5. International Brokerage of Services and Goods; 6. I.T. Industry; 7. Business Process Re-engineering; 8. Sector-wide I.T. networks and beyond; 9. Telecommunications Regulation and Infrastructure; 10. Legislative framework for I.T.

of IT in the civil service which, as noted above, was the responsibility of the former Management Systems Unit.

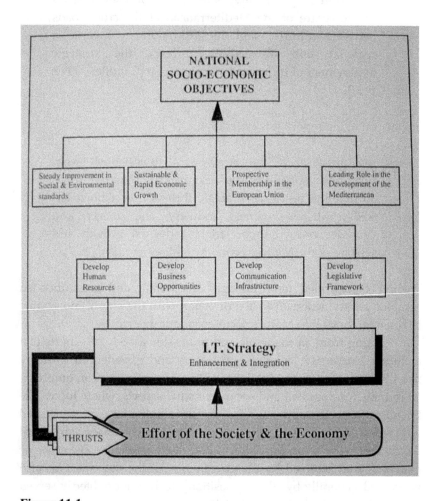

Figure 11.1
Intentions of the NSIT. This diagram captures the essence of the mission statement, which is to integrate IT considerations into Malta's socio-economic development. Like the 1991 ISSP before it, the NSIT was an important document that for many years served as the guiding torch by which IT at a national level would be developed.
Source: Camilleri (1994)

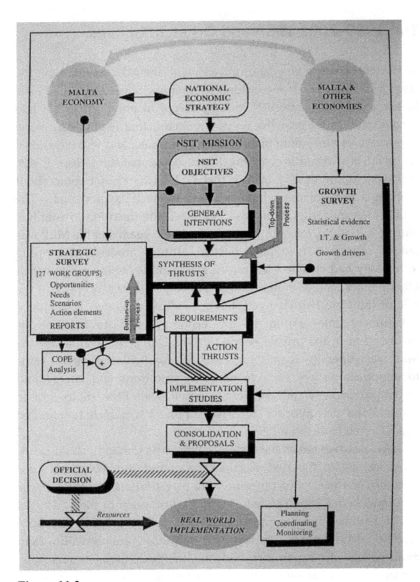

Figure 11.2
NSIT Strategy Formulation Process. A top-down, bottom-up strategy
synthesis depicted in this diagram was effected via two important parallel
studies, namely a strategic survey and a growth survey. Each of the 27 work
groups was to research and report on a distinct aspect of importance to the
development of a viable IT infrastructure and culture for Malta. A computer-
based analytical tool called COPE (Cognitive Policy Evaluation) was used to
synthesise (combine) the work group recommendations.
Source: Camilleri (1994)

The 1999-2001 ISSP and Other Initiatives

In 1996 there was a change of government, the MLP having won the elections. The PN's 1996 electoral programme surprisingly had little to say about information technology except to point out that it had become the fastest growing economic sector, that it provided many opportunities for finding niche markets for Malta, and that it could be the pivot of a nation's economy (Partit Nazzjonalista, 1996). It did, however, follow this by stating that IT benefits cannot come about without a government which believed in its (IT's) potential. The MLP's electoral programme also expressed the intention to continue with IT initiatives, for in the two terms of nine years that the MLP was out of office, its (generally hostile) attitude towards computing technology had changed, as indeed had its views about a number of other political and economic issues. For example, its conception of the role of the state had changed, having indicated its desire to reduce government intervention in the economy, and to increase its involvement in the private sector (Pirotta, 2001). Also, although the MLP was generally against privatisation—particularly when it came to important sectors such as telecommunications and energy and water provision—it nevertheless was left with little choice but to embrace the privatisation initiatives of the PN, which it inherited when elected in October 1996.

At least two issues the general public was unhappy about in the years leading to the 1996 elections and which probably had some influence on the election outcome were privatisation, and the way the MSU was being administered. Within a few years of the MSU's set up, it had become common knowledge that the MSU had been careless with public funds: for example, abnormally high remuneration to expatriates and the methods used in recruiting personnel were among some of the allegations being instigated against it. This made the labour government of the day launch a full enquiry which, in turn, led to a restructuring exercise whence the MITTS was created (see Chapter 6).

An interesting development in the IT area, which took place in this period (mid-1990s), was the Commonwealth Network of Information Technology for Development (COMNET-IT), an initiative of the Commonwealth Secretariat and the Government of Malta.

Established as an independent international foundation in November 1995, COMNET-IT's principal aims were to support Commonwealth member countries in policy-development and "capability-building" for implementing, managing, and using new ICTs. Infrastructural support for the COMNET-IT Foundation has been provided by the Malta Government through its MITTS agency. The Commonwealth Secretariat, through the Commonwealth Fund for Technical Co-operation (CFTC), along with other donors, supported COMNET-IT sponsored programmes.

In 1997, the first ICT and trade related COMNET-IT workshop was held in Malta between May 19-21.[236] Attracting some 40 delegates, this workshop focused on the effects the rapid developments in ICTs were having on the prospects for international trade. Topics discussed included the role of governments, trade promotion, small and medium scale enterprises (SMEs), and infrastructure services and ICT development models. The Workshop was a precursor to the Commonwealth Heads of Government Meeting (CHOGM) held in Edinburgh later that year, and that had as its focus roughly the same themes (trade, investment, and sustainable development). Alfred Sant, then Malta's Prime Minister, was invited to deliver the closing speech. In his address, Sant pointed out that ICTs were 'clearly becoming the conduit for all human endeavour, from managing the utilisation of scare resources to the development of the person and the generation of economic activity', and that the challenge was 'to avoid an increasing divide between "the haves and the have nots" – in all contexts, whether international, regional or local'. What Sant was referring to here is the digital divide.[237] Having touched upon other matters such as SMEs and the information superhighway, he further acknowledged that Malta (and, therefore,

---

[236] The title of this workshop was "Information and Communication Technologies in International Trade, Investment and Sustainable Development – a Commonwealth Perspective". A summary of the main workshop events may be found at: *http://www.comnetit.org/pubs/reports/trdrep97/hilxesrp.html*.

[237] The digital divide has been the subject of a number of studies. It is not new and, as early as 1985 when the Maitland Commission delivered its report ("The Missing Link") to the ITU on 22nd January, it was already of concern to a number of international bodies. More recent initiatives include the Commonwealth Action Programme on the Digital Divide (CAPDD). See, for example, Ayeni & Ramnarine (2005).

presumably also his party) remained committed to the continued renewal of its NSIT and to its Public Service IT Strategy.

It would have been interesting to see how, and to what extent, Labour's vision of the information society would have developed locally had the Labour party spent at least an entire term in office, but disagreements with the MLP parliamentary group led to the early elections of September 1998, which Labour lost.

Back in power, the PN continued with its IT vision by introducing in November 1998 a second ISSP for the years 1999-2001 (Management Efficiency Unit, 1998). This ISSP aimed to build on the principles established in the first ISSP: however, rather than establishing a strategic direction that was solely focused on pure technology, the new Plan focused on inculcating an information resource and strategic management culture which, it was perceived, was still lacking. The primary efforts proposed by the ISSP were therefore directed towards a process of consolidation, maximization and optimization of the information systems that had been created (COMNET-IT, 2000).

The 1999-2001 ISSP established three major thrusts. The first thrust was directed towards the establishment of an institutional framework for an information resource management within the Public Service. It introduced the concept of ownership of the Information Resource Management, for which the establishment of a Central Information Management Unit (CIMU) was proposed. CIMU would assume the functional responsibilities of information technology and systems management, policy formulation, and the drawing up of IT-related legislation. CIMU came into being in February 1999, and it developed the Malta Government portal ("www.gov.mt") and the Public Service Intranet.

The second thrust was directed towards leveraging information technology and systems to support re-generation and continued change in the Public Service. To this effect the Plan recommended that an aggressive stance be undertaken by the Public Service to attain "Government On Line". The strategy for the attainment of "Government On Line" was based on a number of key issues. These issues included:

- best practices for Electronic Service Delivery (e.g. public confidence; assisting business process re-engineering by streamlining internal processes and enabling a 'one-stop' shop service);

- the establishment of a corresponding (e-Services) legislation (see below), and a "one window interface" whereby a Government of Malta website would serve as the single entry point for any interaction with the Public Service;
- a "standards and principles" issue whereby systems would be expected to be consistent (there should be a standard 'look and feel' for all applications), modular, and involve minimal customisation;
- security standards (systems acquired or built would have security standards to ensure that shared information is protected).

To what extent the thrusts envisaged in the ISSP 1999-2001 were successfully realised is debatable; what is certain, however, is that this ISSP triggered the idea of e-Government which was taken up in earnest in the spring of 2001.[238] By then, the Malta Government Network was already in an advanced development phase. With such an infrastructure in place, the stage had therefore been set by the turn of the millennium for the Internet and Intranet technologies to be exploited to the full. The Government Online project, or e-Government, could now become reality. In March 2001, a request for proposal for the design and implementation of the e-Government project was publicly announced by the Ministry for Justice and Local Government (Ministry for Justice and Local Government, 2001). The "request for proposal" document gave summary guidelines to interested parties, and also referred them to a White Paper published by the Office of the Prime Minister in May 2000 articulating the Maltese Government's Vision and Strategy for e-Government (Office of the Prime Minister, 2001). The response was overwhelming, with some 19 consortia having shown interest in the project (Brincat, 2001b).

---

[238] The literature on e-Government is extensive. For a brief discussion of e-Government and its benefits, see Schelin (2003).

Box 11-1
Early Information Technology Policy: A Snapshot

In view of the computer's socio-economic impact, governments worldwide have made considerable efforts to devise some sort of IT-related policy. Various policy strategies have been tried, rejected, and adopted, with countries following different policies as they see fit. This is hardly surprising given that policy decisions are the result of a combination of factors including political ideologies and propagandas, and a nation's exigencies, its wealth, size, and political history. Policy issues have varied also on account of the fact that some nations—particularly in the early data processing years—had the technological capability to design and build computers whereas others did not. Thus, for those countries with the technical knowhow and the financial means for funding R&D projects, policy matters had to deal with manufacturing issues in addition to pure technology adoption. Additionally, there has been diversification in the emphasis of policy issues over the years, a process that reflected both the change in political ideologies as well as that in economic thought. Thus, during the Cold War period, the manufacture and distribution of computers by the United States was properly guarded because of the importance the US government placed on national security. Later, changes in policy reflected the shift that was occuring from Keynesian theory (that in practice took the form of government intervention) to the so-called New Right economics (that partly drew on the work of Adam Smith and Friedrich Hayek) which essentially stressed the non-interventionist, free market approach. Later still, as wide area computer networking, the Internet, and mobile telephony began to gain popularity, the importance of the telecommunications sector grew in proportion, and telecommunications policy—which had always been on any government's agenda—took newer dimensions.

The following gives a very brief summary of computing developments and the early IT policies that selected economies chose to foster. The countries mentioned below were quick to realise the computer's potential, and accordingly attempted to use it as a means by which technology policy could be targeted. Of course, in the case of Europe and the United States, the computer's creation was very much tied to the war effort, and the early policy decisions were often dictated by military, as much as economic, needs.

Development of Computers and IT Policy: USA

Several agencies influenced and shaped IT research, for example the National Science Foundation (NSF), the National Bureau of Standards (NBS) and the Census Bureau. Government funding was primarily military related (e.g. the development of ENIAC, the SAGE early warning air defence system, and

ARPANET). However, government support was not exactly a uniform and coordinated programme, since government agencies and military departments often pursued diverse and conflicting programmes.

In general, government policies were directed at:

1) The development and production of computer systems
2) The labour market in computing, hence the role of government in providing computer education
3) The "regulation" of IBM which grew so big as to dwarf other manufacturers and hence effectively had become a monopolist (like AT&T in telecommunications).

Development of Computers and IT Policy: Europe

In a number of European countries—particularly the industrialised nations such as the UK, France, and the Netherlands—early IT policy was partly driven by strong national feelings of vulnerability to outside competition and pride. The major competitor was, of course, IBM. The three countries just mentioned tried to promote their own national IT champion, whereby the government heavily supported the most promising computer manufacturer, if not creating one. ICL was the UK's national champion; CII that of France; and Philips that of Holland.

One argument in favour of national champions centred around economic theory, for example scale economies: in attempting to reach economies of scale, at least France and Britain tried to capitalize (rather unsuccessfully) on captive empire markets (in spite of its smallness, Malta was one of these for Britain's ICL) or those of the eastern bloc where US manufacturers were not permitted to export. Interestingly, the national champion approach was also extended to a sort of European national (or supranational) champion when Unidata—a pan European company established in 1973 that formed part of France's CII, Germany's Siemens and the Netherlands' Philips—was created to take on IBM. The aim was to have Unidata build a range of computers on par with those of Big Blue but, unfortunately, the venture was not very successful, having encountered difficulty in coordination at various levels.

Development of Computers and IT Policy: Russia

In the former USSR, the design and manufacturing of computers began in the early 1950s and became a main task of national economy. Given the Cold War trade embargoes (e.g. the COCOM—Coordination Committee for Multilateral Export Control—agreement) which prohibited Western exports of military-related equipment, including computers, to the Soviet Union, the development of computing in Russia took place independently of external influences, that is, without contacts with scientists in the West. Moreover, computers supported important projects such as those of atomic energy, satellite technology, and rocketry. Computer research was also shrouded in secrecy.

In Russia, the post-war rate of economic growth was more rapid than most other countries, and a sense of optimism prevailed. This may partly explain the enthusiasm associated with computing research which led to a number of computers being built by the mid-1950s. Like the West, Soviet computer development was dominated by demand for the military sector, but unlike the West where it was later superseded by a civil need for computers, market demand in the Soviet Union did not mature as well, given the command-type economic planning. Throughout the 1950s, Russia also played a pivotal role in China's computing development effort by giving the Chinese the opportunity to learn computer science via the supply of soviet-made components, the description of the manufacturing process, and the parting of expert advice on how to manage computer-related projects.

In 1967 the Soviet government adopted a decree whereby R&D in semiconductor and microelectronic circuitry would be stepped up and industrial facilites for the production of computers for both civil and military use. Cooperation with the computer industries of Bulgaria, Hungary, Czechoslovakia, and Poland was also widened. By the late 1960s, together with the United States, the Soviet Union had also become a world leader in the production of computers.

12

Information Technology Legislation

Computer and Information-related Legislation

The preceding chapter touched on the 1999-2001 Information System Strategic Plan (ISSP 1999-2001) and mentioned the publication of a White Paper which essentially articulated the government's vision of an information society and an information economy in Malta. Of course, the foundations for the attainment of e-Government could be established only if the relevant legislation were in place. Therefore as the 1999-2001 ISSP was being launched, government also discussed the need for the introduction of an Information Practices Act to provide for good governance, and thus gain the necessary trust and confidence needed for the e-Government policy as a whole. In March 1999 an Inter-Ministerial Working Group was set up to develop a compendium of cyber legislation to put together the appropriate legislative framework. Following an exercise of consultation and feedback, three bills were drafted, namely:

(i)   The Electronic Commerce Bill
(ii)   The Data Protection Bill
(iii)   The Computer Misuse Bill

These bills were made law after further consultation of the May 2000

Information Practices White Paper,[239] of which they formed part.

Enacted in 2001 and brought into force in May 2002, the Electronic Commerce Act aimed to facilitate and encourage the use of e-Commerce, communications, transactions, signatures and contracts (*Electronic Commerce Act 2001*).[240] Its intention was also to promote confidence in e-Commerce and communications, therefore enabling the business sector and society to interact with government. The Act was based on the United Nations Commission for International Trade Law (UNCITRAL) model with the necessary amendments to factor in the EU Directives titled "A Common Framework for Electronic Signatures" and "Certain Legal Aspects on Electronic Commerce", respectively (see, for example, Micallef, 2007: p. 391). The Malta Communications Authority (MCA) is the regulator.

The Data Protection Act was endorsed on 14 December 2001 and brought into force in July 2003. This Act was long in coming: as early as 1986 an LLD dissertation by Cannataci had exposed how public data being processed at the former Government Computer Centre at Swatar was vulnerable to misuse, and the thesis therefore had called for the urgent need of such an Act (Cannataci, 1986).[241] In spite of some good arguments put forward by Cannataci in connection with private data misuse, fifteen years had to pass before legislation was formulated. Based on the EU Directive on data protection and also modelled on the Swedish Data Protection Act of 1998, the Maltese act aimed to build the public's trust by outlining the rights of the individual and providing help—through the Data Protection Commissioner—on how to safeguard one's rights. The requirements and criteria for the processing of personal data—nine data protection principles (for example, processing of data fairly and lawfully; in accordance with good practice; data only collected for specific, explicitly stated and legitimate purposes, etc.)—are clearly indicated in Part III of the Act, article 7 (*Data Protection Act 2001*).

---

[239] "White Paper on the Legislative Framework for Information Practices" (CIMU, OPM). This paper was revised and published in 2001 as the "White Paper on the Vision and Strategy for the Attainment of eGovernment".
[240] This Act was initially published as a Bill in the Government Gazette of 29 September 2000.
[241] Cannataci later went on to become Professor of Law with a specialisation in Intellectual Property.

The Computer Misuse Bill was not enacted as a separate Act: instead, the Maltese Criminal Code was amended in order to introduce computer misuse as a criminal offence. Important amendments include the unauthorised access to data; unauthorised prevention or hindrance of others from accessing data; unauthorised destruction or transfer of data; and unauthorised use of other persons' passwords or access codes.[242] Contravention of any of these acts carries a maximum penalty of €116,468 and up to ten years of imprisonment.

Intellectual Property Laws: Software Protection

International Background

In the early days when manufacturers' software packages were free, and custom programs too specific for an organization to be attractive to another user, software protection was barely an issue. However, the rise of the software products industry in the 1960s and 1970s — when software was turned into a product and perceived as just another good — changed all that. Software had become another commodity similar to, for example, music records, and therefore needed protection from illegal copying. Both physical and legal means were employed as a result: the legal issues were widely aired by the legal profession and in the computer trade press as early as the mid-1960s, whereas attempts at finding methods of physically protecting software did not appear until about a decade later.

The four major intellectual property (IP) protection laws, eventually applied also to software, were those of patents, copyright, trade secrets, and trademarks. Of these, copyright was by far the most appealing for software, although software patents have been issued by the thousands, and the trade secret law was also variously applied to some categories of software.[243] As for trademarks, this was used for

---

[242] See Articles 337B-337G of the Criminal Code (BOOK FIRST, Part II, Title IV, Sub-title V "OF COMPUTER MISUSE"), Chapter 9 of the Laws of Malta. Note: the "Contents" section of this Act has not been updated accordingly.

[243] Nicholas (1998: p. 118) notes that a good example of software that should be maintained as a trade secret is a program-trading application (software which makes buy and sell recommendations) since disclosing the trading strategy (as one

registering and protecting brand names, so that when a trade mark was obtained for a successful software product, that same trademark appearing on the product's packaging often served as a powerful advert for the software producer. The registering of a trade mark gives the mark (and, by proxy, the product) statutory recognition as assignable and transmissible property and—unlike patents and copyrights—can last forever (Niblett, 1982, as quoted in Grover, 1990: p. 200).

The problems relating to patents and copyright as applied to software, for example the validity of the patent law vis-à-vis software when the patent law was originally designed to protect tangible artefacts rather than an abstract entity (such as software), are complex and have been discussed widely in the literature.[244] The adoption of the laws themselves by individual countries is an important issue, since this will often determine the scale of software piracy, as well as the extent to which a given company is willing to set up operations in a country where no software copyright and patent laws exist.[245] Balanced regulation and use of intellectual property rights (IPRs) that aim to mitigate the cost of obtaining, maintaining and enforcing IPRs are also very important for ICT firms, particularly innovative small ones, since the rapid growth of software and business method patenting can easily increase the costs of small businesses and the likelihood of infringement (OECD, 2004). Regulatory frameworks, therefore, should aim at balancing the interests of suppliers and users, and protect and manage IPRs without disadvantaging innovative businesses.

In the United States, software or computer programs are not explicitly mentioned in the US patent law,[246] but the US Patent and

---

would be required to do for a patent) would dilute the software, which presumably depends on predicting market movements before they occur.

[244] Numerous works have been written about software copyrights and patents. See, for example, Grover (1990); Galler (1995); Nicholas (1998); Klemens (2005); Bainbridge (2007); and Leith (2007). For a historical perspective on software patents see Campbell-Kelly (2005).

[245] For a recent global piracy survey see the 2008 BSA and IDC document at *http://global.bsa.org/globalpiracy2008/studies/globalpiracy2008.pdf* (BSA & IDC, 2009). Malta's software piracy rate for 2008 is given as 45% (same as for 2005), 4% above the global average.

[246] The U.S. Patent Act (35 USC) is found in Title 35 of the U.S. Code. It may be accessed at, for example, *http://www.uspto.gov/web/offices/pac/mpep/consolidated_laws.pdf*;

Trademark Office has granted patents that may be referred to as software patents since at least the early 1970s.[247] As in Europe, the US was originally reluctant to issue patents for "pure" software, which was seen as being very much akin to the excluded (i.e., unpatentable) categories of "mental acts", including discoveries, mathematical methods and scientific theories. However, following a decision in 1981 by the Supreme Court that 'a claim drawn to subject matter otherwise statutory does not become nonstatutory simply because it uses a mathematical formula, computer program, or digital computer' and a claim is patentable if it contains 'a mathematical formula [and] implements or applies the formula in a structure or process which, when considered as a whole, is performing a function which the patent laws were designed to protect' (Diamond v. Diehr, 1981), software patents in the US began to be granted more openly, and in greater proportions than in Europe.

Europe does not have universal legislation on software patenting, and different countries have adopted their own patent regulations. However, many European countries have based their patent laws on the European Patent Convention (EPC) signed in Munich in 1973.[248] The EPC has a number of exclusions (i.e., certain things are not considered as inventions, and therefore unpatentable), amongst them a computer program. However, the section relating to these exclusions goes on to say that 'the foregoing provision [referring to the exclusions] shall prevent anything from being treated as an invention...*only to the extent that a patent or application for a patent relates to the thing as such*' (my italics) (EPC Article 52(2)). As Bainbridge (2007) notes, the phrase "as such" has been the root of the problem with software (and certain other) patents in Europe. The things in the

---

http://www.bitlaw.com/source/35usc/index.html;
http://www4.law.cornell.edu.uscode/35/.

[247] See, for example, "Software patent" at *http://en.wikipedia.org/wiki/Patenting_of_software#United_States*. An introduction to software patenting (with particular reference to the US) which gives some useful links may be found at *http://www.bitlaw.com/software-patent/index.html*.

[248] As in the US, this does not mean that software patents could not be issued prior to the European Patent Convention. In fact, patent law prior to the EPC made no specific reference to software and thus applications were dealt with as general technology and had to meet the requirements of the 1949 Patent Act as to patentability – i.e., that the invention related to a 'manner of new manufacture'. See Leith, *op. cit.*, p. 11.

exclusion list are not excluded totally and unequivocally, but only if the patent application is directed towards the excluded thing itself. This has caused judicial differences in interpreting the law, and at the same time allowed a number of software-related patents to be issued.

Up to recently, the crucial question therefore was whether software-related inventions should in future be more easily accessible to patent protection in Europe or whether, in view of the assumed idiosyncrasies in the development and economic utilization of software, patents for software should be awarded more restrictively. A major concern was to what extent has the lack of uniform legal regulation Europe-wide hindered (and could hinder) the competitiveness of the software sector and thus also the economic growth of the EU as a whole. Another main concern was the unsatisfactory legal situation pertaining to software patents in Europe, there having been a lack of both clarity and legal certainty. Primarily for these reasons, in February 2002 the European Commission presented a new draft guideline that aimed to regulate the patentability of software in Europe (Proposal 2002/0047 of 20 February 2002). The draft document was fiercely debated in the EU Parliament as well as by the software producing and software utilising industry and the "independent" software developers. Essentially, the controversy broke out because some reasoned that software patents could promote innovation (by protecting it) and therefore encourage incentives for further investments; whereas others—among them developers of the open-source community—were of the opinion that patents undermine fair competition by facilitating the creation of monopolies, thereby hindering innovations (Blind, Jakob & Friedewald, 2005). After many heated debates and revisions of the original EC draft guideline, it was decided by the European Parliament in the summer of 2005 that software will remain unpatentable. Of course, this has not ended the debate, which is surely to continue for some years to come.

Intellectual Property Laws: Maltese Legislation

Patents

Maltese legislation dealing with patents is contained in the Patents and Designs Act of 2000 which came into force on 1 June 2002, and was amended a number of times since.[249] This act incorporates the principal substantive provision of the EPC and is also TRIPS-compliant.[250]

In accordance with the provisions of this Act, and like other European countries that have similar patent legislation (i.e., primarily following the EPC), Malta generally denies any patent protection for computer programs. The Act specifically excludes a computer program from being an invention or a product. Article 4(2) [Part IV - Patentability], states that

> the following, in particular, shall not be regarded as inventions within the meaning of subarticle (1): (a) discoveries, scientific theories and mathematical models; (b) aesthetic creations; (c) schemes, rules and methods for performing mental acts, playing games or doing business and programs for computers; (d) presentations of information.

Further on, in Article 63(1), [Part XVIII - Interpretation], a "product" is defined as

> any industrial or handicraft item, other than a computer program, including *inter alia* intended to be assembled into a complex product, packaging, get-up, graphic symbols and typographic typefaces.

The word "software" is not mentioned.

Patents having effect in European states are typically obtained either nationally, through national patent offices, or via a centralised patent prosecution process at the European Patent Office. Until recently, Malta neither had its own (national) patent office, nor was it a member of the Patent Cooperation Treaty, through which the international filing procedure can be effected. It also did not form

---

[249] *Patents and Designs Act XVII of 2000* (as amended by Acts IX of 2003 and XVIII of 2005), Chapter 417 of the Laws of Malta. This Act superseded the Industrial Property (Protection) Ordinance Chapter 29 dating back to 1899.

[250] TRIPS is the World Trade Organization's Agreement on Trade-Related Aspects of Intellectual Property Rights.

part of the EPC, the legal basis for the European Patent Organization (see Box 12-1 for a brief summary of the EPC and PCT). This, and the fact that Malta has denied patent protection for software, therefore has meant that a local company considering patenting a piece of software in order to protect its invention had no option but to file its patent application in Europe through another jurisdiction. Some have argued that this has rendered the application process to Maltese companies an arduous task involving a complicated and more expensive exercise and, that even if a patent application were successful, the eventual European patent would not automatically have enjoyed local recognition (i.e., even if granted, the patent for a computer-implemented invention would have been completely valueless in Malta) (Ghio, 2005).[251] At the same time, it does not make much sense to only patent in Malta, given Malta's tiny market.

Up to the summer of 2005 before the European Parliament voted overwhelmingly against the patentability of computer-implemented inventions (the CII Directive),[252] Malta—like many other European countries—was waiting to see what that outcome would be before deciding if further changes to the Patents and Designs Act should be effected. Following the European Parliament's decision, Malta did not take any further action as far as legislation is concerned.[253] However, it did go on to expand its membership with international organizations. For example, on 1 December 2006, Malta became the 134th contracting state of the Patent Cooperation Treaty when it deposited its instrument of accession at WIPO. The Treaty entered

---

[251] Ghio's article stirred up some heated debates about software patents, particularly among the local open source community (predominently members of the Malta Linux User Group).

[252] Directive on Computer Implemented Inventions, COM(2002) 92 Final. The CII Directive was geared to harmonise national patent laws and clarify once and for all the current policy conflicts that abound. The *raison d'etre* of the CII Directive was not to broaden the scope of patentability, but rather to unify the myriad of patent laws present in Europe. The European Parliament's thumbs down to the CII Directive has proved somewhat disappointing for some countries that had then to decide what further action to take.

[253] At the time of the CII Directive, Malta's position regarding software patents was that of maintaining the *status quo*: as Malta has a large number of SME's (including many microenterprises), it was felt that it would probably be more beneficial for Malta if software remained unpatentable and protected only by copyright. This was also much of the thinking behind other European countries that voted against the Directive.

into force for Malta on 1 March 2007.[254]   On that date, Malta also joined the European Patent Organization.[255]   However, since Malta had closed the national route via the PCT, in international applications filed on or after 1 March 2007, Malta has only been considered as designated for a European patent and not for a national patent.[256]

Box 12-1
The European Patent Convention and the Patent Co-operation Treaty

The European Patent Convention (EPC) and the Patent Co-operation Treaty (PCT) are two methods by which an applicant, having made an invention, may seek patent protection in a number of signatory states. The PCT was opened for signature in 1970 and the EPC in 1973. Although both instruments aim (and serve) to eliminate a measure of duplication of searches and examinatiions, the PCT is international in character, being a global protection treaty administered by WIPO, the World Intellectual Property Organization. On the other hand, the EPC provides further rationalisation of the patent system in Europe. There is a "relationship" between the EPC and the PCT which is explained below.

Firstly, under EPC's system of Intergovernmental Co-operation, it is possible for someone to file a single patent application (in one of three official languages, namely English, French and German) and obtain a patent in one, several, or all of the EPC's Contracting States. Not being an EPC member essentially means that an owner of a new invention has to apply in each and

---

[254] The accession by Malta has meant that in any international application filed on or after 1 March, 2007, Malta would automatically be designated and, being bound by Chapter II of the Treaty, would automatically be elected in any demand for international preliminary examination filed in respect of an international application filed on or after 1 March, 2007. Also, as of that date, nationals and residents of Malta would themselves be able to file PCT applications. See WIPO (2006).

[255] "Malta joins European Patent Organization". Accessed at *http://www.kooperation-international.de/en/malta/themes/info/detail/data/9916/?PHPSESSID=c33269fafb89cb7622d0c5cb8c6a7*. See also "Accession to the PCT by Malta (MT)" at *http://www.epo.org/patents/law/legal-texts/InformationEPO/archiveinfo/02012007.html*.

[256] For a list of PCT contracting states for which a Regional Patent can be obtained see *http://www.wipo.int/pct/en/texts/pdf/reg_des.pdf*. This list is up-to-date as of 1 January 2009.

every country where protection is sought, using different languages, paying separate fees to the respective patent offices, and charges to the national patent attorneys. The rationale behind the EPC was precisely to provide some means of harmonization by centralising the prosecution in one language and defer the cost of translations until the time of the actual patent grant.

Secondly, an application under the EPC may result from the filing of an international application under the PCT, in other words an applicant (e.g. outside the EPC contracting states) will launch a PCT application and designate an EPC contracting state (or states). In these circumstances, an application will proceed to the European Patent Office (EPO) at the so-called national phase of the PCT process and will be categorised as entry into the "European regional phase". The EPO is one of the two official organs of the European Patent Organisation (the other being the Administrative Council) in charge of examining European patent applications and determining if a patent is likely to be awarded. For PCT applications, apart from the International Bureau of WIPO, a number of countries have patent offices that act as international searching authorities. In the case of a PCT application it is important to understand that it is ultimately the task of the patent office (or one acting on its behalf) of where the patent is sought to decide whether that patent should be granted or not. In this respect, the term "national phase" is used to refer to the final process of having the national (regional) patent office (of where patent protection is sought) determine the grant, or otherwise, of the patent.

In 2007 eleven EPC member countries (including Malta) chose "to close their national route", meaning that it was no longer possible to obtain a national patent protection (i.e., a patent protection from any of these eleven specified nations) through the PCT system without entering into the European phase and obtaining a European patent from the EPO. The prime reason why these countries decided to close their national route is because they have neither the expertise to carry out an extensive prior art search nor the financial means to do so.

Copyright

It has been shown that in formulating a strategy on software protection, no general prescription can be followed. For example, Correra (1993) cites a number of specific examples where different countries have adopted different attitudes regarding copyright laws. In other words, the drafting of that part of the law concerning software copyright is in the hands of individual countries, as is the decision whether to legislate or not, although countries that have not yet legislated on software protection are often pressured by international organizations to do so. The crucial point in formulating a strategy of course is how to obtain a balance between private and public interests, including those of local industries.[257] The regulation of software protection may even reflect certain policy objectives related to the diffusion or production of programs.

That said, in 1988 the Commission of the European Communities (now the EU) issued a Green paper titled "Copyright and the Challenge of Technology" on software copyright protection, and followed this through by a number of directives, the first of which was the 1991 Directive where it expressed its wishes to reinforce the European industry by producing unambiguous harmonised legislation, and urging member states and other European countries to adopt its framework (European Union, 1988 and 1991).[258]

In line with this directive, copyright protection of software in Malta was first made legal in 1992 when the Maltese Copyright Act of 1967 was amended by inserting a section (paragraph (g)) regarding computer software at the end of the list of works comprised in the definition of "literary work" in Section 2(1) of the Act (Callus, 1997).[259] The scope of amending the 1967 Copyright Act was to give protection to computer software and help reduce software piracy.[260] The 1992 amendment to the 1967 Act aimed to meet the EC Directive because

---

[257] Some of the ways in which this balance may be struck are given in Correra (1993: pp. 144-147).

[258] The Commission hinted at the protection of software either by copyright, a copyright-like *sui generis* right, or a mixture of both. The *sui generis* alternative however was rejected in favour of copyright. See Callus (1997).

[259] Instead of "software", paragraph (g) of the 1992 Copyright Act lists "computer program". According to this Act, "computer program" includes computer programs whatever may be the mode or form of their expression including those which are incorporated in hardware, interfaces which provide for the physical interconnection and interaction or the interoperability between elements of software and hardware and preparatory design material leading to the development of a computer program.

[260] To what extent software piracy has been reduced as a result of this amendment is impossible to state since no statistics for software piracy in Malta are available for the early 1990s. Piracy rate in Malta for the years 2003-2007 has remained roughly the same, varying between 45% to 47%. See the BSA and IDC Annual Global Software Piracy Study at
http://global.bsa.org/idcglobalstudy2007/studies/summaryfindings_globalstudy07. pdf.

Malta, although then not a member, had already started preparing to join the EU.

In 2000 a new Act (Act XIII of 2000) was enacted in order to implement Directive 96/9/EC of the European Parliament and of the Council on the legal protection of databases, i.e., in respect of neighbouring rights and certain "sui generis" intellectual-property rights, in substitution of the provisions of the Copyright Act, Cap. 196 (see later). This Act was further amended in 2001 (Act VI of 2001), and again in 2003 (Act IX of 2003). The last amendments incorporated the provisions on inter-member cable retransmission and satellite broadcasting (Directive 93/83/EEC). It also incorporated Directive 2001/29/EC on the harmonisation of certain aspects of copyright and related rights in the information society. By virtue of the new law pertaining to Directive 2001/29/EC, acts which infringe copyright also include acts intended to circumvent technological measures to protect copyright and those which manipulate any electronic rights-management information present in copyrighted material.

The Maltese Copyright Act (2000) as it now (2008) stands provides protection for artistic works, audiovisual works, databases, literary works and musical works, with computer programs or software falling under the literary works category. This protection is offered irrespective of the literary quality of the work.

In accordance with the Maltese Copyright Act (2000), a work will be eligible for copyright if it satisfies the three criteria of qualification, originality and fixation. "Qualification" covers the five works categories referred to above: for some categories, several works are listed which would make them eligible for copyright. "Originality" refers to the fact that a piece of work must be original, i.e., according to the Act, it must have an "original character", although the term "original character" is itself not defined. According to the Act, "fixation" means the embodiment of sounds, images, or both, or digital representations thereof, in any material form, from which they can be perceived, reproduced or communicated through a device. This has been included in view of audiovisual works. Copyright is infringed by any person who, without a licence from the copyright owner, does any of the prohibited acts listed in the Act. A licence is an express or implied authorisation by the copyright owner to do one or more of such acts.

Unlike a trade mark or a patent, a copyright is granted to an eligible work automatically. Therefore there is no need for registration under Maltese law as the Act provides that protection is granted *ipso jure* upon creation of the work. This protection is obviously limited by territoriality, the main connecting factors being domicile or citizenship of the creation. However, through a network of Conventions to which Malta is a party, the litigations presented by territoriality are, to a large extent, reduced. Copyright protection is thus conferred on every work which is eligible for copyright and which is made or first published in Malta or in a State in which such works are protected under an international agreement to which Malta is also a party. In the case of literary, musical or artistic works and databases, such protection shall subsist for 70 years after the end of the year in which the author dies, irrespective of the date when the work is made available to the public; for audiovisual work, it is 70 years after the end of the year in which the last of the following person dies: the principal director, the author of the dialogue and the composer of music specifically created for use in the audiovisual work.

Sui Generis Right of Copyright for Databases

As noted, the 2000 Copyright Act includes "databases" apart from "computer programs". In this Act, a "database" is

> a collection of independent works, data or other materials arranged in a systematic or methodical way and individually accessible by electronic or other means without it being necessary for these materials to have been physically stored in an organized manner but does not extend to computer programs used in the making or operation of a database accessible by electronic means comprised within the term "computer program".

This definition is the same as that given in the (controversial) 1996 European Council Directive on the legal protection of databases.[261]

---

[261] Directive 96/9/EC, Article 1(2). See European Union (2001). This publication is a collection of the seven EC directives (following the 1988 Green paper on copyright), a version of the *acquis comunautaire* in the field of copyright and related rights.

Aplin (2005: p. 44) notes that the fact that the definition refers to 'independent works, data or other materials' suggests that a wide range of material may comprise a database, and that according to Davidson (2003: p. 73), 'works' probably refers to individual copyright works, whereas 'data' are 'facts, especially numerical facts' and 'other materials' probably refer to information generally.

Essentially, the situation regarding databases is as follows. There are two types of protection: either full copyright protection; or what has been termed as 'database right' protection, also known as the *sui generis* right. Full copyright protection is given to those databases which by virtue of their selection and arrangement of the contents constitute the author's own intellectual creation. For full copyright protection the database must qualify as 'original'. The criterion for qualification for 'database right' is that a substantial investment must have been made in the obtaining, verification and presentation of its contents by the database maker. Thus, although a database must be original to qualify for full copyright, it need not be original to qualify for database right; and qualification is regardless of the actual contents, which may or may not have copyright protection in their own right.[262]

Database right is often referred to as the *sui generis* right of database copyright, and as this is considered less important than full copyright, the *sui generis* right of copyright is for fifteen years, rather than the normal seventy years. The law states that protection is for fifteen years following the date of completion of the making of the database, or following the date when the database is first made to the public.

---

[262] The nature of *sui generis* right in respect of databases states that 'Notwithstanding the provisions of article 7, the maker of a database who can show that there has been qualitatively or quantitatively a substantial investment in either the obtaining, verification or presentation of the contents of the database shall have, irrespective of the eligibility of that database or its contents for protection by copyright or by other rights, the right to authorise or prohibit acts of extraction or re-utilization of its contents, in whole or in substantial part, evaluated qualitatively or quantitatively'. However, some exceptions to the *sui generis* right pertaining to databases are also made (for example, the provision of private or educational use of the database, in the case when the database is public). Of course, what constitutes 'substantial investment' is difficult to predict, and this can therefore lead to misinterpretation. See, for example, Aplin (2005: pp. 60-63).

13

I.T. Education and R&D Initiatives

In this chapter we trace, briefly and in roughly chronological order, the policy measures taken by government to promote IT education and related research. A holistic approach to IT education has generally been adopted. In recent years, policy decisions relating to education in general have been driven, in part, by the Lisbon Agenda of 2000, which set out to achieve a set of specific goals by 2010.[263] In the area of R&D, the EU Framework Programmes (FPs) have proved useful in enabling Maltese firms and the University of Malta (UOM) to do collaborative work with foreign firms and institutions, and therefore gain that much-needed experience. Participation in these projects by small firms unaccustomed to this sort of involvement often necessitates some guidance and, in this respect, both Malta Enterprise and the Malta Council for Science and Technology have been instrumental in providing the right help.

Research funding is an important issue. The Framework Programmes are funded by the European Commission so that it is typically a matter of developing an appropriate strategy (e.g. by

---

[263] The Lisbon Agenda (or Strategy) refers to an action and development plan for Europe advocated by the European Council at a meeting held in Lisbon in March 2000. The strategic goal for the new decade articulated by the EU was for Europe to become 'the most dynamic and competitive knowledge-based economy in the world, capable of sustained economic growth with more and better jobs and greater social cohesion'. One of the specific objectives concerned education, whence five key areas were identified, namely: ICT, technological culture, foreign languages, entrepreneurship, and social skills. For a brief introduction, see ESIB (2006).

presenting a well-defined research proposal) for these funds to be secured. However, FPs also have their downside. For example, administrative overhead places additional demands on academic staff, and research projects are based on FP priorities. For this reason and in order to encourage innovation, national funding for R&D is very important. In Malta, government research funding was first made available in 2004, when the National Research, Technological Development and Innovation Programme (RTDI Programme) was launched (see below).

IT Education

The building of a nation-wide IT education programme began with the provision of computer labs in all secondary schools, in accordance with the EU Second Financial Protocol.[264] This exercise was started in 1995 when a number of state schools were each equipped with at least a computer lab of twenty networked PCs per lab. Recognising the importance of computer studies much earlier, many private schools (mostly church schools) had long introduced computer studies as part of their curriculum and simultaneously set up their own computer laboratories, some as early as 1981 (see Chapter 4).

The setting up of computer laboratories in secondary schools was followed approximately one year later by the introduction of a formal ICT syllabus at the secondary level. This syllabus followed much of the various UK syllabi at the same level. However, today's curriculum in secondary schools is also oriented towards the European Computer Driving Licence (ECDL), which is internationally recognised. Two IT-related subjects are offered at the secondary level: one, called "ICT", is compulsory and must be followed by all students up to the last year of schooling; whereas the other, called "Computer Studies", is an optional subject like many others. At the post-secondary level, Computing and IT were already being offered as separate subjects. These could be taken at an Intermediate or an Advanced (pre-University) level. As with other subjects, the

---

[264] Unused loans from the First and Second EU (then EEC) Financial Protocols could be utilised (and were used) for the building of the new Air Terminal, the Solid Waste Recycling Project, and the raising of standards of local educational institutions. See Pollacco (1992: p. 71).

Computing and IT Syllabi are established by the Maltese Matriculation Board (MATSEC). Microcomputer technology and digital electronics could be studied at two technical (and adjacent) institutes, which now form part of the new Malta College of Arts, Science, and Technology (MCAST).

In that same period (c. 1996-1997), a gradual phasing in of ICT equipment in primary classrooms (e.g. multimedia PCs) was also initiated. According to a NSO survey (NSO, 2005) conducted during the scholastic year 2003-2004, primary schools had 16 computers per 100 pupils (i.e., a pupil to computer ratio of about 6:1), whereas secondary schools had 9 computers per 100 pupils (i.e., a pupil to computer ratio of about 11:1). Close to 89% of schools also had a broadband Internet connection, although in the majority of schools, few classrooms actually had Internet access.

Complementing the secondary ICT syllabus, the secondary level Mathematics syllabus was updated to include basic IT-related topics such as certain features of the Logo programming language, the educational programs Cabri and Derive,[265] and the basics of spreadsheet application (Giordmaina, 2000; Zammit, 2004). At both the secondary and post-secondary levels, syllabi have typically been revised every four years since their introduction.

The introduction of computer hardware in schools and the reforms in the school curricula to include ICT are not by themselves sufficient to build the required ICT skills. These initiatives need to be complemented by the right teacher training, regarded as a very important aspect. Primarily under the guidance of the Education Division, programmes were therefore established that aimed to help existing teachers become comfortable with ICT. These programmes included specialised in-service training, and an Internet awareness programme related to child safety.

Teacher training courses at University typically include either the four-year Bachelor of Education (BEd) (Hons) course with specialisation to teach Computing and IT at the primary, secondary, or post-secondary (sixth form) level, or—particularly for those already

---

[265] Cabri is a simple and comprehensive computer program to understand 3D geometry, primarily intended for the final years of primary school. Derive is computer algebra software for doing symbolic and numeric mathematics, suitable at the secondary and post-secondary levels.

in possession of a first degree in a subject other than education—the postgraduate certificate of education (PGCE) which is typically of one year's full-time duration. A requirement of both courses is for students to spend a period of teaching practice, which allows them to gain first-hand experience. In addition, students taking the BEd degree with an aim to teach computer studies are now required to follow a history of computing module.[266] In Malta, the BEd course was first established in the 1950s, and the BEd (Hons) and the PGCE in the late 1970s.

In order to ensure that ICT teachers become very familiar with the subject, these teachers have also each been provided (on a long-term loan basis) with a laptop for their personal use. This allows them to experiment freely with different applications at home, as well as prepare curriculum material (e.g. notes and handouts) at their convenience. The assumption is that through the use of technology they would be better equipped to deliver their subject matter.

ICT Education for One and All

A main policy goal has been for government to provide ICT access to everyone, everywhere, the intention being to spread ICT literacy and simultaneously reduce the digital divide. To this end, a number of initiatives and schemes have been tried out. In 2005, for example, Internet kiosks were located in major towns; and Internet cafes were also encouraged. The Internet kiosks, either because they were expensive or because of the eventual proliferation of laptops and mobile phones with advanced Internet access technology, never became popular and not only were they discontinued, but many have actually been removed.

Local councils were instructed to organize elementary ICT courses for housewives and pensioners, whilst the Employment and Training Corporation (ETC) also designed and organized courses for the unemployed and those who were interested in upgrading their computer skills.[267] The local council and ETC courses were provided

---

[266] This module has been co-ordinated by Mario Camilleri.

[267] The ETC, Malta's public employment service, was set up by an Act of Parliament in August 1990 to provide an employment and training service. It was later identified by the Government as one of the main prime movers towards the attainment of the Lisbon objectives. See Cutajar (2004).

free of charge. At a higher level, the Swatar Training Centre (STC)—which used to form part of MITTS—began offering certificate and diploma courses that could be taken either on a day-release or a part-time evening basis. Sponsorship typically came from employers, or in the case of qualified unemployed persons from the ETC itself. More recently, in order to encourage the take up of computer science diploma and degree courses, a scheme was introduced whereby the entire course fee would be reimbursed at the end of the course provided the applicant successfully completes his or her course.

Government's commitment to provide ICT education for all was outlined in at least two official documents: *The National ICT Strategy 2004-2006* (MIT&I, 2004a), published in 2004, and *HelloIT* (MIT&I, 2004b), published later that year. Both documents emphasised the importance of ICT education at the national level, but *HelloIT*, in particular, was specifically dedicated to explaining the initiatives the government intended pursuing in order to ensure that digital knowledge would be available and affordable to everyone. Fourteen initiatives were identified in the *HelloIT* document (see Table 13.1), most of which have now been carried through.

TABLE 13.1
HelloIT: The Fourteen Initiatives

---

1. myWeb: ICT education for all
2. myWeb for the industry: using ICT's to become more productive
3. myWeb for the public sector
4. Community Technology and Learning Centres
5. European Computer Driving License training
6. Public Internet Access Points and Internet Centres
7. Affordable Hardware for everyone
8. New Broadband Packages
9. Affordable Software
10. Taking Technology Home
11. E-learning: A Virtual Classroom
12. Internet bil-Malti
13. Learning ICT on TV
14. Access to the Internet through electric power lines

Computer Science at the University of Malta

Computing at the University of Malta is discussed fully in Chapter 5, therefore only a few points are included here for completeness.

Computer Science at the University of Malta is a very young discipline. Before the founding of an ICT Faculty in 2007, Computing and IT courses were offered by departments that came under the jurisdiction of the Board of Studies for Information Technology, set up in 1995. This Board oversaw three distinct departments: the Department of Computer Information Systems; the Department of Computer Science and Artificial Intelligence; and the Department of Communications and Computer Engineering. Prospective students wanting to follow the undergraduate BSc IT course (with or without Honours) could choose from three technical streams, namely Informatics (Department of Computer Information Systems), Computer Science (Department of Computer Science & AI), and Computer Systems Engineering (Department of Communications & Computer Engineering). Students taking the BSc course could specialise in one of these three streams, but in the first two years of the course, a core suite of units from all three streams would be offered, with complemetary units in Mathematics, Statistics, Operations Research, and Management (UOM, 2000: p. 9). The degree programme aimed to produce graduates 'fit to occupy responsible positions in the Information Technology industry' (*ibid.*).

An event promoted by the IT Board of Studies has been the annual exhibition of projects by final year students in Engineering and Information Technology. Usually held at the beginning of July, the exhibition is a public showcase of the capabilities of students: the projects reflect the philosophy that technological education is there for the service of the community, since many of the projects are typically both of an academic and practical nature. In 2008, 120 projects were presented, 77 by engineering students and 43 by those of IT (UOM, 2008: p. 24). The event is generally well-attended, attracting industry personnel on the look-out for recruiting young, talented, graduates. Another more recent initiative is the Computer Science Annual Workshop (CSAW) (see Chapter 5).

Over the years, these three departments slowly but steadily expanded. In 2007 the Faculty of Information and Communications Technology was set up which now constituted four departments

(Intelligent Computer Systems, Communications & Computer Engineering, Computer Information Systems, Computer Science). The BSc course was shortened to three years (to conform to the European system), and different types of Master's courses introduced (e.g. by research, or by instruction for conversion degrees). Also, for the first time in Malta's IT history, applications for doctorate research studies in different fields of computing began to be accepted. This reflects the accumulated experience of the senior lecturers and few professors who could now be seen as having the necessary qualities to conduct academic supervision at this level.

Research and Development, and Innovation

The first concrete step by government to promote research in the sciences may be traced back to March 1988 when, in a memorandum from the Minister of Education (Dr. Ugo Mifsud Bonnici) to the Prime Minister (Dr. Eddie Fenech Adami) it was suggested that:

(i)   A National Commission for Science and Technology be established and that it should reside within the Office of the Prime Minister;

(ii) An Inter-Ministerial Committee chaired by the Prime Minister and composed of the respective Ministers for Education, Social Policy and Productive Development be set up (Education Ministry, 1988).

The National Commission was mandated to perform a number of tasks, including finding out what the country has in this field by carrying out a survey of people, equipment and relevant literature; investigating the country's needs in this area; reviewing and proposing educational programmes with the aim of training scientists and technologists; and co-ordinating and assisting in the effort related to the transfer of technology and technological innovation (*ibid.*, p. 4).

Following the discussion of the March memo, the Malta Council for Science and Technology (MCST) was officially created in August 1988. MCST was to assist the government in the formulation and implementation of a National Science and Technology policy, acting as an advisory body and executing a number of tasks according to identified objectives (MCST, 2006: p. 19). These objectives—eleven in all—were spelled out in a letter to the Chair of the Council by the Prime Minister. Three of these included: (i) the submission of proposals and recommendations concerning a national policy for science and technology; (ii) the preparation of short and medium term plans for science and technology activities in Malta; and (iii) the participation in the national socio-economic planning process (*ibid.*).

Following some basic groundwork, including a brief National IT Strategy report, the setting up of working groups, and participation in UNDP-UNESCO programmes, MCST began conceiving and promulgating definite propositions (see, for example, Cassingena Harper, 1999).[268] The first of these was the proposed development in 1992 of the concept of making Malta a regional communications hub. This idea was expounded in a document produced by MCST entitled "Vision 2000: Malta Regional Hub" (MCST, 1992), and was discussed at a special conference on this issue held on 5 May 1992. MCST has maintained that the hub concept was a fundamental premise of national strategic planning, however none other than a former MCST chairman (the late Rev. Prof. Peter Serracino Inglott) later pointed out that Malta was perhaps too ambitious to project itself in this manner, and would probably have been better seeing itself as a "node" rather than a "hub".[269]

The second important exercise MCST undertook was the commissioning of an autonomous and independent study that led to the formulation of the National IT Strategy. The latter was one of seven areas identified in a science and technology policy document presented by the Minister of Education and Human Resources in January 1994, a document that was meant to emphasise government's commitment in this field (Ministry of Education and Human Resources, 1994: pp. 4-5). The National IT Strategy study laid the foundations for Malta's now thriving information economy.

From about 1996, MCST started getting involved in the EU Framework Programmes. The latter are designed to encourage

---

[268] Cassingena Harper argues that the preparation of the National Information Technology Strategy report was significant given that UNESCO's 1985 Mission Report on Malta focused exclusively on Science and Technology policy, with no reference to IT.

[269] Serracino Inglott in a presentation given as part of the *Workshop on ICT Strategies for Islands and Small States*, held in Malta, 17-19 March 1999.

collaborative European research and development by clearly stating a proposed structure for the research (i.e., identifying research priorities), and providing substantial funding. MCST's role has been primarily that of facilitating access by Maltese organizations to these programs (see below). MCST has also been involved in institution-building strategies, when the National Laboratory and the Innovation Relay Centre were set up in 2000 and 2004, respectively.[270] The Malta Innovation Relay Centre, now managed by Malta Enterprise, forms part of the global IRC network, originally involving only European countries, but later expanded to include countries from outside Europe.[271]

Innovation is a key element in long-term economic growth, and collaboration is an important means of fostering innovation. Indeed, in at least one study, it has been shown that "innovating firms" often enter into collaboration partnerships, whereas less innovative ones collaborate correspondingly less (Kitson & Michie, 1998: pp. 107-109). It is also believed that the overall impact of increased innovation and collaboration is improvement in both output and employment growth rates for individual businesses as well as for the economy as a whole. Hence, the idea of the Innovation Relay Centre as a means of fostering close collaboration and technology transfer between different countries and organizations.

In 2001, a Business Incubation Centre was also set up by the former Institute for the Promotion of Small Enterprises (IPSE, now incorporated into Malta Enterprise) to help start up companies overcome the initial difficulties of operating a business. Apart from office space provided at an affordable rental fee, the programme provides for the expert assistance related to the running of the

---

[270] See the websites *http://www.mnl.com.mt* and *http://www.innovationmalta.com/irc* for information about the national laboratory and the information relay centre.

[271] In July 2005, for example, Chile established its own IRC, which aimed to enable European and Chilean companies to work together. See, for example, European Commission (2006: p. 14). For general information about the IRC network (now Enterprise Europe Network) see *http://www.enterprise-europe-network.ec.europa.eu/index_en.htm* (formerly *http://irc.cordis.lu/*). For articles on how companies have benefited from the IRC network, see, for example, the November 2005 issue of *European Innovation* (published by the Communication and Information Unit, European and Industry DG, European Commission).

business (e.g. legal advice), as well as business contacts.[272] The first four companies to move into the new premises (located at Kordin) were firms which had been operating for less than a year (*The Malta Business Weekly*, 2001) (see also Figure 13.1).

Figure 13.1
The Business Incubation Centre at Kordin.
Source: Author's collection

In 2004, the first National RTDI Programme was launched by MCST with the aim of promoting a culture for continuous scientific research and innovation, and providing the technical support for Malta to meet its requirements for being competitive in today's economy (MCST, 2006: p. 35). The RTDI set to encourage public-private sector partnerships by providing financial support for scientific research, from basic and applied research to near-to-market innovations. In 2004, the tiny sum of Lm300,000 (c. US$900,000) was made available to MCST for the first call for proposals. As many as 85 proposals were

---

[272] See *http://www.maltaenterprise.com/documents/KBICbrochureA4.pdf* for more details.

submitted under that call (a perhaps surprisingly large number given Malta's small size), totalling Lm3 million. Given the limited funds, only 15 projects could be funded.[273] Unfortunately, this research budget—the only national funding for scientific research—was not increased for subsequent years, which led to government being criticised. In 2008, for example, 40 high-quality proposals were submitted for evaluation by MCST, requesting a sum of 5.4 million Euros.[274] Again, because of the inconsequential amount of 700,000 Euros (also equivalent to c. US$900,000) available, only 17% of projects could be considered, described as 'a shame'[275] considering that most proposals scored high points for excellence.

Participation in the Framework Programmes

Following ESPRIT (see Box 13-1), the EU commenced with its Fifth Framework Programme (FP5), which covered the period 1998-2002.[276] At that time Malta was still quite unprepared to carry out research of any significance and participation in the FP5 Programme was therefore minimal, but not insignificant given Malta's size and its then relative inexperience in this field.[277] However, with the onset of FP6 the situation in Malta as regards research had improved marginally, since by now MCST had made some efforts in promoting R&D. Private companies and, in particular, the University of Malta had had some exposure to, and familiarity with, the workings of the Framework system, and hence were in a better position to submit quality research proposals and take part in new projects.

FP6 ran from 2002 to 2006 and had an overall budget of nearly 20 billion Euros. Malta's performance in FP6 was very encouraging: a total of 101 participants took part in 98 projects, 6 of which were coordinated by Maltese organizations.[278] Table 13.2 shows a

---

[273] *Ricerka*, Issue 2, December 2005, p. 7.

[274] Malta changed its monetary currency unit to the Euro on 1 January 2008.

[275] *Ricerka*, Issue 7, May 2008, p. 16.

[276] FP5 covered 4 main thematic programmes, namely: quality of life; user-friendly information society; competitive and sustainable growth; and energy, environment and sustainable development. Maltese companies took part in projects relating to health care, aquaculture, IT, and environmentally friendly products. See Kelleher (2001).

[277] Malta took part in 45 projects. See MCST (2006: p. 37).

[278] *Ricerka*, Issue 6, December 2007, p. 19.

breakdown of Malta's participation by Priority Area. It shows that Maltese organizations participated as partners in 1.1% of the funded projects, drawing a total funding of nearly 9 million Euros.

TABLE 13.2
Malta's performance in the Sixth Framework Programme – Breakdown by Priority Area

Priority Area	Total Number of Contracts in FP (All Countries)	Which include MT Participation	% MT	Total Funding (MT)
Life sciences	535	0	0.00	0
IST	1,093	26	2.38	2,244,283
NMP	446	3	0.67	337,066
Aeronautics & space	216	4	1.85	1,001,309
Food	186	5	2.69	488,302
SusDev	598	11	1.84	896,784
Citizens & governance	140	5	3.57	475,010
Policy Support	458	5	1.09	371,612
SMEs	416	6	1.44	382,503
INCO	340	10	2.94	857,995
Coordination	100	3	3.00	79,122
R&I policies	16	0	0.00	0
Research & innovation	224	8	3.57	765,409
Human resources & mobility	3,723	4	0.11	479,437
Research infrastructures	149	4	2.68	317,333
Science and society	143	4	2.80	278,410
Euratom	78	0	0.00	0
Total	8,861	98	1.11	8,974,577

Source: *Ricerka* (December 2007: p. 19)

Although the number of funded projects for Malta is low when compared to other EU countries, when projects per capita are taken into account, Malta ranked second in EU-27 (see Figure 13.2). Although Figure 13.2 shows that projects per capita tend to be high for countries with relatively lower population figures (i.e., there is an obvious correlation between the number of participants and the population in these countries), the fact that Malta scored second is an indication that the will to succeed has not been lacking. In Malta's case, the majority of the projects in FP6 fell under the Information Society Technologies (IST) Thematic priority, covering 26 projects (25%) and drawing over 2.2 million Euros of funding.

For the first year of FP7, Malta netted 3.26 million Euros, when 41 successful Maltese organizations started participating in 35 projects.[279] Analysis (carried out by MCST) of the type of Maltese participants revealed that of the 41 participants, only 6 were private companies, although these companies participated in 10 of the 35 projects. The remaining proposals came from the public sector, research organizations, and the UOM. The low participation rate by private firms obviates the need for a more intensive information campaign, which the MCST has acknowledged.

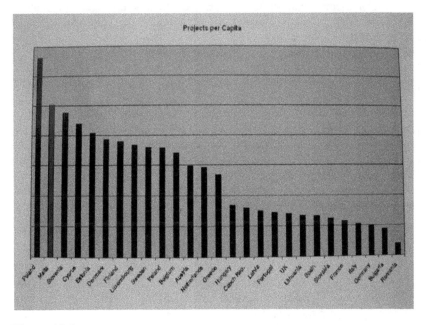

Figure 13.2
Per Capita Participation in FP6
Source: *Ricerka* (December 2007: p. 19)

---

[279] *Ricerka*, Issue 7, May 2008, p. 24.

Box 13-1
ESPRIT and the EU Framework Programmes

Throughout the 1970s and much of the 1980s the United States and Japan held a global lead over their competitors in semiconductors and consumer electronics. Their outstanding performance in high-technology industries began to worry European companies who felt that they were beginning to lag behind their US and Japanese counterparts in a number of key technological areas. The European Commission (EC), in particular, perceived the US's and Japan's dominance as a threat to Europe's economy. To address this apparent imbalance, but also to try to ameliorate the disparities between the technological capabilities of its country members, the EC therefore invited its then twelve member states (the "Big Twelve") to draw up a common strategy for IT research. Named as the European Strategic Programme for Research in Information Technology (ESPRIT), the programme began to be implemented in 1984 after a pilot project was launched the previous year.

The main objective of ESPRIT was to encourage collaborative research between European nations. Traditionally, research and development (R&D) has been an activity conducted by enterprises secretely and independent of competitors. The European Commission however believed that collaboration among industry, university and research institutions across Europe would be an effective means of narrowing the perceived technological gap: collaboration among European firms was thought to be more attractive than alliances with non-European firms (even though many European firms actually preferred to form alliances with others outside Europe). The Commission reasoned that such a strategy would involve less risk and possibly also take advantage of economies of scale.

Up to 1998 the ESPRIT programme consisted of four phases, called ESPRIT I through ESPRIT IV. These phases encouraged collaboration between primarily large electronics and IT firms (including telecommunications companies) with a focus on hard science. These phases were jointly funded by the European Commission and the participating organizations.

Following ESPRIT, the EC then began a series of research programmes, each called the nth Framework Programme for Research and Technological Development. The first of these, initiated in 1998 was the Fifth Framework Programme (shortened for FP5) that lasted until 2002. Although research collaboration and innovation remained dominant characteristics, there was a shift in emphasis in the dimension of this (and the following) Framework Programmes. For example, beginning with FP5 participation was expanded to include small and medium-sized enterprises. The focus was also shifted to "soft" science with an emphasis on socioeconomic research. The nature of the collboration was required to be more competitive (since, formerly, the emphasis was on precompetitive research, i.e., research that was considered to be distant from individual market interests of collaborators).

Whatever their nature, the FP programmes have had two main objectives, namely to: a) strengthen the scientific and technological base of European research; and b) encourage its international competitiveness, while promoting research that supports EU policies. Table B13-1 summarises the research programmes todate. The thematic research areas shown in this table are the priority areas only (for FP6, forming part of the first specific programme called "Integrating and Strengthening the ERA").

Table B13-1
Summary of the ESPRIT and Framework Programmes

Phase/Budget (€ billion)	Name of Programme(s)/Thematic Research Areas
ESPRIT I (1984-1987) / 3.8	European Strategic Programme for Research in Information Technology
ESPRIT II (1987-1992) / 5.4	R&D in Advanced Communications Technologies (RACE-1)
ESPRIT III (1992-1994) / 6.6	R&D in Advanced Communications Technologies (RACE-2)
ESPRIT IV (1994-1998) / 13.2	Advanced Communications Technologies and Services (ACTS)
FP5 (1998-2002) / 15.0	Information Society Technology (IST)

FP6
(2002-2006) / 17.9
	1) Integrating and Strengthening the ERA
	2) Structuring the ERA
	Research Areas:
	    Life sciences, Genomics and Biotechnology for Health
	    Information Society Technologies
	    Nanotechnologies and nanosciences, Knowledge-based functional materials, and new production processes and devices
	    Aeronautics and Space
	    Food Quality and Safety
	    Sustainable Development, Global Change and Ecosystems
	    Citizens and Governance in a Knowledge-based Society

FP7
(2007-2013) / 50.5
	1) Cooperatiion
	2) Ideas
	3) People
	4) Capacities
	5) Nuclear Research
	Research Areas:
	    Health
	    Food, agriculture and fisheries, and biotechnology
	    Information and communication technologies
	    Nanosciences, nanotechnologies, materials and new
	        production technologies
	    Energy
	    Environment (including climate change)
	    Transport (including aeronautics)
	    Socio-economic sciences and the humanities
	    Space
	    Security

14

Conclusion

This study traced the general history of computing in Malta. It charted the adoption of computers and related technology in the private sector and government, the introduction of computers in schools, the rise of the software industry, and the development of telecommunications, its infrastructure and the appropriate legislation that goes with it. The narrative also dealt with political, policy and, to a lesser extent, economic issues. Since the study implicitly makes reference to technology adoption and diffusion, I will conclude by dedicating this last chapter to what some scholars have termed "IT Diffusion Models". To do this, it will be useful to first briefly review the salient themes covered in the preceding chapters. I will then attempt to integrate this material by relating it to suggested IT diffusion models, specifically on how Malta's IT take-up and past government policies fit certain IT diffusion patterns.

Summary Review and Analysis

Use of Tabulators

The 1890 US Census and the 1952 US Presidential Elections hold key positions in the history of American computing. The first event was carried out using Herman Hollerith's newly invented punched card tabulators; the second involved the use of an early digital computer, a Remington Rand UNIVAC machine that correctly predicted the outcome of the election results. Subsequently, in the US, all censuses were done with the help of those technologies.

It was not long before Hollerith's tabulating machines, eventually produced by IBM, were patented in Europe and elsewhere and introduced by large companies and government organizations. Their earliest application was for statistical calculations, and by the 1930s few were those governments in developed countries that had not yet introduced them (see Heide, 2009; Connolly, 1967). Corporate firms, amongst them insurance companies, the banks, the railways and telecommunications providers, were also heavy users.

It is not surprising therefore to find that the former Central Office of Statistics (COS) and the large private brewery of Farsons were the first two entities in Malta to adopt tabulating machines. Malta's statistics office was formed in 1947, following the war. Before its formation, statistics were gathered by different departments and hence there was little need for advanced equipment. With the establishment of the Central Office of Statistics—as it became to be known in 1957—it made sense to automate the processes involved, since the production of statistics had become centralised. The first machines from the BTM company were installed in 1950, with more powerful tabulators and sorters introduced progressively. As noted in the opening chapter, the aftermath of war necessitated the gathering and analysis of new demographic data; and in the late 1950's when Malta began its industrialisation programme, the need for statistics became an important tool for the economy.[280]

Industrialisation needed the training of workers in existing and new industrial skills, as well as professional education in fields such as economics and adminstration. At the time, the professional education and expertise in economics and statistics were lacking. The training of Maltese personnel overseas in these subjects and in the use of tabulators may be seen as part of a government policy that would ensure the right complement of needed personnel.

Other salient points that come out of the COS's case study include: the political controversy related to the Statistics Act, which was seen by some as an "enabling" Act; the exorbitantly high equipment cost in relation to the meagre salaries; and the inappropriate working physical environment (lack of space and excessive machine noise) which was not conducive to productivity

---

[280] Note that although the first population census in Malta was mechanized in the 1950s, the general elections were not computerised until the early 1990s.

and personnel morale. The last point is rarely mentioned in computing history.

Civil Service Reform, DP Services and the First Computers

Although by no means a turning point in Maltese computing history, the late 1960s must be singled out for two computer-related events which are historically significant (see Part II). The first of these was the appearance of private computer bureaus that started offering data preparation and processing services. The second was the government's O&M exercise to reorganize the civil service and introduce modern methods of operations. Government's intention was also to set up a computer centre by the early 1970s.

EDP was seen as one of the newer methods forming part of the O&M process, so that after feasibility studies were conducted, it was decided by the Cabinet to create a computer organization that would, at least initially, meet the demands of the COS, the Treasury, and the Inland Revenue departments. It was anticipated that a sufficiently powerful computer installation would also serve the needs of the then newly set up Malta Development Corporation and the Polytechnic. The computer system plan was, however, never implemented following a change of government which was indifferent to the new technology.

Owing to Malta's small size, the market for data services did not prove sufficiently profitable for the handful of small firms that began offering these services in the late 1960s and early 1970s. These companies were relatively short-lived. One company's intention to expand overseas by providing services to Italian and Libyan customers was also unsuccessful. Later attempts by three other firms that specialised in computer time-sharing proved more fruitful, with two of these firms still extant. These firms had to diversify their business and move into telecommunications and turnkey services following the decline of computer time-sharing systems in the mid-to-late 1980s. The brief account of Computime reveals that time-sharing was not only profitable for the companies that offered it, but an economical alternative for those who made use of it. Indeed, even medium-sized companies employing in excess of a hundred personnel and who therefore could probably have afforded their own small data processing department, preferred to make use of this service. The fact that not just one company but two others were in the computer time-sharing business for a number of years (in a small place like Malta) proves that computer time-sharing was a popular model of computerising business processes.

The two other significant computing events of the 1970s were Barclays Bank's computerisation and that of the Inland Revenue. In this period a few private manufacturing firms also introduced computers. Even so, whereas at the close of the 1970s many countries had thousands of computer installations, Malta only had a handful. The likely reasons for this slow take up of computers are their (then) high cost and government's indifference. The government's reluctance to introduce computers on a national scale in the 1980s resulted in a painfully slow IT diffusion process (up to the early 1990s) that left Malta trailing behind the rest of Europe in computer education and information technology.

Microcomputers and ICT Education

Part III looked at the major computing developments that took place in Malta in the 1980s and set the pace for the rapid uptake of information technology in the 1990s. Worldwide, the 1980s will be remembered for the PC or IT "revolution" and the 1990s for the widespread use of the world wide web. Affordability played a key role here, as did packaged software. Miniaturisation of electronic circuitry and advancements in production processes allowed the microcomputer to be produced in quantity at a reasonable price, resulting in economies of scale which pushed down prices further.

The introduction of microcomputers in Malta had a positive impact on at least two sectors, namely education and the small business sector. Even if the home computer was often used for playing games, it enabled a number of enthusiasts to experiment with it and become more confident with emerging technologies. Importantly, these hobbyists formed computer clubs and helped spread their knowledge of computers: for example the Malta Amateur Radio Club formed its own computer section and began organising computer courses both for their members and the public. Private firms also began specialising in computer training; and at the more professional level, professional bodies such as the Chamber of Commerce and the Malta branch of the Institute of Data Processing and Management played an important role in computing education.

Unfortunately, in spite of private initiatives by non-governmental bodies and private (mainly Church) schools, computer education in state schools was a neglected area that left Malta trailing behind European neighbours in informatics. The thorny issue of unpopular educational reforms in the early 1980s certainly did not help to create an atmosphere conducive to dialogue about IT education's potential.[281] At the tertiary level, computer science was introduced relatively late, however the account given in Chapter 5 reveals that Malta has made up for the time lost in this sphere, and both the University of Malta (UOM) and the Malta College of Arts, Science and Technology now have well-established ICT degrees and diplomas that are comparable to courses offered by Universities of advanced European countries. That account has also shown that at the UOM, as in many other institutions abroad, the Mathematics and Electrical Engineering departments both involved themselves in some aspects of computing for a number of years before establishing the three departments of information systems, computer science (& AI), and computer engineering.

With reference to the small business sector, small companies could benefit from the introduction of the PC because in the early 1980s a number of systems houses were set up that offered turnkey solutions and tailor-made software to suit business requirements.

Government Computer Agencies

Chapter 6 also investigated two "milestones" in the history of Maltese computing, namely the creation of the Government Computer Centre (the Swatar Centre) and the Management Systems Unit. The former was created by the Labour government then in power, the latter by the Nationalists. However both the Computer Centre and the Management Systems Unit (MSU) were also products of their time. The Computer Centre was created in 1981 at a time when many other countries had already introduced similar centres. A decade later, the

---

[281] These educational reforms are discussed in Caruana (1992) and Zammit Mangion (1992).

creation of the MSU reflected the mentality then prevailing of a "management way" of doing things, even in government. The MSU was also part of a process of civil service reform.

The contrast between these two entities showed different political ideologies. Whereas, for example, the Swatar Centre was very much government controlled, the MSU was independent. The Swatar Centre had to operate under strict financial budgets and limited personnel, whereas the MSU was given sufficient funds to be able to recruit expensive foreign consultants and numerous project managers.

Both entities came under attack, however, having been criticised for the way they operated. The Swatar Centre was accused of lacking direction, of neglect in certain operational procedures, and of data privacy abuse at a time when data protection laws in Malta had not yet been implemented. Security presence was always evident at the Centre, but following a bomb which did moderate damage it was heavily guarded as though it were some military base, simultaneously giving it a sense of absolute government ownership. As for the MSU, this was accused of lack of transparency and squandering pubic funds.

Software as an Economic Sector

The computer software and services industry was the subject of Chapter 7 (Part IV). The software companies operating in Malta are a mix of domestic and foreign firms engaged in a wide variety of products and services. Before the mid-1990s there were few incentives for foreign software firms to locate to Malta, and software houses consisted of domestic firms, the oldest ones set up in 1979-1980. From about 1997 onwards foreign firms were encouraged to operate locally. This was a sound foreign investment policy that gave access to foreign markets and sustained growth and development.[282] Malta Enterprise, set up in 2004, has played a key role in the diffusion of ICT, helping recent start-ups in particular. However, this entity did not come from nowhere, since it was preceded by other bodies such as the Malta Development Corporation (MDC, created in 1967), the Malta External Trade Corporation (METCO, created in 1985), and the

---

[282] Foreign investment also enables access to know-how needed for the knowledge society, and brings with it up-to-date software and jobs (Wilson III, 2006).

Institue for the Promotion of Small Enterprises (IPSE, created in 1998). The three bodies, together with the Malta Federation of Industries, were all instrumental in the promotion of Maltese industry. In 2004, it was felt that these three enterprises, which in some areas were duplicating work, should merge.[283]

In their book about software outsourcing, Carmel & Tjia (2005) dedicate an entire chapter about software exporting countries. They use a 3-Tier taxonomy of software exporting countries, where: a) the mature software exporting nations (advanced nations like the UK, the US, Germany, the Netherlands, and places like Ireland, Israel and India) form the Tier-1 group; b) emerging software exporting nations (such as Brazil, Mexico, Malaysia and South Korea) form the Tier-2 group; and c) infant stage software exporting nations (such as Egypt, Indonesia and Bangladesh) make up Tier-3. Of these three tiers, Malta falls somewhere between Tier-2 and Tier-3, possibly closer to Tier-3. Owing to Malta's smallness, which severly restricts its ability to grow large industries, it is unlikely that it will ever join the Tier-1 nations.

Telecommunications Infrastructure

The chapters in Part V have shown that telecommunications was given prominence by both the MLP and the PN, the two major Maltese political parties. The reasons for investing in the telecommunications sector have not always been the same. In the 1970s and 1980s the prime motive for upgrading the telecommunications network was tourism and industrialisation. Together with manufacturing, tourism is today a major industry. In the 1970s and 1980s much effort went into building these two industries, both of major economic importance; and their growth could be severely hampered by the absence of a good telecommunications system.

---

[283] To what extent the merger has been successful or whether it was the best decision is debatable and probably still too soon to tell. In a presentation made at the Malta Business and Finance Forum 2008, Malta Enterprise Chairman, Alan Camilleri, noted that his corporation's role follows that of the former MDC more than those of IPSE and METCO, presumably suggesting that the corporation places great emphasis on the administration of government policies, the attraction of foreign direct investment, and the execution of EU and local programmes that promote and support all types of enterprise in general. See Camilleri (2008).

In the 1990s the main reason for the continued investment in telecommunications is related to the new, knowledge-based, industries and the shift to a services (and knowledge-based) economy that were then (and are still) being promoted.[284] By the mid-1990s it had become clear that a proper and efficient ICT infrastructure was crucial for conducting the new modes of business (e.g. e-commerce) and simultaneously attracting foreign companies to invest locally. The impressive export success of the Dynamic Asian Economies (DAEs) in the late 1980s and 1990s was partly the result of a heavy investment in the ICT infrastructure which they (and, in particular, places like Hong Kong and Singapore) had come to depend on (Freeman, 1996; Kahin & Wilson, 1997). Indeed, by the early 1990s many countries had begun to devise national IT strategies, and Malta was one of those that took similar initiatives. Malta's robust telecommunications infrastructure has also been used to attract foreign remote gaming operators to Malta's shores (see, for example, Micallef, 2008).

Investment in ICTs is of little benefit unless complemented by a corresponding heavy investment in human capital. Whilst a number of initiatives were taken recently to ensure that Malta would not fall victim to the digital divide,[285] of immediate importance in the early years was the the upgrading of the educational system into a modern one comparable to those of the more advanced European countries. In this vein, the setting up of computer laboratories in educational institutions was started rather late in the early 1990s and was quickly followed by the introduction of formal computer syllabi. At the tertiary level an effort was made in the 1990s to tailor different types of IT courses and encourage students to take up computing studies. The upgrading of the educational system, although started late, was executed at a relatively fast pace to the extent that Malta is now

---

[284] Malta, because of its small size and open economy, is very dependent on what happens globally, so that its economy can easily be affected by the economies of other countries, particularly in the manufacturing sector for which a great deal of raw material is imported. A shift towards a services industry and a reduction in manufacturing activities minimises this foreign dependency.

[285] In the preface to the "HelloIT" document, Austin Gatt—then Minister for IT— likened the effort to overcome the digital divide to that of the long battle to eliminate illiteracy whereby the first step in that process was to make learning available and affordable to everyone and to then persuade everyone that life without reading and writing was simply not complete. See MIT&I (2004b).

projecting itself as an ICT centre of excellence (MIT&I, 2004a: pp. 48-49).

Chapter 9 has also shown that the penetration of the Internet and mobile devices in Malta compares favourably with other European countries. The liberalisation process of the telecommunications sector was started in 1990, ten years before the Malta Communications Authority was set up. The latter faced the somewhat difficult task of transforming the electronic communications sector into a competitive one, placing emphasis on consumer choice, services offerings, quality and cost. In the years leading to the start of the telecommunications liberalisation, local pressure groups and the international community (e.g. the EU) were urging the Maltese government to end the monopoly the former Telemalta corporation long enjoyed (by amending the legislation). The Federation of Industry, for example, brought up this issue a number of times and also noted that the local industry was then paying high tariffs for telecommunications services.[286]

IT Policy Issues

Part VI showed that the issue of IT policy only started to be taken seriously in the 1990s. A renewed interest in joining the EU led the Nationalist government of the day to pursue policies that would comply with EU directives. It is doubtful, for example, if the liberalisation and privatisation process, would bave been executed at the modest rate it was, were it not for Malta's application to become an EU member. Prospective membership meant that Malta had to meet certain EU objectives by target dates, and the building of an efficient ICT infrastructure would ensure, at least partly, that some of those objectives were met.

The two major IT policy initiatives were the drawing up of the first Information Systems Strategic Plan (which was followed by others) and the 1994 National Strategy for Information Technology (NSIT). The former had its roots in a combination of external and internal inputs — the external coming from UNESCO's Mission Report of 1985 on National Science and Technology Policy (Cassingena

---

[286] See, for example, "FOI on Telemalta's communications monopoly", *The Sunday Times*, 10 September 1995, p. 21.

Harper, 1998: p. 278). Malta's 1994 NSIT roughly coincided with, or came shortly after, a number of visionary IT strategies and reports on the information superhighways by other countries, including Singapore's (National Computer Board, 1992), the United States' (National Infrastructure Task Force, 1993), the United Kingdom's (CCTA, 1994) and Japan's (Ministry of International Trade and Industry, 1994). The European Union's Bangemann Report entitled "Europe and the Global Information Society" (Bangemann Group, 1994) was also produced in the same year.

Bishop (1999) makes a reference to Malta's NSIT (in writing about that of Barbados) as follows:

> It seems inconceivable, at a time when institutions such as the Commonwealth Secretariat have recognised the particular context of developing countries, that the UK model [which Barbados followed] could have prevailed. Malta, for example, is very similar in many ways to Barbados and has used the mechanism of a national IT strategy for the public sector to create a modern IT infrastructure and several significant information systems. Malta's model would definitely seem more appropriate (p. 262).

Bishop's mention of Malta's IT infrastructure acknowledges Malta's success in the NSIT's implementation.

Diffusion Models and Malta's IT Uptake

In an attempt to try to explain the different IT deployment patterns that occurred worldwide over the past sixty years, Cortada (2008) has suggested eight technology diffusion models that, at one time or another, different countries followed or experienced. These diffusion models are reproduced in Table 14.1. I will now show that, despite Malta's small size, a number of these diffusion models were followed in varying degrees. In effect, this section reinforces Cortada's thesis, but also identifies the key modes by which the uptake of computing and IT in Malta has occurred.

TABLE 14.1

Eight technology diffusion models and their features

Diffusion Model Type	Key Features
Government supported/ private sector driven	Inital government funding; Relies on private sector to do work; Shifts initiative to private sector
National champion driven	National government driven; National government invests in local firms; Local firms become preferred suppliers
Asian private sector driven	Focuses initially on component manufacturing; Government facilitates partnering with foreign firms; Leverages foreign expertise and capital
Planned economy driven	Centralizes control of IT development and manufacturing; Centralizes ownership of manufacturing and distribution; Largely a Soviet model
Industry driven	Private sector vendors of IT create market demand; Vendors develop IT, sell and support it; Governments invest only in high-risk R&D
Corporate driven	Private firms (customers of IT) drive demand; Private firms lead in implement-ation & use of IT; IT used to drive out costs and create new sources of revenues
Applications driven	Compelling uses of IT stimulates diffusion; Pushes vendors to develop new IT products; Creates widely accepted standards
Technology driven	Technical standards facilitate adoption and upgrades; Increases cost effectiveness of IT; Path dependency propels adoption, and constrains growth of alternative standards

Source: Cortada (2008)

Beginning by a process of elimination, the first two diffusion models can be rejected outright because Malta never had an indigenous computer hardware industry, and neither did government invest and promote a particular domestic firm as a preferred technology supporter (a national champion). These two models were typical of the US and the UK experiences with computers in the earlier years.

We can see patterns of the third and fourth models being operational in Malta between the 1960s and late 1980s. As the name suggests, the third model focusing on component manufacture and government initiatives, was predominant in the Far East, whereas the fourth model, a planned economy model, was largely a Soviet one. We start with the latter.

In the 1970s and for most of the 1980s, Malta had a strictly planned economy with central government control. Technology development played hardly any role because the emphasis was then on the development of tourism and new industry. The type of factories that were allowed to operate in Malta were to an extent determined by government, based on agreements with foreign investors that were mutually beneficial to both the investor and the Maltese government. Apart from the textile industry, electronics firms were encouraged to operate locally: the foreign firms were willing to locate to Malta because of cheap Maltese labour; and the Maltese government was glad to host them because these companies could provide employment on a scale few Maltese firms could match and hence partly solve the unemployment problem. Import substitution and export-oriented, labour-intensive industrialisation typified the approach taken by government in that period. A protectionist policy was also in place, with widespread import controls. These controls were primarily meant to secure employment (by protecting items that were assembled or manufactured locally, such as TV sets and confectionery).[287]

---

[287] This type of policy has been adopted by many developing countries. For example, when the British announced their intention to withdraw from their Singapore bases in the late 1960s, the government there also promoted export-oriented, labour-intensive industrialisation. However, by contrast to Malta which was late in promoting and deploying IT, Singapore quickly moved up the value chain by focusing on more capital-intensive and technology-intensive activities: by the late 1970s it had identified information technology as a key technology that would

As for IT, the planned economy approach could be said to have been extended to computing when the Government Computer Centre was created in 1981. Interestingly, just as this model was inefficient in diffusing computing throughout society in the Eastern bloc countries (Cortada, 2008: p. 11), so in Malta it was accompanied by a very slow take up of computing. However, owing to Malta's small size, the Computer Centre helped to dispel the previously held belief that computing was only for the select few, "demystifying" it. It also enabled a number of University students to acquire first-hand experience of data processing.

Turning attention to the third model, it would initially appear that Malta did follow this model from the 1960s to the 1990s, however closer analysis reveals that in fact this only happened partly, and certainly not in the way the model was successfully implemented by places like Singapore, South Korea and Taiwan. I have mentioned that the industrialisation process in Malta began in the early 1960s,[288] and that some foreign electronics firms operated in Malta at different times between the 1960s and the present. These firms, like their counterparts in East Asia, also produced components that went to be used in high-tech products. For example, the British firm of Plessey, which operated in Malta between 1969 and 1981, produced ferrite core memories for computers, as well as various telecommunications equipment; and the former Italian firm of SGS-Ates (now ST Microelectronics) opened its semiconductor fabrication plant locally in 1981 to produce microprocessors. It is still operating.[289]

The downside of Malta's foreign direct investment (FDI) policy — and this is where the approach differed significantly from that of the

---

help improve the country's economic performance. See Hioe (2001), and Wong (1997).

[288] The Malta Development Corporation (MDC) was created in this early industrialisation period (in 1967) as part of *Malta's Second Development Plan 1964-1969*.

[289] ST-Microelectronics has been one of the success stories of Malta. Beginning with a hundred or so employees, it employed in excess of two thousand in 2008, making it the largest private employer in Malta. In spite of the crisis that forced it to begin reducing its workforce in 2009 (primarily because labour costs in Malta have escalated to about 9 times that in Asian countries, it remains a major player in the Maltese economy, accounting for a significant contribution of GDP (between 1% to 2%), important tax revenues to government and substantial imports and exports. See: "Bleak Outlook", *The Malta Business Weekly*, 12 February 2009; and Zahra (2009).

successful East Asian countries — is that the Maltese government (in the 1960s, 1970s and 1980s) did little to specifically encourage and support local industry to acquire the necessary know-how and compete internationally. For example, there was hardly ever an attempt to create purely Maltese start-ups and arrange partnership agreements with foreign firms to enable local enterprises to gain that much needed foreign expertise. This meant that high-tech industry remained foreign. Undoubtedly, a reason for this has to do with tourism which, at the time, was seen as a more important sector to develop and concentrate on.[290]

The industry diffusion model, the fifth of the models, fits Malta's experience from about the 1980s onwards. In this period, as computers became more affordable, new computer vendors (computer bureaus offering computer time-sharing and turnkey solutions) and software firms began advertising, selling and supporting computer systems. Throughout the 1980s, private companies were the main consumers. They ranged from hotels, to insurance agents, to manufacturing concerns. Then, beginning from about 1989, the government also became a heavy consumer as a process of computerisation was effected across the public sector. Trade fair associations played crucial roles by hosting two computer-related annual events, the *Business Fair* and the *Electronika Fair* (later variously called *Informatics Fair*, or *Computer Fair*). The media, too, was instrumental in publicising computing. The *Times of Malta* (later renamed *The Times*), for example, never failed to produce IT and business-related trade fair "supplements" for the occasions. Later (late 1990s) it started including a "Business Section", part of which was dedicated entirely to informatics (aptly called *i-Tech*). Other newspapers roughly followed a similar pattern. The *Malta Business Weekly*, which commenced publication in 1994, also has included a wealth of information about computing matters over the years.

Closely tied to the industry driven model is the corporate model, since it is impossible to speak of a supply side (that characterises the

---

[290] The situation regarding FDI has changed somewhat since. Malta now has a significant number of companies (for its small size) that are involved in exporting high-tech products. These companies employ highly qualified Maltese personnel. Output indicators (as given in, for example, European Innovation Scoreboards) concerning the exports of high-tech products and employment in high-tech manufacturing rank Malta very high. See, for example, EESC (2006).

industry-driven model) from the demand side (that characterises the corporate driven one). In Malta, these two models were predominent. Parts I and II, for example, have shown how one company, ICL, pushed its products for use by private firms through various channels including regular advertising in the local press and the organization of data processing courses as early as the 1960s (when it was then still ICT); and how another company, Philip Toledo Ltd (the official local agent for NCR), had the majority of the cash register and accounting machines market. Then, in the 1980s, new hardware and software vendors appeared that contributed further to the IT diffusion process. These bureaux and software houses targeted the small-to-medium sized businesses that could not afford to have their own data processing department, and that needed guidance in the implementation of computerised systems. In that same period, the Malta Chamber of Commerce and the Malta Branch of the UK's IDPM began popularising computing and ecouraging the use of computers, explaining their benefits if properly used, and if feasibility studies have been carried out. Indeed, in the mid-to-late 1980s, structured systems analysis and design methodologies were commonly advocated. Some practitioners even prepared articles for the local press (see, for example, Alamango, 1990; and Sant Fournier, 1990).

Turning again to the demand side, customers began to realise the potential of technology if successfully managed. Hotels, which are numerous in Malta, introduced hospitality software; travel agents introduced online reservation systems, insurance agents, insurance policy software; and retailers (also very numerous in Malta), auto dealers, and manufacturing concerns all introduced inventory systems. Beginning from roughly the mid-1980s, many firms, large and small, made use of accounting systems and payroll.[291] The dot-com boom of the late 1990s also created a great demand for website development: web programming became a thriving industry. This demand for software created a need for more systems houses, so that an indigenous software industry was in the making. By the late 1990s it had become already reasonably well developed. In Malta's case, it

---

[291] Although we have no statistics about the companies that actually computerised their manual systems, the value of imported computers rose quite sharply in the period 1980-1990 (see Table 4.2, Chapter 4). Since government began its computerisation programme in the 1990s, we can only conclude that this hardware found itself in the private sector.

is a perfect example which shows that, more than specific policies, the software industry came about as a result of the supply-push, demand-pull. It was only from about the late 1990s that government took action to encourage and expand this sector.

Cortada (2008) refers to the application diffusion model as a variant of the corporate model. However, an important characteristic of the application model is that the use of a technology, or an application, becomes so compelling that it almost sells itself, a 'must have' application (p. 9). The way an organization comes to use a particular technology and carry out its business as a result of a particular vendor's application also falls under this model. For example the use of Enterprise Resource Planning (ERP) from the 1990s onwards dictated the way business functions would be carried by those businesses that chose to implement ERP software. Malta is perhaps too small a place (has too few corporate entities) to lead one to conclude anything about this model's adoption. Even so, in more recent years we have begun to see in local newspapers and business magazines adverts advocating the use of ERP systems.[292] Indeed, SAP, Oracle, and Microsoft all opened an office in Malta in the last few years.[293] As for "must have" technologies, in the years 1989-1990 the local banks introduced ATMs practically simultaneously. It was a technology they could not do without if they were to remain competitive. About sixteen years later it was followed by Internet Banking. The same was true of POS systems which minimarkets and supermarkets introduced in a short span of time.

In Malta, the last of the diffusion models—the technology driven model characterised by the adoption of technical standards and the concept of path-dependency—is demonstrated, for example, when Enemalta Corporation decided in 2001 to use the Microsoft platform for all its systems;[294] or when some years later the Maltese government

---

[292] Local magazines that have typically included adverts by software houses about ERP systems include *The Executive*, *The Commercial Courier*, and *The Malta Economic Update*. Major brands of solution suppliers advertised include Autodesk (CAD and animation software), Primavera (project management software), Cognos (business intelligence and performance management software), Microsoft Dynamics NAV (ERP software), and Eyesel (ERP software).

[293] For a brief account of Oracle's presence in Malta see: "From data to pervasive information", *The Malta Economic Update* , No. 12, 2006, p. 70.

[294] "Enemalta signs software standardisation agreement with Microsoft", *The Sunday Times*, 22 July 2001, p. 76.

signed strategic alliances with industry giants like Microsoft, Oracle, and SAP. Other instances could be given of the adoption of a particular technology, although not necessarily a standard. In the late 1980s, for example, the preferred make of computers for schools was that of Research Machines. Over the years the Malta Information Technology and Training Services have also pursued a policy of standards adoption (e.g. PRINCE 2 for project management; ISO 9001:2000, ISO 9126 and BS 7925 for quality assurance; and ISO 17799 for security management) as a matter of best practice.

Concluding Remarks

The diffusion of IT across the globe has occurred in varying degrees and at different pace. Some diffusion patterns have been typical of many countries, whereas others were particular to a selected few. Likewise, IT policy measures at the national level have been varied. The size and scale of a nation's economy, combined with political ideologies have often dictated the type of IT policy a nation followed. Kurihara et al. (2008), Coopey (2004), Heeks (1999), and Kahin & Wilson (1997), for example, illustrate these different policy measures and issues.

As a small island state, Malta, too, had its own particular policy agendas and priorities which, in turn, affected its IT take-up. Its geographical location, mild climate, and rich history have prompted policy makers and governments of the 1960s and 1970s to develop Malta into a tourist base. This may partly have affected the take-up of computing, which then would have been seen as economically unimportant.

Even so, in the 1980s when many countries (including a number of small states) had recognised the potential of information technology, Maltese politicians were slow to understand, and react to, its implications. In that period, it was primarily the private sector that contributed to the IT diffusion process. Government's luddite attitude left the 1980s civil service behind the private sector in the use of technology. By the late 1980s pressure groups and non-governmental organizations were pressing for educational reforms and the modernisation of the civil service. There was also the realisation that science and technology in Malta had been neglected and that it therefore required immediate attention. The Malta Council for Science and Technology and the Mosta Technopark were created in this vain.

Up until the early 1990s policy formulation, generally but especially in IT, was very much an unexplored territory in Malta, and the earlier inexperience in this field undoubtedly impacted the decision process. Clear visions, combined with a determination to succeed often have a bearing on final outcomes. These visions require a collaborative effort (including advice from the international community) to be properly realised. The first Malta National Strategy for Information Technology recognised these fundamental drivers: it involved various players, including foreign expertise, and was drawn following a detailed study of Malta's then IT deficiencies and requirements. More importantly, it with devised with set policy objectives in mind.

In the author's view, Malta's renewed interest in joining the EU in that same period has also helped improve the ICT environment. Prospective EU membership meant that Malta had to comply with EU regulations and implement EU directives. Although not always welcomed, some of these directives have had a positive effect on Malta's socio-economic welfare. To mention one example: deregulation and the liberalisation process in the ICT sector that ended a telecommunications monopoly and introduced competition between ICT vendors and various ISPs have led to reduced prices and a better choice for consumers. EU membership in 2004 also opened up possibilities for Maltese firms to take part in numerous R&D projects, enabling them to gain experience and exposing them to European markets. Prior to the new millennium, R&D in Malta was practically unknown. Malta had lacked the context, the confidence, and the funds to invest in high technology research. Indigenous attempts to break into hi-tech industries had to grapple with a number of problems including the unavailability of venture capital, and a lack of entrepreneurial vision resulting from Malta's educational system and lack of funding. EU membership helped provide the supporting framework and the means to realise Malta's potential in this sector.

Appendices

Appendix A
Malta: A Summary in Figures

Geographical Location:	Mediterranean Sea, European Continent
Area:	316 square kilometers
Capital City:	Valletta
Official Languages:	Maltese and English
Political System:	Parliamentary Democracy
Independence:	21 September 1964 (from the UK)
Republic:	13 December 1974
EU Accession:	1 May 2004
Population:	404,962 (2005 Census)
Population Density:	1,298 per square kilometer
Gross Domestic Product:	€6,200 million (2008) (= US$8,370 million)
GDP per capita:	€15,022 (2008) (= US$20,280)
Human Development Index:	0.902 (2008)
Currency:	Euro (€)

Appendix B
Information Technology Timeline for Malta

1857 > Electric submarine cables link Malta with Sardinia and Corfu. They are laid by the Mediterranean Extension Telegraph Company, John Watkin Brett's firm that would later be incorporated as part of the British company Cable and Wireless.

1859 > First telegraph station at 6-7 Marsamscetto Road, Valletta, is established by the Mediterranean Extension Telegraph Company.

1861 > A number of defensive Forts are directly linked by electric telegraphic cable to the Commander in Chief's headquarters at the Palace in Valletta.

1868 > The first direct electric cable from Malta to Alexandria is completed after John Pender forms his first telegraphic company, the Anglo-Mediterranean Telegraph Company, specifically for this purpose.

1870 > Pender's second telegraph company, The Falmouth, Gibraltar and Malta Telegraph Company, successfully lays a cable between Malta and Gibraltar to link Malta with England via Portugal and Gibraltar.

1882 > Edwardo Rosenbusch is told by the government to install magneto-type telephone sets in a few Police Stations (Birgu, Bormla, Isla, Sliema and Valletta), at the Prison, at the Palace in Valletta, at the Customs House and at Pinto Warehouse. A small telephone exchange is also put into service later that year, operated by Compagnie Générale des Téléphone (a subsidiary of Société Internationale des Téléphones).

1897 > The public is allowed to make use of the telephones at the Police Stations against a payment of 3d (three British pence) for calls between Valletta, Floriana, Bormla, Sliema and Hamrun.

1900 > First experiments are carried out to establish a wireless station.

1914 > Architect Robert Galea, a retired Maltese Royal Engineer Officer, succeeds in building a receiver/transmitter set, which he uses to communicate with an American Merchant Naval vessel.

1922 > Governor issues the Wireless Telegraphy Ordinance by which the public is allowed the use of radio sets provided they obtain a licence for it.

1933 > The telephone service, which up till now had been run privately by the Melita Telephone company, is taken over by government, and a public telephone system starts operating.

1936 > A 14-pair submarine cable is installed between Malta and Gozo which allows up to 14 voice channels.

1937 > Public telephone boots are introduced.

1942 > Valletta telephone exchange is destroyed by bombing, but underground communications system used by the military is unaffected.

1946 > Call for post of Government Statistician (Circular No. 12/46). Captain George Stivala is appointed as the first Maltese Government Statistician with task of setting up the Office.

1947 > Statistics Department starts operating (temporary accommodation with Public Relations Office at 5, Merchants Street).
> First Statistical Abstract for 1946 is issued. It contains a compendium of statistics on the development of the country in the demographic, social and economic fields, covering the period 1936-1946.

1948 > New premises is provided for the COS at 201, Old Bakery Street, Valletta.
> The COS embarks on the first major work: the Census of Population, 1948.
> Two new posts are created: (a) Assistant Statistician; (b) Research Officer.
> Steps are taken to train persons abroad in the use of punched card equipment.

1949 > Contract is signed between the COS and the BTM company for the supply of Hollerith machines.

1950 > Hollerith punched card installation starts functioning.

1953   > NATO's Mediterranean Headquarters, under the command of Lord Admiral Louis Mountbatten is established in Malta.

1955   > Installation of a NATO submarine cable and its associated repeater.

1957   > Philip Toledo introduces NCR Accounting Machines.
> The new automatic telephone exchange at the purposely-built premises at Blata l-Bajda is inaugurated. That year, the number of telephone subscribers stood at about 7,000.

1959   > British Tabulating Machines Company is renamed International Computers and Tabulators Ltd (ICT) after a merger with Powers-Samas. In 1968 it becomes International Computers Ltd (ICL) after further merges.

1962   > A 24 voice channel radio communication system is established between Malta and Gozo. The capacity of this network is extended to 60 voice channels in 1971.
> A small telex circuit is also established with only 6 subscribers. An automatic electro-mechanical exchange is introduced five years later, providing 300 local telex subscribers direct access to foreign subscribers.

1963   > ICT holds a series of lectures at the University of Malta about data processing techniques aimed at junior and senior management.

1964   > The Stolper Report (entitled *Economic Adaptation and Development in Malta*) is published. This is the outcome of a UN mission to tender advice on the economic policies Malta should follow given the eventual rundown of the British services, and serves as a model for the The *Second Development Plan 1964-1969*.
> The *Second Development Plan 1964-1969* is published. Its main aim is industrialisation, efficiency and competitiveness. This plan also announces government's intentions to set up the Malta Development Corporation.
> Philip Toledo introduces the NCR Century series computer.
> Malta obtains independence.

1965   > Malta joins the ITU.

1967   >Philip Toledo introduces the NCR500 series computer with magnetic tape as well as punch tape and punch cards.
> The Malta Development Corporation is set up.

> Trans-World Data Processing Ltd is set up in Malta.
> The first of three reports dealing with re-organization and efficiency in the civil service is drawn up by Gunnar Westermark, a UN expert brought over by the Maltese government specifically for that purpose.

1968   > George Haynes, Vice President and Group Executive International Operations of NCR visits Malta in recognition of the sterling service which Philip Toledo has given to the company.
> Computers In Business (Malta) Ltd is set up as part of the UK company Computers in Business (Holdings) Ltd.

1969   > Official opening of Plessey Components (Malta) Ltd. on 16 September 1969 at San Gwann Industrial Estate. The company produces ferrite core memories for export.
> O.C.R. Data Services Ltd is set up.

1970   > Philip Toledo taken up by NCR and a local branch of the NCR corporation is set up. The NCR branch closes down in 1976 and a distributorship arrangement is again established.

1971   > Cabinet decides to purchase a powerful central computer for government work. A call for tenders is published in the Government Gazette of 9 March 1971. The purchase never materialises, however, after a change of government in the summer of 1971.
> General Elections, MLP wins.

1973   > Malta hosts Honeywell Salesmen for Conference Meeting. Malta then fell within the marketing area of Honeywell Information Systems Italia (the US company affiliate).
> £M12 million are allocated to an expansion programme in telecommunications as part of the 1973-1980 Seven Year Development Plan.
> Barclays Bank Malta introduces the first computer in Malta, an ICL 1902A.

1974   > Malta subsidiary of Cable & Wireless Ltd sold to the Maltese government.

1975   > Telemalta Corporation Act establishes Telemalta as the sole Maltese telecommunications monopoly.
> The Department of Electrical Engineering at the University of Malta is set up.

1976   > The Inland Revenue installs its first computer system, an ICL 1900A. It is also applied to tasks done by the COS, the Treasury, the Social Services and the Agriculture departments.

1978   > Philip Toledo Ltd is entrusted by the NCR Corporation of Dayton, USA, with the management of the Mediterranean Technical Centre in Mtarfa. The Centre provides inhouse training courses for NCR Engineers in the Middle East and North Africa on computers and terminals.

1979   > Computime Ltd is founded. It is the first company to offer online time-sharing services.
> Megabyte Ltd is founded by brothers Thomas and Carmel Galea, both computer engineers.
> Dowty (Malta) Ltd installs an ICL 2903 mainframe on hire terms.
> Philip Toledo Ltd wins its first NCR EDP (computer) system contract.

1980   > Management Computing Services Ltd is founded by Tonio Farrugia and Victor Camilleri, two ex-Barclays Bank employees. It is the second local company to offer time-sharing services.
> The University of Malta acquires its first computer, a MINC-11. It is purchased on the initiative of the Electrical Engineering Department.
> Stella Maris College introduces microcomputers for educational purposes.

1981   > Philip Toledo Ltd appointed HP representatives.
> Intercomp Data Systems is set up to offer turnkey solutions.
> The Government Computer Centre at tas-Swatar, Dingli, is inaugurated.
> Panta Computers Co Ltd is set up to officially represent Prime computers in Malta.
> The first Electronika fair is held in Naxxar.

1982   > Dowty (Malta) Ltd replaces ICL 2903 with ICL ME29 model.
> Farsons installs an ICL ME29 computer.
> An examinable microprocessors and microcomputer technology module is established by the UOM's Electrical Engineering Department.

1983   > Bob Thompson, Area Business Manager for Prime Computer Inc. visits Panta Computers.

> First diploma course in computing and mathematics is launched by the Mathematics Department of the University of Malta.

1985   > Parliament passes a bill (Bill No. 100) which requires every imported computer to be subjected to a customs duty of 20% if manufactured outside the (then) EEC area, and 12% if produced within the EEC.

1986   > Telemalta embarks on a long-term programme of expansion and modernisation. A Long Term Development Plan – known simply as the Master Plan – is conceived with the help of the ITU. The Master Plan document, entitled *The Long Term Development Plan for Telecommunications in Malta*, is officially presented to government by the ITU Secretary General on 18 April 1988.
> The first satellite earth station, a standard B type, is installed at Maghtab. A second F2 type is installed a year later.

1987   > General Election. PN wins election after 16 years of MLP rule.
> The first Bachelor's degree course in Mathematics and Computing is announced. This part-time course commences in September and attracts a record 160 students.
> The UOM installs a multi-user Prime 750 computer.

1988   > Public Service Reform Commission is set up to examine the organization of the Public Service. Complemented by an Operations Review (OR) exercise that aims to articulate a five-year strategic plan, the Commission's findings are published in 1989 in a report titled *A New Public Service for Malta*.
> Malta Council for Science and Technology is established as an advisory body to assist in the formulation and implementation of a National Science and Technology policy.

1989   > Telemalta signs a memorandum of understanding with Racal Vodafone for the setting up of a Cellular Mobile Telephone System. Telecell Ltd (later to become Vodafone (Malta)) is set up and given a 20-year licence to operate the mobile cellular telephone system.
> Public Service Reform Commission publishes its report (*A New Public Service for Malta*).
> A Malta-Sicily microwave system is introduced for the first time.
> Melita Cable Television Ltd is set up, the first company to offer cable TV services in Malta.

1990   > *Information Systems Strategic Plan* for the years 1991-1996 is presented to Cabinet. It is the first "blueprint" for the introduction of information systems across the Public Service. The ISSP is endorsed in early 1991, when the Management System Unit (MSU) is constituted in order to implement it. Apart from the MSU, the Staff Development Organization (SDO), and the Management Personnel Office (MPO) are established as two other "change" agencies responsible for the reform of the public service. The ISSP's 3 main goals are: the distribution of PCs; the development of applications; the introduction of networking (MAGNET).

1991   > An agreement is signed between Maltacom and Melita Cable TV for the latter to use the former's trenches for the laying of fibre optic cables. The construction of the cable network is started that same year.

1992   > General Election. PN wins.
> Authority over the top level domain for Malta is delegated (by IANA) to the University of Malta.
> Melita Cable TV starts laying the cable network

1993   > Melita's cable TV service is officially launched. By 1999 cable TV subscribers stands at c. 70,000.
> MCST is entrusted to formulate the National Information Technology Strategy, the nationwide framework for IT.
> MSU's Business Plan for 1993 is tabled in parliament for members to examine its contents.
> MLP publishes report entitled *Analysis of MSU Business Plan 1993* in which the MSU's 1993 Business Plan is analysed and criticised.
> A fundamental restructuring is effected within the UOM's Faculty of Engineering and the Faculty of Science. The new departments of Electrical Power and Control Engineering, Microelectronics, and Communications and Computer Engineering are created within the Engineering Faculty; and those of Computer Information Systems, and Computer Science and Artificial Intelligence within the Science Department.
> Board of Studies for Information Technology is set up.

1994   > The *National Strategy for Information Technology for Malta* (NSIT) is published. The NSIT is a detailed policy document that involves many working groups from both academia and industry for its design.

> An aggressive project is initiated to introduce technology within classrooms and place IT as a key component of the national curriculum. By the year 2000, over 3,700 PCs have been introduced in state schools.
> The first 4-year BSc Honours course in IT is introduced by the UOM.
> New Computer Building is inaugurated, which houses the departments of Mathematics, Information Systems, and Computer Science & AI.

1995 > The first two licences are issued to two ISP's (Video-on-Line and Electronic Systems Ltd) to provide internet services. By 1999, the number of ISP's stood at 10, with the number of internet subscribers probably not exceeding 15,000.
> The Domain Name Registration Committee for Malta is set up within the University of Malta to manage the DNS for *mt*, the TLD for Malta.
> A new UOM Engineering Building is officially inaugurated in December.

1996 > General Election. MLP wins.
> MLP appoints a consultant to conduct a strategic resource audit on the MSU with the view of identifying key areas that need change.
> Telemalta starts providing Internet services

1997 > MSU is restructured into a new entity called the *Malta Information Technology and Training Services Ltd* (MITTS).
> Telemalta Corporation is made a public liability company to become Maltacom plc.

1998 > The Malta Internet Foundation (also known as NIC (Malta)) is set up.
> A three-year *1999-2001 Information Systems Strategic Plan* (ISSP) for the Public Service is published. This ISSP builds on the 1991-1996 ISSP.
> GSM is introduced in Malta by Vodafone (Malta) Ltd. At this time less than 13% of the Maltese population used mobile phones; by 2006 the mobile penetration rate had reached 86%, but was still slightly below the EU average.
> Vodafone applies for, and is granted, a licence to provide data services.
> Terranet, initially a joint venture company, becomes a fully owned subsidiary of Maltacom.

> MLP leader and Prime Minister Alfred Sant resigns, resulting in a General Election which the PN wins.

1999   > Central Information Management Unit (CIMU) within the Office of the Prime Minster is established to provide leadership in the application of ICTs in the Public Service and to promulgate policies and standards concerning the technologies supplied. CIMU develops the Malta Government portal ("www.gov.mt") and the Public Service Intranet. Following a review of ICT policy, it is closed down on 30 September 2005, when responsibility for broad ICT strategy and planning across the whole public sector falls under the Ministry for Infrastructure, Transport and Communications. MITTS continues assuming responsibility for technical standards, policies and corporate ICT applications. The government portal and the Intranet is later managed by the DOI.
> Mobisle Communications Ltd, a subsidiary of Maltacom, is set up to offer mobile services under the "Go Mobile" brand name.

2000   > Publishing of a White Paper entitled "Vision & Strategy for the Attainment of e-Government in Malta".
> Mobisle Communications Ltd is issued with a mobile communications license. License is issued on condition that Maltacom divests itself of the 20% share it held in Vodafone.
> Reorganization of the former Fellinberg and Technical Institutes into the new MCAST. ICT-related certificate and diploma courses are among the many vocational courses offered at MCAST.
> An Inter-Ministerial Working Group is set up to develop a compendium of cyber legislation.
> Malta Communications Act, 2000 is drawn up, by which the Malta Communications Authority is set up. This Act is officially approved in July 2001.

2001   > A request for proposal for the design and implementation of the e-Government project is publicly announced by the Ministry for Justice and Local Government.
> Liberalisation of cable services.
> Enactment of Data Protection Act.
> Enactment of E-Commerce Act.

2002   > Vodafone is granted a licence to provide International Gateway Services beginning from 1 January 2003.
> Introduction of Multimedia Messaging Service (MMS)

2003   > Liberalisation of fixed line telephony.
> General Elections, PN wins.

2004   > Malta joins the EU.
> Government funding for R&D is made available for the first time.
> *The National ICT Strategy 2004-2006* and *HelloIT* documents
are published.

2005   > Vodafone and Go Mobile are granted rights to use radio
frequencies for the establishment and the operation of a third
generation (3G) mobile communication network. A third operator –
3G Telecommunications Ltd – is granted rights in August 2007.
> Introduction of Digital Terrestrial Television (DDTV) by Multiplus.

2006   > MCST launches National Strategy for Research and Innovation for
2007-2010, entitled "Building and Sustaining the Research and
Innovation".
> Dubai Holding LLC – the parent company of Emirates
International and Telecommunications Malta Ltd, a joint venture
between TECOM Investments and Dubai Investment Group –
acquires the Government of Malta's 60% controlling share in
Maltacom.
> Melita Cable launches its VoIP telephony service (called "Hello").

2007   > Maltacom Group is rebranded and renamed GO in a move that
reflects the company's position as Malta's sole quadruple-play
organization covering fixed voice, mobile, broadband Internet, and
digital television.
> New Faculty of ICT is created at the UOM.

2009   > Work on the construction of the ICT Faculty Building starts at the
UOM tal-Qroqq campus.

Appendix C

A Brief Overview of Tabulating and Sorting Equipment Functions

This appendix explains briefly the main functions of the old tabulating machines, often considered as the forrunners of modern computers. The description is given in roughly the order that the machines would generally have been used for a particular application.

The *mechanical punch* was used to produce coded information on the punch cards. The first step would have been to prepare the source documents for punching. Basic information found on the source documents (e.g. nationality, occupation, etc.) would be given numeric codes. The coded information would then be entered by an operator via a typewriter-like keyboard (the punch machine, or mechanical punch), which would punch holes in the cards at the appropriate fields.

As the punched cards formed the basis on which the entire mechanisation process operated, it was fundamental for the accuracy of the punched-hole recordings to be established at the outset. Therefore a check of the punching of each individual card would be carried out by means of the *electro-mechanical verifier* or by the *hand-punch verifier*.[295] Having placed the punched cards in the card hopper of the verifier, the information from the source document would again be typed in (usually by a different operator) using the verifier machine keyboard. This time, instead of punching holes, the verifier would check if a key depression corresponds to the hole previously punched in the card: if not, the machine would stop and indicate an error (e.g. by switching on a light).[296]

Occasionally, it would have been necessary to transfer particular information from one card to another. For example, in the case of the Water and Electricity billing done at the COS, the rates on the

---

[295] According to Joe D'Amico, an ex-COS employee, these hand-punch machines remained in use up until the early 1980s, even when the Government Computer Centre opened in November 1981.

[296] Some manufacturers, notably Univac and IBM, had combined punching and verifying machines (e.g. IBM's 129 model) which, apart from saving space, also had buffer memory to hold the keyed characters prior to actual punching. This made the punching process faster and allowed for error correction.

consumption card would have had to be copied to new cards for which the latest consumption was to be calculated. This was essentially the function of the *reproducing card punch*. Another use of the reproducer was simply to copy the entire information from perhaps a slightly damaged (worn-out) card to a new card.

The reproducing card machine could also incorporate "mark sensing", whereby pencil marks would be detected by the machine and automatically converted into punched holes. Typical operation speed of this machine was 100 cards per minute. One such machine was already available at the COS by 1958. It was used initially for statistical work, but later also for billing. However, in the opinion of one ex-COS senior operator, the mark sensing unit of this machine was not fool-proof and often gave problems to the extent that mark sensing eventually had to be discontinued.[297]

As the name implies, the *sorter* was used to sort the punched cards, for example by customer account number. The sorter operated at a higher speed of 400 card passages per minute (although later machines could reach speeds of 1100 cards per minute), but in order for a complete sort to take place, the cards had to be put through the machine a number of times depending on the length of the sorting field. Thus, if the cards were to be sorted by account number which consisted of six digits, the cards would have had to be passed through the sorting machine six times. Thus, in reality, for a machine operating at 24000 card passages per hour, the sorting of 24000 accounts would have taken at least six hours. In fact, the sorting operation would take longer because of the operator time involved which typically accounted for about 20% of the machine time.[298]

The *collator* was used to merge two sets of ordered cards to produce one ordered set, as well as for sequence checking. As an example of the collator's function, suppose one set of cards contained the customer ("master" record) details such as the customer code, address, and telephone number, sorted by customer code, and another

---

[297] Interview with Joe D'Amico on 4 May 2005 at the National Statistics Office, Lascaris, Valletta.

[298] Information provided by D'Amico during another meeting on 10 May 2005. For the Maltese 1967 Census of Population, Housing and Employment, when the number of punch cards used was c. 87,100 for housing and 314,300 for population, sorting took something like two weeks to complete, and required a concerted effort on the part of the persons responsible for the sorting operation.

set of cards contained the consumption and payment details, also sorted by customer code. The task of the collator was then to go through both card decks and produce one merged deck with the cards grouped together by customer number. Another use would have been to group consumption cards of one quarter (e.g. the March quarter) with those of another quarter (e.g. the June quarter) primarily for ledger records.

The next step in the process would have been to pass the cards through the *calculator* for calculations. The calculator (as well as the collator and reproducer) was typically programmed using a wired-controlled panel, so that differently wired panels would be used for different operations or jobs. In the case of the Water and Electricity billing, a typical operation for each consumer would have included: (i) calculating the electricity amount due; (ii) deducting rebates allowed for electrical appliances; (iii) dividing water consumption by the number of persons per family and multiplying the result by the appropriate rates according to a "rising scale"; and (iv) adding the water and electricity amounts to produce the final bill total. The machine could carry out these calculations at the rate of about 100 cards per minute, so that if five calculations were performed on each card, roughly 500 calculations per minute were being done, equivalent to approximately eight calculations per second, or a calculation speed of about 125ms. One calculator used at the COS was the model 550 which worked with valves (type 12AU4).[299] This calculator and two tabulators (a 901 tabulator and a senior rolling tabulator) were eventually replaced by the 1004 data processor.

Up to this stage the information would still be on punched cards. The *tabulator*—one of the major units of a punched card system— processed the calculated amounts as well as other relevant data on the different cards to produce a "hardcopy" output in the form of a printed list or tabulations on special pre-printed, continuous, stationery. Final bills, reminders and receipts, as well as statements of accounts which were sent to customers were produced by this machine.

---

[299] Information provided by D'Amico, 4 May 2005 meeting.

Appendix D
IT-related courses at the University of Malta, 2008-2009

For the academic year 2008-2009, five undergraduate degree courses
having an IT component could be followed at the University of Malta.
These were:

- the BSc (Hons) ICT
  (offered by the new Faculty of ICT);

- the BSc (Hons) Business & Computing
  (offered by the Faculty of Economics, Management and
  Accountancy);

- the BSc (Hons) in Science with Computing
  (offered by the Faculty of Science);

- the BCommunications (Hons) with Informatics
  (offered by the Centre for Communication Technology);

- the BEd (Hons) in Computing
  (offered by the Faculty of Education)

Within the Faculty of ICT, students could follow courses from
different "streams", and therefore be awarded a degree in that
particular stream. The undergraduate degree programmes (or
streams) on offer included:

- a degree in Computer Information Systems (CIS)
- a degree in Computer Science (CS)
- a degree in Communications and Computer
  Engineering (CCE)

These three courses merged some aspects from the previous Honours
degree programmes that were offered before the 2008-2009 academic
year. For example, the new CCE course merged aspects of the
Computer Systems Engineering stream in the previous BSc IT (Hons)

degree with the areas of Communications and Computer Engineering previously covered in the BEng (Hons) degree. The new course format was also designed to better prepare engineers working in these fields where a strong emphasis on software design was required backed by a strong background in digital system hardware design.

Other major changes included the course duration and format. Although honours degree programmes at the University of Malta have typically been of four years' duration, these new BSc (Hons) courses now last for three years, and involve a total of 180 credits.[300] The reason for the shortening of the courses' duration is to make them compatible with similar undergraduate programmes offered in many European countries. Many European Univeristies now follow a system known as the Bologna Process consisting of three cycles, the first of which covers a 3-year bachelor's degree. Having successfully followed such a course, students can then engage in employment or move on to the second cycle and obtain a master's degree by studying for a further two years. The third cycle is at the doctorate level.

Finally, students reading for the BSc (Hons) ICT could either opt to specialise or follow a programme of studies that covers all the main areas of ICT without specialisation. Specialisation entails studying some modules (in more detail) and not others. The areas of specialisation are Communications and Computer Engineering; Computer Science and AI; and Computer Information Systems. Table D.1 lists some of the specialisation topics within each of the specialisation areas.

---

[300] The allocation of credits to study-units forming part of graduate and undergraduate courses follows closely the European Credit Transfer and Accumulation System (ECTS) proposed by the European Commission.

TABLE D.1
BSc (Hons) ICT course specialisation areas and specialisation topics,
2007-2008

Specialisation Area	Topics of Specialisation
Communications and Computer Engineering	computer programming; digital system design; computer architecture and organization; embedded systems; VLSI design and fabrication; digital signal processing; algorithms; multimedia communications; computer networks; communication systems; software engineering
Computer Science	data abstraction, encoding and storage; operating systems; formal methods; networking; algorithms and algorithm design; theory of computation; programming languages; software engineeering;database systems; machine architecture and machine language; graphics
Information Systems (Informatics)	computer programming; information system theory; business and systems analysis and design; enterprise wide information resource planning; databases; data warehousing and data mining; e-commerce and applied web engineering; scientific and geographic information systems; customer relation management; IT project management

Appendix E

Letter of Concern by the Chamber of Commerce to the House of Representatives regarding Import Duties on Computers

AN ACT FURTHER TO AMEND THE IMPORT DUTIES ACT, 1976

The Bill provides for the imposition of import duty on computers, collectors' pieces and antiques, to exempt from duty certain video recordings of a cultural nature and to establish rules for the remission of import duty on goods which are found short.

The Computer Section of the Chamber of Commerce met on the 13th of May 1985 to discuss the new act, wherein computers would have to start paying duty on importation.

It was decided to send the following letter to all members of the House Of Representitives.

Dear Sir,

The Computer Section of the Chamber of Commerce, having examined Bill No. 100 of 1985 entitled an Act further to amend the import duties Act 1976, and in particular Section 5(c) thereof, wish to draw your attention to the following points:

1 There exists in Malta a price freeze and a wage freeze. There is an undertaking by Government to hold prices at a fixed level. The introduction of a new customs duty on computers besides other items will increase the eventual selling price to the detriment of the public.

2 Computers today are an essential tool in Industrial Production. They are used extensively on the shop floor and even more in the processing of data in offices i.e. payroll, leave, financial modelling, production planning and so on.

The imposition of customs duty MAY have some small effect on revenue in the short term but the long term effects are disastrous.

3 The need for development of a computer mentality among our children is appreciated by all. Our children are already late in this field compared to other children in Europe. However one of the best resources that the Maltese people have at their disposal and which is not dependent on the importation of raw materials is undoutedly the brain power. Brain power which can be used to write software which could be exported. Such an industry could be built into a worldwide industry in Malta with a reasonable effort. (A major export from Israel today is software and it is second only to Fruit Export!) Duty on computers would stifle such an important industry.

4 Finally the introduction of a percentage duty would have a marginal effect on the cost of the small computer but will become very high on the cost of the larger business computers and the upper limit of duty should be considered carefully if it is to be applied in spite of our representations.

In conclusion, one must mention the recent speeches made by the Government Ministers in reference to computer technology and the need for youths to take up the science of computers which is most commendable.

Yours Faithfully,

Andrew de Domenico
HONORARY SECRETARY

Appendix F
Maltese Software Industry Revenue Estimate

Since few companies have actually furnished sales data, the Maltese software industry revenue (for 2005) had to be estimated indirectly by taking into account the following:

(i)   The sales figures per employee. For those companies that provided sales data, this value ranged from as much as Lm45,000 [= c. US$135,000] (typically for the larger, established companies) to as little as Lm8,000 [= c. US$24,000] (typically for smaller companies or those whose business is not purely software development).

(ii)   Government's reported figure for value added per person which, for 2005, has been estimated at Lm21,000 [= c. US$63,000] per annum (see, for example, Malta Enterprise, 2006a). (The average sales figure per employee obtained from the author's e-survey is Lm21,966.)

(iii)   The number of employees in the software industry sector which, according to the author's estimate, was about 1000 in 2005.

Interestingly, Arora & Gambardella (2005) give the software sales figures per employee for different countries as between c. US$40,000 and US$200,000. Taking these factors into consideration, and in view of the fact that Malta has a proportionately large number of small (< 10 employees) software firms, Lm21,000—which represents roughly a little under three times the 2005 average IT salary) seems to be a reasonable figure to adopt for the sales per employee. This yields Lm21 million [= c. US$63 m.] for the total software sales, or about 1.1% of GDP.

Glossary of Terms

Administrative Statistics. Statistics obtained from administrative records (e.g. social security, employment, housing) primarily for planning purposes.

ADSL. Asymmetric digital subscriber line (ADSL) is a type of broadband communication system that uses the traditional (existing) telephone copper cable pairs to transmit and receive data. Asymmetric refers to the fact that data is downloaded at a different (faster) transmission rate than when it is uploaded. A frequency filter is used to separate the voice frequencies from those used for data.

Asynchronous Transfer Mode. This is a switch-based, wide area network service using fixed length frames known as cells. Fixed length cells assure fixed length processing time by ATM switches, thereby enabling predictable delay and delivery time.

Bottom-up Strategy. This is synonymous with synthesis. In a bottom-up approach, "subsystems" are pieced together to give rise to a bigger, emergent, system.

CASE. An acronym for Computer Aided Software Engineering. It refers to the use of software tools to automate the system development process. These tools can include any program that aids the system developer (e.g. a program debugger), but more often they are sophisticated programs that help automate the system life cycle.

Client/Server Computing. A term used to describe a computer system which is based on a model whereby the application programs running on workstations equipped with graphical displays and sophisticated input/output devices are the "clients" and the system programs providing those facilities and running on either the same machine, or more commonly on other machines to which the clients are connected (usually via a network) are the "servers".

Client/server computing, as it is known today, evolved from the use of networks and networking concepts, in particular local area networks. Thus, the client and server communicate with each other by means of messages in a standard protocol. The client issues a request which the server responds to. With the advent of the Internet and Intranets, client/server computing has become a standard mode of communications.

Comparative Advantage. An economic term used to indicate the relative advantage (as opposed to absolute advantage) a country has over another in a particular economic sector (such as software productivity) in comparison to all other economic activities (such as productivity in all of manufacturing). The comparative advantage may be given as a ratio, for example, in the case of software productivity, the comparative advantage would be the value of the software revenue per employee over the value added per employee for all of manufacturing.

As with absolute advantage, comparative advantage partly (but only partly) explains why certain countries have done well in the software industry. For example, it is found that software production in India was less than those of other countries, as was productivity in all manufacturing, but in comparison to all manufacturing, the software productivity was relatively high, i.e., Indian firms producing software were more productive per unit of labour employed than their counterparts (in India) in manufacturing. Put another way, software was more productive relative to the manufacturing sector in India compared with other countries.

Comparative advantage alone does not explain why some countries and not others have developed an international competitive software industry, nor can it explain by itself why growth has continued even as the initial advantages (such as cheap labour) diminish. For example, company level capabilities, both organizational and technological are among other important factors that sustain growth in the software industry.[301]

---

[301] Sometimes, competitive advantage and comparative advantage are used interchangeably. For example, Israel's long academic involvement in industrial research and development (R&D) has been one of its competitive advantages, a distinctive feature of its IT industry over those of other emerging economies. This competitive advantage attracted large multinational companies (MNCs) to its

Copyright. A copyright on a piece of work is the legal right of its author, composer, or publisher to be the only person allowed to reproduce it. Copyright practically requires no procedural formalities (such as patents and trademarks), so that an author or the creator of a piece of truly original work automatically becomes the sole copyright owner of that work when first published (recorded in some form).

Critical Mass. This is a concept used in a variety of contexts, primarily to describe that a certain "momentum" has been reached for sustainability. In the case of an organization, this sustainability momentum would be its critical mass.

CRM Software. CRM stands for customer relationship management, and CRM software is used for managing a company's interactions with customers and potential sales. The software is used to collect and analyse data in order to take the appropriate actions. It is also useful for marketing.

Customisation. The modification of packaged (mass-market) software to users' needs. It can involve changes done as part of a vendor-provided user exit or changes to the actual source code. When source code changes are made, customization can be a risky process that has implications: each change that is made complicates not only the initial implementation but also every upgrade or new software release. Customisation can thus be very costly.

Customs Union. A kind of preferential trading agreement (allowed under GATT) in which member states (forming the Customs Union) set up common external tariffs. The member states must agree to charge the same tariff rate on each imported good. The EU is an example of a customs union. (The other preferential agreement is the free trade areas, whereby each country's goods can be shipped to the other member without tariffs, but each member country can set their own tariffs against those not belonging to the free trade area.)

---

shores for R&D purposes. MNCs would first open R&D centres (or buy an Israeli technology company and transfer it into an R&D centre) and only later—if all progresses well—move on to manufacturing activities.

Domain Name System. The Domain Name System (DNS) is a method (in reality an application protocol used as part of TCP/IP) to map a symbolic name (such as www.blablabla.com) into the equivalent fully qualified network address. DNS is hierarchically structured (for example, the "com" part forms part of the so-called top-level domain) and allows a computer (actually its location) on the Internet to be identified so that other computers will be able to access it.

Embedded System. A computer system developed for a special purpose and in which the computer (typically a microprocessor-based system or one consisting of a microcontroller) with its software is largely hidden within the application.

With a general-purpose microcomputer system, the user can interact with the system and is able to develop (and change existing) programs, as well as run different applications. However, the program of an embedded system cannot be changed: the user can only perform the pre-programmed functions (as in a mobile phone, a washing machine, or a microwave oven).

Enabling Act. A legislative act that confers on appropriate officials the power to implement or enforce the law.

E-Payment Gateway. An electronic payment (e-Payment) gateway is an infrastructure that allows online payments to be effected. The infrastructure consists of computers and the appropriate software to process, verify, and accept (or decline) credit card transactions on behalf of a merchant through secure Internet connections. Sensitive information such as credit card details is encrypted during the transaction processing. The payment gateway service is typically offered by Internet and web service providers with expertise in secure web programming. In Malta, one of the first payment gateways to be launched was that by MaltaNET in 2004.

ERP Software. Enterprise Resource Planning software is sophisticated business management software which allows an organisation to use a system of integrated applications to manage its system. The ERP software allows a company to integrate all facets of an operation, from development, to manufacturing, to marketing and sales.

FLAG. FLAG (Fiber-Optic Link Around the Globe) is a submarine communications cable laid in the mid-1990s that spans the Earth. It is thousands of kilometers long and connects many nations. FLAG offers a speed of 10 Gigabits per second and uses synchronous digital hierarchy (SDH) technology. It carries over 100,000 voice channels via almost 30,000km of mainly undersea cable.

Frame Relay. A packet switched network whereby charges are based on actual amounts of traffic transmitted rather than fixed monthly rates. The frame relay telecommunication service is designed for cost-efficient data transmission for intermittent traffic in a network. Frame relay puts data in variable-size units called frames and leaves any necessary error correction (retransmission of data) up to the end-points, thereby speeding up the overall data transmission. For most services, the network provides a permanent virtual circuit (PVC), which means that the customer sees a continuous, dedicated connection without having to pay for a full-time leased line. The service provider determines the route each frame takes and charges according to usage.

FSK. FSK (Frequency Shift Keying) is a modulation technique used in telecommunications. It is a method of representing digital data with analogue signals by using a change in the frequency of the transmitted wave. Thus, one frequency would represent a digital logic '0', and another frequency would represent a digital logic '1'.

Gateway. A gateway is one of a handful of network interconnecting devices used to connect telecommunications networks together. The gateway is the most sophisticated of the interconnecting devices, enabling computer networks of different types and using different protocols to communicate together.

Get-up. A term used in intellectual property law, it refers to the arrangement and production style (the general composition, or structure) of a work such as a book or an electronic document.

GSM. Global system for mobile communications (GSM) is a communications standard introduced in the early 1990s. GSM is the most popular standard for mobile telephones, and its ubiquity has meant that users can now use mobile devices practically anywhere in the world. GSM is a cellular network, whereby mobile phones search for "cells" in the immediate vicinity in order to connect to the network. A cell is a geographical (land) area served by at least one fixed-location transceiver (transmitter/receiver) known as a base station (or cell site). GSM was introduced in Malta in 1998.

Harmonization. In international law, harmonization is the process by which different states adopt the same laws. It is an important concept in the European Union for creating common standards across the internal market. The intention is to make laws more uniform and coherent to facilitate free trade and protect citizens.

Horizontal Application. A software application which is developed for use by a broad cross-section of users. Software products typically used by financial and accounting business users (e.g. payroll, book-keeping, accounting systems, and other office automation software such as word processing and spreadsheet) are examples of horizontal applications.

Import Substitution. A policy whereby a lower proportion of a nation's needs is imported. It occurs when certain stages of domestic production replace imported production. Governments encourage import substitution because it promotes domestic value added and employment.

Informative Statistics. Statistics that are often related to social behaviour and methods such as the number of people in worst-off households, the number of children that die before a certain age, the rate of alcoholism, and the number of students that graduate in a given year.

ISO 9001:2000. This is an international standard for quality assurance. The standard specifies requirements for a quality management system whereby an organization would need to demonstrate its ability to consistently provide products that meet customer requirements and satisfaction. The requirements are generic and intended to be applicable to all organizations, regardless of the type, size and product provided.

Legacy Systems. One definition of legacy systems relates to existing systems that will eventually be replaced by a new computerised application. Support of legacy systems is a major issue for software developers who must decide how much effort to put into them since the support of legacy systems may require a number of years. Establishing realistic end-user expectations and defining the work that will be provided during the interim "lame duck" period is essential. Support can either be provided by existing staff or outsourced to another firm. Some software firms specialise in providing support for legacy systems. In Malta, one company that at one time specialised in legacy systems was Philip Toledo Ltd (because of its long experience in the data processing field).

Market Failure. This is a situation where the allocation of production or the use of goods and services by the free market is not efficient. It is often used as a justification for government intervention in free markets.

Market failure often occurs when an agent (e.g. a company) gains market power blocking others and therefore possibly leading to inefficiency due to imperfect competition (e.g. a monopoly) and price discrimination. Some economists view market failure as a problem of an unregulated market system.

Market Reserve Policy. A protectionist policy which disallows imports of foreign goods that compete with domestically-produced offerings.

Marshall Aid. Also known as the Marshall Plan (after the US Secretary of State George Marshall who proposed it), and by the longer title of the European Economic Recovery Program, this was a programme of US economic assistance for European countries affected by World War II. Since Malta was a British colony, it unfortunately did not qualify for Marshall Plan funds, although some aid was eventually forthcoming (from Britain itself) which went towards the building of a new power station.

Memorandum of Understanding. A document describing a mutual agreement between two or more partners. The document is not as binding as a contract but outlines a commitment between the parties to work together towards the same goals.

National Champion. A national champion is a political concept and policy (popular in some European countries in the 1970s) whereby a large, usually private, company is chosen or promoted by government as its "national champion", that is, as a company which is expected to grow and compete with other multinationals, and thus contribute positively to the national economy. The anticipated growth would partly be achieved through government intervention and regulation.

Organizational Inertia. This refers to an inability to make proper decisions or proper analysis in a management environment. The reasons could be varied, for example, the structure may not be aligned with the strategy, the roles and responsibilities of personnel may be unclear, and staff may not have the right skills or training. A key to avoiding organizational inertia is having an unequivocal goal.

Packaged Software. This is commercial, off the shelf, software (COTS), i.e., vendor supplied "packaged" software not designed to any particular customer's specification, but designed instead to meet common needs.

Patent. A patent is an official right granted to a person or a company in recognition of that person's or company's invention. The patent effectively gives the inventor a monopoly to work the invention to the exclusion of others for a period of time (e.g. 20 years). The monopoly is not absolute in the sense that there are a number of checks to curb its abuse. For a patent to be awarded, a number of conditions would need to be satisfied, for example the invention must be new, it must involve an inventive step, and it must be capable of industrial application. According to most patent acts, some things are not considered inventions and therefore cannot be patentable. These include: a discovery, scientific theory or mathematical method; a literary, dramatic, musical or artistic work or any other aesthetic creation whatsoever; a scheme, rule or method for performing a mental act, playing a game or doing business, or a program for a computer; and the presentation of information.

Path dependency. A tendency of a traditional practice or preference to continue even when better alternatives are available. It is related to "lock-in" and "bandwagon effects" (when people do and believe things because others share the same believes). Path dependency was initially developed by economists to explain technology adoption processes. The classic example is that of the QWERTY vs. the Dvorak keyboard. Although it has been argued that persons trained on the use of the Dvorak keyboard (patented in 1936) can achieve higher typing speeds (than on the QWERTY), it never caught up. In telecommunications, path dependency also partly explains why the Postal, Telegraph, and Telecommunications Administrations in many European countries outlived their usefulness: their monopoly proved difficult to eliminate or modify significantly because many actors had become reliant on them.

Permanent Virtual Circuit. A PVC is a virtual (or logical) circuit that is permanently established ahead of data transmission. The word "virtual" signifies that the circuit is not a fixed, circuit-switched physical connection, but an established path (a route) over which the data (i.e., all data packets originating from a network node) will be transmitted. With a normal virtual circuit, the virtual circuit is established and then released or cleared for every tranmission session, but with a PVC the circuit is left permanently established (useful for frequent communications). With virtual circuits, both permanent and temporary, the actual lines may be shared by other users at the same time, yet the virtual circuit appears exclusive to the users who are communicating with each other.

Planned Economy. A type of economy, also sometimes referred to as a command economy, where the government practically has total control over the allocation of resources. Although a planned economy can provide stability, it often limits growth. Moreover it makes the government a dictatorship.

Prototyping. An iterative method of developing a certain kind of system instead of using traditional structured methods. With 'disposable' prototyping, a working model of the computer system is typically constructed at an early stage of the development process so that user requirements may be identified. Once the requirements have been established, the prototype is thrown away. 'Evolutionary' prototyping is when the working model is developed into the final system.

PSK. PSK (Phase Shift Keying) is a method of representing digital data with analogue signals by using a change in the phase of the transmitted wave. It is a modulation technique that allows an analogue waveform to carry digital information: the change of phase of the modulated signal represents a change in the digital value from logic '0' to '1' or vice-versa.

Rapid Application Development (RAD). A popular development method based on prototyping, user participation and high-powered software tools.

Shrink-wrapped software. Another term for commercial, off the shelf, software.

Strategic Alliance. A formal agreement between two or more parties to pursue a set of agreed upon goals, or to meet some business need while remaining independent organizations. The alliance aims for a synergy of the partners involved in the hope that the benefits from the synergy will be greater than those from individual efforts. Benefits accruing from the alliance include technology transfer, economic specialisation, shared expenses and shared risks.

System Integration. Basic system integration work involves the installation of hardware coupled with relatively simple software applications. Higher, value-added, system integration involves large custom projects where a software firm provides a combination of hardware, software, and services, including customised software.

Software Product. A software product refers to a software application (or a suite of applications) that has been designed and developed as a "product", that is, as a packaged item meant to be used by many customers. It typically requires considerable development effort and hence appropriate product management and marketing knowledge.

SSB. Single-side band (SSB) is a refinement of amplitude modulation whereby one of the two frequency bands (known as the side bands) associated with an amplitude-modulated signal is suppressed so that less transmission power and bandwidth is used.

Sui Generis. A Latin term essentially meaning 'one of a kind'. In law, it is used to identify a legal classification that exists independently of other categorizations because of its singularity or due to the specific creation of an entitlement or obligation. For example, in intellectual property, there are certain matters—such as databases—that have specifically coded (i.e., *sui generis*) laws. In the case of a database, a database right is therefore sui generis right: the database right is a property right, comparable to but distinct from copyright, put in place to recognise the effort and investment made in compiling a database.

SWIFT. An acronym that stands for Society for Worldwide Interbank Financial Telecommunications. Founded in 1973, SWIFT supplies secure messaging services and interface software to wholesale financial entities.

Tacit Knowledge. This refers to "intangible" knowledge which is intuitive and difficult to express in practice, i.e., the knowledge that people carry in their minds, based on life experience. In contrast, explicit knowledge can be verbally explained and codified in a document.

Top-down Strategy. A top-down approach is used as a synonym for analysis or decomposition, whereby a system (e.g. involving pure software design, information processing, etc.) is broken down into sub-systems, which are then further divided so that each subsystem is refined in greater detail than the one before it.

Treaty of Rome. The treaty that established the European Economic Community in 1957. The six countries that signed this treaty were

Belgium, France, Italy, Luxembourg, the Netherlands, and West Germany.

Value Added. In economics, value added is the difference between the costs of inputs purchased and the value of the output produced. A product that requires a certain amount of skill to produce would generally have a greater value added than one that requires little skill because a greater part of the final cost will be due to the skilled labour involved. In marketing, value added refers to the creation of a competitive advantage by bundling, combining, or packaging features for greater customer acceptance.

Venture Capital. This refers to funds provided by investors to start-up firms and small businesses with perceived long-term growth potential. It is an important form of funding for small companies that often do not have the required financial means to start operating their business. The investors (who guarantee the funds) are usually wealthy entrepreneurs, investment banks and financial institutions willing to take a certain amount of risk.

Verityper. The verityper was an ingenious "word processor" of the pre-digital aid which could use several different type styles and type in several different natural languages. It allowed the user to, for example, adjust the space between characters and produce right-justified text. It was used primarily as an "office composing" or "cold typesetting" machine to produce camera-ready copies for offset printing.

Vertical Application. An application (software) that is developed for a single or narrowly defined market such as insurance billing, point-of-sale transaction processing, and medical patient records.

VoIP. Voice over IP (VoIP) refers to the method and the technology used for sending voice and multi-media data over Internet Protocol (IP)-based computer networks. VoIP can be implemented using various technologies and protocols, both public and proprietary. Skype may be considered as an example that utilises VoIP.

Bibliography

Agar, Jon (2003), *The Government Machine: A Revolutionary History of the Computer*, Cambridge (Massachusetts): MIT Press.

Adler, Paul S, (ed.) (1992), *Technology and the Future of Work*, Oxford: Oxford University Press.

Alamango, Henry (1990), "Computer Procurement and Implementation", *The Sunday Times Computers Supplement*, 15 July, p. VIII.

Alberts, Gerard (2010), "Appropriating America: Americanization in the History of European Computing", *IEEE Annals of the History of Computing*, Vol. 32, No. 2, pp. 4-7.

Aloisio, F. (1999), "Legal suits entertained by ISPs as internet war rages on", *Malta Business Weekly*, No. 249 (29 July-4 August).

Aloisio, M. (2010), "Computing in Malta: Adoption of a Technology in a Small Island State", PhD dissertation, Department of Computer Science, University of Warwick.

Anderson, R. G. (1978), *Data Processing and Management Information Systems* (2nd Edition), Plymouth: Macdonald and Evans.

Anderson, R. G. (1980), *Organization and Methods* (2nd Edition), Plymouth: Macdonald and Evans.

Aplin, Tanya (2005), *Copyright Law in the Digital Society – The Challenge of Multimedia*, Oxford: Hart Publishing.

Aquilina, Victor (1984), "Has Malta Missed the Bus in Electronics?", *The Sunday Times Trade Fair Supplement* , 1 July, p. XIV.

Arora, A., and Gambardella, A. (eds.) (2005), *From Underdogs to Tigers—The rise and growth of the software industry in Brazil, China, India, Ireland, and Israel*, Oxford: Oxford University Press.

Arthur, B. W. (1996), "Increasing Returns and the New World of Business", *Harvard Business Review*, July-August, 1996: pp. 100-109.

Aspray, William (1990), *John von Neumann and the Origins of Modern Computing*, Cambridge, MA: The MIT Press.

Aspray, W. et al. (eds.) (2006), "Globalisation and Offshoring of Software: A Report of the ACM Job Migration Task Force – Executive Summary and Findings". Available at: http://www.acm.org/globalizationreport/ summary.htm. Accessed: 12 January 2007.

Assimakopulos, D. et. al. (2004), "ESPRIT: Europe's response to US and Japanese Domination in Information Technology", in R. Coopey (ed.), *Information Technology Policy: An International History*, Oxford: Oxford University Press, pp. 247-263.

Attard, Edward (2003), *A History of the Malta Police (1800-1964)*, Malta: Colour Image.

Ayeni, V. O., and Ramnarine, D. (2005), "Sharing expertise between countries and across differing ICT environments – the experience of the Commonwealth reflected through the CAPDD", in G. Milward-Oliver (ed.), *Maitland+20: Fixing the Missing Link*, UK: Anima Centre Ltd, pp. 65-80.

Azzopardi Vella, John (1973), "Planning for an Unaided Economy by 1979", BA (Gen) thesis, Department of Economics, Royal University of Malta.

Baer, Walter S. (2001), "Telecommunication Infrastructure Competition: The Costs of Delay", in William H. Dutton (ed.), *Information and Communication Technologies – Visions and Realities*, Oxford: Oxford University Press, pp. 353-370.

Bainbridge, David I. (2007), *Intellectual Property* (6th Edition), Harlow: Pearson Longman.

Baldacchino, G., and Milne, D. (eds.) (2000), *Lessons from the Political Economy of Small Islands: the Resourcefulness of Jurisdiction*, UK: Macmillan.

Balogh, T. and Seers, D. (1955), *The Economic Problems of Malta*, Malta: Government Printing Office.

Balzan, S. (2006), "Smarting over Smart City", *Malta Today*, 17 September.

Bangemann Group (1994), *Europe and the Global Information Society*, EU: Bangemann Group.

Beauchamp Ken (2001), *History of the Telegraph*, London: IEE.

Behrens, A. (2005), "Brazil", in S. Commander (ed.), *The Software Industries in Emerging Markets*, Cheltenham: Edward Elgar, pp. 189-219.

Belden, Thomas G., and Belden, Marva R. (1962), *The Lengthening Shadow: The Life of Thomas J. Watson*, Boston: Little Brown & Co.

Bell, S. J. (1985), "Computers in Business and Industry", in W. R. Williams (ed.), *Looking Back to Tomorrow – Reflections on the twenty-five years of computers in New Zealand*, Wellington: NZCS, pp. 76-90.

Beniger, James (1989), *The Control Revolution: Technological and Economic Origins of the Information Society*, Cambridge, MA: Harvard University Press.

Bennett, J. M., Broomham R., Murton, P. M., Pearcey, T., and Rutledge, R. W. (eds.) (1994), *Computing in Australia – The development of a profession*, Sydney: Hale & Iremonger and the Australian Computer Society Inc.

Bezzina, John (1962), *Servizzi Pubbliċi f'Malta*, Malta: Department of Information.

Bishop, Stewart (1999), "Outsourcing and government information technology strategy—Relevance of external consultant models in Barbados" in R. Heeks (ed.), *Reinventing Government in the Information Age*, UK: Routledge.

Blind, K., Edler, J., and Friedewald, M. (2005), *Software Patents – Economic Impacts and Policy Implications*, UK: Edward Elgar.

Bonello, J. (2006), "Malta's Potential in the Global Offshore Outsourcing Market", MBA dissertation, University of Malta.

Bonello Du Puis, G. (1987), *Diskors tal-Budget għall-1988*, 25 November, Statement No. 1. (Hard-copy version of budget speech for 1987)

Bonnici, Josef (2000), "A Profile of Malta's Manufacturing Sector", in C. Vella (ed.), *The Maltese Islands on the Move*, pp. 47-54.

Borda, M. (1999), "Economic Self-Reliance and Small Island Developing States", PhD thesis, University of Malta.

Bowe, M., Briguglio. L., and Dean, J. W. (eds.) (1998), *Banking and Finance in Islands and Small States*, Malta: Pinter.

Braun, Ernest (1995), *Futile Progress—Technology's Empty Promise*, London: Earthscan Publications.

Braun, J., and Capito, R. (2002) "The Emergence of EC Telecommunications Law as a New Self-Standing Field Within Community Law", in C. Koenig, A. Bartosch, and J. Braun (eds.), *EC Competition and Telecommunications Law*, The Hague: Kluwer Law International, pp. 51-69.

Briffa, J. (1981), *An Introductory Guide to Telecommunications Facilities*, Malta: Telemalta Corporation.

Briggs, A. (1961), *The History of Broadcasting in the United Kingdom – Vol. 1: The Birth of Broadcasting*, Oxford: Oxford University Press.

Briguglio Lino (1995), "Small Island Developing States and their Economic Vulnerabilities", *World Development*, Vol. 23, Issue 9, pp. 1615-1632.

Briguglio, Lino (1988), *The Maltese Economy – A Macroeconomic Analysis*, Malta: David Moore Publications.

Brincat, I. (2001a), "Lack of Security Hindering Start-ups from Getting Loans", *Malta Business Weekly*, No. 342, 24 - 30 May.

Brincat, I. (2001b), "Top foreign companies interested in e-government initiative", *Malta Business Weekly*, Issue No. 343, 31 May – 6 June.

Broadcasting Ordinance (1961). Ordinance No. 20, Act XX of 1961, Chapter 165 of the Laws of Malta.

Brock, Gerald W. (1994), *Telecommunication Policy for the Information Age – From Monopoly to Competition*, Cambridge, MA: Harvard University Press.

Bromley, Allan G. (1982), "Charles Babbage's Analytical Engine, 1838", in *Annals of the History of Computing*, Vol. 4, No. 3, pp. 196-217.

Bruford, R. (1954), "Cable and Wireless – Early days of Cable Communication in Malta", in L. Barrington (ed.), *Malta Year Book 1954*, pp. 165-166.

BSA & IDC (2009), *Sixth Annual BSA-IDC Global Software 08 Piracy Study*, Washington, DC: Business Software Alliance. Available at: http://global.bsa.org/globalpiracy2008/studies/globalpiracy2008.pdf. Accessed 9 January 2010.

Busuttil, Simon, et al. (1999), *Malta, the EU and You – A Practical Guide*, Malta: PEG.

Business Promotion Act 2001, "An Act to amend the Industrial Development Act". Act IV of 2001, Chapter 325 of the Laws of Malta.

Cachia Zammit, Ray (1985), "Computers in Education", *The Times Electronika Fair Supplement*, 25 April.

Callus, Sharon Ann (1997), "Software Copyright Law —A Comparative Study", LLD Thesis, University of Malta.

Camilleri, Alan (2008), "Why Malta? Projecting Malta as a Business Centre on the International Scene". Presentation given at the Malta Business and Finance Forum 2008. Organized by EMCS, 26 November.

Camilleri, Colin (1990), "A Cost-Effective Computer Based Educational System", BEng thesis, University of Malta.

Camilleri, Juanito (1994), *A National Strategy for IT for Malta*, Malta: University of Malta.

Camilleri, Raymond (ed.) (2004), *Rising to the Challenge – The Lisbon Objectives and Maltese Education Provision*, Malta: Education Division. Proceedings of a national conference organized by the Education Division (Ministry of Education, Youth and Employment).

Camilleri, Reno (2000), "Estimating National Income with some reference to Malta", in Vella, *The Maltese Islands on the Move*, Malta: COS, pp. 55-71.

Camilleri, Reno (1996), "The Compilation of the Retail Price Index in Malta", *Central Bank Quarterly Review*, **29**:1.

Campbell-Kelly, Martin (2005), "Not All Bad: An Historical Perspective on Software Patents", 11 Mich. Telecomm. Tech. L. Rev. 191.

Campbell-Kelly, Martin (2004), *From Airline Reservations to Sonic the Hedgehog—A History of the Software Industry*, Cambridge, MA: The MIT Press.

Campbell-Kelly, Martin (1989a), "The history of ICL", in *The Computer Bulletin*, **1**:9.

Campbell-Kelly, Martin (1989b), *ICL: A Business and Technical History*, Oxford: Oxford University Press.

Campbell-Kelly, Martin and Aspray, William (2004), *Computer: A History of the Information Machine*, Oxford: Westview Press.

Campbell-Kelly, Martin and Garcia-Swartz, Daniel D. (2008), "Economic Perspectives on the History of the Computer Time-Sharing Industry, 1965-1985", in *IEEE Annals of the History of Computing*, Vol. 30, No. 1, January-March, pp. 16-36.

Cannataci, Joseph A. (1986), "Legal Implications of Data Processing Privacy and Data Protection Law", LL.D. thesis, University of Malta.

Carmel, E. and Tjia, P. (2005), *Offshoring Information Technology – Sourcing and Outsourcing to a Global Workforce*, Cambridge: Cambridge University Press.

Caruana, Carmen M. (1992), *Education's Role in the Socioeconomic Development of Malta*, Westport, Connecticut: Praeger.

Cassar, C. (1997), "An Integrated Services Backbone Using Internet Infrastructure". Paper read at the Malta Chartered Professional Engineers' Annual Engineering Conference on Data Communications, Malta.

Cassar, Josette and Dimech Mario (1988), "The Educational Potential of the Personal Computer in the Home and the School for the 11 to 16 year old child". BEd (Hons) Thesis, University of Malta.

Cassingena Harper, Jennifer (1998), "The Internationalisation of Science and Technology Policy: Malta Case Study (1988-1996)". PhD thesis, University of Malta.

Castells, Manuel (1999), *The Information Age: Economy, Society and Culture* (Volumes I, II, & III), New York: Wiley-Blackwell.

CCTA (1994), *Information Superhighways: Opportunities for Public sector applications in the UK*, London: CCTA.

Census of the Maltese Islands, 1948, Malta: COS.

Ceruzzi, Paul E. (2003), *A History of Modern Computing*, (2nd Edition), Cambridge (Massachusetts): The MIT Press.

Child, J., and Loverdige, R. (1990), *I. T. in European Services*, ESRC, UK: Basil Blackwell.

CII Directive (2002), *Directive on Computer Implemented Inventions*, COM(2002) 92 Final.

Cilia, Joseph (2002), "Meeting Industrial and Environmental Needs through Research in Enginnering, *University of Malta Annual Report 2001*, Malta.

"Civil Service Reform", *The Times* [of Malta], 27 March 1989, p. 18.

Clarke, A. (1992), *How the World was Won - Beyond the Global Village*, London: Victor Gollancz Ltd.

Cohen, I. Bernard (1999), *Howard Aiken: Portrait of a Computer Pioneer*, Cambridge, MA: The MIT Press.

Commander, Simon (ed.) (2005), *The Software Industries in Emerging Markets*, Cheltenham: Edward Elgar.

COMNET-IT (2000), "COMNET-IT Review on Member States – Malta", *COMNET-IT Forum*, Issue 5.

Condon, Dan (2002), *Software Product Management: Managing Software Development from Idea to Product to Marketing to Sales*, US: Aspatore Books.

Connolly, J. (1967), *History of Computing in Europe*, USA: IBM World Trade Corporation.

Consiglio, John A. (2005), *The History of Maltese Banking*, Malta: Progress Press.

Consiglio John A. (1979), "History of Maltese Banking" (in 3 parts), in *Heritage*, Issues 14, 21, & 28, Malta.

Coopey, Richard (ed.) (2004), *Information Technology Policy – An International History*, Oxford: Oxford University Press.

Correra, C. M. (1993), "The Legal Protection of Software", in *Software Industry – Current Trends and Implications for Developing Countries*, Vienna: UNIDO, pp. 144-145.

Cortada, James W. (2008), "Patterns and Practices in How Information Technology Spread around the World", in *IEEE Annals of the History of Computing*, Vol. 30, No. 4, pp. 4-25.

Cortada, James W. (1996), *Information Technology as Business History – Issues in the History and Management of Computers*, Connecticut: Westport.

Cortada, James W. (1993), *Before the Computer: IBM, NCR, Burroughs, and Remington Rand and the Industry They Created, 1865-1956*, Princeton (N.J.): Princeton University Press.

COS (1980), *Census of Production 1978 – Summary Tables*, Malta: Central Office of Statistics, p. 62.

COS (1957), *The National Accounts of the Maltese Islands*, Malta: Central Office of Statistics.

Crandall, Robert W. (2005), *Competition and Chaos: U.S. Telecommunications since the 1996 Telecom Act*, Washington, D.C.: Brookings Institution Press.

Criminal Code, Chapter 9 of the Laws of Malta.

Cringely, Robert (1996), *Accidental Empires*, London: Penguin.

Cutajar, J. (2004), "The Contribution of the Employment and Training Corporation towards the realisation of the Lisbon Objectives", in R. Camilleri (ed.), *Rising to the Challenge*, pp. 99-108.

Cutajar, Tony C. (2001), *Ix-Xandir f'Malta*, Malta: Pubblikazzjonijiet Indipendenza.

Data Protection Act 2001. Act XXVI of 2001, Chapter 440 of the Laws of Malta.

Davidson, M. J. (2003), *The Legal Protection of Databases*, Cambridge: Cambridge University Press.

Davis, J., Hirschl, T., and Stack, M. (eds.) (1997), *Cutting Edge—Technology, Information Capitalism and Social Revolution*, London: Verso.

Debono, Carmen (1989), "The role of the ITU in the development of telecommunications in Malta", BA (Hons.) (Public Administration) Thesis, University of Malta.

Delia, E. P. (2002), *Papers on Malta's Political Economy*, Malta: Midsea Books.

Despatch to the Secretary of State (1859), 28 November. National Archives of Malta [NAM:CSG4978].

Despatch to the Secretary of State (1857), 4 August. National Archives of Malta [NAM:CSG829].

Development Plan for the Maltese Islands, 1969-1974 (1964) (known as the *Third Development Plan*), Malta: DOI.

Development Plan for the Maltese Islands, 1959-1964 (1959) (known as the *First Development Plan*), Malta: DOI.

De Wit, Dirk (1994), *The Shaping of Automation – a Historical Analysis of the Interaction between technology and organisatiion 1950-1985*, The Netherlands: Hilversum Verloren.

De Woot, Phillepe (1990), *High Tech Europe: Strategic Issues for Global Competitiveness*, UK: Blackwell.

Diamond v. Diehr (1981), 450 U.S. 175.

Dunning, J. H. (ed.) (1971), *The Multinational Enterprise*, London: George Allen & Unwin Ltd.

Dutton, William H. (ed.) (1996), *Information and Communications Technologies – Visions and Realities*, Oxford: Oxford University Press.

Dyson, K., and Humphreys, P., (eds.) (1986), *The Politics of the Communications Revolution in Western Europe*, UK: Frank Cass & Co. Ltd.

Education Ministry (1988), "Science and Technology Implementation Policy". Memo 288 dated 9 March.

EESC (2006), "Investment in Knowledge and Innovation in Malta: An Overview of the Malta Council for Economic and Social Development", European Economic and Social Council. Available at: http://eesc.europa.eu/lisbon_strategy/esc_contributions/MT-Knowledge-Innovation-long-en.doc. Accessed: 4 April 2008.

Egerton, David (1997), "The Decline of Declinism", *Business History Review*, Vol. 71, No. 2, pp. 210-206.

Electronic Commerce Act 2001. Act III of 2001, Chapter 426 of the Laws of Malta.

Eliassen, K. A. and Sjovaag, M. (eds.) (1999), *European Telecommunications Liberalisation*, London: Routledge.

Ende, J. C. M., van dem (1994), *The Turn of the Tide – Computerisation in Dutch Society 1900-1965*, The Netherlands: Delft University Press.

Englund, C. (1999), "The global mobile market and regulatory aspects" in K. A. Eliassen and M. Sjovaag (eds.), *European Telecommunications Liberalisation*, London: Routledge, pp. 218-237.

European Commission (2006), "IRC Chile links South America to Europe", *European Innovation*, July 2006.

European Union (2001), *The European Community Directives on Copyright and Related Rights*, Directive 96/9/EC.

European Union (1991), *Council Directive 91/250/EEC of 14 May 1991 on the legal protection of computer programs*.

European Union (1988), *Green Paper on Copyright and the Challenge of Technology of 1988*, COM (88) 172 final, June.

ESIB (2006), *The Lisbon Agenda: an Introduction*, Brussels: The National Unions of Students in Europe.

EU-ESIS (2001), *Regulatory Developments – Malta Master Report*, February. Available at: http://www.eu-esis.org. Accessed: May 2007.

EU-ESIS (1999), *Regulatory Developments – Malta Master Report*, July. Available at: http://www.eu-esis.org. Accessed: May 2007.

Fenech. E. (2002), "Manufacturing SMEs: Their role in the Maltese Economy and the Implications of the New Business Promotion Act Incentives", B. Accountancy (Hons.) Thesis, University of Malta.

Flamm, Kenneth (1988), *Creating the Computer – Government, Industry and High Technology*, Washington, D.C.: The Brookings Institution.

Forester, Tom (ed.) (1989), *Computers in the Human Context: Information Technology, Productivity, and People*, UK: Blackwell.

Forester, Tom (ed.) (1985), *The Information Technology Revolution*, Cambridge, Massachusetts: The MIT Press.

Forester, Tom (ed.) (1980), *The Microelectronics Revolution: The Complete Guide to the New Technology and Its Impact on Society*, Cambridge, Massachusetts: The MIT Press.

Framework Directive (2002), *Directive (2002/21/EC) on a Common Regulatory Framework*, March. Directive 2002/21/EC.

Freeman, Christopher (1996), "The Factory of the Future and the Productivity Paradox", in Dutton, William H. (ed.), *Information and Communications Technologies – Visions and Realities*, Oxford: Oxford University Press, pp. 123-142.

Freeport Terminal (Malta) plc. (1999), *Annual Review*, pp. 13 an 32.

Frendo, Henry (1979), *Party Politics in a Fortress Colony: The Maltese Experience*, Malta: Midsea Books Ltd.

Galea, Albert M. (1981), "When Malta turned to computers", *The Times Government Computer Centre Supplement*, 18 November.

Galler, B. A. (1995), *Software and Intellectual Property Protection: Copyright and Patent Issues for Computer and Legal Professionals*, Quorum: UK.

Garson, G. D. (ed.) (2003), *Public Information Technology: Policy and Management Issues*, Hershey, PA: Idea Group Publishing.

Gates, Bill (1995), *The Road Ahead*, New York: Viking Press.

Gazzetta tal-Gvern ta' Malta (1971), 9 March, p. 698.

Ghio, A. (2005), "Patent pending: Protecting Maltese computer-implemented inventions", *iTech*, The Times, 16 June.

Gill, Colin (1985), *Work,Unemployment and the New Technology*, Cambridge: Polity Press.

Giordmaina, Joseph (ed.) (2000) "National Curriculum on its Way", Malta: Ministry of Education. Proceedings of a Conference on the Implementation of the National Curriculum, Malta, 9-11 June.

Giordmaina, Joseph (1987), "Computers in Educational Institutions: A Survey". BEd (Hons) Dissertation, Faculty of Education, University of Malta.

Glover, Bill (2005), "The Evolution of Cable and Wireless", in *History of the Atlantic Cable & Submarine Telegraphy*, http://www.atlantic-cable.com. Accessed: November 2006.

Goldman, J. E. (1998), *Applied Data Communications – A Business-Oriented Approach* (2nd Edition), New York: John Wiley & Sons.

Goldstein, Herman H. (1972), *The Computer from Pascal to von Neumann*, Princeton, NJ: Princeton University Press.

Government Notice (1995), No. 624, 6 October.

Government of Malta (1990), *Information Systems Strategic Plan 1991-1996*.

Government of Malta (1989), *Public Call for Proposals to Develop a Cable Television Service for the Maltese Islands*, January.

Green Paper on the Development of a Common Market for Telecommunications Services and Equipment, COM (87) 290 final, 30 June 1987.

Grover, D. (ed.) (1990), *The Protection of Computer Software – Its Technology and Applications*, BCS Monographs in Informatics, Cambridge: Cambridge University Press.

Habib, Laurence and Cornford, Tony (2002), "Computers in the home: domestication and gender", in *Information Technology & People*, Vol. 15, No. 2, pp. 159-174. Available at: *citeseerx.ist.psu.edu/viewdoc/download?doi= 10.1.1.127.2686&rep=rep1&type=pdf*. Accessed: 20 August 2010.

Hartley, Jean and Rashman, Lyndsay (2007), "How is Knowledge Transferred between Organizations Involved in Change" in Wallace, Fertig & Schneller (eds.), *Managing Change in the Public Services*, Malden, MA: Blackwell Publishing.

Harvey, J. (1998), *Modern Economics*, UK: Palgrave.

Heap, N., Thomas, R., Einon, G., Mason, R. and Mackay, H. (eds.) (1995), *Information Technology and Society – A Reader*, London: Sage Publications.

Heeks, Richard (1999) (ed.), *Reinventing Government in the Information Age*, UK: Routledge.

Heeks, Richard (1996), *India's Software Industry – State Policy, Liberalisation and Industrial Development*, New Delhi: Sage Publications.

Heeks, R. and Grundey, M. (2004), "Romania's Hardware and Software Industry" in Coopey, *Information Technology Policy – An International History*, Oxford: Oxford University Press, pp. 320-338.

Heide, Lars (2009), "Punched-Card Systems and the Early Information Explosion, 1880-1945, Baltimore, Maryland: The Johns Hopkins University Press.

Hendrey, John (1990), *Innovating for Failure*, Cambridge, Massachusetts: MIT Press.

Hills, Jill (2007), *Telecommunications and Empire*, Urbana: University of Illinois Press.

Hioe, William (2001), "National Infocomm Strategy and Policy: Singapore's Experience", *ICA Information No. 74: General Issue*, Singapore: ICA. Available at: http://www-it.fmi.uni-sofia.bg/eg/res/issue74-hioe.pdf. Accessed: 5 March 2010.

Howells, Jeremy (1998), "Innovation and Technology Transfer Within Multinational Firms", in Michie & Grieve Smith (eds.), *Globalisation, Growth and Governance: Creating an Innovative Economy*, Oxford: Oxford University Press, pp. 50-70.

Hudson, Heather E. (1997), *Global Connections: International Telecommunications Infrastructure and Policy*, New York: Van Nostrand Reinhold.

Hyman, Anthony (1982), *Charles Babbage: Pioneer of the Computer*, Princeton, N. J.: Princenton University Press.

Import Duties Act, 1976 (Act No. XXV of 1976).

Industry Today (various years).

Informatics (various years).

Information Society Review (various years).

Informatix (various years).

Ir-Review (various years).

ITU (1992), *Statistical Year Book 1992*, Geneva: ITU.

ITU (1995), *World Telecommunications Indicators*, Geneva: ITU.

ITU Newsletter 7/94.

Jowett, P. and Rothwell, M. (1986), *The Economics of Information Technology*, UK: Macmillan.

Kagami, M., Tsuji, M., & Giovannetti, E. (2004), *Information Technology Policy and the Digital Divide—Lessons for Developing Countries*, UK: Edward Elgar.

Kahin, B. and Wilson, E., (eds.) (1997), *National Information Infrastructure Initiatives – Vision and Policy Design*, Cambridge (Massachusetts): MIT Press.

Kamall, S. (1996), *Telecommunications Policy – Spicers European Union Policy Briefings*, London: Cartermill Publishing.

Kelleher, D. (2001), "Maltese SMEs show strong interest in EU-funded research projects", *The Malta Business Weekly*, No. 347 (14 - 20 June).

Kelleher, D. (1999), "Maltacom in new alliance with Internet providers", *The Malta Business Weekly*, No. 253 (26 August-1 September).

Kellenbach, F. (1999), "From assembly line to electronic highway junction", in van Maarseveen, *A Century Rounded Up: Reflections on the history of the Central Bureau of Statistics in the Netherlands*, Amsterdam: Stichting beheer IISG, pp. 63-70.

Kemeny, John G. and Kurtz, Thomas E. (1968), "Dartmouth Time-Sharing", *Science*, 162, No. 3850, 11 October, pp. 223-228.

Kirkman, Geoffrey S. (2002), "Networked Readiness and Small Island Developing States", Information Technologies Group, Center for International Development at Harvard University. Available at: cyber.law.harvard.edu/itg/libpubs/libpubs.html. Accessed: May 2008.

Kitson, M. and Michie, J. (1998), "Markets, Competition, and Innovation", in J. Michie and J. G. Smith (eds.), *Globalization, Growth, and Governance: Creating an Innovative Economy*, Oxford: Oxford University Press, pp. 101-118.

Kittlaus, Hans-Bernd and Clough, Peter N. (1999), *Software Product Management and Pricing: Key Success Factors for Software Organizations*, Berlin: Springer-Verlag.

Klemens, B. (2005), "Inventions: Why software patents won't work", *IEEE Spectrum*, Vol. 42, No. 7 (INT), July, pp. 49-50 (in 2 parts).

Koenig, C., Bartosch, A. and Braun, J. (eds.) (2002), *EC Competition and Telecommunications Law*, The Hague: Kluwer Law International.

Kopetz, Hermann (1993), "The Software Market: Emerging Trends", in UNIDO, *Software Industry—Current trends and implications for developing countries*, Vienna: United Nations Industrial Development Organization, pp. 75-90.

Kraemer Kenneth L. and Dedrick, Jason (1996), "IT and Economic Development: International Competitveness", in Dutton, William H. (ed.), *Information and Communications Technologies – Visions and Realities*, Oxford: Oxford University Press, pp. 319-334.

Kurihara, Y., Takava, S., Harui, H., and Kamae, H. (eds.) (2008), *Information Technology and Economic Development*, Hershey, PA: Information Science Reference.

Larsen, E. (1977), *Telecommunications: a History*, London: Frederick Muller Ltd.

Lee, J. A. N. (ed.) (1992a and 1992b), "Special Issue: Time-Sharing and Interactive Computing at MIT", *Annals of the History of Computing*, Vol. 14, Nos. 1 and 2.

Lee, K. and Prime, J. (2001), "Overview of US Telecommunications Law", in Walden, I. and Angel, J. (eds.) (2001), *Telecommunications Law*, London: Blackstone Press, pp. 314-345.

Legal Notice (1990), *Wireless Telegraphy (Broadcasting Licence Changes) (Amendment) Regulations*, L. N. 6.

Legislative Assembly Debates (1 May 1950).

Leith, P. (2007), *Software and Patents in Europe*, Cambridge: Cambridge University Press.

Lembke, Johan (2002), *Competition for Technological Leadership--EU Policy for High Technology*, Cheltenham: Edward Elgar.

Lieutenant-Governor's Office Circular No. 12/46, Valletta, 7 February 1946. NAM: CSG 22/13.

Li-Hua, Richard (2004), *Technology and Knowledge Transfer in China*. UK: Ashgate.

Lloyd Ian J. (2008), *Information Technology Law*, 5th edition, Oxford: Oxford University Press.

Malta Communications Authority (2005), *Annual Report and Financial Statements 2004*, Malta: MCA.

Malta Communications Authority (2002), *A National Internet eXchange*, Malta: MCA.

Malta Enterprise (2006a), *ICT Malta: Malta – A Centre of Quality for the ICT Industry*, Malta: Malta Enterprise.

Malta Enterprise (2006b), *The Business Promotion Act in Brief*, Malta: Malta Enterprise.

Malta Government Gazette (various years).

Malta Guidelines for Progress: Development Plan 1981-1985 (1981).

Malta Labour Party (1993), *Analysis of MSU Business Plan 1993*, February, Malta: MLP.

Maltese Copyright Act (2000), *Act XIII of 2000, as amended by Acts VI of 2001 and IX of 2003*, Chapter 415 of the Laws of Malta.

Management Efficiency Unit (1998), *Information Systems Strategic Plan for the Public Service: 1999-2001*, Malta: Office of the Prime Minister.

Management Systems Unit (1997), *MSU/MITTS 1997 Business Plan*, Malta.

Management Systems Unit (1995), *Annual Report 1994/1995*, Malta.

Margetts, Helen (1999), *Information Technology in Government: Britain and America*, London: Routledge.

MCST (2006), *National Strategic Plan for Research & Innovation 2007-2010: Building and Sustaining the R&I enabling framework*, Malta: Malta Council for Science and Technology, Government Printing Press.

MCST (1992), *Vision 2000: Malta Regional Hub*, Malta: Malta Council for Science and Technology.

McFall, D., et al. (2006), "Software Processes and Process Improvement in Northern Ireland". Available at: http://www.infc.ulst.ac.uk/informatics/cspt/documents/Paris_ICSSEA2003.doc, p. 3. Accessed: December 2007.

Melham, Thomas and Camilleri, Juanito (eds.) (1994), *Higher Order Logic Theorem and Its Applications*, 7th *International Workshop*, Vol. 859, Lecture Notes in Computer Science, Malta: Springer.

Messerschmitt, David G. and Szyperski, Clemens (2003), *Software Ecosystem: Understanding an Indispensable Technology and Industry*, Cambridge, Massachusetts: The MIT Press.

Metropolis, N., Howlett, J. and Rota, G. (eds.) (1980), *A History of Computing in the Twentieth Century: A Collection of Essays*, New York: Academic Press.

Micallef, Maria (2008), "Case Study: An Analysis of our iGaming Industry", in *The Executive*, No 13, pp. 71-79.

Micallef, P. E. (2007), "Current Developments – Malta: The Electronic Commerce (General) Regulations" in C. Twigg-Flesner, et al., *The Yearbook of Consumer Law 2008*, UK: Ashgate Publishing, pp. 389-396.

Micallef, Paul (2001), "Building Bridges with Industry", *University of Malta Annual Report 1999-2000*, Malta.

Micallef Trigona, A. (1995), "Maltanet operational soon", *Malta Business Weekly*, No. 58 (30 November-6 December).

Michie, Jonathan and Grieve Smith, John (eds.) (1998), *Globalisation, Growth and Governance: Creating an Innovative Economy*, Oxford: Oxford University Press.

Mifsud, Alex (2000), "Computing in Malta", in C. Vella, *The Maltese Islands on the Move*, pp. 259-270.

Mifsud, Alfred, (1997), *MSU – A Strategic Review and Assessment*, Malta.

Miles, Ian (1990), "Mapping and Measuring the Information Economy", UK: The British Library.

Milward, G. E. (1967), *Organization and Methods: A Service to Management*, London: Macmillan.

Milward-Oliver, Gerald (ed.) (2005), *Maitland+20: Fixing the Missing Link*, UK: Anima.

Ministry for Justice and Local Government (2001), *Request for Proposal for a Strategic Partnership for the E-Government Initiative*, Malta.

Ministry of Education and Human Resources (1994), *A Science and Technology Policy Document*, Malta: Ministry of Education and Human Resources.

Ministry of International Trade and Industry (1994), *Program for Advanced Information Infrastructure*, Japan: MITI.

MITTS (2003), *Malta Information Technology and Training Services Ltd Annual Report 2002*, Malta: MITTS.

MITTS (2000), *10th Anniversary Malta Information Technology and Training Services*, Malta: MITTS.

MITTS (1999), *Malta Information Technology and Training Services Ltd Annual Report & Accounts 1998*, Malta: MITTS.

MITTS (1998), *Management Systems Unit Limited / Malta Information Technology and Training Services 1997 Business Plan*, Malta: MITTS.

MIT&I (2004a), *The National ICT Strategy 2004-2006*, Malta: Ministry for Investment, Industry and Information Technology.

MIT&I (2004b), *HelloIt*, Malta: Ministry for Investment, Industry and Information Technology.

Mizzi, Edgar (1995), *Malta in the Making 1962-1987 – An Eyewitness Account*, Malta: Edgar Mizzi.

Montebello, C. et. al. (1963), *Report of the Board of Inquiry into complaints regarding Bills and Suspensions of Water and Electricity Supplies*, Valletta, Malta, 10 April.

Morgan, D. J. (1980), *The Official History of Colonial Development*, Vols. 1-3, London: HMSO.

Mowrey, D. C. (1996), *The International Computer Software Industry*, Oxford: Oxford University Press.

Muller, J. and Toker, S. (1994), "Mobile Communications in Europe", in Steinfield, Bauer, & Caby, *Telecommunications in Transition – Policies, Services and Technologies in the European Community*, pp. 182-203.

Murdock, G., Hartman, P., and Gray, P. (1995), "Conceptualizing Home Computing: Resources and Practices", in N. Heap, R. Thomas, G. Einon, R. Mason and H. Mackay (eds.), *Information Technology and Society—A Reader*, London: Sage Publications, pp. 269-283.

National Computer Board (1992), *The IT2000 Report: Vision of an Intelligent Island*, Singapore: NCB.

National Infrastructure Task Force (1993), *The National Information Infrastructure Agenda for Action*, USA: NITF.

Nuechterlein Jonathan E. and Weiser Philip J. (2007), *Digital Crossroads: American Telecommunications Policy in the Internet Age*, Cambridge, Massachusetts: MIT Press.

Niblett, B. (1982), "Legal Opinion", *Computer Weekly*, 18 March.

Nicholas, K. (1998), *Inventing Software – The Rise of "Computer-related" Patents*, Connecticut: Quorum Books.

Norberg, A. and O'Neill, J. (1996), *Transforming Computer Technology—Information Processing for the Pentageon, 1962-1986*, Baltimore, Maryland: The John Hopkins University Press.

NSO (2007), *News Release*, No. 24. Available at: http://nso.gov.mt/statdoc/document_file.aspx?id=1935. Accessed: 20 July 2008.

NSO (2006), *ICT-Usage of Enterprises Survey*, Malta: National Statistics Office.

NSO (2005), *NSO News Release No. 239/2005*, Malta: National Statistics Office, 8 November.

OECD (2004), *ICT, E-Business and SMEs*, Paris: Organization for Economic Co-operation and Development. Report prepared for the second OECD Conference of Ministers Responsible for SMEs held in Istanbul on 3-5 June 2004. Available at: http://www.oecd.org/32/28/34228722.pdf. Accessed: 17 November 2005.

OECD (1999), *OECD Science, Technology and Industry Scoreboard 1999*, Paris: Organization for Economic Co-operation and Development.

OECD (1997), "Materials from the Special Session on Information Infrastructures", in B. Kahin & E. Wilson (eds.), *National Information Infrastructure Initiatives – Vision and Policy Design*, Cambridge, Massachusetts: MIT Press, pp. 569-612.

OECD (1979), *The Usage of International Data Networks in Europe*, Paris: Organization for Economic Co-operation and Development.

Office of the Prime Minister (2000), *White Paper on a Vision and Strategy for the Attainment of Electronic Government in Malta*, Malta.

Old University Gazette (1979), Vol. 11, No. 2.

O'Neill, Judy E. (1992), "The Evolution of Interactive Computing Through Time-Sharing and Networking", PhD dissertation, University of Minnesota.

Oslin, George P. (1992), The Story of Telecommunications, Macon, Gerogia: Mercer University Press.

Packard, David (1996), *The HP Way: How Bill Hewlett and I Built Our Company*, New York, NY: Harper Collins.

Paganetto, Luigi (2004), *The Knowledge Economy, Information Technologies and Growth*, UK: Ashgate Publishing.

Partit Nazzjonalista (1996), *Electoral Programme 1996*, Malta: PN Printing Press.

Partit Nazzjonalista (1987), *Programm Elettorali tal-Partit Nazzjonalista – 1987*, Malta: PN Printing Press.

Pirie, Ian G. (1994), "Computer Education in Australian Schools", in Bennett, et al. (eds.), *Computing in Australia – The development of a profession*, Sydney: Hale & Iremonger and the Australian Computer Society Inc., pp. 155-170.

Pirotta, Godfrey A. (2005), "Public Enterprise Implications of Malta's Entry into the European Union", in *The Asia Pacific Journal of Public Administration*, Vol. 27, No. 2 (December), pp. 202-203.

Pirotta, Godfrey A. (2001), "A Farewell to Paternalism Through Public Enterprise? Privatization in the Small Island State of Malta", in *International Review of Public Administration*, Vol. 6, No. 1 (June), pp. 39-48.

Pirotta, Godfrey A. (1992), "First Observation on the Report of the Public Service Commission", in *Economic & Social Studies*, Vol. 6, pp. 49-64.

Pirotta, Joseph M. (1987), *Fortress Colony: The Final Act 1945-1964*, Vols. 1-3, Malta: Studia Editions.

Pollacco, Christopher (2003), *An Outline of the Socio-Economic Development in Post-War Malta*, Malta: Mireva Publications.

Pollacco, Christopher (1992), *Malta-EEC Relations*, Malta: Mireva Publications.

Portelli, Nicolai (2005), "Policy and the information age: the case of electronic government in Malta". B.Com. (Hons.) Thesis, University of Malta. [1.2]

Potter, C. J. (1985), "Computers in Education", in W. R. Williams (ed.), *Looking Back to Tomorrow – Reflections on the twenty-five years of computers in New Zealand*, Wellington: NZCS, pp. 120-133.

Preliminary Report of the 1957 Census, Malta: COS.

Prior-Willeard, Chris (n.d.), "Global Depositary Receipts". Available at: http://www.exchange-handbook.co.uk/index.cfm?section=articles&action=detail&id=78443. Accessed: April 2010.

Public Service Reform Commission (1989), *A New Public Service for Malta – A Report on the Organization of the Public Service*, Malta: Government Printing Office.

Pugh, Emerson W. (1995), *Building IBM: Shaping an Industry and Its Technology*, Cambridge, MA: The MIT Press.

Pullicino, David (1988), "Views on the Development of the Financial Markets", *Informatics*, January, 1989, pp. 5-6. Publication of a talk titled "Improvements in Banking Service through Computer Use" delivered to IDPM members at the Chamber of Commerce on 18 October 1988.

Report on the working of the Central Office of Statistics (Incorporating the Electoral Registry) (various years), Malta: COS.

Report on the working of the Posts and Telephone Department for the Years 1949-56, Malta: Government Printing Press.

Report on the Working of the Telephone Department for the Years 1966-72, Malta: Government Printing Press.

Reports on the Working of Government Departments (various years), Malta: Government Printing Press.

Ricerka (various years).

Rifkin, Jeremy (1995), *The End of Work — The Decline of the Global Labor Force and the Dawn of the Post-Market Era*, New York: G. P. Putnam's Sons.

Robens, A. (1967), *Joint Mission for Malta Report*, Malta: DOI.

Rose, Michael (1971), *Computers, Managers and Society*, Middlesex: Penguin Books.

Royal Univeristy of Malta Annual Report (various years).

Samsone, Kurt (1999), "What should the role of the telecommunication regulator be in relation to Internet Service Providers?", BA (Hons.) Communication Studies Thesis, University of Malta.

Samut-Tagliaferro, A. (1979), "British Military Communications on Malta and Gozo", *Armed Forces of Malta Journal*, No. 32, pp. 6-7.

Sands, A. (2005), "The Irish Software Industry" in Arora & Gambardella, *From Underdogs to Tigers — The rise and growth of the software industry in Brazil, China, India, Ireland, and Israel*, pp. 41-71.

Sant Fournier, Julian (1990), "Methodologies of Systems Analysis and Design", *The Sunday Times Computers Supplement*, 15 July, p. XXIV.

Scarlett, Theresa (1999), "Mobile phone service set to become more affordable", *The Sunday Times* [of Malta], 19 December, p. 43.

Schelin, S. H. (2003), "E-Government: An Overview", in G. D. Garson (ed.), *Public Information Technology: Policy and Management Issues*, Hershey, PA: Idea Group Publishing, pp. 120-137.

Schmitz, A. (1985), *Technology and Employment Practices in Developing Countries*, London: Croom Helm.

Seven Year Development Plan 1973-1980 (1973), Government of Malta.

Spiteri, J. E. (1997), *Malta: an Island in Transition*, Malta: Progress Press.

Spiteri, Lino (1982), *Diskors tal-Budget ghall-1983*, 16 November, Statement Number 1.

Stanlake, G. F. (1983), *Introductory Economics* (4th Edition), Harlow, UK: Longman.

Steinfield, C., Bauer, J. M. and Caby, L. (eds.) (1994), *Telecommunications in Transition – Policies, Services and Technologies in the European Community*, London: Sage Publications.

Stolper, W., Hellberg, R. and Callander, S. (1964), *Economic Adaptation and Development in Malta: report of the United Nations Economic Mission*, Malta.

Tabone, Joseph V. (2007), "Chairman's Message", in *Annual Report and Financial Statements 2006*, Malta: MCA, pp. 4-5.

Telegraphs and Telephones Ordinance – Telephone Service Regulations 1972 (1972), Chapter 125 of the Laws of Malta.

Telemalta Corporation Act (1975), Act XVI, Chapter 250 of the Laws of Malta.

Temin, P. and Galambos, L. (1989), *The Fall of the Bell System: A Study in Prices and Politics*, Cambridge: Cambridge University Press.

Terterov, Marat (ed.) (2003), *Doing Business with Malta*, London: Kogan Page.

Thake, D. (1999), "Cable Internet – the issues involved", *The Times* [of Malta], 6 September, p. 11.

Thatcher, M. (1999), "Liberalisation in Britain: From monopoly to regulation of competition", in Eliassen & Sjovaag, *European Telecommunications Liberalisation*, pp. 93-109.

The Commercial Courier (August-September 2006).

The Malta Business Weekly (various years).

The Malta Chronicle (3 January 1933).

The Malta Economic Update (2006), "From data to pervasive information", No. 12, p. 70.

The Malta Economist (various years).

The Malta Independent on Sunday (various years).

The Malta Year Book 1956, "The Balogh Report", pp. 195-198.

The Review (various years).

The Royal University of Malta Gazette (various years).

The Sunday Times of Malta (various years).

The Sunday Times [of Malta] (various years).

The Sunday Times Computers Supplement (various years).

The Sunday Times Information Technology Supplement (various years).

The Times [of Malta] (various years).

The Times Government Computer Supplement (18 November 1981).

The Year Book 1990, "Telemalta Corporation", pp. 265-270.

The Year Book 1987, "Telemalta Corporation", pp. 251-255.

Times of Malta (various years).

Torero, Maximo and von Braun, Joachim, (eds.) (2006), *Information and Communication Technologies for Development and Poverty Reduction*, Baltimore: The Johns Hopkins University Press.

Tunstall, J. and Palmer, M. (1990), *Liberating Communications – Policy Making in France and Britain*, Oxford: NCC Blackwell.

Twigg-Flesner, C., Parry, D., Howells, G. and Nordhausen, A. (2008), *The Yearbook of Consumer Law 2008*, UK: Ashgate Publishing.

Ungerer, H. and Costello, N. P. (1990), *Telecommunications in Europe*, Brussels: Office for Official Publications of the EC.

UNCTAD (2009), "About ASYCUDA". Available at: http://www.asycuda.org/aboutas.asp. Accessed: 1 February 2009.

UNIDO (1993), *Software Industry—Current trends and implications for developing countries*, Vienna: United Nations Industrial Development Organization.

University of Malta Annual Report (various years).

University of Malta Gazette (various years).

UOM (2008), *Round Up 2007*, Malta: University of Malta. Available at: *www.um.edu.mt/__data/assets/pdf_file/0010/52498/roundup07.pdf*. *Accessed: 3 October 2008*.

UOM (2000), *BSc IT & BSc IT (Hons.) Course Catalogue 2000/2001*, Malta: Board of Studies for Information Technology.

US Congress (1993), *U.S. Telecommunications Services in European Markets*, Office of Technology Assessment, OTA-TCT-548, Washington, DC: U.S. Government Printing Office.

van Maarseveen, J. (1999), "A bird's eye view of CBS history", in van Maarseveen, *A Century Rounded Up: Reflections on the history of the Central Bureau of Statistics in the Netherlands*, pp. 13-46.

van Maarseveen, J. G., et al. (eds.) (1999), *A Century Rounded Up: Reflections on the history of the Central Bureau of Statistics in the Netherlands*, Amsterdam: Stichting beheer IISG.

Vardalas, J. N. (2001), *The Computer Revolution in Canada: Building National Technological Competence*, Cambridge, MA: MIT Press.

Varian, Hal R., Farrell, Joseph, & Shapiro, Carl (2004), *The Economics of Information Technology: An Introduction*, Cambridge: Cambridge University Press.

Veglio, John and Duncan John Leslie (1968), *Memorandum of Association*, Computers in Business (Malta) Ltd, Malta.

Vella, Catherine C. (ed.) (2000), *The Maltese Islands on the Move*, Malta: Central Office of Statistics.

Vella, J. T. (1989), "Computer Education and the IDPM", *The Sunday Times Computer Supplement*, 16 July, p. IX.

Venkatesh, Alladi and Vitalari, Nichoas (1990), *A Longitudinal Analysis of Computing in the Home*, Project NOAH, Graduate School of Management, and Public Policy Research Organization, University of California, Irvine. Available at: http://crito.uci.edu/papers/1990/ ProjectNOAH1Reportcopy.pdf. Accessed: 20 August 2010.

Walden, I. and Angel, J. (eds.) (2001), *Telecommunications Law*, London: Blackstone Press.

Walker, J. (1996), "The Case 1107". Available at: http://www.fourmilab.ch/documents/univac/case1107.html. Accessed: 14 May 2006.

Wallace, James, and Erickson, Jim (1992), *Hard Drive: Bill Gates and the Making of the Microsoft Empire*, New York: John Wiley.

Wallace Mike, Fertig Michael & Schneller Eugene (eds.) (2007), *Managing Change in the Public Services*, Malden, MA: Blackwell Publishing.

Webster, Frank (ed.) (2004), *The Information Society Reader*, London: Routledge.

Westermark, Gunnar (1969), *Report on Efficiency Development in the Malta Government*, Second Report, Malta.

Westermark, Gunnar (1971), *Report on Efficiency Development in the Malta Government*, Final Report, Malta. NAM:GMR 3252, National Archives.

White, E. (1983), *Channels and Modalities for the transfer of Technology to Public Enterprises in Developing Countries*, Yugoslavia: ICPE.

Wiener, Norbert (1950), *The Human Use of Human Beings: Cybernetics and Society*, Boston, MA: Houghton-Mifflin.

Williams, Michael, R. (1985), *A History of Computing Technology*, Englewood Cliffs, N.J.: Prentice-Hall.

Williams, W. R. (1985) (ed.), *Looking Back to Tomorrow – Reflections on the twenty-five years of computers in New Zealand*, Wellington: NZCS.

Wilson III, Ernest J. (2006), *The Information Revolution and Developing Countries*, Cambridge, Massachusetts: The MIT Press.

Winsbury, Rex (ed.) (1981), *Viewdata in Action – a comparative study of Prestel*, UK: McGraw-Hill.

Winston, Brian (1998), *Media, Technology and Society: A History: From the Telegraph to the Internet*, UK: Routeledge.

WIPO (2006), "Malta Accedes to WIPO's Patent Cooperation Treaty", WIPO News & Events Update 283, Geneva, 12 December. Available at: http://www.wipo.int/edocs/prdocs/en/2006/wipo_upd_2006_283.html. Accessed: March 2008.

Wireless Telegraphy Ordinance (1922), Chapter 49 of the Laws of Malta.

Wong, Poh-Kam (1997), "Implementing the NII Vision: Singapore's Experience and Future Challenges", in B. Kahin and E. Wilson (eds.), *National Information Infrastructure Initiatives – Vision and Policy Design*, Cambridge (Massachusetts): MIT Press, pp. 24-60.

World Economic Forum (2007), *Global Information Technology Report 2006-2007*. Available at: http://www.weforum.org/en/initiatives/gcp/Global%20Information%20Technology%20Report/index.htm. Accessed: August 2008.

Yates, J. (2005), *Structuring the Information Age--Life Insurance and Technology in the Twentieth Century*, Baltimore, Maryland: The John Hopkins University Press.

Yost, Jeffrey R. (2005), *The Computer Industry*, Westport, Connecticut: Greenwood Press.

Zahra, Charlot (2009), "Economists react to possibility of ST shut-down", *Business Today*, 28 January. Available at: http://www.businesstoday.com.mt/2009/01/28/t4.html. Accessed: January 2010.

Zammit, Lawrence (2004), "ICT Literacy & Education in Malta", in R. Camilleri (ed.), *Rising to the Challenge – The Lisbon Objectives and Maltese Education Provision*, Malta: Education Division, pp. 83-96.

Zammit, Saviour (1997), "Provision of Data Services". Paper read at the Chartered Professional Engineers' Annual Engineering Conference on Data Communications, Malta.

Zammit, Sylvana (2006), "Heads of Agreement of SmartCity@Malta Signed", *MaltaMedia Online Network*, 27 March. Available at: http://www.maltamedia.com/news/2005/bf/article_9404.shtml. Accessed: 18 April 2007.

Zammit-Lewis, Edward (1999), "The Role and Powers of the Telecommunications Regulator under Act XXXIII of 1997", LLD Thesis, University of Malta.

Zammit Mangion, J. (1992), *Education in Malta*, Malta: Studia Edition.

Zuboff, Shoshana (1989), *In The Age Of The Smart Machine: The Future Of Work And Power*, UK: Basic Books.

Index

ABOUT THE AUTHOR

Mario Aloisio was introduced to computers in 1979 when, as a physics undergraduate, he began his industrial training at ICI's research laboratories in Runcorn, Cheshire, UK. After graduating from the former Preston Polytechnic (now the University of Central Lancashire), he returned to his native country, where he spent several years developing software mostly for Maltese firms. Apart from Malta, Dr. Aloisio worked in England, Germany and Libya. In the Libyan Desert he did contract work with Independent Oilfield Services Ltd (IOSL), writing software and program documentation for a real-time SCADA system used by the Waha Oil Company.

After a long spell in industry, Dr. Aloisio decided to gain further academic qualifications in computing. He finished a graduate diploma (at honours degree level) in Information Technology at De Montfort University in 1992, then began working as a teacher at a Maltese Technical Institute. He later joined the University of Malta Junior College where he currently lectures in computing. His work at the Junior College provided him with the opportunity to further his academic and research skills: in 2004 he began doctoral studies at the University of Warwick on a part-time basis. His PhD dissertation, supervised by Martin Campbell-Kelly (with Steve Russ as mentor) and completed in 2010, primarily dealt with the history of computing in Malta.

Currently an IEEE member, but formerly also a Chartered Member of the BCS, the former IDPM, and the ACM, Dr. Aloisio's academic interests varied over the years and have included: the history of computing, the history of the telegraph, machine translation, image processing for machine vision, voice recognition, and real-time systems.